Dictionary of Ecodesign

This guide to the terminology of sustainable design is the first dictionary of its kind and provides accurate and relevant information on ecodesign terminology and topics to students, lecturers, conservation associations and advocates, designers, and all those whose work impinges on the environment.

The dictionary has ecological, environmental, scientific, and design terms from professions as varied as engineering, physics, chemistry, biology and ecology, public policy, architecture, landscape architecture, and urban planning. By consolidating terms from the various disciplines, the dictionary provides a useful source of reference for technical, scientific, and design explanations and definitions.

There is an increasing number of terms used in this growing field; this illustrated dictionary provides over 1500 terms to provide a common language and terminology for everyone who is interested in environmental conservation and design.

Ken Yeang is an architect, planner and ecologist whose design, masterplanning and built works are at the cutting edge of green design. He is Chairman of Llewelyn Davies Yeang (UK) and principal of its sister firm, Hamzah & Yeang (Malaysia). With a PhD from Cambridge University, Yeang has authored six books on ecodesign. Yeang has received over 35 awards for his designs and is regarded as one of the foremost designers, theoreticians and thinkers in the field of green design and planning. He is regarded as the inventor of the 'bioclimatic skyscraper'. *The Guardian* magazine in 2008 refers to Yeang as one of the 50 people who could save the planet.

Lillian Woo is an economist and political consultant, who has consulted in hundreds of state and federal campaigns, including US President. She has specialized in public policy and regulatory issues.

Woo holds graduate degrees from Columbia University. She has authored two books.

Yeang and Woo are currently working on a new book, *Ecomimesis: Ecological Design for the Built Environment Using Ecosystem Properties Processes as a Model.*

Dictionary of Ecodesign
An Illustrated Reference

Ken Yeang and Lillian Woo

Routledge
Taylor & Francis Group

LONDON AND NEW YORK

First published 2010
by Routledge
2 Park Square, Milton Park, Abingdon, Oxon OX14 4RN

Simultaneously published in the USA and Canada
by Routledge
270 Madison Avenue, New York, NY 10016, USA

Routledge is an imprint of the Taylor & Francis Group, an informa business

© 2010 Ken Yeang and Lillian Woo

Typeset in Optima by
Taylor & Francis Books
Printed and bound in Great Britain by
The MPG Books Groupd in the UK

British Library Cataloguing in Publication Data
A catalogue record for this book is available from the British Library

Library of Congress Cataloging in Publication Data
Yeang, Ken, 1948-
  Dictionary of ecodesign : an illustrated reference / Ken Yeang and Lillian Woo.
    p. cm.
  Includes bibliographical references.
  1. Sustainable design–Dictionaries. I. Woo, Lillian C. II. Title.
  NK1520.Y43 2010
  720'.47–dc22
                    2009034679

ISBN13 978-0-415-45899-3 (hbk)
ISBN13 978-0-203-86440-1 (ebk)

Contents

Figures

Tables

Preface

Addressing environmental devastation and climate change have become imperatives that preoccupy the daily concerns and work of not just those in the design field and those whose work impinges in one way or the other on the environment, but also the public at large, seeking to grapple with a new set of ideas and terminologies and trying to find out what they mean, how they could affect their lives, and what individuals can do in response.

The intention of this first comprehensive eco-design dictionary is to provide definitions and explanations currently used by the various professionals involved in designing products, structures, and infrastructures, and in land development and use, and who contribute to public policies that have significant effects on environmental conditions and the Earth's ecological balance.

The forecast for life on Earth is seriously grim. Demographers predict a world population that will use up resources more quickly than the environment can replenish them. At the same time, environmentalists and ecologists warn that the ecosystem will be despoiled beyond repair through human consumption and waste, unless there are changes in lifestyle and design, and greater stewardship of the biosphere. In an attempt to stem this tide, ecodesigners in many disciplines are creating new solutions to existing practices in an attempt to reduce waste of materials; to reduce pollution of air, land, and water; to reuse materials to conserve natural resources; to recycle humanmade and natural components; and to integrate the designed system seamlessly with its ambient ecosystems, thereby achieving a benign relationship with the environment.

We include terms and explanations in this dictionary reflecting the many disciplines that have an impact on the environment and atmosphere. In addition to basic science terms, and those that apply to environmental and ecological areas, the various professions that have developed terms and phrases for their specific fields include agriculture, biology, ecology, chemistry, the many specialties of engineering, physics, architecture, landscape architecture, industrial design, environmental protection, energy, urban and regional planning, and public policy, as well as regulations and environmental agreements and pacts.

We are aware that such an endeavour cannot be totally comprehensive, and we will have missed many current and key terms and/or have left some out inadvertently, or due to limitations of publication. In this regard, we seek your help in letting us know what we should have included, so that future editions can be improved.

We hope the definitions and terms will be useful and pertinent to all seeking a better ecological balance in the world through their lives, their work, and their designs, and to anyone whose studies or responsibilities necessitate learning these ecodesign terms.

We would like to acknowledge the impressive quality and extent of research by the many government agencies as well as university researchers around the world. Their constant additions to the existing body of knowledge and innovative solutions are invaluable as the world grapples with problems with the environment. We would like thank Charles Culp for his review of the manuscript and invaluable suggestions; Thomas Regan for his assistance with illustrations; and George Mann for reference and topic suggestions—all three from Texas A&M University; and Francesca Ford, our commissioning editor, for her patience and great assistance. Illustrations by Freya Cobbin.

Ken Yeang and Lillian Woo

A

Abiotic   Nonbiological, nonliving portion of the ecosystem. Abiotic components include chemicals that are present in soil, water and air, solar radiation, and various aspects of climate. These are the counterpart of the biotic portions of the ecosystem. In ecosystems in nature, as well as in ecomimetic designs, both abiotic and biotic components are necessary to balance the ecosystem, and a change in one will affect the balance and diversity of the other.

As most of the existing built environment is abiotic, one of the goals of ecodesign is to ensure our built environment includes both abiotic and biotic elements that complement each other and form a whole. *See also: Biotic; Ecosystem*

ABS   *See: Acrylonitrile butadiene styrene resin*

Absolute humidity   Amount of water held in the air—the ratio of the mass of water vapor to the volume of the water. It is also commonly referred to as the density of the water vapor. It is the measurement of pounds of water per pound of dry air, or grams of water per kilogram of dry air. The technical definition, from the 2005 *ASHRAE Handbook*, is that water vapor density (d_v) equals the mass of water (M_w) held in a volume of air (V): $d_v = M_w/V$.

The humidity ratio is the ratio of the mass of water to the mass of dry air. The warmer the air, the more water it can contain. Because absolute humidity changes as air pressure changes, it is defined in chemical engineering terms as mass of water vapor per unit mass of dry air (also

known as the mass mixing ratio), which is much more rigorous for heat and mass balance calculations. Mass of water per unit volume would be defined as volumetric humidity.

Humidity levels in regions of the world determine the natural biodiversity as well as architectural design. For example, the most humid cities on Earth are generally located closer to the equator near coastal regions, which are naturally humid zones. Cities in South and Southeast Asia seem to be among the most humid. Some areas in India and Thailand have high humidity during the rainy seasons; parts of Australia have high humidity from December to April; Kuala Lumpur and Singapore have high humidity all year long. In the USA, the most humid cities are in Texas and Florida along the coast.

In ecodesign, knowledge of the relative humidity levels during the course of a year in a particular region or location will help with the design of the passive mode strategy that can be adopted. *See also: Mass mixing ratio; Relative humidity; Passive mode design*

Absorption   1. Physical or physiological process by which substances are absorbed—for example, the uptake of water, nutrients, light, and airborne particles by tissues, cells, air, and soil. Absorption levels affect decisions to use chemicals and materials that emit evaporative fluids and gaseous particles, some of which are pollutants. Government and international regulatory agencies have identified some fluids and airborne particles that are harmful to the environment and to human health. *See also: Air* *pollutants; Biological contaminants; Pollutants; Soil contaminants; Water pollutants*

2. Change of short-wave radiation (e.g. from the Sun) to long-wave radiation when it strikes a surface. The total amount of radiation striking a surface equals the amount of energy absorbed by the surface, plus the amount reflected off that surface, plus the amount transmitted. For example, photovoltaic cells absorb the Sun's heat, which can then be converted into electricity.

Water and moisture absorption in walls and penetration through insulating materials has an impact on building physics, and condensation effects can result in mold.

Absorption cooling   A cooling process, such as an air conditioner, driven by a heat source such as solar-heated water or natural gas, not by electricity. As a solar cooling technique, absorption cooling uses steam or an open flame to generate cooling. It is most frequently used to air-condition large commercial buildings. The use of solar energy for cooling generates clean energy and significantly reduces greenhouse gas emissions and carbon dioxide emissions. For example, large, high-efficiency, double-effect absorption chillers using water as the refrigerant are common in the Japanese commercial air-conditioning market.

There has been a growing interest in absorption cooling. In order to lower costs where peak demand rates and overall electricity rates are high, and natural gas prices are reasonable, there may be increased use of absorption chillers. For example, hotels are installing more small, built-in absorption refrigerators, and recreational vehicles are using absorption refrigerators because they do not require electricity.

Some of the negative effects of absorption cooling include complexity of operation, increased on-site pollutants if natural gas provides the energy, and very high temperatures (possibly >300 °F; >149 °C) to operate.

Because absorption chillers can make use of waste heat, they can essentially provide free cooling in certain facilities. Absorption cooling systems can most easily be incorporated into new construction, although they can also be used as replacements for conventional electric chillers.

Absorption cooling has a coefficient of performance (COP) of less than 1 (one). *See also:* **Coefficient of performance (COP); Solar cooling**

Absorption heat pump   *See: Heat pump*

Absorption process   General term used by designers for processes used in industrial plants to remove gaseous contaminants and environmental pollutants to minimize their emission into the environment. *See also:* **Scrubbers**

Accretion   Build-up of sediment along the bank or shore of a body of water such as a river or stream. It can result in flooding of adjacent areas if the sediment or loessial deposits impede the natural flow of water and increase silting and diversion of waterways. Silting can affect water quality. Ecodesign tries to eliminate accretion as it can significantly affect the aquatic ecology of water bodies.

Acetone   Major soil and air contaminant. It evaporates easily, is flammable, and dissolves in water. It is also called dimethyl ketone, 2-propanone, or beta-ketopropane. It is a compound that is also found naturally in the environment. Acetone occurs naturally in plants, trees, volcanic gases, forest fires, and as a product of the breakdown of body fat. It is present in vehicle exhaust, tobacco smoke, and landfill sites.

Acetone is used to make plastic, fibers, drugs, and other chemicals. It is also used to dissolve other substances. Industrial processes contribute more acetone to the environment than natural processes. Discharge onto the land and into mature ecosystems leads to contamination and to brownfield sites that will require decontamination and rehabilitation. *See also:* **Soil contaminants; Brownfield site**

ACEA agreement A voluntary agreement between the Association des Constructeurs Européens d'Automobiles (ACEA; the European Automobile Manufacturers' Association) and the European Commission to limit the amount of carbon dioxide emitted by automobiles sold in Europe. *See also: Emissions standards, automobile; Fuel economy regulations, automobile*

ACH Air change per hour. *See: Air change*

Acid deposition Wet or dry deposits of atmospheric emissions of acid particles, such as sulfur and nitrogen compounds, from industrial processes onto the Earth's surface—either ground or surface water. The wet forms are called acid rain and can fall to Earth as rain, snow, or fog. The dry forms are acidic gases or particulate matter. Acid rain adversely affects the environment and an ecosystem's key species and vegetation.

It should be noted that rainwater has always been—and probably always will be—acidic. The natural acidity is caused by carbon dioxide in the atmosphere. When water and carbon dioxide combine, they form carbonic acid (H_2CO_3). Gases from other natural sources such as volcanoes also add to the acidity of rainwater. *See also: Acid rain*

Acid gas Air pollutant with acid content contained in a gas. Usually a by-product of incomplete combustion of solid waste or fossil fuels. This leads to leaf discoloration and possible degradation of biotic life. In ecological assessments of pollution, such as in cities, the extent of discoloration can be used as an index of aerial pollution of a locality.

Acid-neutralizing capacity (ANC) Measure of the ability of water or soil to neutralize added acids. This is achieved through the reaction of hydrogen ions with inorganic or organic bases, such as bicarbonate—hydrogen carbonate (HCO_3)—or organic ions. ANC's acid-neutralizing ability helps decrease the harmful effects of acid deposition on the ecosystem.

Acid rain The acidity of rain depends on two factors: the presence of acid-forming substances such as sulfates; and the availability of acid-neutralizing substances such as calcium and magnesium salts. Clean rain has a pH value of about 5.6. By comparison, vinegar has a pH of 3. The occurrence of acid rain is most prevalent in industrial areas.

Common use of the term "acid rain" designates pollution produced when acid compounds formed in the atmosphere are mixed into rain, fog, snow, or mist. The acid compounds include a combination of sulfur dioxide (SO_2) and nitrogen oxides (NO_x)—the products of burning coal and other fuels, and of other anthropogenic industrial processes. Acid rain can take the form of both wet and dry deposition.

Prior to falling to Earth, sulfur dioxide (SO_2) and nitrogen oxide (NO_x) gases and their particulate matter derivatives—sulfates and nitrates—can contribute to visibility degradation and harm to public health.

Acid rain damages forests, freshwater lakes and streams, coastal ecosystems, and soils. These acids also help release heavy metals into groundwater, which has an adverse impact on the environment, plants, animals, fish, human health, and property. In addition, acid rain accelerates the decay of building materials and paints, and of buildings themselves, as well as the decay of dead plant materials.

Ecodesign of large-scale industrial processes tries to minimize or eliminate emissions that result in acid rain. *See also: Wet deposition; Dry deposition*

Acidification Environmentally, acidification is the process whereby emissions from large-scale industrial processes produce air pollution, mainly ammonia (NH_3), sulfur dioxide (SO_2), and nitrogen oxide (NO_x). The air pollution is converted into acid substances and acid rain, which can seep into the groundwater, contaminate the groundwater and soil, and degrade local ecosystems. Chemically, it refers to reducing the pH of a substance, making it more acidic. *See also: Acid rain*

Acrylonitrile butadiene styrene (ABS) resin, ($C_8H_8C_4H_6C_3H_3N)_n$ Designated as a hazardous air pollutant (HAP) by the USEPA, which has set national emissions standards for ABS resin. ABS resin has a very significant impact on the environment because styrene plastics are widely used in many products. ABS is a "polymerized alloy" of the three materials—acrylonitrile, butadiene, and styrene. It is a member of the group styrene plastics.

ABS resin is used for auto body parts, suitcases, and toys. In plumbing, ABS pipes are black (whereas PVC pipes are white). ABS is also used in plastic pressure-pipe systems. Butadiene and styrene (in ABS), when combined, become benzene-like in both form and function. Benzene is a known human carcinogen.

An important ecodesign consideration is to avoid using products that contain HAPs. *See also: Benzene*

Activated carbon Also known as activated charcoal. Result of burning a carbon material such as wood and applying steam treatment to increase its surface area. Used to adsorb organic materials to control air or water pollution. Activated carbon can be specified and used in ecodesign to adsorb organic materials to control air and water pollution.

Activated sludge Product of a biological process in which microorganisms present in the aeration tanks of sewage treatment plants help decompose the organic material and transform inorganic substances into environmentally acceptable forms. The typical microbiology of activated sludge consists of approximately 95% bacteria and 5% higher organisms (protozoa, rotifers, and higher forms of invertebrates). It is commonly used in secondary treatment of sewage. *See also: Secondary wastewater treatment*

Active façade Also known as an active wall. As part of an energy conservation system, exterior walls can be designed to absorb heat and serve as a heat storage wall. Absorption and storage of heat in the wall mass helps decrease dependency on mechanical heating and cooling systems of the building, and results in reduced energy consumption. *See also: Thermal storage; Trombe wall; Building envelope*

Active gas collection Technique that forcibly removes gas from a landfill by attaching a vacuum or pump to a network of pipelines in the landfill or surrounding soil to remove the gases. Gas collected from the landfill may be flared or collected for energy recovery for use as a fuel. In some applications, the fuel collected from landfills is inexpensive and renewable. Landfill gas has about 50% of the Btu content per volume of natural gas.

Active solar energy *See: Solar energy*

Active system Term used to describe the energy source and systems for a building. Active systems depend on electromechanical systems to provide energy transformation and transportation within a structure. As they depend on energy resources, they are much more expensive in cost and use of resources than passive systems. The opposite would be a passive system, which refers to low-energy design. *See also: Passive mode design; Passive system*

Adaptable buildings Buildings not only designed for present use and long-term durability, but also that can be adapted for future users and other uses. Flexibility may include building layout, environmental systems, and energy sources. This adaptability assists in the conservation of building materials by reusing those already in place, by eliminating the use of new natural sites for construction, and by not disrupting the ecosystems of other sites.

Adaptation   Refers to a central idea in evolutionary biology—an organism's ability to change its metabolism and habits in order to cope with environmental pressures and changes and to survive in a new environment. The adaptive changes may be metabolic, structural or behavioral, but must be part of the generic potential of the organism.

The collapse of an ecosystem's functions indicates that organisms in a specific ecosystem have limited ability to adapt to anthropogenic as well as natural and climatic influences. The result is the establishment of new ecosystem balances resulting from these changes. *See also: Ecosystem*

Adaptive radiation   Evolution of new species to fill vacant and new ecological niches in changed environments, usually after mass extinction.

Adaptive reuse   In architecture, term used to describe the process of adapting old structures for new purposes and functions. Many architects retain some of the original design elements of the existing building while renovating it for new uses. Adaptive reuse of buildings is essentially a process that assists in closing the material loop by recycling existing building stock. It involves considered conservation of land and historical value, more responsible redevelopment of older buildings in the urban core, and hence reduction of sprawl. It is the built environment equivalent of brownfield reclamation.

One measure of the effectiveness of adaptive reuse is a performance assessment of a building's energy use based on present-day energy efficiency standards.

Add-on control device   A secondary device, such as an incinerator or carbon absorber, that is added to an exhaust system to prevent air pollution. The device removes pollutants from the exhaust gases. The control device usually does not affect the process being controlled and thus is "add-on" technology, as opposed to a scheme to control pollution through altering the basic process itself.

The device removes polluting particulate emissions which chemically damage buildings and infrastructure and affect the soil, water, and organisms that absorb them.

Adiabatic   Thermodynamic process in which no heat is transferred to or from the working fluid in a system. An adiabatic change in a gas is a change in volume and pressure of a volume of gas without heat transfer between the system and the outside. The opposite system would be a process with maximum heat transfer to or from the surroundings, causing the temperature to remain constant. In ecodesign, an adiabatic system is more efficient than one that loses heat during its operation.

For example, in a steam turbine, the adiabatic efficiency is the ratio of the work done per pound of steam to the heat energy released, and is theoretically capable of transformation into mechanical work during the adiabatic expansion of a unit weight of steam. *See also: Steam turbine*

Adipic acid   Organic compound with the formula $(CH_2)_4(COOH)_2$. It is considered the most important dicarboxylic acid. Its production is a major source of the greenhouse gas nitrous oxide (N_2O). The majority of the 2.5 billion kg of adipic acid produced annually is used as monomer for the production of nylon.

Adsorb   To take up and hold a gas, liquid, or dissolved substance on the surface or in the body of a solid substance. For example, activated charcoal has the ability to adsorb pollutants such as volatile organic compounds (VOCs).

Adsorbent   Porous solids that trap polluting emissions on their surfaces. Most common adsorbents are activated carbon, activated alumina, silica gel, and molecular sieves. Adsorbents become saturated after a period of use and must be regenerated or replaced. Researchers indicate that adsorbents impregnated with permanganate show promise for controlling indoor formaldehyde. Elimination of pollutants promotes healthier species and environments.

Advanced technology vehicle   A vehicle that combines new engine/power/drivetrain systems to improve fuel economy and efficiency. This includes hybrid power systems and fuel cells, as well as some specialized electric vehicles. This type of vehicle is considered an improvement over gas engine cars and trucks for the short term, but transport professionals stress the need for longer-term major solutions to transportation and the movement of people and materials in the built environment.

Aeolian soil   Soil transported from one area to another by the wind. Contaminated soil cannot be contained at its point of origin and can be spread from one area to another by the wind. The contamination may adversely affect the health and diversity of the biotic ecosystem. Government environmental agencies currently monitor and regulate soil contaminants.

Aerated static pile   Forced aeration method of composting in which a free-standing composting pile is aerated by a blower moving air through the perforated pipes located beneath the pile. The aeration speeds decomposition and the creation of humus. In ecodesign, this method closes the materials cycle. *See also: Materials cycle*

Aeration   Process that promotes biological decomposition of organic matter through contact with oxygen. The process may be passive, when it is exposed to air, or active, when a mixing or bubbling device introduces the air.

Aerobic bacteria   Microorganisms that require free oxygen or air to live and contribute to the decomposition of organic material in soil or composting systems.

Aerobic treatment   Also known as aerobic digestion. Process in which microbes decompose complex organic compounds in the presence of oxygen and use the resulting released energy for reproduction and growth.

Aerobism   Ability to grow where free oxygen is present. The presence of oxygen increases the growth of microbes and decomposition of organic material.

Aerosols   Colloidal particles suspended in a gas. Air pollutants as a collection of airborne solid or liquid particles, sized between 0.01 and 10 mm, that linger in the atmosphere for at least several hours. Aerosols may be either natural or anthropogenic, and may affect the climate in one of two ways: directly through scattering and absorbing radiation; and indirectly through acting as condensation nuclei for cloud formation or modifying the optical properties and lifetime of clouds. The term "aerosol" is often confused with "aerosol spray", which refers to the propellant in spray containers.

The burning of fossil fuels and biomass results in aerosol emissions into the atmosphere. Aerosols absorb and emit heat, reflect light, and, depending on their properties, can either cool or warm the atmosphere. Sulfate aerosols are emitted when fuel containing sulfur, such as coal and oil, is burned. These aerosols reflect solar radiation back into space and have a cooling effect. Carbon black results from incomplete combustion of fossil fuels and biomass burning, such as forest fires and land clearing, and is believed to contribute to global warming. Other aerosols emitted in small quantities from human activities include organic carbon and associated aerosols from biomass burning. For a complete list *See: **Air pollutants**. See also: **Carbon black***

Afforestation Planting of new forests on land that historically has not contained forests. Afforestation and revegetation are important in ecodesign, not only to counterbalance current timber-harvesting and deforestation practices, but also to provide new trees and plants to absorb carbon emissions. New forests expand the possibilities of new species and a new ecosystem balance.

Afterburner Device that controls air pollution by incinerating organic compounds into carbon dioxide and water. At the same time, the energy consumption and impacts of carbon dioxide emissions are serious considerations in using afterburners. In ecodesign, it is believed that the overall long-term benign effects of large-scale industrial production systems on the total environment are more important than short-term incremental solutions.

Agricultural biotechnology Technology that alters living organisms or parts of organisms to make or modify products; improves plants or animals; or develops microorganisms for specific agricultural uses. Includes the tools of genetic engineering. Biotechnology research and tools have produced some crops that are more resistant to specific plant diseases and insect pests and cheaper to grow; more effective pest control through biotechnology can result in decreased use of synthetic pesticides.

In ecodesign, agricultural technology can be used to further the development of integrated food production systems.

Agricultural by-products Also known as agriproducts. Agricultural crops and materials that are being manufactured or used as biodegradable products. These products are being developed as biodegradable substitutes for nonbiodegradable crops and materials. For example, biopolymers made from potato starch and corn starch have the same characteristics as nonbiodegradable plastic; soy-based products for construction include water sealants for concrete, soybean oil paints, and solvents for use as adhesives, which reduce formaldehyde requirements; rice and wheat straw are used in strawboard, a construction material used for partitions; animal wool and plant fibers are used for products ranging from clothing to packaging.

In ecodesign, the use of biodegradable products reduces wastes deposited in landfills and closes the ecological loop by reintegrating materials used in the human built environment back into the environment.

Agricultural wastes Term that includes both organic (animal and plant) and non-natural wastes. Plant wastes, such as tree cuttings and crop residues, are biodegradable. The two environmentally harmful agricultural wastes are excess fertilizer and herbicides that filter through the soil and contaminate groundwater; and animal waste and crop residues that can result in eutrophication in lakes, rivers, and estuaries. Excess fertilizer can also seep into water bodies and cause eutrophication. Agricultural waste-management systems help minimize damage to the environment.

This issue presents an ecodesign challenge to rethink large-scale food production so that agricultural wastes can be managed and minimized, and damage to the environment is minimized.

Agroecosystem The effect that agricultural practices such as human-made structures, croplands, pasture, and livestock have on the atmosphere, soils, surface drainage, and groundwater.

Air analysis Analysis of air to determine contaminant levels and the presence of various forms of air pollution, including carbon monoxide, hydrocarbons, particulate matter, photochemical oxidants, and sulfur oxides. Government regulatory agencies have set emissions standards for major air pollutants.

Air change   Measure of how quickly air in an interior space is replaced by outside or conditioned air by ventilation or infiltration. It is an indication of how well a space is ventilated, its air tightness, compared with published standards, codes, or recommendations. When a quantity of air equal to the volume of a room is supplied or depleted, it is known as "one air change". This is typically measured in air change per hour (ACH). It is particularly important in hospitals, schools, offices, and other environments, such as airplanes, in which bacteria and viruses causing infectious diseases can be carried through the air.

In ecodesign, the assessment of ACH is a requisite for designing buildings that utilize natural ventilation systems. *See also:* **Passive mode design**

Air emissions   Gases and particles that are put into the air or emitted from various sources, the majority of which are produced anthropogenically. There are four major categories of emission: point, mobile, biogenic, and area. Point sources include factories and electric power plants. Mobile sources include cars and trucks, lawnmowers, airplanes, and anything else that moves and emits pollution into the air. Biogenic sources include trees and vegetation, gas seeps, and microbial activity. Area sources consist of smaller, stationary sources such as dry cleaners and degreasing operations. Of the four categories, only biogenic emissions provide elements that help the natural ecosystem and its maintenance. The other three categories generally contain pollutants that damage the environment, property, and human health, and impede biological processes.

Air exchanger   *See: Heat recovery ventilator*

Air mass   1. In weather applications, an air mass refers to a large body of air that has similar temperature and moisture properties throughout. The best source regions for air masses are large, flat areas where air can be stagnant long enough to take on the characteristics of the surface below. For example, maritime tropical air masses (mT) develop over the subtropical oceans and transport heat and moisture northward into the land surface. Conversely, continental polar air masses (cP) transport colder and drier air southward.

Once an air mass moves out of its source region, it is modified as it encounters different conditions. For example, as a polar air mass moves southward it encounters warmer land masses and is heated by the ground below. Air masses typically clash in the middle latitudes, producing turbulent weather.

The point at which two different air masses meet is called a front—the transition area between two air masses of different density. Fronts extend in both horizontal and vertical directions; the term frontal surface (or frontal zone) refers to both horizontal and vertical components of the front.

One important component of ecodesign is to address global warming. The potential for severe

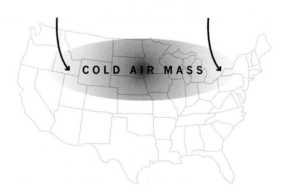

Figure 1 Continental polar air mass
Source: University of Illinois-UC

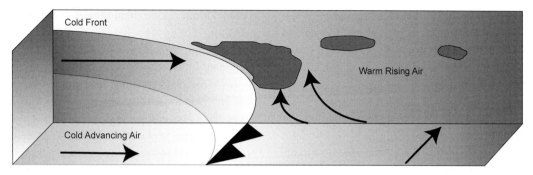

Figure 2 Air mass fronts
Source: University of Illinois

weather and flooding increases as more warm fronts meet cold ones.

2. Air mass is sometimes known as air mass ratio. It is equal to the cosine of the zenith angle (angle from directly overhead to a line intersecting the Sun). Air mass is an indication of the length of the path travelled by solar radiation through the atmosphere. An air mass of 1.0 means the Sun is directly overhead and the radiation travels through one atmosphere thickness.

Air pollutants Air contaminants with concentrations heavy enough to prevent the normal dispersive ability of the air and interfere with biological processes, particularly human health, or produce other harmful environmental effects. Six common air pollutants are:

- particle pollution (often referred to as particulate matter)
- ground-level ozone
- carbon monoxide
- sulfur oxides
- nitrogen oxides
- lead.

These pollutants can be hazardous to the environment and to health. Of the six, particle pollution and ground-level ozone are the most widespread health threats. Other air pollutants include aerosols, asbestos, chlorofluorocarbons (CFCs), criteria air pollutants, hazardous air pollutants (HAPs), hydrochlorofluorocarbons (HCFCs), mercury, methane, propellants, radon, refrigerants, and volatile organic compounds (VOCs). Some sources of air pollution include factories, power plants, dry-cleaners, cars, buses, trucks, windblown dust, and wildfires.

Ecodesigns can help develop new types of industrial process that do not produce polluting emissions and do not exceed the carrying capacity of the natural environment to absorb these emissions. *See also: **Air toxins; Criteria air pollutants; Hazardous air pollutants; Indoor air pollution; Particulate matter; Volatile organic compound;** and individual entries for pollutants listed above.

Air pollution control systems Systems used to eliminate or reduce airborne pollutants such as smoke, ash, dust, sulfur, nitrogen oxides, carbon monoxide, odors, and hydrocarbons. Systems include nitrogen oxide control devices, flue gas particulate collectors and desulfurization units.

In ecodesign, it is believed that the overall long-term benign effects of large-scale industrial production systems on the total environment are more important than short-term incremental solutions.

Air quality standard Mandatory standard set by USEPA for the maximum permitted contaminant concentrations in the air.

Air shed Air supply of a specific geographical area, usually defined by topographic barriers or atmospheric conditions that confine air emissions. Air sheds can vary in size, from small areas within valleys to urban-wide and even region-wide air sheds where the effects of urban air pollution, such as ozone, may extend over a wide area.

Tools such as emissions inventories, air quality monitoring, atmospheric dispersion modeling, and predictions of trends in emissions and pollution levels should be used to obtain information for effective air quality management.

Ecodesign can help develop and implement an air quality management plan which includes determination of air, influences on that air and how they might change over time; use of monitoring data and national guidelines to establish reduction targets; and management and reduction strategies.

Air-source heat pump The most common type of heat pump. Transfers heat from outdoor air to indoor air during the heating season and works in reverse during the cooling season. Can provide efficient heating and cooling for homes, particularly in warm climate zones. When properly installed, an air-source heat pump can deliver 1.5 to three times more heat energy to a home than the electrical energy it consumes. This is possible because a heat pump moves heat rather than converting it from a fuel (as with combustion heating systems).

In *cooling mode,* an air-source heat pump indoor coil contains boiling refrigerant which absorbs heat from the air stream passing through the indoor coil (evaporator). As the liquid evaporates, it pulls heat from the air in the house. The refrigerant gas then proceeds to a compressor. After the gas is compressed, it passes into the outdoor coil and condenses when heat is extracted through the condenser coil. The liquid refrigerant then goes to an expansion device, where the high-pressure liquid becomes a low-pressure liquid. This liquid then proceeds to the evaporator coil, where the process repeats.

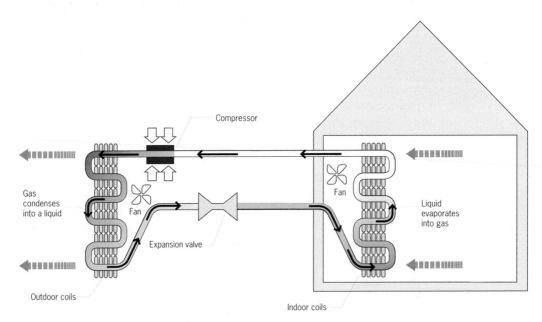

Figure 3 Air-source heat pump: cooling
Source: US Department of Energy

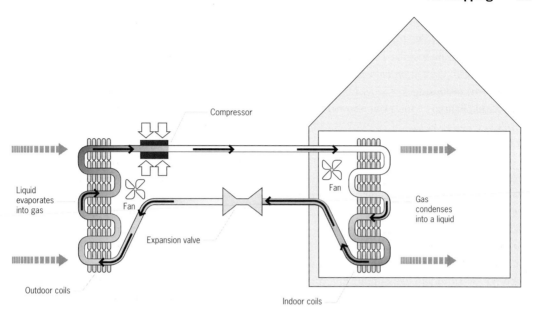

Figure 4 Air-source heat pump: heating
Source: US Department of Energy

In *heating mode*, the process works in reverse. Heat transfers from the outside to the inside using the outside coil as an evaporator and the inside coil as a condenser. A reversing valve provides the ability to reverse the direction of the refrigerant flow. As the liquid evaporates in the outside coil, it pulls heat from the outside air. After the gas is compressed, it passes into the indoor coil and condenses, releasing heat to the inside of the house. The pressure changes caused by the compressor and the expansion valve allow the gas to evaporate at a low temperature outside and condense at a higher temperature indoors. In heating mode, when the outside air approaches 32 °F (0 °C) or less, air-source heat pumps lose efficiency and generally require a back-up (resistance) heating system.

Most central heat pumps are split-systems— they each have one coil indoors and one outdoors. Supply and return ducts connect to a central fan, which is located indoors. For homes without ducts, air-source heat pumps are also available in a ductless version called a mini-split heat pump. In addition, a special type of air-source heat pump called a reverse-cycle chiller generates hot and cold water rather than air, allowing it to be used with radiant floor-heating systems in heating mode.

The efficiency and performance of present-day air-source heat pumps is 1.5 to two times greater than those available 30 years ago. This improvement in efficiency has resulted from technical advances and options such as thermo-expansion valves, electronic controls, high-efficiency compressors, and higher-efficiency heat exchangers. *See also: **Heat pump***

Air sparging   Contaminant reduction process. Injection of air or oxygen into groundwater to strip or flush volatile contaminants up through the groundwater as air bubbles and captures them with a vapor-extraction system. *See also: **Vapor-extraction system***

Air stripping   Treatment system that removes volatile organic compounds (VOCs) from contaminated groundwater or surface water by forcing an air stream through the water and causing the compounds to evaporate. *See also: Steam stripping; Volatile organic compound*

Air-to-air exchanger   *See: Heat recovery ventilator*

Air toxins   Air pollutants that may cause cancer or other serious health problems and produce adverse environmental and ecological effects. Air toxins may include benzene, perchloroethylene, and methylene chloride. Government agencies have set emissions standards and regulate levels of emission. *See also: Air pollutants*

Airborne   Suspended in the atmosphere.

Airflow patterns   1. Ecodesign architecture specifies the use of passive mode systems to provide horizontal or vertical spaces in atria or façades for airflow as well as light flow for buildings. 2. In eco masterplanning, i) landscape design can create different airflow patterns and can be used to direct or divert the wind by causing a pressure difference; ii) city and urban planning designs can apply analysis of the natural airflow patterns of a specific location—as well as the altered air flow of densely populated areas—to new developments and urban areas to maximize the benefits of the airflows. 3. Airflow patterns and ventilation effectiveness in buildings can be analyzed by computer models and existing codes. Building analysis includes simulation of single and multizone air flow and predictions of the efficiency of ventilation systems as well as the spread of airborne contaminants. 4. Urban planners and architects factor natural airflow patterns of a specific location to maximize them in laying out a city or new development. 5. Natural weather flow patterns may be altered by dense developments and cities.

Albedo   Ratio of solar radiation reflected to incident solar radiation. Amount of solar reflectance from a surface or object. For example, snow-covered surfaces have a high albedo; soil albedo ranges from high to low; low albedo is found in vegetation-covered surfaces and oceans. The albedo of the Earth varies due to cloudiness, snow, ice, clear areas, and land-cover changes.

The Earth and its atmosphere typically reflect about 4% and 26%, respectively, of the Sun's incoming radiation back to space over the course of one year. As a result, the Earth–atmosphere system has a combined albedo of about 30%, a number that is dependent on the local surface make-up, cover, and cloud distribution.

The proportion of absorbed, emitted, and reflected incoming solar radiation causes fluctuations in temperature, winds, ocean currents, and precipitation. The climate system remains in equilibrium as long as the amount of absorbed solar radiation is in balance with the amount of terrestrial radiation emitted back to space.

The Earth's albedo values are very important in shaping local and global climates through the radiation budget, determined as the difference between the amount of absorbed short-wave radiation (input) and the outgoing long-wave radiation (output). For example, clouds control the amount of energy that may reach the Earth's surface. As mean cloudiness varies geographically with lowest values observed in the subtropics and highest values in the mid to high latitudes, the variation of surface reflectance has a significant impact on the distribution of absorbed solar radiation at the surface. Approximately half the incident solar energy is absorbed by the Earth's surface. This energy is then used to heat the land and oceans and drive the hydrological cycle.

The harmful effects of an urban heat island put a burden on environmental preservation, energy consumption, and thermal comfort. These problems need to be considered in ecodesign. Simple methods to reduce heat island effects are to plant more trees, add more urban landscaping, and install more roof gardens.

High-albedo materials can lower temperatures effectively when exposed to solar radiation. Research has shown that high-albedo coatings on building exterior walls are effective in mitigating high temperatures in the urban environment. Conversely, dark pavement areas have low albedo and absorb and retain heat longer, adding to the heat island effect.

Solar absorptance of various materials (percentage of heat retained from solar radiation):

Flat, nonmetallic surfaces	0.85–0.98
Red brick and tile, concrete and stone, rusty steel and iron	0.65–0.8
Uncolored concrete	0.65
Yellow and buff brick and stone	0.50–0.7
White and light cream brick, tile, paint, paper, whitewash	0.30–0.5
Aluminum paint, gilt, bronze paint	0.30–0.50
Polished brass, copper	0.30–0.50
Polished aluminum reflector sheet	0.12

See also: **Reflectivity**

Algae Primitive plants, usually aquatic, capable of synthesizing their own food by photosynthesis. They are important biota in the ecosystem balance.

Algal blooms Spurts of algal growth that degrade water quality and indicate potentially hazardous changes in local water chemistry. Ecodesign should avoid the rampant growth of algal blooms that have been attributed to high nutrients introduced into water by fertilizer runoff and other chemicals high in nitrogen. Algal blooms can cause eutrophication of lakes, rivers, and streams, and death of fish and other aquatic life.

Alkali 1. Substance that can neutralize an acid. 2. Soluble salts in soil or water, both surface and groundwater.

Alkaline fuel cell (AFC) Type of fuel cell. Alkali fuel cells operate on compressed hydrogen and oxygen. They generally use a solution of potassium hydroxide (KOH) in water as their electrolyte and can use a variety of nonprecious metals as a catalyst at the anode and cathode. Operating temperatures inside alkali cells are around 150–200 °C (302–392 °F).

Because they produce potable water in addition to electricity, they were the first type widely used in the US space program to produce electrical energy and water on board a spacecraft, which is essentially a closed ecosystem.

Alkali cells need very pure hydrogen, or an unwanted chemical reaction will form a solid carbonate that interferes with chemical reactions inside the cell. As most methods of generating hydrogen from other fuels produce some carbon dioxide, the need for pure hydrogen has slowed work on alkali fuel cells in recent years. This fuel cell also needs large amounts of a costly platinum catalyst to speed up the reaction. Most of these alkali fuel cells are being designed for transport applications. See also: **Fuel cells**

Alkyl benzene Any member of the benzene family. Benzene is a known human carcinogen. See: **Benzene**

Allelopathy The production and secretion by some plants of chemical substances that inhibit the growth of competing species. This process is a retardant to plant succession and an inhibitor to increased biodiversity.

Alley cropping Planting of crops in strips with rows of trees or shrubs on each side.

Alluvial Formed by flowing water; usually refers to the soil found in floodplains or deltas. Alluvial soil is generally composed of clay, silt, sand, gravel, or similar detrital material carried in the water flow until being finally deposited at the mouth of a stream or river. Alluvial soil has little or no change from the original materials of which it is composed. If alluvial soil blocks the mouth of a stream or river, the water may be diverted and/or have its quality altered.

Alpha radiation   Form of radiant energy made up of helium nuclei. A particle ejected from the nucleus of a radioactive particle. Although the alpha particle has low penetrating power, it has adverse health effects when in direct contact with human tissue.

The health effects of alpha particles depend heavily on how exposure takes place. The greatest exposure to alpha radiation for average citizens comes from the inhalation of radon, a radioactive gas formed in the decay of uranium. Radon is an air pollutant that can accumulate in buildings and is known to be carcinogenic. *See also: Ionizing radiation; Radon*

Alpine tundra   One of the two types of tundra (the other being arctic tundra). Tundra is the coldest biome on Earth. Alpine tundra is located on mountains throughout the world at high altitude where trees cannot grow. The growing season is approximately 180 days. The nighttime temperature is usually below freezing. Unlike the arctic tundra, the soil in the alpine tundra is well drained. The plants are very similar to those of arctic tundra, and include tussock grasses, dwarf trees, small-leafed shrubs, and heaths. Animals living in the alpine tundra are also well adapted: pikas, marmots, mountain goats, sheep, elk, grouse-like birds, beetles, grasshoppers, and butterflies.

Any changes to the prevailing temperatures may alter the existing ecosystem. Global warming may result in changes to the alpine tundra. *See also: Arctic tundra; Tundra*

Alternating current (AC)   One of the two types of electrical current (the other being direct current). The direction of AC is reversed at regular intervals or cycles. The most common AC waveform is a sine (or sinusoidal) waveform.

The electrical system in the USA and many countries operates on 110/125 volts of AC. Other countries operate on 220/225 volts of AC. With the exception of Argentina and Bahrain, which use both alternating and direct current, and India, Madeira, and South Africa, which use direct current in certain areas, homes and businesses in all other countries use AC electricity exclusively. *See also: Direct current*

Alternative energy   Energy derived from non-traditional sources such as compressed natural gas, solar, water, or wind. The use of alternative energy will help decrease reliance on petroleum, coal, and natural gas, all of which are non-renewable energy sources. In ecodesign, the use of alternative energy contributes to decreased reliance on nonrenewable energy sources: petroleum, coal, and natural gas.

Alternative fuel   Fuel that can replace ordinary petroleum gasoline and may have energy-efficiency and pollution-reduction benefits. Alternative fuels can be derived from natural gas (such as propane, compressed natural gas, or methanol) or from biomass materials (such as ethanol, methanol, or soy diesel). Alternative fuels also include gasohol, which is a gasoline–alcohol mixture, and liquefied petroleum gas. *See also: Clean fuels; Compressed natural gas*

Alternative-fuel vehicle (AFV)   Any flexible-fuel or dual-fuel (or bi-fuel) vehicle designed to operate on at least one alternative fuel. Because of the expense of petroleum fuel and environmental concerns, more automakers are manufacturing alternative-fuel vehicles. Because vehicles collectively are significant consumers of energy, the hybrid vehicle helps decrease the demand for fuel. However, it is not a long-term solution. In ecodesign, transportation professionals propose a broader long-term view and design of vehicles and transportation systems that are more energy efficient. *See also: Dual-fuel vehicle*

Alternator Also known as an AC generator or a synchronous generator. An electrical device that produces a sinusoidal electric current that reverses direction many times per second.

Aluminum (Al) Metal with atomic number 13. Aluminum is light-weight and essential to modern transportation, food storage, and energy conversion equipment. It is toxic to trees and fish. Aluminum has a higher level of embodied energy than steel and requires considerably less energy to recycle.

Ambient air Any unconfined portion of the atmosphere: open air, surrounding air. Ambient air may contain hazardous air pollutants which are regulated by government agencies.

Ambient lighting Light from all sources in an area producing composite, general illumination. High-intensity and dense lighting, although ambient, can cause light pollution. Light pollution can be a composite of glare, sky glow, and omnipresence of lights. According to environmentalists, the extensive use of electricity to provide lighting is expensive, is generated by fossil fuel power plants, disrupts nocturnal wildlife, and can cause visual overload and stress in humans.

Ecodesigns of buildings should optimize the use of natural ambient light and minimize the use of electrical lights. Natural ambient lighting can be achieved by appropriate orientation of façades, larger window areas, use of light shelves and light pipes, and avoidance of deep floor plans. See also: **Light pollution**

Ambient noise Background noise associated with a given environment. Ambient noise is formed as a composite of sounds from all sources, with no particular dominant sound. Ambient noise is an important consideration in buildings and other public places. In the past few decades the level of ambient noise from countless sounds—

from vehicles to nonstop music and cellphone conversations—has increased substantially. Environmentalists feel that it has reached a level considered to be noise pollution. Loud ambient noise can damage hearing as well as threaten the quality of the occupational environment, street environment, and human lives.

Sound levels (in dB):

Normal conversation	60
Main road traffic	70
Heavy traffic	85
Truck, shouted conversation	90
Subway	90–115
Motorcycle	95–110
Crying baby, car horn	110
Pneumatic drill, ambulance siren	120
Jackhammer, power drill	130
Bicycle horn	143

See also: **Noise pollution**

Ambient temperature 1. Temperature of the surrounding air. Certain temperature of air, water, or earth around people or the environment.

2. Temperature within an enclosed space to which human beings are accustomed. Room temperature is usually indicated by general human comfort, with a common range of 18–23 °C (64–73 °F), although people may be acclimatized to higher or lower temperatures.

3. Certain temperature within settings of scientific experiments and calculations.

4. Temperature of a medium, such as gas or liquid, which comes into contact with or surrounds an apparatus or building element.

In ecodesign, the occupant of the enclosed space ultimately determines the ambient temperature for an acceptable comfort level. If the occupant can develop greater tolerance for warmer comfort levels in the summer and colder comfort levels in the winter, less energy will be required to maintain ambient temperatures and comfort conditions.

Amensalism   A type of interaction between biota in the ecosystem. Unequal interaction of one population with another: one is adversely affected and the other is not. *See also: Commensalism; Mutualism; Parasitism; Symbiosis*

American Society for Testing and Materials (ASTM)   Publishes standards covering a wide range of materials, equipment, and systems.

American Society of Heating, Refrigerating and Air-Conditioning Engineers (ASHRAE)
Organization that has actively developed building energy standards. It publishes standard test specifications, practices, classifications, and terminology in over 130 industrial segments. ASHRAE'S Standard 90.1 Energy Conservation in New Building Design is used extensively in various building codes in the USA, including the Model Energy Code.
   One of the standards set by ASHRAE is for thermal environmental conditions for human occupancy, which specifies conditions in which a specified fraction of the occupants will find the environment thermally acceptable. The standard is intended for use in design, commissioning, and testing of buildings and other occupied spaces and their HVAC systems and for the evaluation of thermal environments. Because it is not possible to prescribe the metabolic rate of occupants, and because of variations in occupant clothing levels, operating set points for buildings cannot be mandated practically by this standard. The standard does, however, provide a general guideline for environmental design systems and energy consumption. If the acceptable thermal comfort level can be lowered, energy consumption can also be lowered in a built structure.

Amorphous silicon   Also known as thin-film silicon. Type of photovoltaic (PV) cell material. Silicon photovoltaic cells have lower manufacturing cost than crystalline PV cells, but also have lower efficiency per area. *See also: Appendix 4: Photovoltaics*

Ampere (amp)   Standard unit of measure of electrical current. The amount of current that flows in a circuit at an electromotive force of one volt and at a resistance of one ohm.

Anaerobic decomposition   Also known as anaerobic digestion. Breakdown of bio-waste such as manure and municipal solid waste as feedstock by water and microorganisms that can survive in the partial or complete absence of oxygen. In ecodesign, methane gas produced in this breakdown is captured and contained to power turbines which generate electricity. *See also: Biomass electricity*

Anaerobic lagoon   Liquid-based manure-management system characterized by waste residing in water to a depth of at least 6 feet (2 m) for a period ranging between 30 and 200 days in partial or complete absence of oxygen.

Anaerobism   Ability to grow where there is no air or free oxygen.

Angle of incidence   Angle the Sun's ray makes with a line perpendicular to the surface. A surface that directly faces the Sun has a solar angle of incidence of zero, but if the surface is parallel to the Sun (sunrise striking a horizontal rooftop), the angle of the incidence is 90°. In ecodesign, the angle of incidence is used to help design fenestration, and to calculate the placement of sunshades and solar collector orientation and inclination to maximize collection of the Sun's heat.

Angstrom   Named after A. J. Angstrom, a unit of length used to measure electromagnetic radiation equal to 0.0000000001 m.

Anhydrous   Chemical compound that contains no water.

Anhydrous ethanol 99–100% alcohol (1% H_2O is allowable); neat ethanol.

Anion Negatively charged ion; an ion that is attracted to the anode. Negatively charged molecules such as $SO_4^{(2-)}$ or NO_3 in combination with hydrogen (H^+) act as strong acids and are found in acid rain.

Anode 1. Positive pole or electrode of an electrolytic cell or vacuum tube. One of four components of a fuel cell (anode, cathode, electrolyte, and interconnect). Its properties include electrical conductivity, thermal expansion, compatibility, and porosity. It must function in a reducing atmosphere. It is the source of electrical current.

2. Terminal or electrode from which electrons leave a system.

3. Negative electrode, the source of electric current in a battery.

See also: **Cathode; Electrolyte; Fuel cells; Solid oxide fuel cell**

Anoxia Condition of complete deprivation of an oxygen supply. If a body of water is anoxic, no fish can live in it. In lakes, rivers, and streams that experience eutrophication, algal blooms choke out the oxygen and the fish die. Eutrophication does not have to be anoxic; it can also be hypoxic. *See also:* **Algal blooms; Hypoxia**

Anthropogenic Made by people or resulting from human activities; not occurring naturally. Usually used in the context of emissions and environmental changes that are produced as a result of human activities. For example, greenhouse gases and thinning of the ozone layer have been attributed to industrialization worldwide.

Anthropogenic heat Human-made heat generated by buildings, people, or machinery. It is small in rural areas and larger in dense urban areas. It is usually not large enough to be a

significant factor in summertime heat island formation, but has a more significant impact on wintertime heat islands. *See also:* **Heat island**

Antioxidant Chemical that is added to a material or substance to prevent or slow the oxidation of that material. Antioxidants are used in automobile tires, food additives, and various vitamins. In ecodesign, antioxidants retard the biodegradation process and the reintegration of materials into the natural environment.

Aphotic Without light; unable to promote photosynthesis. Plants are unable to grow in aphotic conditions. In ecodesign, aphotic conditions may inhibit the incorporation of internal biotic constituents and internal landscaping into the built environment.

Apparent day A solar day. An interval between successive transits of the Sun's center across an observer's meridian; the time measured is equal to clock time.

Apparent temperature 1. Measure of relative discomfort due to combined heat and high humidity. It was developed by R. G. Steadman in 1979, and is based on physiological studies of evaporative skin cooling for various combinations of ambient temperature and humidity.

2. Temperature determined by using the measure radiance.

Aquaculture Farming of plants and animals that live in water, such as fish, shellfish, and algae.

Aquatic corridor Area of land or water that protects the quality of a stream, river, lake, wetland, or other body of water; usually an actual body of water which is an adjacent buffer or a fringe of adjacent upland area. In ecodesign, an aquatic corridor is part of the natural infrastructure and serves as a buffer against contaminants flowing into a body of water or wetland and a protection for the biota of that body of water.

Aquatic ecosystems   Salt or freshwater ecosystems, include rivers, streams, lakes, wetlands, estuaries, and coral reefs. An aquatic ecosystem also includes all the living organisms that inhabit it.

Aqueous   Something made up of water.

Aquiclude   Underground area with low perviousness located above or below an aquifer. Preserves the purity of the water from contaminant seepage.

Aquifer   Geological formation that stores or transmits water, such as wells and springs, and yields enough water supply for human use. There are two types of aquifer: confined and unconfined. *See also: Confined aquifer; Unconfined aquifer*

Architectural program   A document that serves as the basis for design. It stipulates the physical provisions needed to support the operational requirements in a built form. An architectural program includes names, numbers, sizes, and descriptions of spaces and adjacency diagrams, and may also include lists of major furnishings and equipment for each space, significant architectural characteristics of each space, and consequential engineering requirements. In ecodesign, environmental considerations should also be incorporated into the architectural program.

Arctic tundra   One of two types of tundra (the other being alpine tundra). Arctic tundra is located in the northern hemisphere, encircling the North Pole and extending south to the coniferous forests of the taiga. The arctic is characterized by cold, desert-like conditions, a growing season of 50–60 days/year, and an average winter temperature of –34°C (–30°F). However,

the arctic tundra can sustain life because its average summer temperature is 3–12°C (37–54°F). Rainfall may vary in different regions of the arctic. Yearly precipitation, including melting snow, is 15–25 cm (6–10 inches). Soil is formed slowly. There is a layer of permanently frozen subsoil called permafrost, consisting mostly of gravel and finer material. When water saturates the upper surface, bogs and ponds may form, providing moisture for plants.

There are no deep root systems in the vegetation of the arctic tundra; however, there are still a wide variety of plants that are able to resist the cold climate. There are about 1700 kinds of plant in the arctic. The fauna in the arctic is also diverse, including herbivorous and carnivorous mammals, and a wide variety of fish and insects. Reptiles and amphibians are few or absent because of the extremely cold temperatures. Because of constant immigration and emigration, the population continually oscillates.

The recent loss of arctic sea ice has been attributed by scientists to changes in the interactions between wind, weather, ice drift, and ocean currents and, most importantly, to an increased influence of greenhouse gases. Artic experts are assessing the massive shrinking of the Arctic ice cap, and are trying to determine the implications for the future of this biome. Experts are assessing this recent phenomenon—coupled with the wind shifts since 2000 that have pushed huge ice masses out of the Arctic basin and into open waters, resulting in melting of these masses—so they can forecast what will happen in the near future. *See also: Alpine tundra; Tundra*

Area fill   Landfill method that compacts the refuse in cells and then uses soil cover to separate and cover the cells. This is usually done in layers and in separate phases. It is a controlled process to contain and manage landfills. Area fill is designed to prevent spills and haphazard dumping, and is a method to prevent insects and animal scavengers from ravaging the landfill and increasing the hazards of disease spread. In ecodesign, the discarded and dumped residue and waste materials should be reused, recycled, and reintegrated into the environment, thus slowing the depletion of natural resources. *See also: Landfill*

Aromatics   Hydrocarbons based on the ringed six-carbon benzene series or related organic groups. Benzene, toluene, and xylene are the principal aromatics, known as the BTX group. They represent one of the heaviest fractions in gasoline. Benzene is a known carcinogen, and the discharge of aromatics into the environment causes contamination. *See also: Benzene*

Array   Any number of solar photovoltaic modules or solar thermal collectors or reflectors connected together to provide electrical or thermal energy. *See also: Appendix 4: Photovoltaics*

Arsenic (As)   Water pollutant and soil contaminant. Heavy metal, member of the nitrogen family. Tends to accumulate in the food chain. Arsenic in groundwater is largely the result of minerals dissolving from weathered rocks and soils. Arsenic and its compounds are used as insecticides, pesticides, and herbicides. It is carcinogenic. *See also: Heavy metals; Soil contaminants; Water pollutants*

Artificial photosynthesis   Seeks to replicate the natural process of photosynthesis, which converts sunlight, water, and carbon dioxide into carbohydrates and oxygen and splits water into hydrogen and oxygen by using energy from sunlight. Research on artificial photosynthesis focuses on several areas: producing carbon-based foods; producing oxygen; using water resources more efficiently to combat salinity, which damages crop lands in many parts of the world; using CO_2 from the atmosphere and direct solar conversion

to reduce global warming; and reducing CO_2 emissions from fossil fuels by the photoproduction of hydrogen for use in hydrogen engines or hydrogen fuel cells to generate clean energy.

Replication of photosynthesis uses solar energy directly to split water into oxygen and hydrogen. The hydrogen produced can be used as a fuel, which is considered clean, nonpolluting fuel. Another component of artificial photosynthesis is to convert sunlight, water, and carbon dioxide into carbohydrates and oxygen. Scientists studying the conversion of CO_2 to carbon monoxide (CO)—a crucial step in transforming CO_2 to useful organic compounds such as methanol—are trying to mimic what plants do when they convert CO_2 and water to carbohydrates and oxygen in the presence of chlorophyll and sunlight. Some scientists are using artificial catalysts made from transition metal complexes such as rhenium complexes. These catalysts absorb solar energy and transfer electrons to CO_2, releasing CO. Other research teams have been able to mimic "water oxidation catalysis" that occurs in natural photosynthesis. Water oxidation is accomplished by immobilizing a ruthenium catalyst on an electrode, placing it in an aqueous solution, and applying a voltage, which results in a rapid turnover of oxidizing water to oxygen.

Splitting water into hydrogen and oxygen is a complex process and requires a large amount of energy from sunlight and metal catalysts to activate the stable water molecules. The two-step process involves i) water oxidation that produces oxygen along with protons and electrons; and ii) combining the protons and electrons to make molecular hydrogen. Making hydrogen by splitting water would not add CO_2 to the atmosphere, and hydrogen produced from water does not contain carbon monoxide so it does not subject fuel cell electrodes to poisoning. *See also: Photosynthesis*

Asbestos   An air pollutant. Name given to a number of naturally occurring, fibrous silicate minerals whose properties include chemical and thermal stability and high tensile strength. Asbestos was commonly used as an acoustic insulator, thermal insulator, and fire-proofer, and in other building materials. Many products in use today contain asbestos.

Asbestos is made up of microscopic bundles of fibers that may become airborne when asbestos-containing materials are damaged or disturbed. When these fibers get into the air they may be inhaled into the lungs, where they can cause significant health problems. Asbestos contamination in vermiculite and vermiculite products has become a health and environmental concern. There are specific bans on asbestos in New Zealand, Australia, the European Union, and the USA. The bans include the following specific asbestos-containing products: flooring felt, rollboard, and corrugated, commercial, or specialty paper. In addition, the regulation continues to ban the use of asbestos in products that have not historically contained asbestos, otherwise referred to as "new uses" of asbestos. *See also:* **Air pollutants; Indoor air pollution; Vermiculite**

ASHRAE   *See:* **American Society of Heating, Refrigerating and Air Conditioning Engineers**

Aspect ratio   Ratio of length to width of an object.

Asphalt cement concrete (ACC)   Commonly known as "asphalt", ACC makes up approximately 90% of all paved surfaces in the USA. It is a hardened mixture of 7% asphalt cement binder and 93% aggregate. Asphalt, an impervious surface, absorbs emissions from vehicles and other airborne pollutants as well as heat from the Sun. Large expanses of paved areas contribute to the heat build-up of a location.

Assemblage   Interacting populations of organisms in a selected habitat. The number and

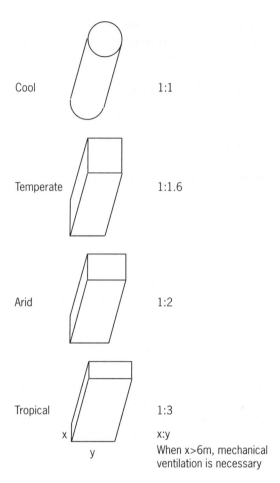

Figure 5 Optimum aspect ratios of buildings

population density of various species is an indicator of the balance and health of a particular ecosystem.

Assimilation   Ecodesign for assimilation specifies that pollutants from the built environment should be of the type and size that can be disposed into the biosphere within its capacity to assimilate those emissions by self-cleansing and self-renewal, and without contamination. The assimilative capacity of the ecosystem varies over time and space.

Asthenosphere   Section of the Earth that lies beneath the lithosphere. Volcanic eruptions originate in this area, which is about 124 miles (199.6 km) thick and sustains a very hot but not molten temperature.

ASTM   *See: American Society for Testing and Materials*

Atmosphere   Thin layer of gases surrounding the Earth. If it is not affected by anthropogenic factors, the atmosphere is normally composed of 78% nitrogen, 21% oxygen, 0.9% argon, and active greenhouse gases such as 0.03% carbon dioxide and ozone. In addition, the atmosphere contains water vapor, highly variable in amount but typically 1% volume mixing ratio. The atmosphere also contains clouds and aerosols. There is no place where the atmosphere ends, it just becomes thinner and thinner until it merges with outer space.

The greenhouse gases found in the atmosphere allow sunlight to enter the atmosphere freely. The gases with greenhouse properties that occur in nature are water vapor, CO_2, methane, and nitrous oxide. When sunlight strikes the Earth's surface, some of it is reflected back towards space as infrared radiation (heat). Greenhouse gases absorb this infrared radiation and trap the heat in the atmosphere. Over time, the amount of energy sent from the Sun to the Earth's surface should be about the same as the amount of energy radiated back into space, leaving the temperature of the Earth's surface roughly constant.

Other gases that exhibit greenhouse properties are anthropogenic, including gases for aerosols. Anthropogenically produced gases with greenhouse properties have affected the atmosphere and climate significantly since large-scale industrialization began around 150 years ago. Levels of several important greenhouse gases have increased by about 25% since then. During the past 20 years, about three-quarters of human-made CO_2 emissions were from burning fossil fuels.

Concentrations of carbon dioxide in the atmosphere are naturally regulated by numerous processes, collectively known as the "carbon cycle" (Figure 7). The movement (flux) of carbon between the atmosphere and the land and oceans is dominated by natural processes such as plant photosynthesis. While these natural

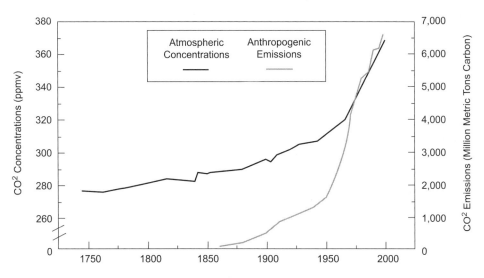

Figure 6 Trends in atmospheric concentrations and anthropogenic emissions of CO_2
Oak Ridge National Laboratory, Carbon Dioxide Information Analysis Center, http://cd/ac.esd.oml.gov

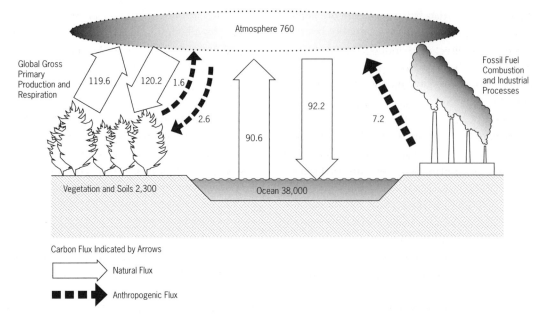

Figure 7 Global Carbon cycle (billion metric tons carbon)
Source: Intergovernmental Panel on Climate Change (2001) *Climate Change 2001: The Scientific Basis*

processes can absorb some of the net 6.1 billion metric tons of anthropogenic CO_2 emissions produced each year (measured in carbon equivalent terms), an estimated 3.2 billion metric tons is added to the atmosphere annually. The Earth's positive imbalance between emissions and absorption results in the continued growth of greenhouse gases in the atmosphere.

Given the natural variability of the Earth's climate, it is difficult to determine the extent of change caused by humans. Computer-based models indicate that rising concentrations of greenhouse gases generally produce an increase in the average temperature of the Earth. Rising temperatures may, in turn, produce changes in weather, sea levels, and land-use patterns, commonly referred to as climate change.

Assessments generally suggest that the Earth's climate has warmed over the past century, and that human activity has contributed substantially to that warming. A principal challenge of eco-design is to assist in reversing current global warming trends by addressing human activities

that have contributed to the warming. *See also:* **Greenhouse gases**

Atmospheric deposition Term used for air-borne solids, liquids, or gaseous materials that either remain in the air or become sediment on the soil or in water bodies. Some of the sedimentation is benign, while other parts contain contaminants such as acid rain, greenhouse gas emissions, and particulates.

Atmospheric deposition can be a major source of air pollution. Contaminants can travel long distances from their origins to become pollution problems in other states and nations. For example, in the USA fossil fuel combustion annually discharges almost 50 million tons of sulfur and nitrogen oxides in the atmosphere. These pollutants are diluted in the atmosphere and become acid rain. Power plants burning coal, oil, and natural gas account for about 70% of the sulfur dioxide emissions in the USA. Cars and trucks, coal-burning power plants, and industrial boilers and heaters account for most of the nitrogen oxide emissions. Mercury is also an airborne contaminant.

There are direct and indirect health effects associated with the various pollutants in atmospheric deposition. Inhalation exposures to acid deposition precursors may exacerbate existing respiratory conditions. Atmospheric deposition is known to leach heavy metals such as mercury from rocks, causing possible contamination of water supplies and increased exposure to humans through the consumption of fish. Mercury exposure effects include damage to the senses and brain. Exposure to other heavy metals can damage the kidneys and nervous system.

While many government agencies monitor the pollutant emissions in wet deposition and set reduction rates for SO_2 and NO_x emissions, there remains a need to decrease its effects on air and water quality, agriculture, watersheds, forests, human health, and the surrounding ecosystem. *See also: Acid rain; Air pollutants*

Atmospheric lifetime The approximate amount of time it would take for the anthropogenic increment of an atmospheric pollutant concentration to return to its natural level (assuming emissions cease) as a result of either being converted to another chemical compound, or being taken out of the atmosphere via a sink. The amount of time depends on the pollutant's sources and sinks as well as its reactivity. The lifetime of a pollutant is often considered in conjunction with the mixing of pollutants in the atmosphere. A long lifetime will allow the pollutant to mix throughout the atmosphere. Average lifetimes can vary from about a week (sulfate aerosols) to more than a century (CFCs and CO_2). Emissions of atmospheric pollutants individually and collectively are monitored and regulated by government and international agencies. *See also: Assimilation*

Atmospheric pressure Force exerted by the movement of air in the atmosphere, usually measured in units of force per area. For fuel cells, atmospheric pressure is generally used to describe a system where the only pressure acting on the system is from the atmosphere and no external pressure is applied.

Atomic Energy Act Refers to the US federal law that administers and regulates the production and uses of atomic power. The act was originally passed in 1946 and has been amended many times since then. Other countries also have laws that regulate and govern the use of atomic power.

Atomic Energy Agency, International *See: International Atomic Energy Agency (IAEA)*

Attainment area Geographical area in which levels of a criteria air pollutant meet the health-based primary standard (in the USA, National Ambient Air Quality Standards, NAAQS) for the pollutant. Government environmental protection agencies set national pollutant limits. *See also: Criteria air pollutants; Nonattainment area*

Autoclave Device that uses steam to sterilize equipment and deactivate bacteria, viruses, fungi, and spores.

Autogenic Endogenous, coming from within a community or organism. Changes to the organism or locality are affected by internal (endogenous) factors rather than external factors.

Autotroph Organism that uses carbon dioxide as its primary source of carbon. It synthesizes food molecules from inorganic molecules by using an external energy source. For example, green plants, which get their energy from sunlight through photosynthesis, are a major group of autotrophic organisms. *See also: Heterotroph; Lithotroph*

Autotrophic layer Green belt or ecosystem.

Avalanche diode Specialized diode that acts as a relief valve for excess voltage. A diode that conducts in the reverse direction when the reverse bias voltage exceeds the breakdown voltage. These are electrically very similar to Zener diodes (and are often mistakenly called Zener diodes), but break down by a different mechanism: the avalanche effect. This occurs when the reverse electric field across the p–n junction causes a wave of ionization, reminiscent of an avalanche, leading to a large current. Avalanche diodes are designed to break down at a well defined reverse voltage without being destroyed. The difference between the avalanche diode (which has a reverse breakdown above about 6.2 V) and the Zener diode is that the channel length of the former exceeds the "mean free path" of the electrons, so there are collisions between them on the way out. The only practical difference is that the two types have temperature coefficients of opposite polarities. Avalanche diodes are sometimes used in combination with Zener diodes. *See also: Diode; Schottky diode; Zener diode*

Azimuth angle Angle between true south and the point on the horizon directly below the Sun.

B

B100 100% neat biodiesel, a renewable, biodegradable fuel. *See also: Biodiesel*

B20 Blend of biodiesel fuel with 80% petroleum-based diesel and 20% biodiesel. It can be used in diesel vehicles with no modifications to their engines, fuel systems, or refueling infrastructure. *See also: Biodiesel*

Background extinction Extinction of species as a result of changes in environmental conditions in an ecosystem.

BACT *See: Best available control technology*

BAF *See: Biological aerated filter*

Baghouse Municipal waste combustion facility air emissions control device, consisting of a series of fabric filters through which flue gases are passed to remove particulates prior to atmospheric dispersion.

Bake out 1. Artificial acceleration of the outgassing process.

2. In various physics and engineering vacuum devices, such as particle accelerators, semiconductor fabrication, and vacuum tubes, refers to a period where a part or the entire device is placed in a vacuum chamber (or its operating vacuum state, for devices that operate in a vacuum) and heated, usually by built-in heaters. This drives off gases, which can then be removed by a vacuum pump system.

3. In building construction, refers to a process using heat to remove volatile organic compounds (VOC) such as solvents used in paint, carpets, and other building materials from the building after construction. The building is heated to a much higher temperature than normal and left at that temperature for an extended period to encourage such compounds to vaporize into the air, which can then be vented.

Balance of system (BOS) Term used in connection with photovoltaic systems. It can mean all components and costs of a photovoltaic (PV) system, other than the photovoltaic modules/array. It includes design costs, land, site preparation, system installation, support structures, power conditioning, operation and maintenance costs, indirect storage, and related costs.

It can also describe one of the subsystems of a complete PV energy system. It is the subsystem that enables the PV-generated electricity to be properly applied to the load. The BOS typically consists of structures for mounting the PV arrays or modules and power-conditioning equipment that adjusts and converts the DC electricity to the proper form and magnitude required by an AC load. The BOS can also include storage devices such as batteries, so PV-generated electricity can be used during cloudy days or at night. *See also: Photovoltaic (PV)* and associated entries; *Appendix 4: Photovoltaics*

Bali Roadmap Agreement adopted by participating nations during the United Nations Climate

Change Conference in Bali, Indonesia in December 2007. It outlines a two-year process of meetings to finalize a binding agreement in 2009 in Denmark. Affirming scientific evidence of global warming, the convention addressed: i) the need to reduce emissions and the risks of further global warming; ii) policies, incentives, and financial support to halt deforestation and forest degradation and to preserve tropical rain forests; iii) international cooperation to protect poorer nations against climate change impacts; iv) assistance to help developing countries adapt to green technologies to reduce or avoid carbon pollution. Four meetings in 2008 developed specific goals and strategies to implement the Bali Roadmap, with the intention of expanding the Kyoto Protocol. *See also:* **Kyoto Protocol**

Bamboo   A strong, renewable building material that can be substituted for hardwoods. Bamboo is not a tree, it is a giant grass. It has the ability to reach full height in one growth spurt of about two months. When bamboo is harvested, the root system is unharmed and healthy, ready to produce more shoots, just like a grass lawn. Bamboo grows in tropical temperate climates, and for thousands of years people in Asia, Africa, and South America have used it as a building material, for furniture, weapons, writing and musical instruments, fuel, food, and medical products.

Some varieties of bamboo grow to timber proportions, 120 feet (37 m) high and 13 feet (4 m) diameter. Thick bamboo poles are two or three times stronger than comparably sized wood timber. Bamboo can be harvested in seven years compared with 10–50 years for softwoods and hardwoods, yielding up to 20 times more than wood. One bamboo clump can produce 200 poles in the five years it takes one plant to reach maturity. Bamboo can be sustainably harvested and replenished with virtually no impact on the environment. *See also:* **Cork**

Bara Costantini   Passive solar heating system invented by Bara Costantini, which uses a heavy internal wall with a ventilated air gap to store solar energy and improve summer comfort. *See also:* **Passive solar heating**

Barium (Ba)   Major soil contaminant. Metallic chemical element found as a carbonate or sulfate; often used in alloys. Monitored by USEPA. Studies have shown that barium causes health problems through exposure. *See also:* **Soil contaminants**

BAS   *See:* **Building automation management system**

Base cations   Regarded as the most prevalent exchangeable weak acid cations in the soil. They include positively charged ions such as magnesium (Mg), sodium (Na), potassium (K), and calcium (Ca). Base cations are important in sustaining ecosystems because their deposition serves as nutrients for the forest ecosystem and vegetation, and has an impact on surface pH. Their deposition is important to determine critical loads for acidity; as base cations increase in the soil, they counteract acidity in the soil and add alkalinity to it.

The base cations (Na^+, K^+, Ca^{2+}, Mg^{2+}) are known to be present in ambient air and in precipitation. The deposition of these base cations in ecosystems helps neutralize the acidifying inputs from the deposition of SO_x and NO_x. Base cations are emitted to the atmosphere as particles through natural processes such as soil erosion and rock weathering, and from sea salt, as well as through anthropogenic activities such as combustion of coal and wood fuel, limestone quarrying, industrial processes like cement manufacture and concrete batching, iron and steel manufacture, glass manufacture, construction and demolition activities, materials handling and storage, and dust from traffic and exhaust emissions of potassium from lead-replacement gasoline.

The UK International Review Group on Acid Rain (1997) reported a decline in the base cation deposition in Europe and North America since the early 1970s. The review group also found a decrease in base cation effectiveness in reducing SO_2 emissions. Other international research groups indicate that base cation data are relatively uncertain.

Basel Convention   The Basel Convention on the Control of Transboundary Movements of Hazardous Wastes and their Disposal is an international agreement on hazardous and other wastes. The Convention has 170 signatories, and seeks to protect human health and the environment against the adverse effects resulting from the generation, management, transboundary movements, and disposal of hazardous and other wastes. The Basel Convention was enacted in 1989 and became effective in 1992.

Batch heater   Also known as an integral collector storage system or bread box system. Simple passive solar hot water system which consists of one or more storage tanks placed in an insulated box that has a glazed side facing the Sun. Cold water first passes through the solar collector, which preheats the water. The water then continues on to the conventional backup water heater, providing a reliable source of hot water. They are useful only in mild-freeze climates because the outdoor pipes could freeze in severe cold weather. During the winter, they should be protected from freezing or drained. *See also: **Solar collector, residential use***

Batesian mimicry   Mimicry adaptation that helps preserve certain species and maintain biodiversity. Refers to two or more species that are similar in appearance, but only one of which is armed with spines, stingers, or toxic chemistry, while its apparent double lacks these traits. The second species has no defense other than resembling the more toxic species and is protected from certain predators by its resemblance to the unpalatable species, which the predator associates with a certain appearance and a bad experience. Mimicry is used by both predator and prey.

Batesian mimicry is named for Henry Walter Bates, a British scientist who studied mimicry in Amazonian butterflies during the mid- and late-nineteenth century. Examples of Batesian mimicry are the several species of butterflies that mimic toxic Heliconid butterflies. Another butterfly mimic is the nontoxic *Papilio memmon* of Indonesia. Each female butterfly (regardless of coloration) can produce one or more different female forms that mimic any of five other species of foul-tasting butterflies. Batesian mimicry is also found in venomous coral snakes and the harmless milk and king snakes. Both snakes are marked with alternating yellow, red, and black bands, causing possible predators to avoid both. The deadly coral snake has bands in the order red, yellow, black; while the harmless species have the pattern red, black, yellow, although there are exceptions. *See: **Meullerian mimicry***

Battery   1. Energy storage device that produces electricity by a chemical action. It consists of two of more electrochemical cells enclosed in a container and electrically interconnected in an appropriate series/parallel arrangement to provide operating voltage and current levels.

2. Applies to a single cell if it constitutes the entire electrochemical storage system.

Research conducted independently by a number of countries, the European Union (EU), and the United Nations has shown that there are adverse environmental and health effects from large quantities of heavy metals (such as cadmium and nickel), acid and alkali that leak from discarded batteries. Batteries dumped into landfills will disintegrate and leak toxic substances into groundwater, soil, and air, eventually polluting the food people consume.

The most commonly used batteries are portable cadmium, lead–acid, automotive, industrial, and disposable ones. Disposable batteries are known as dry batteries and cannot be recharged. Because of their toxicity, disposable batteries increase pollutant hazards in landfills. In the USA alone, 84,000 tons of alkaline batteries are thrown away annually. AA, AAA, C, D, and 9-volt batteries that power electronic games, toys, portable audio equipment, clocks, smoke detectors, and various other household items comprise 20% of the hazardous materials households produce each year across the USA.

Many countries have already passed laws that prohibit dumping of spent batteries into landfills. Programs to protect nature from the often toxic substances contained in batteries were scheduled to be enacted in all 25 EU countries by 2008. The regulation requires 19 of the EU's 25 members to set up programs for collecting spent consumer batteries. Austria, Belgium, Germany, France, the Netherlands, and Sweden already have such systems in place. The law bans some portable cadmium batteries and prohibits dumping in landfills or burning of automotive and industrial batteries, most of which are already collected. The EU wants to ensure all such batteries, which make up about 86% of the market, are collected. By 2012, a quarter of all batteries sold must be collected once they run out. By 2016, the target will rise to 45%. Distributors will be required to take used batteries back at no charge. The rules also determine how batteries must be recycled once collected. Battery producers and distributors will bear the cost of most of the bill for implementing the recycling.

Battery electric vehicle (BEV)   A type of hybrid vehicle engine. It uses chemical energy stored in rechargeable battery packs, and an electric motor and motor controller instead of an internal combustion engine. Some confusion arises because the industry often refers to BEVs when it means electric cars.

The hybrid electric vehicle (HEV) uses both an electric motor and an internal combustion engine. It is not considered a pure BEV because it operates in a charge-sustaining mode. *See also: Hybrid electric vehicle; Hybrid engine*

Battery, sugar   Recently developed, the sugar battery is an environmentally friendly prototype battery that runs on sugars and can generate enough electricity to power a music player and a pair of speakers. The bio-battery's casing is made of a vegetable-based plastic. It measures 1.5 inches (3.9 cm) along each edge, and works by pouring sugar solution into the unit, where enzymes break it down to generate electricity. Current tests show an output of 50 milliwatts. It is still in development for eventual commercial use.

Beadwall   A form of movable insulation that uses tiny polystyrene beads blown into the space between two window panes. Polystyrene is a nonbiodegradable plastic. An insulation substitute made from plant-based plastics would decrease the adverse effects of synthetic polymers on the environment.

Beam radiation   Solar radiation that is not scattered by dust or water droplets.

Beaufort scale   Measures wind speed on a scale from 0–12. Zero is the lowest, calmest wind speed of 19 km/h or less; 12 is the highest, hurricane-force wind speed of 118 km/h or more (see Table 1).

Bedrock   Consolidated rock.

BEES   *See: Building for Economic and Environmental Stability*

Beijing Agreement   1999 Amendment to the Montreal Protocol. *See also: Montreal Protocol on Substances that Deplete the Ozone Layer*

Table 1 Beaufort scale

Beaufort number	Wind speed km/h	mph	Description	Wave height m	ft	Sea conditions	Land conditions
0	<1	<1	Calm	0	0	Flat	Calm
1	1–5	1–3	Light air	0.1	0.33	Ripples, no crests	Wind motion visible
2	6–11	3–7	Light breeze	0.2	0.66	Small wavelets	Leaves rustle
3	12–19	7–10	Gentle breeze	0.6	2.0	Large wavelets	Leaves in motion
4	20–28	13–17	Moderate breeze	1.0	3.3	Small waves	Small branches move
5	29–38	18–24	Fresh breeze	2.0	6.6	Moderate waves	Small trees sway
6	39–49	34–40	Strong breeze	3.0	9.9	Large waves, foam	Large branches move
7	50–61	31–38	High wind, near gale	4.0	13.1	Sea heaps up	Whole trees in motion
8	62–74	39–46	Fresh gale	5.5	18.0	Breaking crests	Twigs broken
9	75–88	47–54	Strong gale	7.0	23.0	High waves	Large branches break
10	89–102	55–63	Whole gale/ storm	9.0	29.5	Very high waves	Trees uprooted
11	103–117	64–72	Violent storm	11.5	37.7	Extreme waves	Widespread damage
12	>118	>73	Hurricane force	>14	>46	Huge waves	Widespread damage

Benthic Occurring at or near the bottom of a body of water.

Benthic organisms Also known as benthos. Organisms, including worms, clams, and crustaceans that live at the bottom of freshwater and marine ecosystems.

Bentonite Sodium-rich volcanic ash that can be used as a substitute for regular cement, which has chlorides and emits carbon. Because it expands when wet and can absorb several times its dry weight in water, it is used in drilling mud in the oil and gas well-drilling industries, as a sealant for spent nuclear fuel, for quarantining metal pollutants of groundwater, and as a base liner for landfills and slurry walls. Its waterproof characteristics work well in below-grade walls and in forming other impermeable barriers.

Benzene (C$_6$H$_6$) Major soil contaminant and toxic chemical. A colorless liquid with a sweet odor, it evaporates into the air very quickly and dissolves slightly in water. It is highly flammable, and is formed from both natural processes and human activities. It ranks in the top 20 chemicals for production volume in the USA. It is used to make other chemicals, which are used to make plastics, resins, and nylon and synthetic fibers. It is also used to make some types of rubber, lubricants, dyes, detergents, drugs, and pesticides.

Industrial processes are the main source of benzene in the environment. It can pass into the air from water and soil, and can attach to rain or snow and be carried back down to the ground. It breaks down more slowly in water and soil, and can pass through the soil into underground water. Benzene does not build up in plants or animals. Studies have shown that plants remove benzene from the air, along with formaldehyde, and airborne microbes.

Natural sources of benzene include volcanoes and forest fires. Benzene is also a natural part of crude oil, gasoline, and cigarette smoke. *See also:* **Soil contaminants; Toxic chemicals**

Berm Elongated pile of soil, usually human-made, used to control and direct the flow of surface water runoff. Berms may also be used to provide wind protection and insulation, to block out noise, and to screen operations from public view. In ecodesign, a vegetated berm can be used to bring vegetation up the sides of a building.

Beryllium (Be) A metal that has adverse effects on human health. Emitted from ceramic and propellant plants, foundries, and machine shops.

Best available control technology (BACT)
Pollution control standard originally mandated by the USA's Clean Air Act. It has subsequently been adopted and used by state governments in the USA. The USEPA determines what air pollution control technology will be used to control a specific pollutant to a specified limit. The factors used to determine best available control technology include energy consumption, total source emission, regional environmental impact, and economic costs. BACT applies to agricultural, chemical, and mechanical processes that produce emissions. It is the current USEPA standard for all polluting sources and is determined on a case-by-case basis.

Best management practices Term used to describe the most effective organization, strategy and planning, operations, and management in many professional areas. For example, best management practices to contain pollution would be the most effective and practical method designed to minimize harm to the environment.

Beta radiation Beta radiation is emitted during the radioactive decay of many beta-active, unstable nuclides. Examples of pure beta-emitters are the radionuclides strontium-90, with a half-life of 27.7 years; and tritium, 12.3 years. The beta particle, which is an electron, is emitted when a neutron in a nucleus is transformed into a proton. Eye-glasses or thick clothing are often sufficient to stop beta radiation. Unprotected skin exposed to very strong beta radiation may burn as a result of a large skin dose. The greatest risk is associated with ingestion with food, or inhalation. *See also:* **Ionizing radiation**

BEV   *See:* **Battery electric vehicle**

Bi-fuel vehicle   *See:* **Dual-fuel vehicle**

BIFP   *See:* **Building integrated food production**

BIM   *See:* **Building information modeling**

Bin method Method of predicting heating and/or cooling loads using instantaneous load calculation at different outdoor dry-bulb temperatures, and multiplying the result by the number of hours of occurrence of each temperature.

Binary cycle geothermal power An alternative source of energy. One of three main geothermal power technologies: dry steam, flash steam, and binary cycle. Hot geothermal fluids are passed through one side of a heat exchanger to heat a working fluid in a separate adjacent pipe. The working fluid, usually an organic compound with a low boiling point, such as iso-butane or iso-pentane, is vaporized and passed through a turbine to generate electricity. This system enables working fluids to boil at lower temperature than water, so electricity can be generated from reservoirs with lower temperatures. The binary cycle system is self-contained and produces virtually no emissions. Geothermal energy is an alternative energy source that utilizes the heat of the earth for direct heating or production of electricity. *See also: Dry steam geothermal power; Flash steam geothermal power; Geothermal power technology*

BIPV *See: Building integrated photovoltaics*

Bioaccumulation Process in which chemicals such as PCB and DDT are retained by plants and animals and increase in concentration over time. Depending on the ability of fauna and flora to accumulate toxic chemicals, the biodiversity of an area could decrease, thereby altering the balance of the ecosystem.

Biochemical oxygen demand (BOD) 1. Also known as biological oxygen demand. BOD is a measure of the amount of oxygen used by microorganisms, such as aerobic bacteria, in the oxidation of organic matter. Natural sources of organic matter include plant decay and leaf fall. Plant growth and decay may be accelerated when nutrients and sunlight are overly abundant due to human influence. Urban runoff carries pet wastes from streets and sidewalks; nutrients from lawn fertilizers; leaves, grass clippings, and paper from residential areas, which increase oxygen demand. Oxygen consumed in the decomposition process robs other aquatic organisms of the oxygen they need to live. Organisms that are more tolerant of lower dissolved oxygen levels may replace a diversity of more sensitive organisms.

2. Chemical procedure to determine the time it takes biological organisms to use up oxygen in a body of water. It is used in water quality management and assessment, ecology, and environmental science. BOD is not an accurate quantitative test, although it could be used as an indication of the quality of a water source.

Bioclimatic design *See: Passive mode design*

Bioclimatology Branch of climatology that deals with the effects of the physical environment on living organisms over an extended period; study of the effects of climatic conditions on living organisms.

Bioconversion Conversion of biomass to ethanol, methanol, or methane. Converting plants and microorganisms into energy.

Biodegradable Characteristic of a substance that can be broken down by a living organism into simple compounds such as carbon dioxide and water.

Biodegradable material Material that can be reduced to simple compounds by organisms through decomposition; generally, organic material such as plant and animal matter and other substances originating from living organisms, or artificial materials that are similar enough to plant and animal matter to be put to use by microorganisms.

In ecodesign, the use of benign biodegradable materials, such as those used for packaging, enables the materials used in the built environment to be reintegrated into the natural environment. This process will change a throughput pattern of use into a closed loop in the ecosystem. As in ecomimicry, the waste from one organism becomes the food for another.

Examples of substances and the time they take to biodegrade:

Banana peel	2–10 days
Sugar cane pulp products	1–2 months
Cotton rags	1–5 months
Paper	2–5 months

Rope	3–14 months
Orange peels	6 months
Wool socks	1–5 years
Cigarette filters	1–12 years
Tetrapaks (plastic composite milk cartons)	5 years
Plastic bags	10–20 years
Leather shoes	25–40 years
Nylon fabric	30–40 years
Tin cans	50–100 years
Aluminum cans	80–100 years
Plastic six-pack holder rings	450 years
Diapers and sanitary napkins	500–800 years
Plastic bottles	nonbiodegradeable
Styrofoam cup	nonbiodegradeable

See also: *Ecomimicry*

Biodegradable plastics   Plastics made from plant-based materials that decompose when exposed to microorganisms. Examples are copolymers made of plant materials such as wheat and corn starch, and synthetic polymers made by polymerization of starch and cellulose with polystyrene. This new plastic can eventually replace traditional synthetic polymer-based plastics made from nonrenewable fossil fuels. *See also: Plastics*

Biodegradation   The process by which organic substances are broken down by living organisms. The term is often used in relation to ecology, waste management, environmental remediation (bioremediation), and to describe plastic materials, due to their long life span. Organic materials can be degraded aerobically, with oxygen, or anaerobically, without oxygen. A term related to biodegradation is biomineralization, in which organic matter is converted into minerals. *See also: Biomineralization*

Biodiesel   Renewable fuel that can be manufactured from soybean or rapeseed oils, animal fats, recycled restaurant greases, or microalgae oils. It is safe, biodegradable, and reduces air pollutants such as particulates, carbon monoxide, hydrocarbons, and air toxins. It is produced through transesterfication, in which the organic oils are combined with ethanol or methanol in the presence of a catalyst to form ethyl or methyl ester. These esters can be blended with conventional diesel fuel or used on their own.

Biodiversity   Also known as biological diversity. Variety and variability among living organisms and the ecological complexes in which they occur. Biodiversity can be considered at four levels: i) species diversity; ii) habitat diversity—the number of different physical environments with their own range of organisms that occur with an ecosystem; iii) niche diversity—the variety of relationships that occur between organisms and their habitat; iv) genetic diversity, which is essentially the gene pool. Biodiversity enhancement is a principal consideration in ecodesign. *See also: Williams alpha diversity index*

Bioenergy   1. Renewable sources of energy, such as the Sun's energy stored in plant matter and animal waste (known as biomass). Biomass fuel sources are considered renewable because they replenish themselves more quickly than the sources of fossil fuels.

2. Application of technology to biomass resources to produce energy-related products, including electricity; liquid, solid, and gaseous fuels; heat, chemicals, and other materials. *See also: Biomass fuel; Biomass electricity*

Bioengineering   Science on which all biotechnological applications are based. Often refers to genetic engineering. *See also: Biotechnology*

Bioenhancing plastics   Plastic materials that carry additives to stimulate plant growth, prevent erosion in arid climates, and carry plant seeds embedded in growth stimulants.

Bioethanol   *See: Ethanol*

Biofilter   Indoor vegetation serves as a biofilter to improve internal air quality (IAQ) by eliminating formaldehyde, benzene, and airborne microbes, and by absorbing carbon dioxide and releasing oxygen. Some of the best plants for biofiltering are the areca palm golden pothos, rubber plant, English ivy, spider plant, and Boston fern. *See also: Bamboo*

Biofuel   *See: Biomass fuel*

Biogas   Combustible gas produced from the anaerobic decomposition of organic material in a landfill. Material is primarily methane, carbon dioxide, and hydrogen sulfide. *See also: Biomass fuel*

Biogasification   Process of decomposing biomass with anaerobic bacteria to produce biogas.

Biogenic   Produced by the actions of living organisms.

Biogenic hydrocarbons   Naturally occurring compounds, including volatile organic compounds (VOCs) that are emitted from trees and vegetations. High-VOC-emitting tree species such as eucalyptus can contribute to smog formation. Species-specific biogenic emission rates may influence the selection of trees for large-scale planting, especially in areas with high ozone concentrations.

Biogeochemical cycle   Movement through the Earth's system—atmosphere, hydrosphere, lithosphere, and biosphere—of key chemical constituents essential to life: carbon, nitrogen, oxygen, and phosphorus.

Biogeofilter system   Experimental system that treats both wastewater and sewage. This system takes the nitrogen and phosphorus still remaining after septic tank treatment and uses it as a hydroponic solution to grow plants. The plants absorb the decomposed nitrogen and phosphorus, thereby cleaning the water of these pollutants. *See also: Hydroponic*

Biogeographical area   A region or ecosystem that has unique biological, water, and land characteristics.

Biohazard   Organisms and/or microorganisms, such as bacteria and viruses, that are a threat to human health. Medical waste, such as toxins, can also have an adverse effect on human and animal health.

Biointegration   Fundamental principle of ecodesign, based on the concept of biological integrity. Its basic premise is to design the built environment to integrate benignly and seamlessly with the natural environment, which includes the biosphere.

Biological aerated filter (BAF)   Wastewater treatment process that uses active biomass attached to fixed media in an aerobic environment to remove contaminants.

Biological contaminants   Also known as microbiologicals or microbials. Living organisms, or agents derived from them, that can be inhaled and may cause many types of health problem.

Biological integrity   Balanced ecosystem in which an environment can maintain a balanced, integrated community of organisms.

Biological oxygen demand   *See: Biochemical oxygen demand (BOD)*

Biological toilet   *See: Composting toilet*

Biomarker   1. Measure used to identify a toxic effect in an individual organism; it can also be used in extrapolation between species.

2. Indicator of an event or condition in a biological system or sample that provides a measure of exposure, effect, or susceptibility.

Biomass Any organic matter, particularly cellulosic or lignocellulosic matter, which is available on a renewable or recurring basis. May include trees, plants, pulp and paper operation residue, plant fiber, agriculture and forestry wastes, urban wood wastes, landfill wastes, and animal wastes. Biomass resources also include land and water crops grown solely for energy purposes, known as energy crops. In ecomimetic ecodesign, the imitation/created ecosystem should include biotic and abiotic parts to form a balanced whole. *See also: Ecomimicry; Energy crops*

Biomass electricity Use of organic biomass as the feedstock or source of fuel. There are a number of ways to generate electricity from biomass: i) direct-fired or conventional steam, ii) pyrolysis, iii) co-firing, iv) biomass gasification, v) anaerobic digestion, vi) landfill gas collection, and vii) modular systems.

- *Direct-fired or conventional steam* boilers burn bioenergy feedstocks directly to produce steam, which in turn creates electricity.
- *Pyrolysis* The process in which biomass is combusted at high temperatures and decomposed in the absence of oxygen. *See: Pyrolysis*
- *Co-firing* combines biomass with coal to generate energy. The biomass used in this process is usually woody and herbaceous, such as poplar, willow, or switchgrass.
- *Biomass gasification* Heat conversion of solid biomass into a flammable gaseous form, syngas. Can be used in a combined-cycle gas turbine or another power-conversion technology such as a coal power plant. The biogas is cleaned and filtered to remove problem chemical compounds, and can be used in power-generation systems called combined cycles, which combine gas turbines and steam turbines to

produce electricity. *See: Biomass gasification; Gasification*
- *Anaerobic digestion* Biological process in which methane, released by the interactions of bacteria and archaea, is contained and used to create energy. *See: Anaerobic decomposition*
- *Landfill gas* By-product of the decomposition of solid waste. Consists of 50% methane, 45% CO_2, and 4% nitrogen; uses technology similar to anaerobic digestion to generate electricity.
- *Modular systems* use some of the same technologies as the methods above but are suited to much smaller-scale use, such as in villages, farms, and small industry. They have great potential for use in developing countries, where biomass is abundant and electricity is scarce.

Biomass feedstock Term used to describe large quantities of biomass source.

Biomass fuel Organic materials (biomass) are converted to liquid or gaseous fuels such as ethanol, methanol, methane, and hydrogen. They are burned for energy purposes. Sources for biomass fuel include agricultural residue, pulp/paper mill residue, urban wood waste, forest residue, energy crops, landfill methane, and animal waste. When plants (biomass) are burned, the sugars contained in the plants, the polymer of 6-carbon sugars, break down and release energy exothermically, giving off CO_2, heat, and steam. The by-products of this reaction can be captured and manipulated to create electricity, known as biopower (or biomass power). Biomass fuels also can produce heat and steam. Fuels can be derived from biomass sources through conversion methods such as direct combustion boiler and steam turbines, anaerobic digestion, co-firing, gasification, and pyrolysis. The co-firing method mixes biomass with coal.

As an energy source, biomass is renewable, more evenly distributed over the Earth's surface, and uses less capital-intensive technologies. It ranks second to hydropower in renewable primary energy production. *See also: Biomass; Biomass electricity; Biopower*

Biomass gasification   Conversion of biomass into a gas or thermal gasification, in which hydrogen is produced from high-temperature gasifying and low-temperature pyrolysis of biomass. *See also: Biomass electricity; Gasification*

Biomass power   *See: Biomass electricity; Biomass fuel; Biopower*

Biomass pyramid   Total distribution of organisms in each trophic level (see Figure 8).

Biome   Geographical region of the world that has a distinctive climate and environment that affects the living organisms and vegetation within it. The climate and geography of a region determines what type of biome can exist in that region. Major biomes include deserts, forests, grasslands, tundra, and several types of aquatic environment. Each biome consists of many ecosystems, whose communities have adapted to the small differences in climate and environment within the biome. All living things are closely related to their environment. Any change in one part of an environment, such as an increase or decrease in a species of animal or plant, causes a ripple effect of change through other parts of the environment.

Biomimicry   Also known as biomimetics. Using nature as a model and imitating it. Nature

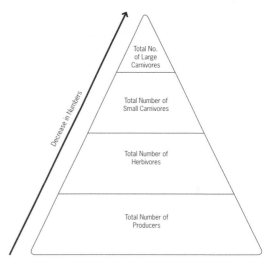

Figure 8 A biomass pyramid

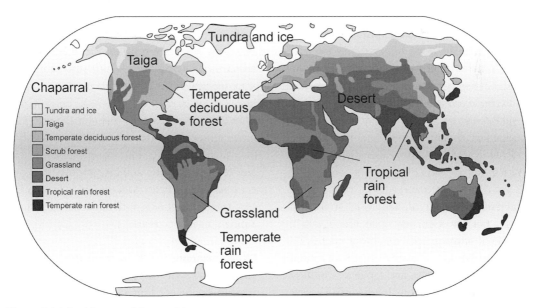

Figure 9 Major biomes of the world

provides an endless source of models and principles for invention. A corollary is ecomimicry as a fundamental design strategy in ecodesign. Examples of natural processes that can be used in human communities include use of solar energy using photosynthesis or creating artificial photosynthesis; recycling of waste; and increasing energy efficiency. *See also: Bionics; Ecomimicry*

Biomineralization   The process by which living organisms produce minerals, usually to harden or stiffen existing tissues. Examples include silicates in algae and diatoms, carbonates in invertebrates, and calcium phosphates and carbonates in vertebrates. These minerals often form structures such as sea shells and the bone in mammals and birds. Other examples include copper, iron, and gold deposits involving bacteria. *See also: Biodegradation*

Bionics   Also known as bionical creativity engineering. The application of systems and methods found in nature to the design of modern technology, engineering, and systems in the built environment. *See also: Biomimicry*

Biophilia   Genetic tendency of humans to respond positively to nature, particularly plants. This has influenced the use of plants internally and externally in the built environment in ecodesign. Research has shown that humans respond positively to nature and plants: for example, hospital patients heal more quickly, stay in hospital for shorter periods, and require less medication when they have views of nature and plants.

Bioplastics   Instead of traditional petroleum-derived plastics, bioplastics are biodegradable and compostable plastics made from renewable raw materials, such as starch (including, but not limited to, corn, potato, and tapioca), cellulose, soybean oil, lactic acid, and hemp oil. Bioplastics are not hazardous in production and

decompose back to carbon dioxide, water, and biomass in the environment when discarded. Corn starch is currently the main raw material being used in the manufacture of bioplastic resins. This is generally regarded as a more sustainable process, as it relies less on fossil fuels and produces less greenhouse emissions. *See also: Biodegradable plastics; Bioenhancing plastics; Bioregenerative plastics*

Biopolymer   Biopolymers are polymers that are biodegradable. The materials for production of these polymers may be based on agricultural plant or animal products, and may be renewable or synthetic. There are four main types of biopolymer, based on starch, sugar, cellulose, and synthetic materials.

Biopower   Also known as biomass power. Electricity produced as a by-product of burning biomass fuels. Methods used include direct firing, co-firing, gasification, pyrolysis, and anaerobic digestion. *See also: Biomass electricity; Biomass fuel*

Bioregenerative plastics   Polycaprolactone film completely biodegrades within three months with no residues. These films, used on paper products, are water-resistant and have potential uses in many types of container for liquids. *See also: Bioplastics; Biodegradable plastics*

Bioregion   A subset of the biosphere. Each bioregion contains characteristic fauna and flora that have adapted to the region's climate, soils, and landforms, and each bioregion has its own ecosystem. Examples include tropical rain forests, open woodlands and savannas, tundra and alpine areas, and deserts.

Bioremediation   Used in tandem with phytoremediation. Use of biological processes to remove pollutants from a contaminated environment, such as the ability of trees and vegetation to remove pollution from rainwater. Green roofs and shade trees mitigate urban runoff and nonpoint-source nitrogen and phosphorus pollution through these processes. *See also: Phytoremediation*

Biosphere   All forms of life that exist on Earth; all ecosystems and living organisms in the atmosphere, on the land or in the oceans, including derived dead organic matter such as litter, soil organic matter, and oceanic detritus.

Biosphere 2   An enclosed structure in Oracle, Arizona, USA covering 3.14 acres, originally built by Space Biosphere Ventures to be an artificial, closed ecological system. Constructed between 1987 and 1991, it was used to study ecosystems. It studied the manipulation of a biosphere without harming the external environment. Biosphere 2 was the largest closed system ever created. The sealed nature of the structure allowed scientists to monitor the ever-changing chemistry of the air, water, and soil contained within.

The biosphere included a 850 m² (1,017 yd²) ocean with a coral reef, a 450 m² (538 yd²) mangrove wetlands, a 1900 m² (2,272 yd²) savannah grassland, a 1400 m² (1,674 yd²) fog desert, a 2500 m² (2,990 yd²) agricultural system, a human habitat with living quarters and office, and a below-ground-level technical facility. Heating and cooling water circulated through independent piping systems, and electrical power was supplied from a natural gas energy center through airtight penetrations.

Bioswales   Swaled drainage course with gently sloped sides (less than 6%) and filled with vegetation, compost and/or riprap. The water's flow path, along with the wide and shallow ditch, are designed to maximize the time water spends in the swale, which aids the trapping of pollutants and silt from surface runoff water. Used for sustainable drainage systems in ecodesign and ecomasterplanning to return rainfall back to the land and to prevent flooding. Commonly used around parking lots, where automotive pollution is collected by the paving and then flushed by rain. The bioswale, or other type of biofilter, wraps around the parking lot and treats the runoff before releasing it to the watershed or storm sewer (see Figure 10).

Biotechnology (biotech)   Technologies based on biology, especially when used in agriculture, food science, and medicine. The United Nations Convention on Biological Diversity defines biotechnology as: "Any technological application

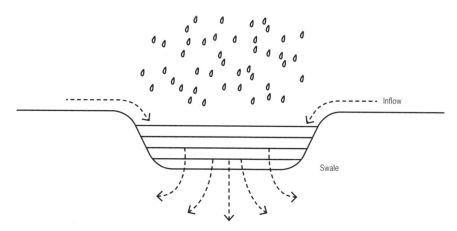

Figure 10 Use of bioswales for site-water management

that uses biological systems, living organisms, or derivatives thereof, to make or modify products or processes for specific use."

Biotechnology is often used to refer to genetic engineering technology of the 21st century, but the term encompasses a wider range and history of procedures for modifying biological organisms according to the needs of humanity, going back to the initial modifications of native plants into improved food crops through artificial selection and hybridization. Bioengineering is the science on which all biotechnological applications are based. With the development of new approaches and modern techniques, traditional biotechnology industries are more able to improve the quality of their products and increase the productivity of their systems. Before 1971, the term "biotechnology" was used primarily in food processing and agriculture. Since the 1970s it began to be used by the western scientific establishment to refer to laboratory-based techniques being developed in biological research, such as recombinant DNA or tissue culture-based processes, or horizontal gene transfer in living plants, using vectors such as *Agrobacterium* to transfer DNA into a host organism.

The term can be used in a much broader sense to describe the whole range of methods, both ancient and modern, used to manipulate and change organic materials to reach the demands of food production. Biotechnology combines disciplines including genetics, molecular biology, biochemistry, embryology, and cell biology, which in turn are linked to practical disciplines including chemical engineering, information technology, and robotics. Patho-biotechnology describes the exploitation of pathogens or pathogen derived compounds for beneficial effect.

Biotic   Refers to living organisms.

Biotic integrity   Ability to support and maintain balanced, integrated functionality in the natural habitat of a given region.

Bipolar plates   Conductive plate in a fuel cell stack that acts as an anode for one cell and a cathode for the adjacent cell. *See also: Fuel cells*

Black body   Theoretical object that absorbs 100% of the radiation that hits it. Therefore it reflects no radiation and appears perfectly black. It is the opposite of an object that has 100% albedo reflectivity.

Black water   Nonpotable wastewater generated by households, particularly toilet waste. If black water contains fecal matter and urine, its pathogens and high content of organic material need to decompose before they can be reused in the built environment or released safely into the environment. *See also: Gray water*

BLAST   Building Loads Analysis and System Thermodynamics, a building energy simulation program developed in the 1970s by the US Department of Defense.

Blowdown   Minimum discharge of recirculating water so that when materials are released into water, the concentration of materials will not exceed limits established by best management practices.

BMS   *See: Building automation management system*

BOD   *See: Biochemical oxygen demand*

Body burden   Amount of various contaminants retained in a person's tissues.

Bog   *See: Wetlands*

Bone (oven) dry   Refers to solid biomass fuels, such as wood, having zero moisture content.

Borlaug, Norman   Instrumental figure in the Green Revolution. In a project funded by the

Rockefeller Foundation, Ford Foundation, and other agencies in the 1940s, Dr Borlaug, an American, began working as a plant pathologist and geneticist in Mexico to develop high-productivity wheat. The varieties proved very successful, and subsequent research was done on corn and rice. Dr Borlaug was awarded the 1970 Nobel Peace Prize. *See also:* **Green Revolution**

Boron (B) Chemical element commonly used as the dopant in photovoltaic devices or cell materials. *See also:* **Photovoltaic (PV) and associated entries; Appendix 4: Photovoltaics**

BOS *See:* **Balance of system**

Bottle bill Law that requires the use of returnable beverage containers to encourage recycling and reuse.

Box culvert Mechanism to prevent road flooding. Channel or conduit placed beneath roads to allow water or other effluent to travel from one side of the roadway to the other without flooding the surface of the road. The culvert prevents washouts and erosion of the road. Box culverts usually are constructed of metal pipe or concrete. *See also:* **Culvert**

Bread box system *See:* **Batch heater**

Breathing wall A totally vegetated façade. Instead of a horizontal green roof, a breathing wall is vertical greening, which develops and uses a stable plant and microbial community using hydroponic growing media that will improve internal air quality. Studies have shown that the more diverse an ecosystem, the better it can absorb carbon dioxide and nitrogen. *See also:* **Green roof**

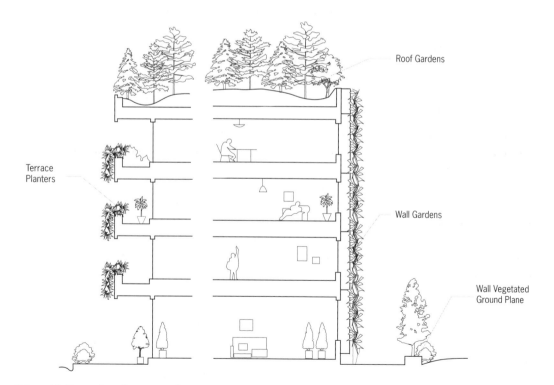

Roof Gardens

Terrace Planters

Wall Gardens

Wall Vegetated Ground Plane

Figure 11 Examples of green wall systems

BREEAM   *See: Building Research Establishment Environmental Assessment Method*

Brightness ratio   Ratio of luminosity (brightness) of an object to brightness of adjacent spaces or objects; this ratio describes varying levels of comfort.

British thermal unit (Btu)   Amount of heat required to raise the temperature of 1 lb of water by 1°F; equal to 252 calories.

Brown belt   *See: Heterotrophic layer*

Brownfield site   Abandoned, idle, or underused industrial and commercial facilities or sites that are environmentally contaminated and often hazardous to humans. Also known as brownfield land. The expansion, redevelopment, or reuse of these sites is complicated by the presence (or potential presence) of a hazardous substance, pollutant, or contaminant. The sites may be in urban, rural, or suburban areas. In ecomasterplanning, the rehabilitation of these lands in cities would allow the land to be used for urban growth and development, leaving existing arable and vegetated lands intact as greenfield sites. *See also: Greenfield site*

Brundtland Report   In 1987 the Brundtland Report, officially known as the United Nations report *Our Common Future*, alerted the world to the urgency of making progress toward economic development that can be sustained without depleting natural resources or harming the environment. The Brundtland Report highlights the three fundamental components of sustainable development: the environment, the economy, and society. *See also: World Commission on Environment and Development*

Btu   *See: British thermal unit*

BTX   Industry term referring to the group of aromatic hydrocarbons: benzene, toluene, and xylene. Benzene is a known carcinogen. *See also: Aromatics*

Bubble approach   Method to control air pollutant emissions that allows a manufacturing plant to consider emissions from several sources as combined emissions from that plant.

Buffer zone   Neutral area used as a protective barrier separating two conflicting forces. For example, an area adjacent to an estuarine shoreline, wetland edge or stream bank where ecological processes and water pollution control functions take place.

Buffering capacity   Resistance of water or soil to changes in pH (acidity). Tolerance to changes in pH determine the continued ability of fauna and flora in a particular locality to remain as part of that ecosystem. *See also: Carrying capacity*

Building automation management system (BAS)   In the UK known as a building management system (BMS); also known as energy management systems or energy management and control systems. Automated management systems or energy management and control systems in buildings. System that controls energy-consuming equipment in a building so that the building can operate more efficiently while maintaining a comfortable environment. BAS is used to achieve higher energy efficiency through procedures and methods that ensure improvement of energy flow and use. In addition to saving energy, these systems may also reduce the costs of overall building maintenance. This system may also include other features, such as maintenance planning, fire safety and physical safety functions, and security. A BAS consists of sensors, controllers, actuators, and software. An operator interfaces with the system via a central workstation.

Building configuration using passive mode design   Passive mode building design focuses

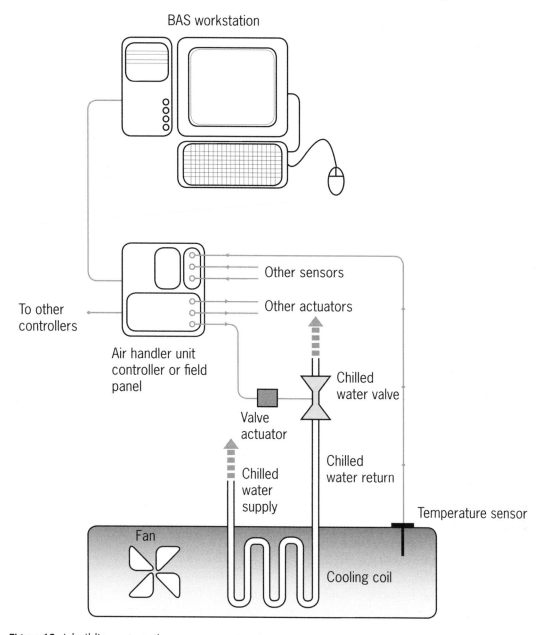

BAS workstation

Other sensors

Other actuators

To other
controllers

Air handler unit
controller or field
panel

Chilled
water valve

Valve
actuator

Chilled
water
supply

Chilled
water return

Temperature sensor

Fan

Cooling coil

Figure 12 A building automation management system

on spatial arrangements and layouts that maximize the energies of the ambient environment.
It is important that the building form is appropriate to the Sun path and winds for that latitude
to reduce energy consumption. *See also:* **Passive
mode design**

Building envelope The outer elements of a
building that enclose the internal space: foundations, roof, walls, windows, doors, and floors.
The primary functions of the building envelope
are to provide shelter, security, solar and thermal
control, moisture control, internal air quality

control, access to daylight and view to outside, fire resistance, acoustics, cost effectiveness, and aesthetics. The building envelope both protects the building occupants and plays a major role in regulating the indoor environment. The design and performance of the building envelope are important aspects of ecodesign. *See also: Insulation; Active façade*

Building for Economic and Environmental Stability (BEES) A rating and software product developed by the US National Institute of Standards and Technology's Building and Fire Research Laboratory. It is a life-cycle assessment (LCA) tool for built structures. Analysis is broken into two general categories, economic and environmental. The LCA has 12 criteria by which to analyze the structure. The process provides the user with some flexibility when defining and comparing the importance of one criterion versus another. The software package

includes comprehensive economic and environmental considerations. BEES, like other software of the same genre, is designed to increase sustainability within the built environment. BEES 4.0 is available free. *See also: Life-cycle assessment*

Building information modeling (BIM)
Introduced by Autodesk in 2002, the term refers to the creation and use of coordinated, consistent, computable information about a building project in design—information used for design decision-making, production of high-quality construction documents, predicting performance, cost estimating and construction planning, and, eventually, for managing and operating the facility. Subsequent models may include ecodesign considerations.

Building integrated food production (BIFP)
The design and integration of food production technology into the built form, such as roofs, terraces, and façades, and the use of hydroponics.

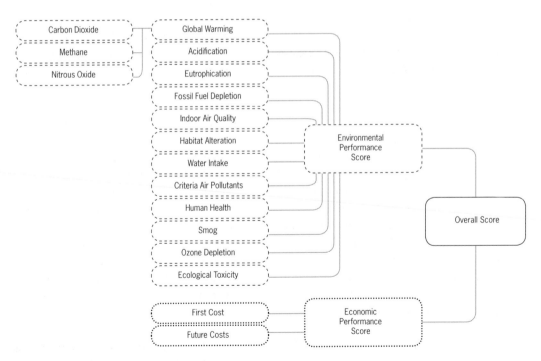

Figure 13 BEES 4.0
Source: US National Institute of Standards and Technology

Producing food within buildings contributes to greater nutritional self-sufficiency and is a component of ecodesign.

Building integrated photovoltaics (BIPV)   The design and integration of photovoltaic technology into the building envelope, typically replacing conventional building materials. The integration may be in: i) vertical façades, replacing view glass, spandrel glass or other façade materials; ii) semitransparent skylight systems; iii) roofing systems, replacing traditional roofing materials; iv) shading eyebrows over windows; or v) other building envelope systems. *See also: Photovoltaic (PV)* and associated entries; *Appendix 4: Photovoltaics*

Building mass, passive mode   Ecodesign approach using the thermal mass of building materials to absorb heat and then release the heat back into the built form's internal space during periods when the building is not actively gaining heat from the Sun or other source. *See also: Passive mode design; Trombe wall*

Building Research Establishment Environmental Assessment Method (BREEAM)   Environmental assessment method created in 1990 for buildings in the UK. It established standards for sustainable development and measures achievement of those standards, and has been adopted formally by the British government as the benchmark to measure the environmental performance of buildings. BREEAM provides guidance on minimizing the adverse effects of buildings on the global and local environment. It aims to reduce energy usage both in the construction and management of a building, as well as to promote a healthy, comfortable indoor environment for end-users. BREEAM assesses the performance of a building in the following areas:

- Management—overall management policy, commissioning site management, and contractors and procedures issues.

- Energy use—operational energy and CO_2 issues; energy-efficient heating and cooling, and controlled metering.

- Health and wellbeing—indoor and external issues affecting users' health and wellbeing. Examples include fresh air provision and ventilation, lighting and lighting control, provision of local temperatures, and eliminating risk of Legionnaires' disease.

- Pollution—air and water pollution issues. Examples include refrigerant recovery, specification of HCFC- and CFC-free materials in construction, and low-emission boilers.

- Transport—transport-related CO_2 and location-related factors. Examples include provision of secure facilities for cyclists, coordination with local public transport systems, and consideration of national public transport systems.

- Land use—use of brownfield rather than greenfield sites; treatment/capping of contaminated land.

- Ecology—conservation of ecological values and enhancement of the site. Where possible, use of sites of low ecological value. Use of environmental and ecological assessments to advise on improvements to the site, such as habitat creation within the site.

- Materials—consideration of the environmental implications of building materials, including life-cycle impacts. Examples include specification of timber from renewable and managed sources, provision of storage for recycling, and specification of asbestos-free materials.

- Water—consumption and water efficiency. Examples include installation of low-water-content WCs, installation of water systems with leak detection, water metering, gray water recycling.

See also: Comprehensive Assessment System for Building Environmental Efficiency (CASBEE); Green building rating systems; Green Globes;

Leadership in Energy and Environmental Design (LEED)

Built-up roof (BUR)   Class of low-slope roof that consists of layers of reinforcing felt between layers of either asphalt or coal-tar bitumen. The reflectivity of built-up roofs depends on the color of the surface layer. Four surfacing options are aggregate, smooth, mineral cap, and protective coating.

Butane   Gas derived from natural gas or crude oil. It is a common component of gasoline and liquefied petroleum gas.

C

Cadmium (Cd) Major soil contaminant. Chemical element used in certain types of solar cell and battery. Toxic heavy metal that tends to accumulate in the food chain. *See also: Heavy metals; Soil contaminants*

CAFE *See: Corporate Average Fuel Economy*

CAI *See: Clean Air Initiative*

Calcination 1. Chemically, a process of heating a substance in a crucible or over an open flame until it is reduced to ashes.

2. A thermal treatment process applied to ores and other solid materials to bring about a thermal decomposition, phase transition, or removal of a volatile fraction. The calcination process normally takes place at temperatures below the melting point of the product materials. Goals of calcination are: i) to drive off water present as absorbed moisture; ii) to drive off CO_2 or sulfur dioxide or other volatile constituents; iii) to oxidize part or all of the material. Examples are: i) decomposition of hydrated minerals, as in calcination of bauxite to remove crystalline water as water vapor; ii) decomposition of carbonate minerals, as in the calcination of limestone to drive off carbon dioxide; iii) decomposition of volatile matter contained in raw petroleum coke.

California low-emission vehicle regulations The US State of California's automotive emissions standards are stricter than the USA's national-tier regulations. There have been two major phases. The first began in the 1990s and ended when the Low Emission Vehicle II (LEV II) standards began to be phased in for 2004. Several states other than California now use the same restrictions. These include Maine, Massachusetts, New York, Oregon, Vermont, and Washington, and are frequently referred to as "CARB states" in automotive discussions because the regulations are defined by the California Air Resources Board (CARB). *See also: Emissions standards, designations*

Calorie Amount of heat needed to raise the temperature of 1 g of water by 1°C. One calorie is equal to approximately 4 Btu.

Cap Layer of clay or other impermeable material installed over the top of a closed landfill to prevent entry of rainwater and to minimize leachate.

Cap and trade *See: Emissions trading*

Capital stock Property, plant, and equipment used in the production, processing, and distribution of energy resources.

Carbon black Product of incomplete combustion of fossil fuel, wood, and biomass. Consists of soot, charcoal, and/or possible light-absorbing refractory organic matter. Black carbon can also be also be found naturally in sediments, soils, aerosols, and graphite forms.

Carbon capture and storage *See: Geological sequestration*

Carbon cycle   Cyclic movement of carbon circulating through the air, plants, animals, and soil. Carbon exists everywhere in the atmosphere as a gas, as dissolved ions in the hydrosphere, and as solids. Organisms extract carbon from their nonliving environment. For life to continue, carbon must be recycled.

There are four main reservoirs of carbon exchange: atmosphere, terrestrial biosphere (including freshwater systems), oceans, and sediments (including fossil fuels). The carbon exchanges between reservoirs occur because of various chemical, physical, geological, and biological processes. The ocean contains the largest pool of carbon near the Earth's surface, but most of the pool is not involved with rapid exchange with the atmosphere. Pathogenic production of CO_2 may result in greenhouse gases.

Carbon exists in the abiotic environment as: carbon dioxide (CO_2) in the atmosphere and dissolved in water (forming HCO_3^-); carbonate rocks (limestone and coral, $CaCO_3$); deposits of coal, petroleum, and natural gas derived from once-living things; and dead organic matter (such as humus in the soil). Carbon enters the biotic world through the action of autotrophs: primarily photoautotrophs, including plants and algae, that use the energy of light to convert carbon dioxide to organic matter, and to a small extent chemoautotrophs—bacteria and archaea that do the same but use the energy derived from an oxidation of molecules in their substrate.

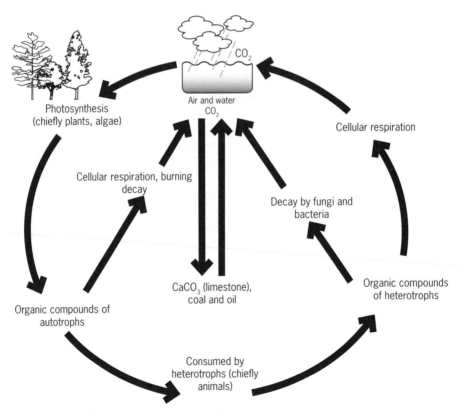

Figure 14 The carbon cycle
Source: US Environmental Protection Agency

Carbon returns to the atmosphere and water by respiration (as CO$_2$), burning, and decay producing CO$_2$ if oxygen is present, methane (CH$_4$) if it is not. Carbon is released from changes in land use. Much of the carbon stored in trees and soils is released to the atmosphere when forests are cleared and cultivated. Some of the release occurs rapidly with burning; some of it occurs slowly as dead plant material decomposes. When forests regrow on cleared land, they withdraw carbon from the atmosphere and store it again in trees and soils. The difference between the total amount of carbon released to the atmosphere and the total amount withdrawn from the atmosphere determines whether the land is a net source or sink for atmospheric carbon.

Studies indicate that between 1850 and 2000, about 155 Pg of carbon were released to the atmosphere from changes in land use world-wide (1 petagram [Pg] = 1 billion metric tonnes = 1000 × 1 billion kg). The amount released each year generally increased over the period, and by the 1990s the rate of release averaged about 2 Pg of carbon per year.

Carbon cycle disruption The carbon cycle can be disrupted in the biosphere by activities that change the concentration of CO$_2$ in the biosphere. One of these activities is fossil fuel combustion, which is prevalent worldwide.

Carbon dioxide (CO$_2$) A gas that occurs naturally and is formed during respiration, organic decomposition, and burning fossil fuels and biomass, as well as by land-use changes and industrial processes. It is the

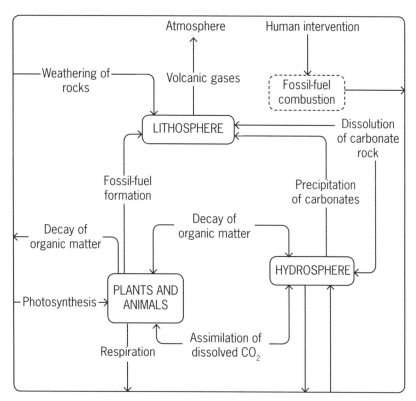

Figure 15 Disruption to the carbon cycle in the biosphere due to fossil fuel combustion
Source: US Environmental Protection Agency

principal anthropogenic greenhouse gas that affects the Earth's radiative balance. It is the reference gas against which other greenhouse gases are measured, and has a global warming potential of 1. CO_2 is removed from the atmosphere (sequestered) when it is absorbed by plants as part of the biological carbon cycle.

When considered with the other factors in the global carbon equation (the atmosphere, fossil fuels, and the oceans), the increase in atmospheric CO_2 is only half of what would have been expected from the increased amount of fossil fuel consumption and forest burning. Research has found that increased CO_2 levels lead to increased net production by photoautotrophs. There is also evidence that some of the apparent imbalance in the global accounting of CO_2 has been due to increased growth of forests, especially in North America, and increased amounts of phytoplankton in the oceans. *See also:* **Carbon cycle**

Carbon emission   Refers to carbon dioxide (CO_2). The movement (flux) of carbon between the atmosphere and the land and oceans is dominated by natural processes such as plant photosynthesis. While these natural processes can absorb some of the net 6.2 billion metric tons (7.2 billion metric tons less 1 billion metric tons of sinks) of anthropogenic CO_2 emissions produced each year (measured in carbon equivalent terms), an estimated 4.1 billion metric tons are added to the atmosphere annually. This imbalance between greenhouse gas emissions and absorption results in the continuing increase in atmospheric concentrations of greenhouse gases. *See also:* **Carbon cycle; Carbon dioxide; Carbon footprint**

Carbon footprint   Measure of the amount of carbon dioxide (CO_2) emitted through combustion of fossil fuels. Environmentalists advocate the use of alternative and renewable fuels and

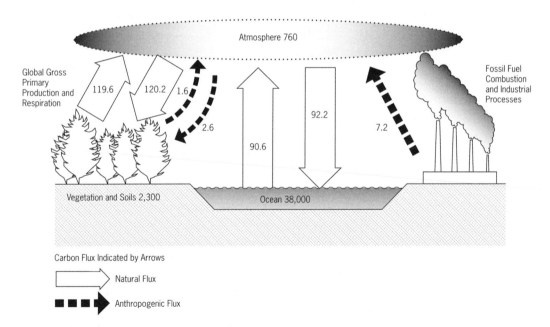

Figure 16 Global carbon cycle 2007 (billion metric tons carbon)
Source: Intergovernmental Panel on Climate Change (2007), *Climate Change 2007: The Physical Science Basis* (see also Figure 7)

biofuels to decrease CO_2 emissions and the damage CO_2 does as a greenhouse gas.

Carbon monoxide (CO) Common air pollutant. Toxic gas or liquid that results from incomplete oxidation of carbon in combustion of carbon-based fuels, including gasoline, oil, and wood. It is also produced by incomplete combustion of many natural and synthetic products. It is a health hazard when present at high levels in the air. Reacts with the Sun's radiation and other chemical compounds to form ozone. *See also: Air pollutants; Ozone precursors*

Carbon negative The use of bioenergy to decrease potential environmental degradation through global warming and atmospheric pollution. Relatively recently coined term.

Carbon neutral Refers to neutral (meaning zero) total carbon release, which is the result of balancing the amount of carbon released with the amount sequestered or offset. Various special interests attempt to promote a use of the term that refers to carbon reduction, which is clearly not neutral. The term has two common uses.

- The practice of balancing carbon dioxide (CO_2) released into the atmosphere from burning fossil fuels with renewable energy that creates a similar amount of useful energy, so that the carbon emissions are compensated; alternatively, of using only renewable energies that do not produce any CO_2.
- The practice of carbon offsetting by paying others to remove or sequester 100% of the CO_2 emitted from the atmosphere. This offset can be achieved by planting trees; or by funding carbon projects that may lead to the prevention of future greenhouse gas emissions; or by buying carbon credits to remove (or "retire") them through carbon trading. These practices are often used in parallel,

together with energy conservation measures, to minimize energy use.

Carbon reservoir Carbon as the principal element in the biogeochemical cycle. Global forests contain approximately 80% of the carbon stored in land vegetation. Large stores of carbon in the biosphere are necessary for continued carbon cycle balance in the biosphere.

Carbon sequestration Part of the carbon cycle. Uptake and storage of carbon. Trees and plants absorb carbon dioxide, release oxygen and store the carbon. Fossil fuels store carbon until it is burned. *See also: Carbon cycle; Carbon reservoir; Carbon sink*

Carbon sink A pool or reservoir that absorbs or takes up released carbon from another part of the carbon cycle. The four sinks, which are regions of the Earth within which carbon behaves in a systematic manner, are: i) atmosphere, ii) terrestrial biosphere (including freshwater systems), iii) oceans, and iv) sediments (including fossil fuels).

Carbon tetrachloride (CCl_4) Used in producing chlorofluorocarbons (CFCs). Its use in solvents was discontinued when it was found to be carcinogenic.

Carcinogen Any substance known to cause or aggravate cancer.

Carrying capacity Food, habitat, water, and other essential components in the ecosystem that support an organism or population. This is based on the premise that the population of an organism within an ecosystem is in equilibrium. For the human population more complex variables, such as sanitation and medical care, are sometimes considered part of the necessary infrastructure. A fundamental strategy of eco-masterplanning is to ensure a new built form or human activity can be accommodated within the carrying capacity and resilience of the ecosystems in that specific locality. *See also: Buffering capacity*

CASBEE   *See: Comprehensive Assessment System for Building Environmental Efficiency*

Cascading energy   Repeated sequential use of recoverable waste heat, with each successive application requiring a lower temperature or quality level until the waste heat is no longer useful or needed. This process maximizes the use of generated heat and minimizes wasted heat. *See also: Recoverable waste heat*

Casinghead gas   Natural gas coproduced with crude oil from an underground formation.

Catalyst   Chemical substance that increases the rate of a reaction without being consumed. In a fuel cell, a catalyst facilitates the reaction of oxygen and hydrogen.

Catalytic converter   Air pollution-control device that removes organic contaminants by oxidizing them into carbon dioxide and water through a chemical reaction using a catalyst. Required in all automobiles sold in the USA and used in some types of heating appliance. *See also: Catalyst*

Catalytic hydrocracking   Refining process that uses hydrogen and catalysts with relatively low temperature and high pressure for converting middle-boiling or residual material to high-octane gasoline, reformer charge stock, jet fuel, and high-grade fuel oil. This process converts waste or mediocre material into usable fuel.

Catchment basin   Also known as catchment area, drainage area, or drainage basin. 1. Geographical area draining into a river or reservoir. It is usually the lowest point of land that receives runoff from rain. Serves as a buffer zone between dry land and a body of water. The level of wetness of a catchment basin determines the density of a stream network and the influence of vegetation types on river or reservoir ecology. *See also: Watershed*

2. Government agencies regulate underground storage tanks to minimize leakage, spills, and corrosiveness, and require catchment basins to contain spills. Catchment basins, in this context, are also called "spill containment manholes" or "spill buckets". Basically, a catchment basin is a bucket sealed around the fill pipe. The basin should be large enough to contain any spills that may occur when the delivery hose is uncoupled from the fill pipe. A typical delivery hose can hold about 14 gallons of fuel. Basins range in size from those capable of holding only a few gallons to those that are much larger—the larger the catchment basin, the more spill protection it provides.

Cathode   1. Negative pole or electrode of an electrolytic cell; or vacuum tube where electrons enter (current leaves) a system. In an electrolytic cell, the negative electrode. In a fuel cell, one of four functional component elements: anode, cathode, electrolyte, and interconnect. In a fuel cell, air flows along the cathode (which is also known as an air electrode). When an oxygen molecule contacts the cathode interface, it catalytically acquires four electrons from the cathode and splits into two oxygen ions. The oxygen ions diffuse into the electrolyte material and migrate to the other side of the cell, where they meet the anode (the positive pole), react catalytically, and give off water, carbon dioxide, heat, and electrons. The electrons go through the anode to the external circuit and back to the cathode, providing a source of useful electrical energy in an external circuit. The most common material for cathodes is lanthanum manganite ($LaMnO_3$).

2. Positive terminal of a battery.

See also: Anode; Electrolyte; Fuel cells; Solid oxide fuel cell

Cation   Positively charged ion. *See also: Base cations*

CDD   Cooling degree day *See: Degree day*

Cell barrier   Thin region of static electric charge along the interface of the positive and negative layers in a photovoltaic cell. The barrier inhibits the movement of electrons from one layer to the other, so that higher-energy electrons from one side diffuse preferentially through it in one direction, creating a current and therefore a voltage across the cell. Also called a depletion zone or space charge. *See also: Photovoltaic cell; Appendix 4: Photovoltaics*

Cellulose insulation   Type of insulation composed of waste newspaper, cardboard, or other forms of waste paper. Use of recycled materials conserves resources and energy that would otherwise be used to manufacture new building materials.

Cellulosic ethanol   Ethanol fuel that is made from cellulose in waste materials such as rice straw or sawdust, or low-value crops such as switchgrass, rather than from sugar or starch from food crops such as corn, sugar cane or sugar beet. *See also: Ethanol*

Cellulosic technology   The use of bacteria to convert the hard, fibrous content of plants— cellulose and lignin—into starches that can be fermented by other bacteria to produce ethanol. Two good sources of fibrous plant material are switchgrass and willow trees, although any material, from farm waste to specially grown crops or trees, would work. One estimate is that there are a billion tons of currently unused waste available for ethanol production in the USA. Cellulosic technology can produce a very efficient ethanol, but the technology is too expensive at present to produce ethanol cost-effectively. If production costs of cellulosic technology can be lowered, then it can be used to manufacture ethanol. While researchers continue to study the effects of ethanol as a world-wide fuel, the key considerations are agricultural land-use policy and the effects of fuel crops and increased nitrogen runoff on water quality, water-related problems in hypoxic zones, and climate change.

Cement   Building material made by grinding calcined limestone and clay to a fine powder. Mixed with water, the silicates and aluminates in the cement harden to a mass that is impervious to water. The use of fly ash, magnesium oxide, and nitrogen dioxide-absorbing components in cement has been found to be less damaging to the environment. These substitute components can decrease the pollutant potential of traditional Portland cement, which contains and emits CO_2, SO_2, and NO_x. Researchers indicate that cement plants using conventional materials accounted for 5% of global emissions of CO_2 in 2007. The use of an industry by-product such as fly ash can save natural resources and land. *See also: Bentonite; Fly ash cement; Magnesium oxide cement; Pollution-absorbing cement; Portland cement; Sulfur-based cement*

Central receiver   *See: Concentrating solar collector*

Central receiver solar power plant   *See: Power tower*

CERCLA   *See: Comprehensive Environmental Response Compensation and Liability Act*

Cetane   Ignition performance rating of diesel fuel. Diesel equivalent of gasoline octane.

CFD   *See: Computational fluid dynamics*

Chemicals, toxic   *See: Toxic chemicals*

Chemosynthesis   Process in which certain organisms extract inorganic compounds from the environment and convert them into organic nutrients without the presence of sunlight.

Chimney effect   *See: Stack effect*

Chlorinated hydrocarbons   Chemicals that contain chlorine, carbon, and hydrogen. They are used in insecticides, but tend to accumulate in the food chain. Many of these compounds have been banned, such as DDT and chlordane.

Chlorinated solvent   Toxic chemical. Organic solvent containing chlorine atoms, which was invented to replace hydrocarbon solvents. Used in aerosol spray containers, highway paint, and dry-cleaning fluids. Chlorinated solvents are: i) methylene chloride (CH_2Cl_2), used in pharmaceuticals, chemical processing, aerosols, food extracts, and surface treatments including paint stripping and urethane foam blowing; ii) tetrachloroethylene (perchloroethylene, C_2Cl_4), used in dry-cleaning and metal cleaning; iii) trichloroethylene (C_2HCl_3), used in metal cleaning and specialty adhesives. It takes six to eight days for trichloroethylene to break down, and five to six months for tetrachloroethylene to break down. *See also: Toxic chemicals*

Chlorinated teratogen (TCDD)   Highly toxic hydrocarbons, generally known as "dioxins", produced when chlorinated compounds such as vinyl are burned and when ground wood pulp is bleached with chlorine. Dioxins have carcinogenic properties. About 75 chemical compounds are included in the dioxins.

Chlorination   Addition of chlorine to drinking water, sewage, or industrial waste to disinfect or to oxidize undesirable compounds.

Chlorofluorocarbons (CFCs)   Air pollutants and toxic chemicals. Greenhouse gases covered under the 1987 Montreal Protocol. They are used for refrigeration, air conditioning, packaging, insulation, solvents, and aerosol propellants. They are not destroyed in the lower atmosphere, so they drift into the upper atmosphere, where they break down ozone. The Montreal Protocol banned the use of chemicals responsible for ozone damage, including CFCs. The CFCs are being replaced by other compounds, including hydrochlorofluorocarbons (HCFCs) and hydrofluorocarbons (HFCs), which are greenhouse gases covered under the Kyoto Protocol.

When CFCs are released into the atmosphere, they react with ozone (O_3) to form free chlorine (Cl) atoms and molecular oxygen (O_2), thereby destroying the ozone layer which protects the Earth's surface from the Sun's harmful ultraviolet rays. The chlorine liberated during ozone breakdown can react with still more ozone, making the CFCs particularly dangerous to the environment. CFCs can remain in the atmosphere for more than 100 years. *See also: **Air pollutants**; **Montreal Protocol on Substances that Deplete the Ozone Layer; Toxic chemicals***

Chloroform (CHC_{13})   Major soil contaminant. Chloroform may be released to the air as a result of its formation in the chlorination of drinking water, wastewater, and swimming pools. Other sources include pulp and paper mills, hazardous waste sites, and sanitary landfills. USEPA has classified chloroform as a member of Group B2, a probable human carcinogen. *See also: **Soil contaminants***

Chlorophenoxy   Class of herbicides that have adverse effects on human health.

CHP   Combined heat and power. *See: **Cogeneration***

Chromium (Cr)   Metal found in natural deposits as ores containing other elements. It is also found in plants, soil, volcanic dust and gases.

The greatest use of chromium is in metal alloys such as stainless steel; protective coatings on metal; magnetic tapes; and pigments for paints, cement, paper, rubber, composition floor-covering and other materials. Its soluble forms are used in wood preservatives.

The two largest sources of chromium emission in the atmosphere are from the chemical manufacturing industry and the combustion of natural gas, oil, and coal. When released to land, chromium compounds bind to soil but are not likely to migrate to groundwater. They are very persistent in water as sediments. There is high potential for accumulation of chromium in aquatic life. It can damage living things and can have adverse effects on human health, and tends to accumulate in the food chain. Levels of chromium are regulated by the US Safe Drinking Water Act. This law requires USEPA to determine safe levels of chemicals in drinking water.

Chronic acidification   Surface waters that remain acidified regardless of variations in hydrological conditions. Persistent high levels of acidity in water may affect and alter the organisms and plant species that live in that ecosystem.

Circular metabolism model   Design of products, built structures, facilities, or infrastructures based on the flow of materials and energy through the built environment over its life cycle, from its source to its eventual reuse, recycling, or reintegration—a circular pattern from origin back to origin. This principle in ecodesign asserts that all designs should be made with the eventual goal of dismantling, reuse, recycling, and eventual benign reintegration back into the natural environment. *See also: Design for disassembly*

Circulating fluidized bed   A type of furnace or reactor in which the emission of sulfur compounds is lowered by the addition of crushed limestone in the fluidized bed, thereby decreasing the need for stack gas cleanup equipment.

The particles are collected and recirculated after passing through a conventional bed and cooled internally by a boiler. Since sulfur in various combinations with gases such as oxygen or fluorine is a toxic chemical and can cause acid rain, lower sulfur emissions minimize their adverse effects on the environment.

Cistern   Receptacle for holding liquids, usually water. Cisterns are often built to catch and store rainwater.

CITES   *See: Convention on International Trade in Endangered Species of Wild Fauna and Flora*

Clean Air Act   The original US Clean Air Act was passed in 1963 to regulate and control air pollution. The current air pollution control program is based on 1970 amendments to the Act. The 1990 Clean Air Act Amendments are revisions of the 1970 law, include emissions standards for mobile and stationary sources, and are enforced by USEPA.

The European Union (EU) has the same goals, strategies, and regulations for its member countries. Some European countries have enacted their own standards and regulations for clean air. Examples include, but are not limited to, Germany and the United Kingdom. *See also: Clean Air Initiative*

Clean Air Initiative (CAI)   Global organization whose goal is to improve air quality in cities through research, technology sharing, and partnerships. There are regional partnerships in Asia, Latin America, Sub-Saharan Africa, Europe, and Central Asia.

Clean diesel   Evolving definition of diesel fuel with lower emission specifications, which limit sulfur content to 0.05% weight.

Clean energy technology   Clean energy technologies use renewable energy sources—the

Sun, wind, water, and plant matter—to produce electricity, heat, and transportation fuel.

Clean fuels   Low-pollution fuels that can replace ordinary gasoline. Also known as alternative fuels, they include gasohol (gasoline–alcohol mixtures), natural gas, and liquefied petroleum gas.

Clean Water Act   Enacted by US Congress in 1972, the Federal Water Pollution Control Act was designed to control water pollution. As amended in 1977, this law became commonly known as the Clean Water Act. The Act established the basic structure for regulating discharges of pollutants into the waters of the USA. It gave USEPA the authority to implement pollution control programs such as setting wastewater standards for industry. The Clean Water Act also continued requirements to set water quality standards for all contaminants in surface waters. The Act made it unlawful for any person to discharge any pollutant from a point source into navigable waters unless a permit was obtained under its provisions. It also funded the construction of sewage treatment plants under the construction grants program, and recognized the need for planning to address the critical problems posed by nonpoint-source pollution.

There are water regulations to protect consumers in almost every country of the world. They are based on recommendations made by the World Health Organization (WHO), which is part of the United Nations. WHO's goal is to see the gradual raising of general health levels in all countries in the world.

Cleanup   Term used to describe remedial actions following the release, or threat of release, of hazardous substance(s) that could adversely affect humans and the environment. Other terms used for this action include remedial action, removal action, response action, and corrective action. *See also: Brownfield site*

Clearcut   Cutting and harvesting all the trees and/or forests at one time, leaving vast expanses of exposed fallow land. This practice can result in erosion, soil runoff into streams and bodies of water, sediment accumulation, flooding, and dislocation of species that live in the biota.

Cleavage of lateral epitaxial films for transfer (CLEFT)   Process for making inexpensive gallium arsenide (GaAs) photovoltaic cells. Thin film of GaAs is grown on a thick single-crystal GaAs substrate and then cleaved from the substrate and incorporated into a cell, allowing the substrate to be reused to grow more thin film GaAs. Gallium arsenide is a high-efficiency, low-cost solar cell and semiconductor material.

CLEFT   *See: Cleavage of lateral epitaxial films for transfer*

Climate   1. The characteristic condition of the atmosphere near the Earth's surface at a certain location/point on Earth. It is the long-term weather of that area, and includes the region's general pattern of weather conditions, seasons, and weather extremes such as hurricanes, droughts, or rainy periods. Two of the most important factors determining an area's climate are air temperature and precipitation.

2. Prevailing average weather conditions at a specific location for a long period, normally more than 70 years.

World biomes are controlled by climate. The climate of a region will determine what plants will grow there, and what animals will inhabit it. All three components—climate, plants, and animals—create the make-up of a biome.

A basis for bioclimatic or passive mode design is an understanding of the climate of a given locality. Ecodesign utilizes all passive mode strategies before adopting other low-energy designs.

Climate change   Refers to all forms of climatic inconsistency, but especially to significant

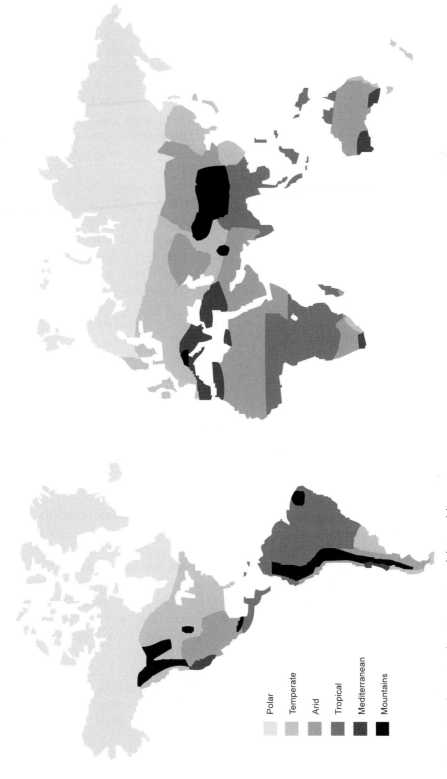

Figure 17 The main climatic regions of the world
Source: Intergovernmental Panel on Climate Change (IPCC)

Polar
Temperate
Arid
Tropical
Mediterranean
Mountains

change from one prevailing climatic condition to another. Sometimes used synonymously with the term "global warming". However, scientists use the term in a wider sense, including natural changes in climate as well as climatic cooling.

Climate feedback   Interaction between processes in the climate system. An initial process triggers changes in a second process that, in turn, influences the initial one. Positive feedback intensifies the original process, and negative feedback reduces it.

Climate system (Earth system)   Five physical components that are responsible for climate and its variations: atmosphere, hydrosphere, cryosphere, lithosphere, and biosphere.

Closed-circuit system design strategy   One of four design strategies to manage materials and energy in buildings and its servicing systems. Impact on the surrounding ecosystem is minimal with this system because most of the processes take place within the built environment as far as possible through continuous reuse and recycling. *See also: Combined open-circuit system design strategy; Once-through system design strategy; Open-circuit system design strategy*

Closed-loop active system   Solar heat transfer system. Pumps heat transfer fluids such as glycol and water antifreeze through solar collectors. Heat exchangers transfer the heat from the fluid to the water stored in the tanks. Similar concept to closed-loop geothermal heat pump system.

Closed-loop biomass   Term defined by the US Comprehensive National Energy Act of 1992: any organic matter from a plant that is cultivated exclusively to be used to produce energy. This does not include wood, or agricultural wastes, or standing timber.

Closed-loop geothermal heat pump systems
Also known as indirect systems. Geothermal heat systems that circulate a solution of water and antifreeze through a series of sealed loops of piping. Once the heat has been transferred into or out of the solution, the solution is recirculated. The loops can be installed in the ground horizontally or vertically, or they can be placed in a body of water, such as a pond.

Closed-loop recycling   Process of reusing an old product by recycling it into the same thing again so that it can be used once more. For example, turning old aluminum cans into new aluminum cans, or old glass jars into new glass jars, old newspapers into new newsprint, old plastic bags into new ones.

CNG   *See: Compressed natural gas*

Coastal wetland   Land along a coastline, extending inland from an estuary that is covered with salt water for most or all of the year.

Coastal zone   Shallow part of the ocean that extends from the high-tide mark on land to the edge of a shelf-like extension of continental land masses.

Coefficient of performance (COP)   The efficiency ratio of the amount of heating or cooling provided by a heating or cooling unit to the energy consumed by the system. COP is used as a measure of the steady-state performance or energy efficiency of heating, cooling, and refrigeration appliances. The higher the COP, the more efficient the system. For example, electrical heating has a COP of 1.0.

Coevolution   Process in which two or more species reciprocally affect each other's evolution so that new features or behaviors result. This natural process, in response to changes in an ecosystem, helps preserve biodiversity. For example, an evolutionary change in the morphology of a plant might affect the morphology of a herbivore that eats the plant, which in turn might affect the evolution of the plant, which might affect the evolution of the herbivore.

Coevolution happens most often when different species have close ecological interactions with one another. These ecological relationships include: predator/prey and parasite/host, competitive species, and mutualistic species. Plants and insects represent a classic case of coevolution—one that is often, but not always, mutualistic. Many plants and their pollinators are so reliant on one another, and their relationships are so exclusive, that biologists have good reason to think the "match" between the two is the result of a coevolutionary process.

Co-firing electricity   *See: Biomass electricity*

Cogeneration   Also known as combined heat and power (CHP). Use of a heat engine or power station to generate both electricity and useful heat simultaneously. Almost all cogeneration utilizes hot air and steam for the process fluid. CHP is thermodynamically a more efficient use of fuel: 70% compared with 35% for conventional plants. It captures the by-product heat for domestic or industrial heating purposes such as making steam, heating water, chilling water, or compressing air. This means less fuel is consumed to produce the same amount of useful energy. Cogeneration plants are commonly found in district heating systems of large towns, hospitals, prisons, oil refineries, paper mills, wastewater treatment plants, and industrial plants with large heating needs.

Common CHP plant types are i) gas turbine plants using waste heat in the flue gas of gas turbines; ii) combined-cycle power plants adapted for CHP; iii) steam turbine CHP plants using the waste heat in the steam after the steam turbine; iv) molten carbonate fuel cells.

Collector efficiency   Ratio of solar radiation captured and transferred to the collector (heat transfer) fluid for solar thermal system or the ratio of incident solar radiation (energy) to energy output.

Collector, flat-plate   *See: Flat-plate solar thermal/ heating collector*

Collector, solar   *See: Solar collector*

Combined heat and power system (CHP) *See: Cogeneration*

Combined open-circuit system design strategy One of four design strategies to manage materials and energy in buildings and their servicing systems. A combination of open- and closed-circuit systems reduces the environmental impact of the once-through system by emitting no more discharges than can be absorbed by the ecosystem. *See also: Closed-circuit system design strategy; Once-through system design strategy; Open-circuit system design strategy*

Commensalism   A type of interaction between species in the biosphere. Describes the relationship humans have with other species. Commensalism is the interaction in which one participant has great benefit while the other receives neither benefit nor harm. *See also: Amensalism; Commensalism; Mutualism; Parasitism; Symbiosis*

Commercial waste   Waste from premises used mainly for a trade or business or for sport, recreation, education, or entertainment. It does not include household, agricultural, or industrial waste. Recycling, reusing, or upcycling would reduce waste.

Commissioning   Initial operation of a building that includes testing and adjusting HVAC, electrical, plumbing, and other systems to assure proper functioning and adherence to design criteria. Commissioning also includes the instruction of building representatives in the use of the building systems.

Committee on the Environment (COTE)
Committee of the American Institute of Architects, which works to advance, disseminate, and advocate—to the profession, the building industry, the academy, and the public—design practices that integrate built and natural systems and enhance both the design quality and environmental performance of the built environment.

Complete mix digester A type of anaerobic digester that has a mechanical mixing system in which temperature and volume are controlled to maximize the anaerobic digestion process for biological waste treatment, methane production, and odor control. This device speeds organic decomposition and creation of humus.

Composite Material created by combining materials differing in composition or form on a macroscale to bring about specific characteristics and properties. In ecodesign, the use of composite materials tends to inhibit their recycling.

Composite mode The composite use of various low-energy designed options for each season of the year. It is generally a composite of passive mode, mixed-mode, full mode, and productive mode, all designed to act in tandem as a low-energy design. In design terms, composite mode depends on operable components in the built structure or infrastructure to facilitate the different systems and modes used in a specific climate condition (see Figure 18).

Compost Aerobically decomposed remnants of organic materials. Compost is often used to enrich the soil in gardening and agriculture and as erosion control, land/stream reclamation, wetland construction, and landfill cover.

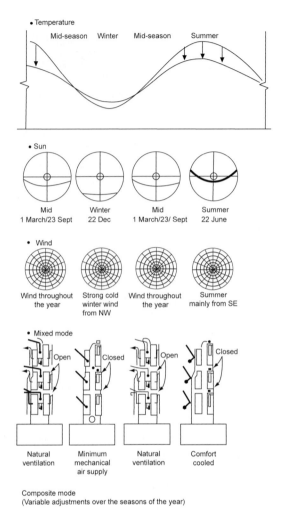

Composite mode
(Variable adjustments over the seasons of the year)

Figure 18 Composite mode (variable adjustments over the seasons of the year)

Compost pile Decomposition of organic material into humus.

Compost system Confined compost in an aerated enclosure so that it can be mechanically mixed or ground, receive air, and create suitable temperatures for proper decomposition into humus.

Composting Process of degrading organic material by microorganisms in aerobic conditions. A natural biological process that reduces the waste stream into a product that can be

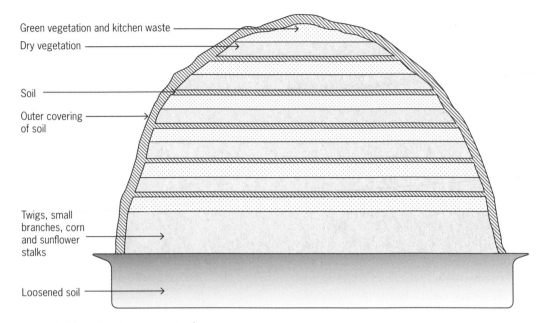

Green vegetation and kitchen waste

Dry vegetation

Soil

Outer covering of soil

Twigs, small branches, corn and sunflower stalks

Loosened soil

Figure 19 A biointensive compost pile

used as a soil amendment. It has become an alternative for managing yard/garden waste.

Composting toilet   Self-contained toilet that uses the process of aerobic decomposition to break down feces into humus and odorless gases.

Compound paraboloid collector   Form of non-imaging solar concentrating collector that does not track the Sun.

Comprehensive Assessment System for Building Environmental Efficiency (CASBEE)   Assessment tool to measure the environmental performance of buildings in Japan. *See also: Building Research Establishment Environmental Assessment Method (BREEAM); Green building rating systems; Green Globes; Leadership in Energy and Environmental Design (LEED)*

Comprehensive   Environmental   Response Compensation and Liability Act (CERCLA) US federal law enacted in 1980 and amended in 1986, which governs the cleanup of hazardous,

toxic, and radioactive substances. The act created a fund, known as the Superfund, to finance the investigation and cleanup of releases of hazardous substances.

Compressed natural gas (CNG)   A substitute for gasoline or diesel fuel. It is considered to be an environmentally "clean" alternative to those fuels. It is made by compressing natural gas, which is mainly composed of methane (CH_4), in a percentage range of 70–98%. It is stored and distributed in hard containers. Currently, CNG is used in light-duty passenger vehicles and pickup trucks, medium-duty delivery vans, postal trucks, and street sweepers, and in transit and school buses. CNG must be stored on board a vehicle in tanks at high pressure—up to 3600 lb per square inch (252 kg/cm^2). A CNG-powered vehicle gets about the same fuel economy as a conventional gasoline vehicle on a gasoline gallon equivalent (GGE) basis. CNG vehicles require a greater amount of space for fuel storage than convention gasoline power vehicles. As it is a compressed gas rather than a liquid like gasoline,

CNG takes up more space for each GGE. This makes it difficult to design smaller vehicles that look and operate like the vehicles people are accustomed to.

The US Department of Energy's Energy Efficiency and Renewable Energy (EERE) research estimates that the use of natural gas as a vehicle fuel will decrease nonmethane hydrocarbon emissions by 50–75%; decrease carbon monoxide emissions by 90–97%, decrease carbon dioxide emissions by 25%, and decrease nitrogen oxide emissions by 35–60%.

CNG is often confused with liquefied natural gas (LNG). While both are stored forms of natural gas, the key difference is that CNG is in compressed form while LNG is in liquefied form. CNG has a lower cost of production and storage compared with LNG as it does not require an expensive cooling process and cryogenic tanks. CNG requires a much larger volume to store the same mass of natural gas and the use of very high pressures: 3000–4000 lbf/in^2 (pound force per square inch); 20,670–27,500 kPa (kilopascals); 205–275 bar; 209–280 kg/cm^2. *See also: Gasoline gallon equivalent; Liquefied natural gas*

Computational fluid dynamics (CFD)   Analysis tool to compute the performance of ventilation and wind flow to create internal conditions of comfort.

Concentrating solar collector   Also known as a concentrator. Solar collector that uses reflective surfaces to concentrate sunlight onto a small area, where it is absorbed and converted to heat or, in the case of solar photovoltaic (PV) devices, into electricity. The main types of concentrating collector are: compound parabolic, parabolic trough, fixed reflector moving receiver, fixed receiver moving reflector, Fresnel lens, and central receiver. Concentrating PV modules must track the Sun and use only the direct sunlight because the diffuse portion cannot be focused onto the PV cell.

Concentrating solar power system (CPS)   Solar power plant that collects and concentrates solar energy in sunlight to generate electricity. These plants consist of two parts: one that uses mirrors to focus solar energy and converts it to heat; and a second that converts the heat energy to electricity.

There are three kinds of CPS systems. *See also: Dish/engine system; Parabolic trough; Power tower*

Concentrator solar cell   New generation of solar cell. Using mirror-and-lens systems, higher light intensity can be focused on the solar cells. These systems track the Sun, always using direct radiation. The parabolic trough solar thermal collector also uses a highly reflective surface. *See also: Parabolic trough*

Conduction, thermal   Heat flow between adjacent molecules. Molecules can be within a single substance, or in two separate bodies in direct contact. Conduction occurs when warmer molecules transfer part of their energy to the colder molecules.

Conductivity, thermal   Measure of heat transfer over a period of time caused by direct molecular interaction. Influenced by a material's thickness, area, and thermal conductivity, and by the difference in temperature. In the case of thermal mass used in a built structure, the mass absorbs and stores heat during sunny periods then releases it when heat is needed or wanted. The ability of a mass to store heat depends on the material's specific heat conductivity as well as the convective heat transfer.

Confined aquifer   Also known as an artesian aquifer. Groundwater that is below a layer of solid rock or clay, which is the confining layer. A well that goes through a confining layer is known as an artesian well. Protection of water by the confining layer decreases the probability of contamination seeping into the aquifer. *See also: Aquifer; Unconfined aquifer*

Conservation 1. Maintenance and preservation of resources and environmental quality in a specific ecosystem.

2. Environmentally, it refers to proper management of a specific biosphere.

3. Term used to describe efficient energy use, production, or distribution that results in a decrease of energy consumption while providing the same level of service.

Environmental conservation is the fundamental basis for sustainability and ecodesign.

Conservation easement Practice used to apply and enforce preservation of natural resources. For example, a landowner may grant rights to a specific parcel of land to a recipient. Easement gives the recipient the right to enforce restrictions, but the recipient does not assume ownership. A wildlife management agency, for example, may have easement in forested floodplains from private landowners that help manage wildlife and fish.

Conservation tillage farming Use of minimum tilling of the soil to prevent erosion.

Consumer Environmentally, refers to organisms that feed off living or dead organic material The two categories of consumer are: macroconsumers, larger animals; and microconsumers, bacteria and fungi.

Contaminant Any physical, chemical, biological, or radiological substance or matter that has an adverse effect on air, water, or soil.

Contaminated ecosystem Design site type measured by condition of ecosystem characteristics and features. These are brownfield sites. *See also: Brownfield site; Ecodesign site types*

Contaminated sediment USEPA lists it as a major water pollutant. Five major types of pollutant are found in sediments, as follows.

- Nutrients, including phosphorus and nitrogen compounds such as ammonia.
- Elevated levels of phosphorus, which can promote the unwanted growth of algae. This can lead to decreased oxygen in the water when algae die and decay.
- High concentrations of ammonia, which can be toxic to benthic organisms.
- Bulk organics—a class of hydrocarbons that includes oil and grease. Halogenated hydrocarbons or persistent organics are very resistant to decay. DDT and polychlorinated biphenyls (PCBs) are in this category. Polycyclic aromatic hydrocarbons (PAHs) include several petroleum products and by-products.
- Metals, such as iron, manganese, lead, cadmium, zinc, and mercury; and metalloids such as arsenic and selenium.

See also: Water pollutants

Contamination Introduction into water, air, or soil of microorganisms, chemicals, toxic substances, wastes, or wastewater in concentrations that make the medium unfit for its next intended use. Also applies to surfaces of objects, buildings, and various household and agricultural products.

Continuous flow energy resources There are direct and indirect forms of continuous flow energy resources: direct forms include flow of precipitated water, tidal effects of water, geothermal heat, wind power and climate energy; indirect forms include photosynthesized energy, biomass, and waste products used as fuel.

Contributory value The indirect benefits that predator–prey species add to the ecosystem. This relationship provides population stability of harvested species and species diversity. The loss of any species represents a decrease in the overall utility value of ecosystems.

Convection   Heat flow when a fluid such as a gas or liquid is involved. Fluid is heated and then moves from one place to another.

Convention on International Trade in Endangered Species of Wild Fauna and Flora (CITES)
Formed in the 1960s. An international treaty was drawn up in 1973 to protect wildlife and plants through international trade control and was signed by 80 countries, members of the World Conservation Union. CITES came into effect in 1975 and now has a membership of 136 countries. Member countries ban commercial international trade in an agreed list of endangered species, and regulate and monitor trade in others that might become endangered.

Convergent evolution   Evolution of species from different origins but under similar environmental conditions that produce species with similar function, appearance, and traits. The similarities are the result of adaptive solutions to similar environmental conditions. This evolution ensures survival of the species and biodiversity. An example is the evolution of functionally similar but distinct antifreeze proteins in divergent species of fish, one group found near Antarctica and the other group found in the Arctic; more obvious examples include the multiple origins of wings (bats, birds), and eyes.

Conversion   *See: Downcycling*

Cool roof   Roofing material that has high solar reflectance or albedo. These materials reflect a large portion of the Sun's energy. Cool roofs also may have a high thermal emittance and thus release a large percentage of absorbed heat. This keeps the material cooler and helps to reduce the heat island effect. There are two types of cool roof: those used on low-slope or flat buildings (primarily commercial); and those used on steep-slope buildings (primarily residential). Most cool roof applications for low-slope buildings have a smooth, bright, white surface to reflect solar radiation, reduce heat transfer to the interior, and reduce summertime air conditioning demand. Most cool roof applications for steep-slope buildings come in various colors and can use special pigments to reflect the Sun's energy. On a hot, sunny, summer day, traditional roofing materials may reach summertime peak temperatures of up to 190 °F (88 °C). By comparison, cool roofs reach peak temperatures of only 120 °F (49 °C). *See also: Green roof*

Cooling pond   A body of water used to cool the water that is circulated in an electric power plant.

Cooling tower   A structure used to cool power plant water; water is pumped to the top of the tubular tower and sprayed out into the center and is cooled by evaporation as it falls, and then is either recycled within the plant or discharged.

COP   *See: Coefficient of performance*

Copenhagen Agreement   1992 amendment to the Montreal Protocol. *See also: Montreal Protocol on Substances that Deplete the Ozone Layer*

Cork   The bark of a species of oak tree (*Quercus suber*) which grows in western Spain and Portugal. These woodland regions account for over 80% of the world's cork production. Cork is harvested in the oak forest for only two months a year. By law, each tree has its bark harvested every nine years. A tree can live for 150–250 years, and is usually harvested at least 15 times during its life. Trees regenerate their bark, which is a renewable material. Like bamboo, cork is considered a green alternative to hardwood floors. It is a durable and sustainable material.

Cork has a unique cell structure and organic characteristic that makes it soft to walk on; it repels dust, bugs, and mildew, and is a good thermal and sound insulator. Because of its high fire-resistance qualities, cork is used in rocket technology. In buildings, cork can be used for its antivibrational, thermal, and acoustic absorbing properties. It can also be used for seals and gaskets, in expansion joints, and for intumescent strips. It has even been used for building exteriors. Granules of cork can also be mixed into concrete. The composites made by mixing cork granules and cement have low thermal conductivity, low density, and good energy absorption. *See also: Bamboo*

Corn   Also known as maize. An energy crop used to produce biofuel, mostly ethanol. Ethanol produced from cellulosic materials produces fewer pollutant emissions than fossil fuels when combusted. Decreased emissions of greenhouse gases such as CO_2 is a benefit of ethanol. Researchers have found that extensive cultivation of corn for use as a biofuel would have a negative impact on water because of its higher nitrogen fertilization rate and greater nitrogen runoff. A higher nitrogen content in water would result in hypoxic zones and possible eutrophication of rivers, lakes, and streams.

The diversion of corn as a food crop to an ingredient for biofuel may contribute to a shortage of food worldwide. Researchers have suggested other crops, such as rapeseed and soybeans, and cellulosic fibrous plants such as switchgrass and willow trees, as alternative ingredients for biofuel.

Corporate Average Fuel Economy (CAFE)   US automobile fuel efficiency standard, established by Congress in 1975 as the sales-weighted average fuel economy expressed in miles per gallon (MPG) of a manufacturer's fleet of passenger cars or light trucks with a gross vehicle weight rating (GVWR) of 8500 pounds or less, manufactured for sale in the USA. CAFE was originally intended to improve the average fuel economy of cars and light trucks (trucks, vans, and sport utility vehicles) sold in the USA in the wake of the 1973 Arab oil embargo. The goal was to double new car fuel economy by 1985.

The USA has the lowest standard of fuel economy of any nation in the world, including China; the European Union and Japan have fuel economy standards almost twice as high as the USA. US Congress specifies that CAFE standards must be set at the "maximum feasible level", which includes: i) technological feasibility; ii) economic practicability; iii) effect of other standards on fuel economy; iv) need of the nation to conserve energy. *See also: Fuel economy, automobile; Fuel economy regulations, automobile*

Corrective action   *See: Cleanup*

COTE   *See: Committee on the Environment*

Cover crops   Crops planted immediately after harvest to prevent soil erosion. Common cover crops are rye, clover, and alfalfa.

CPS   *See: Concentrating solar power system*

Cradle to cradle   Process of rethinking the way people live, work, travel, design, build, and consume so that production not only is efficient, but also minimizes waste. A phrase invented by Walter R. Stahel in the 1970s and popularized by William McDonough and Michael Braungart in their 2002 book of the same name. In cradle to cradle production, all material inputs and outputs are seen as either technical or biological nutrients. Technical nutrients can be recycled or reused with no loss of quality; biological nutrients can be composted or consumed. By contrast, cradle to grave refers to a company taking responsibility for the disposal of goods it has produced, but not necessarily putting products' constituent components back into service.

Cradle-to-grave-analysis

See: Life-cycle assessment

Criteria air pollutants   Group of common air pollutants regulated by USEPA based on health and environmental effects. These pollutants are, or could be, harmful to people. The criteria pollutants are carbon monoxide (CO), lead (Pb), nitrogen dioxide (NO_2), ozone (O_3), particulate matter, and sulfur dioxide (SO_2). There are also a large number of compounds that have been determined to be hazardous, called air toxics. *See: Air pollutants*

Crossdrain   Channel or dips constructed across a road to intercept surface water runoff and divert it before erosive runoff volumes and concentrations occur.

Cryosphere   Frozen water in the form of snow, permanently frozen ground (permafrost), floating ice, and glaciers. Fluctuations in the volume of the cryosphere cause changes in ocean sea level, which have a direct impact on the atmosphere and biosphere. *See also: Arctic tundra*

Crystalline silicon   Type of photovoltaic cell material; made from a slice of single crystal silicon or polycrystalline silicon.

Cube law   In reference to wind energy, for any given instant, the power available in the wind is proportional to the cube of the wind velocity; when wind speed doubles, the power availability increases eight times. This is an important calculation both for wind energy generation and for prediction of natural winds that affect ocean and Arctic ice movements. Cube law ignores real system losses in wind friction. Depending on the system, the exponent can range from about 2.7 to 2.8 or so.

Culvert   Corrugated metal or concrete pipe used to carry or divert runoff water from a drain, usually installed under roads to prevent washouts and erosion. *See also: Box culvert*

Cyanide, organic and inorganic   Chemical pollutant and soil contaminant. Cyanide is a carbon–nitrogen chemical unit that combines with many organic and inorganic compounds. The most commonly used form, hydrogen cyanide, is used mainly to form the compounds needed to make nylon and other synthetic fibers and resins. Other cyanides are used as herbicides. Most cyanide release is from steel mills and metal heat-treating industries. Studies indicate that cyanide has the potential to harm human health. *See also: Soil contaminants*

D

Darrieus wind turbine A type of vertical-axis wind turbine used to generate electricity. The turbine consists of aerofoils mounted vertically on a rotating shaft or framework. This design of wind turbine was patented in 1931 by French aeronautrical engineer George Darrieus.

In theory, the Darrieus type is supposed to be as efficient as the propeller type if wind speed is constant, but in practice this efficiency falls short because of physical stresses and limitations imposed by a practical design and wind speed variation. There are also major difficulties in protecting the Darrieus turbine from extreme wind conditions and in making it self-starting. *See also: Horizontal-axis wind turbine*

Daylighting Passive and active ecodesign strategy to use daylight in place of artificial light that requires generated electrical energy. In the passive mode, fenestration can add diffuse light to a space, often using overhangs and other structural elements to block direct sunlight, while allowing diffuse light to enter. Light shelves, light pipes, and holographic glass can be use to enhance daylight entering internal spaces. In the active mode, using artificial lighting, autmomated controls can be added to lighting fixtures to increase/decrease fixture lumens to maintain a predetermined light level in selected areas, such as double switching. Daylighting can use vertical fenestration, skylights, tubular light pipes, light shelves, and a variety of diffuser methods. *See also: Light pipe; Light shelf; Tubular skylight*

DCE *See: Dichloroethylene*

DDC *See: Direct digital controls*

DDT *See: Dichloro-diphenyl-trichloroethane*

Debris flow Rapid movement of water-charged mixtures of soil, rock, and organic debris down steep stream channels.

Debt-for-nature swap Method of promoting environmental conservation. The swap usually involves an organization, usually nongovernmental, which purchases a less-developed country's foreign debt. In exchange, the country uses funds to establish conservation programs. It was created in 1984 by the World Wildlife Fund in response to exploitation of the environment by developing nations. The program was begun in Central America. Currently there are programs in Central America, South America, and Africa.

Decibel (dB) Unit used to measure the intensity of a sound. On the decibel scale, the smallest audible sound (near total silence) is 0 dB. A sound 10 times more powerful is 10 dB. A sound 100 times more powerful than near total silence is 20 dB. A sound 1000 times more powerful than near total silence is 30 dB.

Decibel levels (dB):

Near total silence	0
Whisper	15
Leaves rustling	40

Normal conversation	60
City traffic, car	70
Vacuum cleaner	80
Lawnmower, passing motorcycle	90
Thunder, chainsaw	100
Car horn	110
Rock concert, jet engine	120
Gunshot, firecracker	140

*See also: **Noise pollution***

Deciduous   Parts of a plant or animal that shed annually, such as tree or plant leaves or deer's antlers. Deciduous trees and forests are found in North America, South America, Europe, Asia, Australia, and Africa. Deciduous forests are defined as forests with a majority of tree species that lose their foliage at the end of the typical growing season. These forests have distinctive ecosystems, understory growth, and soil dynamics.

Two distinctive types of deciduous tree and forest are found around the world. i) Temperate deciduous forest biomes are found in America, Asia, and Europe. They grow in climatic conditions with great seasonable temperature variability, with growth occurring during warm summers, leaf drop in autumn, and dormancy during cold winters. These seasonal communities have diverse life forms that are influenced by the seasonality of their climate, mainly temperature and precipitation rates. These varying and regionally different ecological conditions produce distinctive forest plant communities in different regions. ii) Tropical and subtropical deciduous forest biomes are found in tropical and subtropical latitudes of South America, Africa, and Asia. These forests have developed in response to seasonal rainfall patterns, not to seasonal temperature variations. During prolonged dry periods the foliage is dropped to conserve water and prevent death due to drought. Leaf drop is not seasonally dependent as it is in temperate climates; it can occur any time of year and varies by region of the world.

Decompose   In ecosystems, the process of breaking down organic matter through bacterial or fungal action. In ecodesign, the concept can be used, with limitations, to close the loop to biointegrate materials back into nature.

Decomposer   Organism that breaks down dead organic molecules into simpler ones. Bacteria and fungi are decomposers. In ecodesign, decomposers close the loop within the ecosystem.

Deconstruction   An ecodesign strategy to design a new built structure or product for deconstruction or selective dismantling at the end of its useful life. Deconstruction may include reuse, remanufacture, and recycling of various components of the structure or product. In ecodesign it is design for disassembly.

Dedicated natural gas vehicle   Vehicle that operates only on natural gas. Reduces emissions and also enhances the life of an engine.

Deep ocean sequestration   A method to reduce carbon emissions that adversely affect the environment. Deliberate injection of captured carbon dioxide (CO_2) deep into the ocean so that it can be isolated from the atmosphere for centuries. While the technology allows direct injection of CO_2 into the ocean depths, research continues on the biological, physical, and chemical impacts that might occur from interactions with the marine ecosystem.

Deep plan   Architectural design for a built structure that locates the core areas away from external windows. A deep plan building can cost 50% less to heat than a shallow plan building, but will receive less natural daylight in the deeper parts of the floor plate. Generally, floor plans should not be more than 15 m from glass to glass so that the deepest part of the floor plate will be able to receive natural daylight. The core type that provides minimum air conditioning load is the double core configuration, in which the opening is from north to south and the core runs from east to west.

Deep saline aquifer Deep underground rock formation composed of permeable materials, contains highly saline fluids.

Deforestation Practices or processes that result in the conversion of forested lands to nonforest uses, often involving the disruption and destruction of mature ecosystems. Researchers believe deforestation increases the greenhouse effect in two ways: i) burning or decomposition of wood releases carbon dioxide (CO_2); ii) trees are no longer present to remove CO_2 from the atmosphere. In ecodesign, deforestation should take place only, if at all, where land is not ecologically sensitive.

Degasification system Health safety measure. Method used to remove methane from a coal seam that could not otherwise be removed by standard ventilation fans and would pose a substantial hazard to coal miners. The system may be used prior to or during mining activities. Methane recovery also reduces the build-up of greenhouse gases released to the atmosphere.

Degradable plastics *See: Biodegradable plastics*

Degree day Term used to indicate the heating or cooling load on a facility. One heating degree day (HDD) would occur when the outside temperature was one degree below a reference value (usually 65 °F) for one day. Daily HDDs can be added up for the year to provide the total HDDs for a year. Cooling degree days (CDDs) can be determined similarly. Often used to indicate the amount of annual heating or cooling demand in a particular geographical area.

Delineation of designed system's boundary In site-related designs, the boundary is more than the legal delineation—land title lines—of the

site itself. The ecodesign and ecological planning boundary is the natural extent of the ecosystem within which the design, including the roads, utilities, and various buildings, is located. Key considerations in ecodesign are the effects of those structures on ecological communities, such as zones of sediments, nutrients, and energy.

Delta Sediment deposit found at the mouth of a river.

Demography Study of human population in various categories such as density, population size, growth, age distribution, and socioeconomic characteristics. *See also: Human population*

Dense nonaqueous-phase liquid (DNAPL) Nonaqueous-phase liquids such as chlorinated hydrocarbon solvents or petroleum fractions with a specific gravity more than 1.0 sink through the water column until they reach a confining layer. Because they are at the bottom of aquifers instead of floating on the water table, it is difficult to detect their presence.

DNAPL contaminants result from degreasing operations, underground disposal, and leaking underground storage tanks. DNAPL contaminants can affect groundwater quality as they migrate to the water table. *See also: Light nonaqueous-phase liquid; Nonaqueous-phase liquid*

Department of Energy US Cabinet-level department, enacted into law on August 4, 1977, by President James E. Carter to formulate, administer, and regulate energy policies in the USA.

Depletion zone *See: Cell barrier*

Deposition Atmospheric deposition is the process by which heavier chemical constituents settle out from the atmosphere to the Earth's surface. They include precipitation (wet deposition) such as rain, snow, or fog, and particulate and gas deposition (dry deposition). Some atmosphere-borne chemicals become components of acid rain.

Depuration   Process of reducing the number of disease-causing pathogenic organisms that may be present in shellfish by using a controlled aquatic environment as the treatment process.

DER   *See: Distributed energy resources*

Derived-from rule   Designation of any waste material produced from the storage, treatment, or disposal of hazardous wastes as also hazardous.

Desertification   Land degradation in arid, semi-arid, and dry sub-humid areas resulting from various factors, including climatic variations and human activities. The United Nations Convention to Combat Desertification (UNCCD) defines land degradation as a reduction or loss, in arid, semi-arid, and dry sub-humid areas, of the biological or economic productivity and complexity of rainfed cropland, irrigated cropland, or range, pasture, forest, and woodlands resulting from land uses or from a process or combination of processes, including processes arising from human activities and habitation patterns, such as: i) soil erosion caused by wind and/or water; ii) deterioration of the physical, chemical, and biological or economic properties of soil; iii) long-term loss of natural vegetation.

Desiccant   Material used to dry or dehumidify air.

Desiccant cooling   Using desiccant materials such as silica gel and certain salt compounds. Desiccant cooling systems are designed to dehumidify and cool air. *See also: Solar cooling*

Design for disassembly (DFD)   Designing to allow and facilitate dismantling and disassembly of a structure's component parts for continuous reuse, recycling, and reintegration at the end of its useful life. In ecodesign, this process leads to closing of the loop in the use of materials in the built environment. DFD is facilitated by modular coordination and preassembled construction components, and by mechanical connection of materials instead of chemical bonding of materials.

Designer bugs   Popular term for microbes developed to degrade specific toxic chemicals at their source in toxic waste dumps or in groundwater.

Detention basin   Excavated area of land used to collect surface water runoff for the purpose of creating a constant outflow from the basin. It is a small storage lagoon intended to slow storm water runoff and to prevent surface flooding, as well as to allow surface water to return to groundwater. An ecodesign site planning strategy for sustainable drainage, it provides a water infrastructure for the site. *See also: Bioswales*

Dew point temperature   Temperature at which moisture from the air begins to condense.

DFD   *See: Design for disassembly*

Diazinon   Insecticide, banned by USEPA in 1986. Because of its toxicity it could not be used in open areas such as sod farms and golf courses, but it was not banned for agricultural, domestic, or commercial establishment uses.

Dibenzofurans   *See: Furans*

Dichloro-diphenyl-trichloroethane (DDT)   Because of its toxicity, persistence in the environment, and accumulation in the food chain, this insecticide was banned by USEPA in 1972. It has a long half-life of 15 years and a tendency to accumulate in the fatty tissue of some animals.

Dichloroethylene (DCE)   Toxic chemical pollutant; an industrial chemical that is not found naturally in the environment. Also called 1, 1-dichloroethylene. DCE is used primarily in the production of polyvinylidine chloride (PVC) copolymers as an intermediate for synthesis of organic chemicals. It is also used to make certain plastics, such as flexible film food wrap and packaging materials. It is also used as flame-retardant coating for fibers and carpet backings. It can cause respiratory problems and may damage the nervous system, liver, and lungs. A substance to avoid in ecodesign. *See also: Toxic chemicals*

Diffuse solar radiation   The component of light that has been reflected, typically from numerous surfaces. The intensity of solar radiation decreases as the inverse of R^2, where R is the distance to the Sun. *See also: Direct solar radiation; Solar radiation*

Diode   Electronic device that allows current flow in one direction (forward bias) and inhibits current flow in the opposite direction (reverse bias). Most diodes are based on semiconductor p–n junctions. In a p–n diode, conventional current can flow from the p-type side (the anode) to the n-type side (the cathode), but has difficulty flowing in the opposite direction. Another type of semiconductor diode, the Schottky diode, is formed from the contact between a metal and a semiconductor rather than by a p–n junction. Avalanche and Zener diodes conduct in the reverse bias direction when a reverse bias voltage level reaches a specified voltage. *See also: Avalanche diode; Schottky diode; Zener diode*

Dioxin   Tetrachlorodibenzo-para-dioxin. Anthropogenic toxin created during combustion, chlorine bleaching, and other types of chemical manufacturing. It is one of the more toxic human-made compounds. It is harmful to human health and the environment. Seventy-five chemical compounds are included in the category of dioxins. *See also: Toxic chemicals*

Direct carbon fuel cell   New type of fuel cell based on a process called direct carbon conversion. Carbon particles are joined in an electrochemical process with oxygen molecules to produce CO_2 and electricity. The source of carbon fuel can be any type of hydrocarbon, including coal, lignite, natural gas, petroleum, petroleum, coke, and biomass. Because carbon, not hydrogen, fuels this cell, hydrogen is released as a by-product of the cell reaction and could potentially be captured for use in a separate hydrogen-powered fuel cell. Claims of up to 64% efficiency have been made. The carbon fuel particles can be produced through pyrolysis of hydrocarbons, a thermal decomposition method that is the source of carbon black for tires, ink, and other applications in manufacturing industries. Because this is a high-temperature cell, its best use would be for stationary applications, particularly in combination with CHP, utilizing the waste heat energy.

The direct carbon fuel cell technology was developed at Lawrence Livermore National Laboratory. The technology uses aggregates of extremely fine carbon particles from 10 to 1000 nm in diameter, distributed in a mixture of molten lithium, sodium, or potassium carbonate at 750–850 °C (1,382–1,562 °F). Total cell efficiencies are projected to be 70–80%, with power generation in the 1 kW/m² range, sufficient for practical applications. *See also: Fuel cells*

Direct cooling   Cooling achieved by various methods and devices: keeping heat out by avoiding direct solar gain; shading roofs and overhangs; use of wing walls and vegetation; ventilation; underground construction; and evaporative cooling.

Direct current (DC)   Electricity produced by i) batteries, static, and lightning; and ii) high-voltage electricity.

i) DC is most commonly used in low-voltage applications, especially those powered by batteries or solar power systems (both of which can produce only DC). Most automotive applications use DC, although the alternator is an AC device that uses a rectifier to produce DC. Most electronic circuits require a DC power supply. Applications using fuel cells, which mix hydrogen and oxygen together with a catalyst to produce electricity and water as by-products, also produce only DC. In low-voltage applications a voltage is created, and possibly stored, until a circuit is completed. When it is, the current flows directly, in one direction, and at a specific, constant voltage. For example, DC is used to power flashlights, pocket radios, portable CD players or virtually any other type of portable or battery-powered device. A car battery, approximately 12 V, is as high a DC voltage as most people ever use.

ii) High-voltage DC (HVDC) is used for long-distance point-to-point power transmission and for submarine cables, with voltage from a few kilovolts to approximately one megavolt. In this case DC electric power transmission systems are used for bulk transmission of electrical power instead of using the more common alternating current (AC) systems. High-voltage transmission reduces the energy and power lost in the resistance of the wires. Power in a circuit is proportional to the current, but the power lost as heat in the wires is proportional to the square of the current. However, power is also proportional to voltage, so for a given power level, higher voltage can be traded off for lower current. Thus the higher the voltage, the lower the power loss. Power loss can also be reduced by reducing resistance, commonly achieved by increasing the diameter of the conductor, but larger conductors are heavier and more expensive. High voltages cannot easily be used in lighting and motors, so transmission-level voltage must be reduced to values compatible with end-use equipment. The transformer, which only works with alternating current, is an efficient way to change voltages. An advantage of HVDC is the ability to transmit large amounts of power over long distances with lower capital costs and with lower losses than AC. Depending on voltage level and construction details, losses are quoted as about 3% per 1000 km. High-voltage DC transmission allows efficient use of energy sources remote from load centers. HVDC can carry more power per conductor, because for a given power rating the constant voltage in a DC line is lower than the peak voltage in an AC line.

With the exception of Argentina and Bahrain, which use both AC and DC, and India, Madeira, and South Africa, which use DC in certain areas, homes and businesses in all other countries use AC electricity exclusively. *See also:* **Alternating current**

Direct digital controls (DDC)   Computer software that allows programmed control of heating and cooling functions. These programs can increase the efficiency of mechanical systems. For example, DDC systems can be programmed to reduce the air flow under low occupancy conditions.

Direct-fired or conventional steam electricity
See: **Biomass electricity**

Direct gain   Occurs when sunlight enters a space before being intercepted. Greenhouses, solar floor/wall systems and skylights are examples.

Direct heat pump system   *See:* **Open-loop geothermal heat pump system**

Direct irrigation   Surface watering system that releases small amounts of water through emitters placed near plants.

Direct methanol fuel cell (DMFC)   One type of fuel cell. Fuel cells produce electricity without any moving parts, without burning a fuel, without combustion, and without waste products or harmful pollutants, but significantly improve electrical power generation efficiency. DMFCs are powered by pure methanol, which is mixed with steam and fed directly to the fuel cell anode. As methanol has a higher energy level than hydrogen, DMFCs do not have many of the fuel storage problems of the cells that use hydrogen, although it has less energy density than gasoline or diesel fuel. DMFCs are similar to regenerative proton-exchange membrane cells in that they both use a polymer membrane as the electrolyte. However, in the DMFC the anode catalyst itself draws the hydrogen from the liquid methanol, eliminating the need for a fuel reformer. Efficiencies of about 40% are expected with this type of fuel cell, which would typically operate at a temperature of 120–90 °F (49–88 °C). Higher efficiencies are achieved at higher temperatures.

DMFCs are relatively new compared with other fuel cells powered by pure oxygen. Potential applications include transport, portable power including cellular phones and laptop computers, auxiliary power for instrumentation and vehicles, and as a battery replacement for combat personnel and for battlefield applications. In addition, when compared with conventional internal combustion engines, the fuel cell system's increased efficiency will lower fuel consumption and reduce criteria pollutants and carbon monoxide emissions, which contribute to global warming. *See also: Fuel cells*

Direct radiation   Light that has traveled a straight path from the Sun to the Earth's surface with minimal scatter.

Direct solar gain   Also known as solar heat gain or passive solar gain. Refers to the increase in temperature in a space, object, or structure that results from solar radiation. The amount of solar gain increases with exposure to the Sun. Use of solar gain for passive or active solar heating decreases reliance on nonrenewable energy sources such as oil and coal.

Direct solar radiation   Sunlight arriving directly from the Sun. This causes an increase in temperature for the material absorbing the solar radiation. The radiation absorbed by a substance can then be re-radiated as heat at longer infrared wavelengths. *See also: Diffuse solar radiation; Solar radiation*

Dish/engine system   Type of concentrating solar power system. An electric generator that uses sunlight as its fuel instead of gas or coal to produce electricity. The main components of the system are: i) the solar concentrator, which collects direct beam energy from the Sun and concentrates it on a point on a receiver dish; and ii) the power converter, which is made up of a thermal receiver and an engine/generator. The thermal receiver absorbs the concentrated solar beam, converts it to heat, and transfers the heat to the engine/converter.

Disinfection by-products   Listed by USEPA as a major water pollutant. To protect drinking water from these disease-causing pathogens, water suppliers often add a disinfectant such as chlorine. However, certain microbial pathogens, such as *Cryptosporidium*, are highly resistant to traditional disinfection practices. Disinfectants themselves can react with naturally occurring materials in the water to form by-products, such a trihalomethanes and haloacetic acids, which may pose a health risk. *See also: Water pollutants*

Disposable   Item that can be thrown away after it has been used, with little or no consideration for its return and reintegration back into ecological systems. In ecodesign, the term "disposable items" refers to the part of the present throughput flow of materials in the built environment in which materials are extracted from the Earth, manufactured for use, used and disposed of after their useful life. The increase in disposable items and materials has increased landfills, wastes, and contamination. An ecodesign goal is to avoid designating disposable materials and to seek to reuse, recycle, and reintegrate all materials back into the natural environment.

Dissolved oxygen   Oxygen present in water, vital for fish and aquatic life. Its presence is also an indicator of a water body's ability to support aquatic life.

Distillate fuel   General classification for the petroleum fractions produced in conventional distillation operations. Used primarily for space heating, diesel engine fuel (including fuel for railroad engines and agricultural machinery), and electric power generation. The usual designations for these products are No. 1, No. 2, and No. 4 fuel oils; and No. 1, No. 2, and No. 4 diesel fuels.

Distributed energy resources (DER)   Variety of small modular power-generating technologies that can be combined with energy management and storage systems and used to improve the operation of the electricity delivery system, whether or not those technologies are connected to an electricity grid.

District heating   A heating system in which steam or hot water for space heating or hot water supply is piped from a central boiler plant or electric power/heating plant to a cluster of buildings. Generally regarded as more efficient use of energy than individual heating systems. *See also: Cogeneration*

Diurnal shifts   Difference between day and night temperatures.

Diversion power plant   One of the three types of hydropower facility. *See also: Hydroelectric power plant; Impoundment power plant; Pumped storage plant*

Diversity   *See: Biodiversity*

DMFC   *See: Direct methanol fuel cell*

DNAPL   *See: Dense nonaqueous-phase liquid*

Dobson unit   Measurement unit of the amount of ozone in the atmosphere.

DOE-2 computer simulation model   US Department of Energy computer simulation of hourly building energy consumption. DOE-2 was released in the 1970s and has been the mainstay for computer simulation worldwide. Recently Energy Plus, a new DOE simulation program, has been released and is considered a successor to DOE-2. *See also: Energy Plus*

Dopant   Chemical element (impurity) added in small amounts to an otherwise pure semiconductor material to modify the electrical properties of a material. An n-dopant introduces more electrons; a p-dopant creates electron vacancies (holes).

Doping   Addition of dopants to a semiconductor. The process of intentionally introducing impurities into an extremely pure (also referred to as intrinsic) semiconductor in order to change its electrical properties. The impurities are dependent on the type of semiconductor. *See also: Semiconductor*

Dose–response function   Relationship between the effects on (response of) an organism or system and the amount (dose) of the material to which the organism/system is exposed. Usually used in pollution control.

Double envelope   Construction designed to save energy. Occupied space surrounded on four of its six sides (north and south walls, roof and floor) by an airspace. The airspace is enclosed by an outer shell consisting of the roof, north and south wall, and exposed earth underneath the floor. East and west walls are single walls. *See also: Building envelope; Thermal envelope house*

Double-layered façade system Used in eco-design as a mixed-mode approach in which there is a partial use of mechanical and electrical systems and partial use of renewable source of energy. The double-layered façade system wraps a secondary glass skin—double-skin glazed façade—around the built form, outside the weather-excluding membrane. This decreases energy use by trapping warm air, allows breezes through on temperate days, and creates a stack effect, siphoning ventilation on still days. Ventilated double skin also has an intermediate shading device, which deflects most of the incoming solar radiation back through the external glass. The proportion of absorbed solar radiation is converted in "sensible" heat and radiated back into the air space between the inner and outer glass units. *See also: **Mixed-mode design; Stack effect***

Downcycling The recycling of a material into a material of lesser quality. Examples are the recycling of one grade of plastic into lower-grade plastic products; or the recycling of concrete into use as a lower-grade aggregate. The term was made popular by William McDonough and Michael Braungart in the book *Cradle to Cradle: Remaking the Way We Make Things (2002)*. The terms downcycle and downcycling were first used by Reiner Pilz of Pilz GmbH and Thornton Kay of Salvo Llp in 1993, along with the terms upcycle and upcycling. In the cyclic flow of materials in ecosystems, the waste from one organism becomes the food for another. *See also: **Upcycling***

Drainage basin *See: **Catchment basin***

Drainback system A type of active solar water heater system. Drainback systems are non-pressurized, closed-loop systems using water as the heat-transfer fluid. They use pumps to circulate water through the collectors. Because the water in the collector loop drains into a reserve

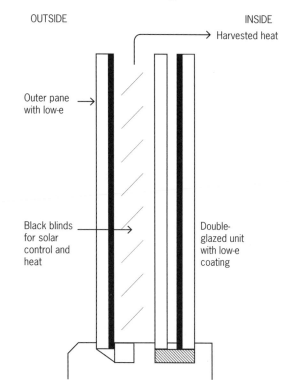

OUTSIDE   INSIDE

→ Harvested heat

Outer pane with low-e →

Black blinds for solar control and heat →

Double-glazed unit with low-e coating

Figure 20 Double-layered façade system

tank when the pump stops, this system works well in colder climates.

Dredged material A major water pollutant. Dredging is the removal of material from the bottom of lakes, rivers, harbors, and other water bodies. Most dredging is done to maintain and keep navigation channels, anchorages, and berthing areas safe for the passage of boats and ships. Dredging of contaminated areas may also be to reduce the exposure of marine biota and humans to contaminants, and/or to prevent the spread of contaminants to the other areas of the water body. Sediments in and around cities and industrial areas are often contaminated with a variety of pollutants. These pollutants are introduced to waterways from point sources such as combined sewer overflows, and municipal and industrial discharges and spills, or may be introduced from nonpoint sources such as surface runoff

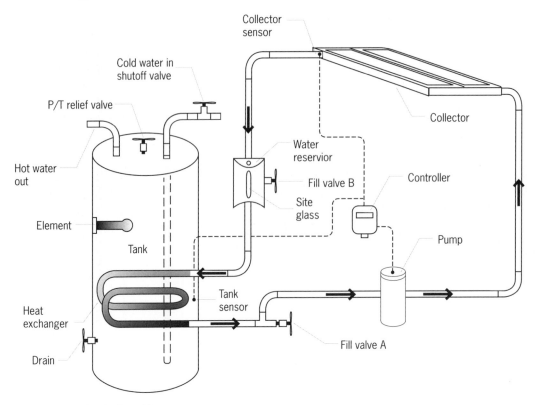

Figure 21 Drainback closed-loop system

and atmospheric deposition. *See also: Water pollutants*

Drinking water standards Standards established by regulatory agencies to protect the health of the public. Potable water is measured by the amount of suspended particles in the water, its clarity and odor, and a threshold of micro-organisms present that may be harmful to health.

Drip irrigation Also known as micro-irrigation. Technology using a network of plastic pipes to carry a low flow of water under low pressure to plants. Water is applied much more slowly and at a lower volume than with sprinkler irrigation. This system maintains a balance of air and water in the soil and provides water to plant roots. It is an efficient method of getting water to

agricultural crops and to planters in buildings. In ecodesign, drip irrigation minimizes the use of water and maximizes efficiency, and is preferred to the sprinkler system.

Dry bulb temperature Temperature of the air as measured by a standard thermometer. The accuracy and resolution of the measurement depends on the sensor used to determine the temperature.

Dry cell Battery with a captive electrolyte. Dry cell batteries can be used in radios, calculators, toys, watches, pacemakers, and hearing aids. As primary batteries that cannot be recharged, dry cells are often discarded after they are discharged. Their chemical and metal components contaminate and pollute landfills and other repositories of waste.

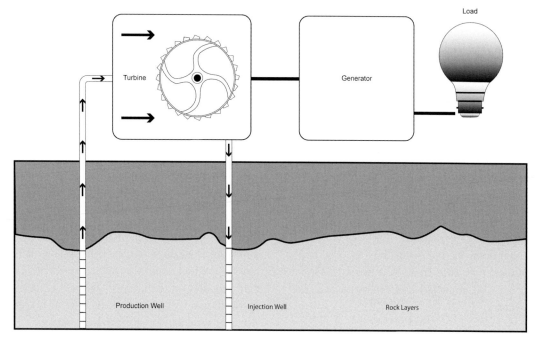

Figure 22a Dry steam power plant schematic
Source: US National Renewable Energy Laboratory

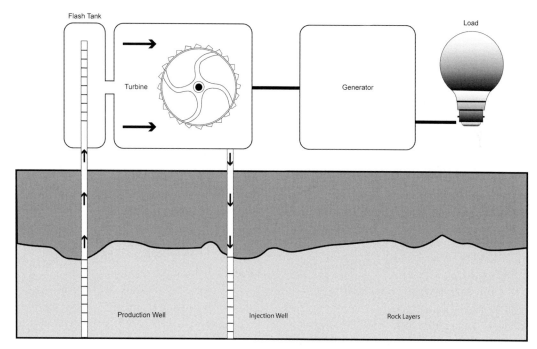

Figure 22b Flash steam power plant schematic
Source: US National Renewable Energy Laboratory

Dry deposition   A form of acid rain, composed of dust- or smoke-containing acid chemicals falling to the ground when the weather is dry. Dry deposited gases and particles stick to the ground, buildings, homes, cars, trees, and streets, and can be washed into runoff by rain. They can also be carried by wind.

Dry rock geothermal energy   Extraction of geo-thermal heat by pumping water through hot rocks.

Dry scrubber   Air pollution control device. 1. Gravel bed that filters and collects particulate matter from gas streams.
  2. Process of removing SO_2 by inserting a chemical into SO_2 to form a solid particulate that can be collected and removed. *See also: Scrubbers*

Dry steam geothermal power   One of three main geothermal power techniques. Dry steam power plants use very hot (>455 °F; >235 °C) steam. Steam goes directly through a pipe to a turbine to spin a generator that produces electricity. Small amounts of CO_2, nitric oxide, and sulfur are emitted. It is the oldest type of geothermal power plant, first used in Italy in 1904 (see Figures 22a and 22b). *See also: Binary cycle geothermal power; Flash steam geothermal power; Geothermal power technology*

Dry toilet   *See: Eco-toilet*

Dual-fuel vehicle   Also known as a bi-fuel vehicle or flexible fuel vehicle. Vehicle designed to operate on a combination of an alternative fuel and a conventional fuel. Includes vehicles using a mixture of gasoline or diesel and an alternative fuel in one fuel tank. Also refers to vehicles that can operate on either an alternative fuel, a conventional fuel, or both, simultaneously using two fuel systems. *See also: Hybrid engine*

Dust-to-dust   energy   cost   *See: Life-cycle assessment*

E

E10 A type of alternative fuel. Gasohol, an ethanol mixture that contains 10% ethanol and 90% unleaded gasoline.

E85 A type of alternative fuel—a fuel mixture that usually contains a mixture of up to 85% denatured fuel ethanol and gasoline or other hydrocarbon by volume. On an undenatured basis, the ethanol/gasoline mixture component ranges from 70 to 83% and 15% gasoline by volume. E85 as a fuel is widely used in Brazil and Sweden and is becoming increasingly common in the USA, mainly in the midwest where corn is a major crop and is the primary source material for ethanol fuel production. It is also available across most of the Maxol chain in Ireland.

E93 Ethanol mixture that contains 93% denatured ethanol and 5% gasoline by volume.

EAHE (EAHX) Earth–air heat exchanger. *See: Earth cooling tube*

Earth berm *See: Berm*

Earth cooling tube An underground heat-exchanger loop that can capture or dissipate heat to or from the ground. It uses the Earth's near-constant subterranean temperature to warm or cool air or other fluids for residential, agricultural, or industrial uses.

It is a long underground metal or plastic pipe, through which air is drawn. As air travels through the pipe, it gives up some of its heat to the soil and enters the house as cooler air. The use of moving air as a cooling mechanism reduces the requirement for large electro-mechanical cooling systems such as air conditioners. Earth cooling tubes can supplement conventional central heating or air conditioning systems, as only blowers are required to move the air. In a warm, humid region it is possible for humidity to condense in the tube, creating an environment for mold growth.

If building air is blown through the heat exchanger for heat recovery ventilation, in Europe this is called an earth tube (also known as an earth cooling tube or earth warming tube); in North America an earth–air heat exchanger (EAHE or EAHX). These systems are known by several other names, including air-to-soil heat exchanger, earth channel, earth canal, earth–air tunnel system, ground tube heat exchanger, hypocaust, subsoil heat exchanger, and underground air pipe. *See also: Earth tube*

Earth-coupled ground-source heat pump Type of geothermal heat pump that uses sealed horizontal or vertical pipes, buried in the ground, as heat exchangers through which a fluid is circulated to transfer heat. Energy research indicates that GSHPs typically provide efficiency increases of over 50% in the heating mode and 20% in the cooling mode.

Earth sheltered design Uses earth as a major component of a building's thermal control system. Earth tempering can be achieved through three primary methods: direct, indirect, and isolated. i) In the direct system, the building envelope is in contact with the earth, and conduction through the building elements, primarily walls and floor, regulates the interior temperature. ii) In the indirect system, the building interior is conditioned by air brought through the earth, such as in earth tubes. iii) The isolated system uses earth temperatures to increase the efficiency of a heat pump by moderating temperatures at the condensing coil. A geothermal heat pump is an example of an isolated system. Earth-sheltered homes are typically built with concrete, which has high thermal mass. In the winter, passive solar features can maintain comfort levels by warming the thermal mass. Earth sheltered homes usually have lower maintenance and operating costs. *See also: Earth tempering; Underground home*

Earth tempering Use of earth as part of a structure's energy systems. *See also: Earth sheltered design*

Earth tube A method to bring air into an earth sheltered home. Cooler earth temperature is transferred to air brought into a house through a tube(s) buried in the ground. Outside air is brought through the tube(s) either by fans or natural convection. In a warm, humid region it is possible for humidity to condense in the tube,

creating an environment for mold growth. *See also: Earth cooling tube*

Ecocell An architectural ecodesign device that consists of slots and incisions inserted at regular intervals into the built form, cutting across all floors, and creating vertical integration of the built form's ecology from the uppermost levels down into the lowest levels. The slots and incisions create a cellular void. These cellular voids have a spiral ramp and bring daylight into the inner parts of the built form, allowing rainwater harvesting and reuse, letting vegetation enter the inner parts of the built form down from the uppermost roof level, and providing natural ventilation and recesses for the provision of recycling systems within the built form. There may be a series of ecocells within the built form so that they cut through all floors from roof terrace to basement. Ecocells may also be integrated horizontally.

Ecodesign Also known as sustainable design; ecological design of the human built environment; green architecture; green design. Managed use of an ecosystem's processes and nonrenewable resources through ecomimicry. Its main objectives are physical and mechanical integration of built forms and infrastructures with the ecosystem features and processes of a given site; prevention of resource depletion of energy, water, and raw

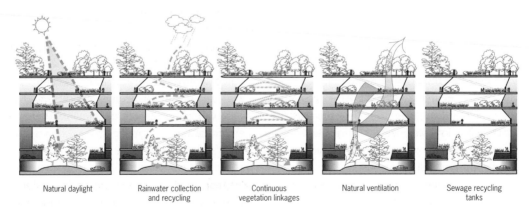

| Natural daylight | Rainwater collection and recycling | Continuous vegetation linkages | Natural ventilation | Sewage recycling tanks |

Figure 23 An ecocell

materials; prevention of environmental degradation caused by facilities and their infrastructure throughout their life cycle; and the creation of biointegration between the built environment and the natural environment. It includes any form of design that minimizes environmentally destructive impacts by integrating physically, systematically, and temporally with the natural environment's living processes. There are six primary principles governing sustainable design.

- Balance ecosystem abiotic and biotic components by integrating the designed system's inorganic mass with biomass.
- Reduce dependency on non renewable energy, and increase efficiency in energy use through bioclimatic design, daylighting, natural ventilation, passive solar systems, active and interactive walls, and roof gardens. Automated systems in buildings increase energy efficiency of building's environmental system
- Minimize resource depletion and waste by using materials that can be reused, recycled, and reintegrated back into nature.
- Through site selection and planning, preserve existing ecosystems and biodiversity through ecological corridors, land bridges, undercrofts and other horizontal integration and green infrastructure. Determine compatibility of the type and form of the human and built impositions and activities with the site's ecology and resilience.
- Use compact space in building and development to reduce heat island effects, urban micro-climate effects, and fragmentation of ecosystem habitats.
- Water management through drainage infrastructure that manages rainfall and run-off through bioswales, retention ponds, filter drains, infiltration devices, and permeable surfaces. This will reduce pollution and flooding, create buffer strips for wetland habitats, and enable water purification, and recycling and reuse through collection.

Utilizing an ecodesign or sustainable design philosophy encourages decisions at each phase of the design process that will reduce negative impacts on the environment and the health of the occupants, without compromising the bottom line. It is an integrated approach that encourages cooperation and compromise. An integrated approach has a positive impact on all phases of a building's life cycle, including design, construction, operation and decommissioning. *See also: Ecomimicry; Interactions matrix*

Ecodesign site types   Classification of site types based on ecosystem characteristics and features. The site with the highest biodiversity, and that has been least affected by human acts and features, is at the top of the taxonomy of site types.

Taxonomy of site types as basis for ecodesign:

- ecologically mature
- ecologically immature
- ecologically simplified
- mixed artificial
- monoculture
- zero culture
- contaminated

See also: Ecologically mature ecosystem; Ecologically immature ecosystem; Ecologically simplified ecosystem; Mixed artificial ecosystem; Monoculture ecosystem; Zero culture ecosystem; Contaminated ecosystem

Eco-efficiency   Term introduced at the Rio Earth Summit in 1992. Doing more with less— use of less energy, fewer materials and resources, less disruption to the ecosystem. Since 1992 the concept of eco-efficiency has been internationally recognized as a method that can contribute to the sustainability of society.

Ecogadget   Term to describe solar collectors, wind generators, photovoltaics, and biodigesters that are attached to buildings. In eco-master planning, the "gray" infrastructure essentially consists of these eco-engineering systems.

Ecological corridor Connections between existing fragments of vegetation to create large, spatially interconnected, continuous greenways, parks, and open spaces as a green infrastructure or nature's infrastructure. This ecodesign strategy provides a region-wide nexus of green corridors to repair habitat fragmentation; to span across impervious surfaces such as roads; to improve the interactions and movement of species from one area to another; and to create a larger habitat with more opportunities for sharing resources within the ecosystem. Devices used to create these corridors include landscaped bridges and undercrofts.

Ecological diversity There are three types of diversity within ecosystems: i) compositional diversity such as species, genetic, community, and ecosystems; ii) functional diversity, which includes the ecological interactions among species through competition, predation, mutualism, and ecological functions as well as episodic natural disturbances; iii) structural diversity, in which plants and animals occupy space efficiently through size, shape, and distribution of species, habitats, and communities across the landscape. *See also: Biodiversity*

Ecological flow management Comprehensive approach to ecodesign, which includes site selection, use of materials, energy, and materials regeneration considerations following the usable life cycle of a building, all aimed at minimizing adverse impacts on the ecosystem.

Ecological footprint Productive land necessary to support humans in their lifestyle.

Ecological health *See: Ecological integrity*

Ecological indicator Measurable, quantitative information on the ecological structure and function of the biotic and abiotic variables in a specific ecosystem. These measurements indicate an ecosystem's health and sustainability, and may be used as indices in ecodesign masterplanning.

Ecological integrity Also known as ecological health or ecological resilience. Describes an ecosystem's ability to survive and maintain itself after sustaining damage. Types of damage that may endanger eco-integrity are: increased waste, decreased keystone species, disease or predation, migration, and disease.

Ecological monitoring Assessing changes that take place in an ecosystem as a result of anthropogenic activities, such as forest clearance, land devastation, and building construction. Monitoring assessments can be carried out using biosensors, aerial satellite monitoring, or ground monitoring. Ecodesign involves constant ecological monitoring of sensitive sites after the imposition of development and built systems to determine consequences of the operations of the build systems on the natural environment.

Ecological niche Description of either the role played by a species in a biological community, or the total set of environmental factors that determine distribution.

Ecological processes Metabolic functions of ecosystems—energy flow, elemental cycling, and the production, consumption, and decomposition of organic matter.

Ecological resilience *See: Ecological integrity*

Ecological risk assessment Formal analysis or model to estimate the effects of human actions on natural resources and to interpret the significance of those effects. Includes initial hazard identification, exposure and dose–response assessments, and other risks.

Ecological succession Process by which organisms occupy a site and gradually change environmental conditions by creating soil, shade, shelter, or increased humidity. These changes constitute constant development and flux of an ecosystem. Changes are orderly and predictable within an ecosystem over time from the initial or pioneer community to a final stage or climax. The last—climax—community is stable and can sustain itself with very little change in biodiversity of species, if there are no major catastrophic natural events or anthropogenic influences. In ecodesign, an evaluation of the state of succession of the ecosystem is made prior to any built development on the site.

Ecologically immature ecosystem Category of site type in ecodesign. Immature ecosystems are sites that are recovering from damage and are in the process of regeneration. The basis for planning and ecodesign for this type of site depends on the condition, characteristics, and features of the specific site. *See also: Ecodesign site types*

Ecologically mature ecosystem Category of site type in ecodesign. Ecosystem characterized by high biodiversity; pristine or largely undisturbed by people for a long time. *See also: Ecodesign site types*

Ecologically simplified ecosystem Category site type in ecodesign. Ecosystem characterized by extreme damage caused by grazing, burning, logging, loss of biotic components. *See also: Ecodesign site types*

EcoLogo Launched by the Canadian federal government in 1988, EcoLogo is a designation of eco-friendly products and services. It sets standards and certifies products in more than 120 categories. EcoLogo is North America's oldest environmental standard and certification organization.

Ecology Study of the structure and function of nature; the relationship between organisms and their environment.

Ecomasterplanning Masterplanning based on ecological concepts. Environmentally benign and seamless biointegration of i) green (eco) infrastructure, ii) engineering infrastructure, iii) water management infrastructure, and iv) infrastructure of buildings and enclosures.

Ecomimesis Imitation of ecosystems by design. Important to ecodesign principles. *See also: Biomimicry*

Ecomimicry Design of human communities and built environment that emulates the model of nature's ecosystems. *See also: Ecodesign*

Ecosystem Interacting system of a biological community (biotic) and its nonliving environmental surroundings (abiotic). A geographical area that includes all living organisms (people, plants, animals, microorganisms), their physical surroundings (soil, water, air, habitats), and the natural cycles that sustain them. Ecosystems can be protected through environmental planning that addresses all the factors, both natural and human, affecting an ecosystem of a given region. An example of protecting an ecosystem is the watershed approach, in which all pollution sources and habitat conditions in a watershed are considered in developing strategies for restoring and maintaining a healthy ecosystem. State and federal regulations seek to protect ecosystems that support plant, animal, and aquatic life through a combination of regulatory and voluntary programs designed to reduce the amount of pollutants entering their environment (see Figure 24).

Ecosystem equilibrium Also known as steady state. Idealized balance of energy and material without substantial loss of nutrients. The human-made built environment is part of the equilibrium.

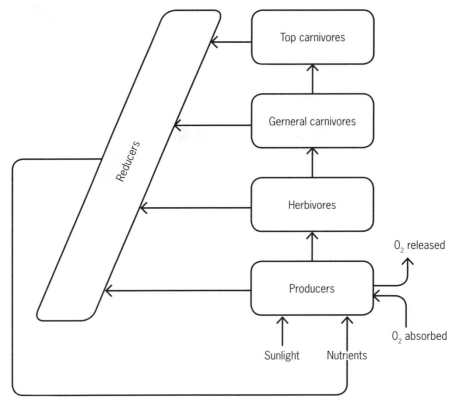

Figure 24 An ecosystem cycle

Eco-toilet   Also known as a dry toilet. Water-less sewage system in which urine and feces are collected in a specially designed chamber that diverts the urine to one receptacle and feces into another, dries and sanitizes the feces, and makes it safely usable as fertilizer. The container with urine can be taken directly to agricultural fields, diluted with water, and used as a fertilizer.

Ecotone   Ecological zone or boundary where two or more distinctly different ecosystems meet.

Edaphic   Pertains to soil nutrients, temperature, moisture level, and the climate of a specific locality. Edaphic factors are primary components in balancing ecological nutrient cycles.

Efficiency factor   Ratio of output energy over input energy.

Effluent   Waste stream flowing into the atmosphere, surface water, groundwater, or soil.

E_h   Measurement of the total hemispheric illumination on the unobstructed plane of the ground from both the Sun and sky.

El Niño   Spanish name for the male child. Term used to describe a cyclical warm current of water. It refers to a normally weak, warm current appearing annually around December along the coast of Ecuador and Peru. It usually lasts only a few weeks to a month or more, but every three to seven years, an extreme El Niño event may disrupt the ocean–atmosphere system in the tropical

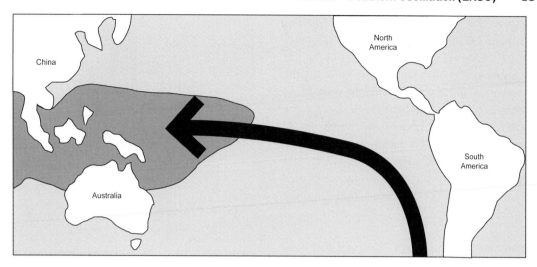

Figure 25 El Niño—movement
Source: National Oceanic and Atmospheric Administration

Pacific, with significant economic consequences worldwide as well. It has a significant impact on weather around the globe.

The National Oceanic and Atmospheric Administration believes that El Niños are not caused by global warming. Clear evidence exists from a variety of sources (including archaeological studies) that El Niños have been present for hundreds, and some indicators suggest maybe millions, of years. However, it has been hypothesized that warmer global sea surface temperatures can enhance the El Niño phenomenon, and it is also true that El Niños have been more frequent and intense in recent decades. Recent climate models that simulate the 21st century with increased greenhouse gases suggest that El Niño-like sea surface temperature patterns in the tropical Pacific are likely to be more persistent.

Since the late 1950s, there have been nine major El Niño events: 1957–58, 1965, 1968–69, 1972–73, 1976–77, 1982–83, 1986–87, 1991–92, and 1994–95. The 1982–83 El Niño was the strongest of the 20th century. The possible interrelationship between El Niño and global weather patterns, especially the simultaneous droughts in the Soviet Union, Africa, Australia, and Central

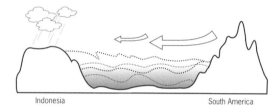

Figure 26a Normal (non-El Niño) conditions
Source: National Oceanic and Atmospheric Administration

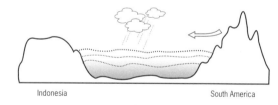

Figure 26b El Niño conditions
Source: National Oceanic and Atmospheric Administration

America, was first realized in 1972–73. Relationships between El Niño and other global weather anomalies are known as teleconnections. *See also: El Niño—Southern Oscillation (ENSO)*

El Niño—Southern Oscillation (ENSO)   A global event resulting from large-scale interaction between the ocean and the atmosphere. The Southern Oscillation, a more recent discovery than El Niño, refers to an oscillation in the surface pressure (atmospheric mass) between the southeastern tropical Pacific and the Australian–Indonesian regions. When the waters of the eastern Pacific are abnormally warm (an El Niño event), sea level pressure drops in the eastern Pacific and rises in the west. The reduction in the pressure gradient is accompanied by a weakening of the low-latitude easterly trades.

Elastomeric roof coatings   Coatings that have elastic properties and can stretch in the summer heat and return to their original shape without damage. Elastomeric coatings include acrylic, silicone, and urethane materials.

Electric vehicle (EV)   Vehicle powered by electricity, generally provided by a very large direct current battery motor. The battery, which is commonly either lead–acid or nickel-based, is rechargeable. Depending on the terrain, EVs average 60 miles (97 km) on a full charge before they need to be recharged. Uses no fossil fuel and its contaminant emissions are minimal. Electric vehicles qualify in the zero-emission vehicle (ZEV) category for emissions. *See also:* **Smart fortwo car**

Electrical generator   *See: Generator*

Electrical grid   Integrated system of electricity distribution, usually covering a large area.

Electrochemical cell   Device containing two conducting electrodes, one positive and the other negative, made of dissimilar materials (usually metals) immersed in a chemical solution (electrolyte) that transmits positive ions from the negative to the positive electrode and forms an electrical charge. One or more cells constitute a battery. A simple electrochemical

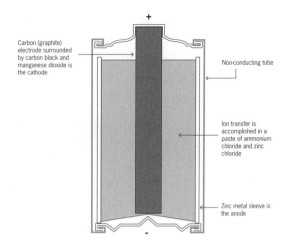

Carbon (graphite) electrode surrounded by carbon black and manganese dioxide is the cathode

Non-conducting tube

Ion transfer is accomplished in a paste of ammonium chloride and zinc chloride

Zinc metal sleeve is the anode

Figure 27 A copper-zinc battery—previously the most common small battery, now replaced by the alkaline battery
Source: US Department of Energy

cell can be made from copper and zinc metals with solutions of their sulfates. In the process of the reaction, electrons can be transferred from the zinc to the copper through an electrically conducting path as a useful electric current.

An electrochemical cell can be created by placing metallic electrodes into an electrolyte where a chemical reaction either uses or generates an electric current. Electrochemical cells that generate an electric current are called voltaic cells or galvanic cells, and common batteries consist of one or more of these cells. In other electrochemical cells, an externally supplied electric current is used to drive a chemical reaction that would not occur spontaneously. Such cells are called electrolytic cells. One type, the dry cell, cannot be recharged once it has been discharged, and must be discarded, increasing contamination and pollution in landfills and other waste repositories through its metal and chemical components.

The accumulator lead acid battery is a secondary electrochemical cell because it can be recharged. A car battery is an example of this cell type. A fuel cell changes energy from combustion directly into electrical energy. It is used in spacecraft and nonnuclear submarines because its only by-product is water. *See also: Dry cell*

Electrochromic windows Windows that can be darkened or lightened with the application of a voltage. Small voltage applied to the windows will cause them to darken; reversing the voltage causes them to lighten. The windows consist of up to seven layers of materials. The electrochromic layer is typically tungsten oxide (WO_3). To darken the windows, a voltage is applied across two transparent conducting oxide layers. The voltage drives the ions from the ion storage layer and into the electrochromic layer. To lighten the window, the process is reversed. Until the cost of production can be decreased substantially, electrochromic windows will remain prohibitively expensive for general consumer use.

Electrode A conductor that provides electrical contact with another material, typically as a pole of a battery or fuel cell. Electrons enter or leave an electrolyte through the electrode conductor. Electrodes are components of batteries and fuel cells, which have a negative electrode (anode) and a positive electrode (cathode). *See also: Battery; Fuel cells*

Electrodeposition Electrolytic process in which a metal (substrate) is given an electrically conducting coating and placed in a liquid solution (electrolyte) containing metal ions, such as gold, copper, or nickel. A wide range of film thicknesses can be built. In thermal oxidation, the substrate is heated to 800–801,100 °C (1472–1,441,832 °F).

Electrolysis A chemical change in a substance that results from the passage of an electric current through an electrolyte. For example, commercial hydrogen is produced by separating the elements of water—hydrogen and oxygen—by charging the water with an electrical current. The same process takes place in fuel cells.

Electrolyte Liquid or solid substance that can conduct an electrical current. Used as a conducting solution in fuel cells. One of four components—anode, cathode, interconnect, and electrolyte—of a fuel cell, an electrolyte is a substance that conducts electrical current by movement of its dissociated positive and negative ions to the electrodes. For movement to take place, the electrolyte must have high ionic conductivity and no electrical conductivity. Because they generally consist of ions in solution, electrolytes are also known as ionic solutions, but molten electrolytes and solid electrolytes are also possible. Electrolytes commonly exist as solutions of acids, bases, or salts. Some gases may act as electrolytes under conditions of high temperature or low pressure. *See also: Anode; Cathode; Fuel cells; Solid oxide fuel cell*

Electrolytic cell   *See: Electrochemical cell*

Electromagnetic energy Energy generated from an electromagnetic field produced by an electric current flowing through a wire.

Electromagnetic field (EMF) Created by an electric current, typically a wire. Electric fields result from the strength (voltage) of the charge, and magnetic fields result from the motion (amperage) of the charge. The health impacts of EMFs, including increased risk of cancer, are subjects of continued research.

Electromagnetic radiation Electromagnetic radiation encompasses a wide range of energies. For example, power lines radiate 60 Hz electromagnetic radiation, which is nonionizing. Visible light is also electromagnetic radiation. Microwaves transfer energy to water molecules as the microwave frequency oscillates at approximately a water molecule's dipole resonant frequency. Collectively, electromagnetic radiation makes up the electromagnetic spectrum. Examples of the width of an electromagnetic energy spectrum include AM bands, aircraft and shipping bands, radio, TV, FM radio, microwave, radar, infrared light, ultraviolet light, x-ray and gamma rays, and higher energy waves. The shorter the wavelength, the higher the energy. Ultraviolet and higher-energy electromagnetic radiation can be ionizing and may break chemical bonds, and thus may cause damage to cells in living tissue.

Electrostatic precipitator   A particulate pollutant cleaning device, an electrostatic precipitator removes small particles from indoor air on an electrostatic surface. Usually can be cleaned with soap and water; some units produce small amounts of ozone. These devices are not effective in removing gaseous contaminants. Some precipitators can be installed in furnace ductwork and walls, while others are portable. Also called an electronic air cleaner.

Embodied energy   Energy expended from an energy source to extract, manufacture, and transport a building's materials, as well as that required to assemble and finish it. This usually includes the energy cost of the means of transport back to the originating station after delivery to the construction site. As buildings become increasingly more energy efficient, the energy required to create a building becomes proportionally more significant compared with the energy required to operate and run it. This is particularly true because some materials, such as aluminum, require a vast amount of energy in their manufacture.

EMCON   Methane generation model used for estimating the production of methane from municipal solid waste landfills. Named after EMCON Associates for Consolidated Concrete Ltd, the Australian company that created the model in 1980.

EMCS   *See: Energy management and control system*

EMF   *See: Electromagnetic field*

Emissions controls   Methods to reduce emissions into air, water, or soil. Wastewater treatment plants, in-plant solid and toxic waste reduction methods, and particulate collectors are some ways to decrease emissions. In the USA, commonly used to describe the technologies employed to reduce the air pollution-causing emissions produced by automobiles. Life cycle emissions are produced in activities associated with the manufacturing, maintenance, and disposal of the automobile, and include such items as volatile solvents used in manufacture, outgassing of synthetic materials, maintenance requirements of oil, batteries, and filters, and contaminated lubricants, tires, and heavy metals. *See also: Emissions, automobile*

Emissions   Release of pollutants into the air from a source.

Emissions, automobile   The emissions produced by a vehicle fall into three basic categories: i) tailpipe emissions, including hydrocarbons, nitrogen oxides, carbon monoxide, and carbon dioxide; ii) evaporative emissions, produced from the evaporation of fuel through gas tank venting and running losses; iii) refueling losses, which contribute to urban smog as these heavier molecules stay closer to ground level.

Motor vehicles generate three major pollutants: hydrocarbons (general formula for saturated hydrocarbon: C_nH_{2n+2}); nitrogen oxides (NO_x); and carbon monoxide (CO). Hydrocarbons react with NO_x in the presence of sunlight and elevated temperatures to form ground-level ozone. It can cause eye irritation, coughing, wheezing, and shortness of breath and can lead to permanent lung damage. NO_x also contribute to the formation of ozone, the formation of acid rain, and water quality problems. CO is a colorless, odorless, deadly gas. It reduces the flow of oxygen in the blood stream and can impair mental functions and visual perception. In urban areas, motor vehicles are responsible for as much as 90% of CO in the air. Motor vehicles also emit large amounts of carbon dioxide, which has potential to trap the Earth's heat and contribute to global warming. *See also:* **Emissions standards, automobile**

Emissions, control of nonroad engines

"Nonroad" is a term that includes a diverse collection of engines, equipment, and vehicles. Also referred to as "off-road" or "off-highway", the nonroad category includes outdoor power equipment, recreational vehicles, farm and construction equipment, boats, and locomotives. Most nonroad equipment and vehicles are powered by engines that burn gasoline or diesel fuel. Pollution from these engines comes from byproducts of the combustion process (exhaust) and, for gasoline-fueled engines, from evaporation of the fuel itself. USEPA estimates that emissions from nonroad engines contribute as much as 15–20% of unhealthy pollution in cities across the USA. Pollutants from nonroad sources include hydrocarbons, nitrogen oxides (NO_x), particulate matter, carbon monoxide (CO), and carbon dioxide (CO_2). Individual countries and international organizations have enacted standards and regulations for nonroad engine emissions.

In the USA, the 1990 Clean Air Act specifically directed USEPA to study, and regulate if warranted, the contribution of nonroad engines to urban air pollution. Since then USEPA has documented higher-than-expected emission levels across a broad spectrum of engines and equipment, and in 2007 amended emissions standards to reduce emissions of oxides of nitrogen, hydrocarbons, sulfur in fuel for diesel engines, and particulate matter. The regulations apply to small spark-ignition lawn and garden equipment, diesel-fueled farm and construction equipment, commercial marine vessels, gasoline fueled personal watercraft, recreational spark ignitions vehicles such as snowmobiles, all-terrain vehicles, dirt bikes, go-carts, and locomotives, among others. In addition, a 2005 USEPA proposal established emissions controls for oxides of nitrogen for new commercial aircraft to conform to the United Nations International Civil Aviation Organization and international standards, and for new engines utilized on commercial aircraft including small regional jets, single-aisle aircraft, twin-aisle aircraft, and 747s and larger aircraft.

The European Union established nonroad engine emissions standards in 1997 and amended the regulations in 2002 and 2004. They address gaseous emissions such as CO, HC, and NO_x as well as particulates. Its executive board, the European Commission, amended emissions standards for gaseous and particulate emissions of nonroad engines so they would be comparable with USEPA standards. This proposal also covers engines used on inland watercraft and self-propelled railcars, but not the huge diesel electric locomotive categories typical of the USA, or large ocean ships.

The United Nations Economic and Social Council amended in 2005 its 1998 Global Agreement of nonroad engine emission tests and standards. Many of its regulations, such as United Nations Economic Commission for Europe (UNECE) Regulation #96, address specific emissions. #96 sets emissions limits on compression ignition engines used in agricultural and forestry tractors.

Japan established nonroad emissions standards in 1991 and last amended them in 2004.

These reductions in NO_x and PM emissions from nonroad diesel engines will provide enormous public health benefits.

Emissions standard Maximum amount of air polluting discharge legally allowed from a single source, mobile or stationary.

Emissions standards, automobile State and federal government and/or international organizations have established standards for pollutants from automobiles. The target set by the Kyoto Protocol was an 8% reduction of emission in all sectors of the economy compared with 1990 levels by 2008–12. Research indicates that passenger cars account for more than half the transport-related carbon dioxide (CO_2) emission in the USA, and about half that in the European Union, with air transport accounting for less than 20% in both. For example, the US CAFE emission limits are mandatory, and the European emission limits for exhaust emissions of new vehicles sold in the EU member states are voluntary, under the ACEA agreement. The emissions standards are defined in a series of standards and regulate the emission of nitrogen oxides (NO_x), hydrocarbons, carbon monoxide (CO), and particulate matter. Vehicles regulated include cars, trucks, trains, tractors and other machinery, and barges, but exclude seagoing ships and airplanes. In late 2006 the European Commission announced its proposal for a legally binding limit of CO_2 emissions from cars. In addition, the European Conference of Ministers of Transport and the Organization of Economic Cooperation and Development monitor vehicle emissions and air quality to ensure CO_2 levels continue to decrease.

The Clean Air Initiative (CAI) with active operations in Asia, Latin America, sub-Saharan Africa, Europe, and Central Asia, also monitors air quality and focuses on decreasing emissions through improved fuel quality, emissions control technology, and alternative fuels. Although many of these regions include developing nations, the same emissions regulations apply. Economically developed countries including Russia, China, India, and Japan have instituted their own emissions standards for vehicles in addition to those of the CAI. *See also: ACEA agreement; Clean Air Initiative; Corporate Average Fuel Economy (CAFE); Kyoto Protocol*

Emissions standards, designations　The California Air Resources Board initiated, and the US federal government concurred, low emissions

standard designations for: i) inherently low-emission vehicles (ILEV); ii) partial zero-emission vehicles (PZEV); iii) super-ultra-low-emission vehicles (SULEV); iv) ultra-low-emission vehicles (ULEV); and v) zero-emission vehicles (ZEV).

Emissions trading　Also known as cap and trade or offset allowances. This practice uses economic incentives to achieve reductions of pollutant emissions. Usually administered by a government agency, emissions trading plans set a limit or cap on the amount of a specific pollutant that can be emitted. The agency issues credits or allowances to individual companies or other groups to emit the pollutant up to the specified limit. The total amount of credits cannot exceed the maximum amount of emissions set by the agency. If a company pollutes more than its allowance, it must buy credits from those who pollute less than their allowance, or face heavy penalties. This transfer of credits is referred to as a trade. In economic terms, the buyer pays for polluting, while the seller benefits for having reduced emissions. There are currently several very large trading systems, most notably the European Union. The carbon market makes up the bulk of trade pollutants.

Emissivity　Indication of a surface's ability to emit heat by radiation, to let go of heat via radiant energy. The lower the emissivity, the better the radiant barrier qualities of a material. Emissivity is measured on a scale of 0 to 1, with 1 indicating 100% emittance. Highly polished aluminum, for example, has an emittance of less than 0.1; a black, nonmetallic surface has an emittance of more than 0.9. Most nonmetallic, opaque materials at temperatures encountered in the built environment have emittance values between 0.85 and 0.955. Most foil-type radiant barriers have emissivity of 0.05 or below, which means 95% of the radiant heat is being blocked. Heat retention or minimized heat loss reduces reliance on electromechanical heating systems.

Encapsulation   A method of sealing one substance within a protective envelope using another material. For example, liquid used to provide a protective coating over asbestos-containing materials and fibers, which helps prevent emission of asbestos into the atmosphere.

Endangered species   Animals, birds, fish, plants or other living organisms threatened with extinction by anthropogenic or natural changes in their environment.

Endemism   Geographical locality in which species are restricted to a single region.

Endocrine disruptors   Toxic chemicals—synthetic chemicals that either mimic or block hormones and disrupt the body's normal functions when absorbed into the body. This disruption can happen through altering normal hormone levels, halting or stimulating the production of hormones, or changing the way hormones travel through the body, thus affecting the functions they control. Chemicals that are known human endocrine disruptors include diethylstilbesterol, dioxin, polychlorinated biphenyls (PCBs), DDT, and some other pesticides. Many chemicals, particularly pesticides and plasticizers, are suspected endocrine disruptors based on limited animal studies. *See also:* **Toxic chemicals**

Endothermic   A heat-absorbing reaction, or a reaction that requires heat.

Energetics   In ecology, the study of the ecosystem's energy exchanges and metabolism or efficiencies. Energetics converts the biomass of an ecosystem into energy units.

Energy   The capacity to do work. Various types of energy include heat, light, sound, potential, chemical, kinetic, and electrical. All these energies flow in and out of buildings.

Energy cost   Monetary cost to produce a unit of energy, such as a kilowatt hour.

Energy crops   Crops grown specifically for their fuel value. These include food crops such as corn and sugar cane, and nonfood crops such as poplar trees and switchgrass. Currently two energy crops are under development: short-rotation woody crops, which are fast-growing hardwood trees harvested in 5 to 8 years; and herbaceous energy crops, such as perennial grasses, which are harvested annually after taking 2–3 years to reach full productivity. Barley, rapeseed, sugar beet, sorghum, and wheat are also energy crops.

Energy intensity   Ratio of energy consumption to a measure of the demand for services, such as total floor space, number of buildings, or number of employees.

Energy management and control system (EMCS)   A computer system with sensors, actuators, and programming to conserve energy in buildings. Energy management programs range from starting and stopping equipment, to performing energy optimization on complicated groups of lighting, heating, and cooling equipment. Various communication protocols exist, including open protocols and proprietary protocols, which enable the computer system to acquire data and control remote equipment. These devices are used in ecodesign to conserve the use of nonrenewable energy in buildings, and are part of the full mode system in ecodesign. *See also:* **Full mode design**

Energy Plus   Energy simulation model created by the US Department of Energy. It is a successor to DOE-2. Energy Plus models heating, cooling, lighting, ventilating, and other energy flows, as well as water, in buildings. While originally based on the most popular features and capabilities of BLAST and DOE-2, Energy Plus includes some new simulation capabilities, such as time steps of less than an hour, modular systems and plant integrated with heat balance-based zone simulation, multizone air flow, thermal comfort, water use, natural ventilation, and photovoltaic systems. *See also: BLAST; DOE-2*

Energy Policy Act of 1992 (EPAct) A comprehensive US Congress package that mandated and encouraged energy efficiency standards, alternative fuel use, and the development of renewable energy technologies. Public Law 102-486, October 24, 1992. Also authorized the Federal Energy Regulatory Commission to order the owners of electric power transmission lines to transmit or "wheel" power for power generators, including electric power providers, federal power marketing authorities, and exempt wholesale generators.

Energy recovery ventilator (ERV) Mechanical equipment that features a heat exchanger combined with a ventilation system to provide controlled ventilation into a building. An ERV with humidity regulation incorporates a method to remove excess humidity or add humidity to the ventilating air that is being brought into a built structure. Equipment was first introduced as air-to-air heat exchangers in the colder regions of the USA, Canada, Europe, and Scandinavia in the 1980s. In these areas, tightly built modern houses were developing problems with internal air quality and excessive humidity during the winter. The air-to-air heat exchanger brought in fresh outside air to combat these problems, and preheated it at the same time. These products are now called heat recovery ventilators. *See also: Heat recovery ventilator*

Energy Star US government program to promote energy efficient consumer products.

Engine Machine that transforms energy into mechanical energy.

Engineered controls Method of managing environmental and health risks by placing a barrier between contamination and the rest of a site, thereby limiting exposure pathways.

Engineered sheet materials Sheet materials made of recycled content or reconstituted materials. Recycled content sheet products are made from recycled newsprint, agricultural by-products, or waste wood. Reconstituted materials use chipped or stranded small-diameter trees as their wood source. This material is then bound together into forms suitable for building. Some of these products contain recycled post-consumer paper, by-product gypsum and recovered gypsum, wood chips from "non-commercial" trees, and annually renewable agricultural fibers. Materials include: hardboard made from waste wood; wallboard made from perlite, gypsum, and recycled post-consumer newsprint; 100% recycled newsprint fiberboard; and fiberboard made from straw. Oriented-strand board (OSB) is a reconstituted material that is now commonly used. *See also: Oriented-strand board*

Engineered siding and trim Recycled-content materials (engineered) include substances salvaged from the waste stream, such as sawdust, paper, steel, and aluminum. Recycled trim refers to the reuse of trim salvaged from building demolition. Reconstituted and recycled-content siding materials resist cracking and other deterioration and have greater longevity over wood siding. Fiber-cement materials, for example, offer very long warranties and have zero flame-spread. Steel and aluminum siding materials are predominantly fabricated from recycled material. Although the embodied energy is high when the materials are originally made, they require much less energy in a recycled form. They can also be recycled again after use in a building. Regarded as closing the loop in built systems in ecodesign.

Engineered structural materials *See: Wood, structurally engineered*

Enhanced greenhouse effect Natural greenhouse effect is increased by anthropogenic emissions of greenhouse gases. Human activities such as fossil fuel consumption increase concentrations of carbon dioxide (CO_2), methane (CH_4), nitrogen oxides (NO_x), chlorofluorocarbons (CFCs), hydrochlorofluorocarbons (HCFCs), and other photochemically important gases, trap more infra-red radiation, and create warmer climates.

ENSO *See: El Niño—Southern Oscillation*

Enthalpy Mathematical quantity used in thermodynamic calculations; equal to the internal energy of a substance plus the pressure multiplied by the volume ($h = u + pv$).

Entrained bed gasifier Type of gasifier that converts biomass into clean fuel and is regarded as a renewable source of energy in ecodesign. In an entrained bed gasifier the feedstock (biomass, waste products) is suspended by the movement of gas so that it moves through the gasifier. Among the different types of gasifier, entrained bed reactors are reported to achieve the highest gasification rates. These reactors operate with feed and blast (air/steam) in co-current flow with extremely short residence time and high temperature and pressure. This type of gasifier generates product gas at high temperature and lowest heating value with the highest oxygen consumption. *See also: Gasifier*

Entropy Measure of the disorder of a system.

Environment Total physical and biological environment in which an organism lives. For human beings, environment includes the social structure.

Environmental assessment methods and standards for buildings *See: Green building rating systems*

Environmental contamination Term for release into the environment of radioactive, hazardous, and toxic materials.

Environmental cost Monetary costs of the impacts of resource depletion, pollution, and disturbance of habitats, and their rehabilitation.

Environmental desensitization Mechanism designed to decrease the impact of contaminants on humans, other fauna, and flora. Examples include buffer zones between degraded areas such as landfills and inhabited areas; or scented vapor applied to an odor-contaminated area. Consideration needs to be given to the ecological resilience of the ecosystem.

Environmental impact statement Assessment of an action on an environment and the environmental consequences that may result. In the USA, a federal requirement for major projects.

Environmental indicator Species with specific tolerance limits that provides information about the environment in which it grows, such as a plant that grows in areas of high acidity. The environmental conditions that allow certain species to survive successfully. Used in ecodesign to assess the environmental consequences of human interventions and built systems.

Environmental integration in design Designing within the limitations of the ecological consequences of the proposed building. Design that achieves the highest possible level of bio-integration for that particular ecosystem, even more than the predetermined standards of green building rating systems. *See also: Green building rating systems*

Environmental medium or compartment Medium through which pollutants are transported. The media include air, water, soil, and biota.

Environmental Protection Agency, US   *See: US Environmental Protection Agency*

Environmental rehabilitation restoration   Repair to sites and ecosystems damaged by anthropogenic activities or natural disasters.

Environmental risk   1. Potential for adverse effects on living organisms associated with pollution of the environment by effluents, emissions, wastes, or accidental chemical releases.
    2. Depletion of natural resources.

Environmental sustainability   Maintenance of an environment, ecosystems, and natural resources for future generations. The primary principle of ecodesign.

Environmentally preferable   Products and activities that damage the environment less than competing products and activities.

EPA, US   *See: US Environmental Protection Agency*

EPAct   *See: Energy Policy Act of 1992*

Epilimnion   Upper layer of a thermally stratified lake. This water is turbulently mixed at some point during the day and, because of its exposure to wind, can freely exchange dissolved gases such as O_2 and CO_2 with the atmosphere. Research indicates that the rise in global temperatures results in greater stratification in temperate zone lakes because increased heating by the Sun will create larger gradient differences between lake strata and less mixing of the strata. In temperate and subarctic regions, small annual temperature increases have a great effect on the timing and intensity of stratification in lakes. If the hypolimnion does not receive oxygen from the atmosphere or enough light penetration for photosynthesis, subsurface algae will not develop the nutrients they need. This will alter algal assemblages and, subsequently, the food chains in lakes.

Epiphyte   Plant, fungus or microbe sustained entirely by nutrients and water received, by means other than a parasite, from within the canopy in which it lives.

Episode, pollution   Environmental event that results in concentrations of atmospheric pollution or water pollution.

Epoxies   Nonbiodegradable plastics.

Equivalent temperature differential   Factor used to determine solar radiation gain through an opaque wall.

Ergonomics   Applied science that investigates the impact of people's physical environment on their health and comfort.

Erosion   Wearing away of land surface by wind or water, intensified by land-clearing practices related to farming, residential, or industrial development, road building, or logging.

ERV   *See: Energy recovery ventilator*

Estuary   Location where fresh and salt water mix, such as a bay, salt marsh, or where a river enters an ocean.

ETBE   *See: Ethyl tertiary butyl ether*

Ethane (C_2H_6)   Flammable gas; explosive when mixed with air. Structurally, the simplest hydrocarbon that contains a single carbon–carbon bond. A by-product of oil refining, it is also the second most important constituent of natural gas, and occurs dissolved in petroleum oils.

Ethanol (C_2H_5OH)   An alternative fuel, ethanol is an alcohol-based fuel produced by fermenting and distilling starch crops that have been converted into simple sugars. Feedstocks for this fuel include corn, barley, wheat, grain sorghum, sugar beet, cheese whey, and potatoes. Ethanol can also be produced from cellulosic biomass including trees and grass—this is bioethanol. Ceullosic feedstocks include corn stalks, grain straw, rice hulls, sugar cane bagasse, switchgrass, and wood chips. Ethanol is most commonly used to increase octane and improve the emissions quality of gasoline.

Ether   Toxic chemical. 1. Light, volatile, flammable liquid used chiefly as a solvent, and formerly as an anesthetic. Solvents containing ether are dimethyl ether, an aerosol spray propellant; diethyl ether, a common, low-boiling solvent (boiling point 34.6 °C (92.28 °F)); dimethoxyethane, a high-boiling solvent (boiling point 85 °C (185 °F)); dioxane, a cyclic ether and high-boiling solvent (boiling point 101.1 °C (213.98 °F)); and tetrahydrofuran, a cyclic ether, one of the most popular simple ethers used as a solvent.

2. Any of a class of organic compounds characterized by an oxygen atom attached to two carbon atoms. *See also: Toxic chemicals*

Ethyl tertiary butyl ether (ETBE)   Fuel oxygenate used as a gasoline additive for increased octane and engine knock reduction.

Ethylbenzene   Toxic chemical. Ethylbenzene is a colorless liquid found in a number of natural products including coal tar and petroleum. It is also used in manufactured products such as gasoline, paint, insecticides, and ink. It is used primarily to make styrene. It is also used as a solvent in fuels and as a component of other chemicals. Breathing very high levels can cause dizziness and throat and eye irritation. It can be released into the air, soil, and water. *See also: Toxic chemicals*

Eutrophic   Pertaining to a lake or other body of water characterized by large nutrient concentrations, such as nitrates and phosphates, resulting in high productivity of algae. *See also: Mesotrophic; Oligotrophic*

Eutrophication   1. Reduction of the amount of oxygen dissolved in water. The results may include increased algal blooms, reduced water clarity, periods of hypoxia, decline in health of fish and shellfish, loss of seagrass beds and coral reefs, ecological changes in food webs, and a shift toward species that can adapt to these conditions.

2. A slow aging process during which a lake, estuary, or bay evolves into a bog or marsh and eventually disappears. During the later stages of this process, the water body is choked by plant life that result from higher levels of nutritive compounds such as nitrogen and phosphorus.

Ev   *See: Exposure value*

EV   *See: Electric vehicle*

Evacuated-tube collector   Mechanism in which fluid (such as water or diluted antifreeze) is heated by the Sun in a solar hot water system. Evacuated-tube collectors are made up of rows of parallel, transparent glass tubes. Each tube consists of a glass outer tube and an inner tube, or absorber. The absorber is covered with a selective coating that absorbs solar energy well, but inhibits radiative heat loss. The air is withdrawn (evacuated) from the space between the tubes to form a vacuum, which eliminates conductive and convective heat loss. Evacuated-tube collectors are used for active solar hot water systems.

Evaporation   The conversion of a liquid to a vapor (gas), usually by means of heat.

Evaporative cooling   Physical process by which a liquid or solid is transformed into the gaseous state. For this process a mechanical device uses the outside air's heat to evaporate water that is held by pads inside the cooler. The heat is drawn out of the air through this process and the cooled air is blown into the home by the cooler's fan. *See also: Solar cooling*

Evapotranspiration   Combines the process of evaporation and transpiration to utilize and dispose of wastewater. Transpiration is the process whereby plants take in water through their roots and convert it to vapor, which is given off through the leaves. A typical evapotranspiration system consists of a septic tank for pretreatment (removal of solids) followed by distribution into a shallow sand bed covered with vegetation. In ecodesign, gray water (wastewater from baths, showers, laundry, and lavatory sinks) flows from the house through the septic tank and into the evapotranspiration bed. The gray water is distributed through perforated pipes. Once in the sand, gray water is taken into the plant root system. Underneath the bed is either a plastic lining or a very impermeable soil, which prevents the gray water from seeping into the ground. Black water (primarily wastewater from toilets and kitchen sinks) flows into a sewer line or an alternative treatment.

Exothermic   Chemical reaction that gives off heat.

Exotic species   Term used to characterize species that are not indigenous to a region.

Exposure pathway   Path from sources of pollutants via soil, water, or food to humans and other species or settings.

Exposure value (Ev)   Measurement of the total light from the sky, plus the light reflected from the ground and surrounding objects near window openings. It is the illumination from the sky on the plane of the vertical fenestration or window wall and parallel to the wall outside the window but beyond any obstructing part of the building, such as overhangs and louvers.

Extensive green roof   Term for a rooftop garden that has thinner soil (usually 6 inches/15 cm or less in depth) and shallow-rooted plants such as turf grass or groundcover, and does not require artificial irrigation. Good for self-sustaining plant communities and roof gardens. *See also: Cool roof; Green roof; Intensive green roof*

Extruded polystyrene (XEPS)   Fabricated type of foam core used as a structural wall panel. Like all polystyrenes, it is a polymer made from the monomer styrene, a liquid hydrocarbon that is commercially manufactured from petroleum by the chemical industry. USEPA has estimated that it takes approximately 2000 years for polystyrene to decompose. *See also: Polystyrene*

F

Facultative bacteria Bacteria that grow equally well under aerobic and anaerobic conditions.

FCCC *See: United Nations Framework Convention on Climate Change*

Federal Water Pollution Control Act *See: Clean Water Act*

Feedstock *See: Biomass feedstock*

Fen *See: Wetlands*

Fenestration Openings in a structure: windows, doors, skylights. Key consideration in bioclimatic aspects of ecodesign.

Fiber optics Invented in the early 1970s, demand for optic fibers has grown very quickly. The most common uses are telecommunications, medicine, military, automotive, and industrial. The fibers used in telecommunications are long, thin strands of very pure glass about the diameter of a human hair. They are arranged in bundles called optical cables, and used to transmit light signals over long distances by confining as much light as possible in a propagating form. Short-distance communication cables can be constructed using plastic fibers. Optical fiber can be used as a medium for telecommunication and networking because it is flexible and can be bundled as cables. It is especially advantageous for long-distance communications, because light propagates through the fiber with little attenuation compared with electrical cables.

Optical fibers can be used as sensors to measure strain, temperature, pressure, and other parameters. Their small size, and the fact that no electrical power is needed at the remote location, give fiber optic sensors advantages over conventional electrical sensors in certain applications. Optical fibers are also used in hydrophones for seismic or SONAR applications. Optical fiber sensors for temperature and pressure have been developed for downhole measurement in oil wells. The fiber optic sensor is well suited for this environment because it can function at temperatures that would be too high for semiconductor sensors. Research is being carried out on the use of fiber optics as light pipes. Fiber optics can be used as lighting devices in ecodesign to bring natural daylight into deep parts and basements of buildings.

Fill factor Ratio of a photovoltaic cell's actual power to its power if both current and voltage were at their maximums. Key characteristic in evaluating cell performance.

Fingerjoint Term used for the method of gluing pieces together in the production of structurally engineered wood from recycled/reconstituted wood material.

Fire ecology Conservation management of forests and prairies by using proactive fires to reduce the accumulation of decaying organic matter and litter that would fuel uncontrolled random fires that could destroy entire forests and prairies. The controlled fires allow forest ecosystems to retain their natural balance. Many species of plants and other processes regenerate after a fire and maintain a healthy ecosystem. Fire reacts differently to environmental factors (topography, climate, vegetation type) or to the present health of the stand (insect invasion, build-up of fuel load). Controlled fires are usually conducted by professional foresters and ecologists.

Fischer–Tropsch fuel   Diesel fuel made from natural gas using a method known as the Fischer–Tropsch process. This process synthesizes hydrocarbons and other aliphatic compounds. A mixture of hydrogen and carbon monoxide is reacted with an iron or cobalt catalyst. Fischer–Tropsch fuels are liquid under ambient conditions, have a high cetane number, and have effectively no sulfur content. They can be used in existing diesel engines.

Fixed receiver moving reflector   Type of concentrating solar collector. *See also: Concentrating solar collector*

Fixed reflector moving receiver   Type of concentrating solar collector. *See also: Concentrating solar collector*

Flamespread   Wood performance under fire conditions.

Flashpoint   Lowest temperature under specific conditions at which a substance will begin to burn.

Flash steam geothermal power   One of three main geothermal power technologies: binary cycle, dry steam, and flash steam. When hot water (>360 °F; >182 °C) is pumped to a generator, it is released from the pressure of the deep geothermal reservoir. The drop in pressure results in vaporization to steam, which spins a turbine to generate electricity. Small amounts of carbon dioxide, nitric oxide, and sulfur are emitted. Hot water not flashed into steam is returned to the geothermal reservoir through injection wells (see Figure 22b). *See also: Binary cycle geothermal power; Dry steam geothermal power; Geothermal power technology*

Flat-plate solar photovoltaic module   An arrangement of photovoltaic cells or material mounted on a rigid flat surface with the cells exposed to incoming sunlight. *See also: Photovoltaic (PV)* and associated entries; *Appendix 4: Photovoltaics*

Flat-plate solar thermal/heating collector   Large, flat box with or without glass cover and dark-colored metal plates inside that absorbs and transfers solar energy to a heat transfer fluid. This is the most common type of collector used in solar hot water systems for homes or small buildings.

Flexible fuel vehicle   *See: Dual-fuel vehicle*

Flocculation   Process by which clumps of solids in water or sewage aggregate through biological or chemical action so they can be separated from water or sewage as part of the ecodesign sewage handling.

Flood plain   Any land area that is susceptible to being inundated by water from any source. It is usually a strip of relatively flat and normally dry land beside a stream, river, or lake that is covered by water during a flood. In ecodesign site planning, the designer considers the relationship of the flood plains and the natural drainage flows of the locality as part of the water management system.

Flue gas   Air emitted from a chimney after combustion in a burner. It can include nitrogen oxides, carbon oxides, water vapor, sulfur oxides, and particles and many chemical pollutants.

Flue gas desulfurization   Equipment, commonly known as scrubbers, used to remove sulfur oxides from the combustion gases of a boiler plant before discharging into the atmosphere. *See also: **Scrubbers***

Fluidized bed combustion Type of furnace or reactor in which fuel particles are combusted while suspended in a stream of hot gas.

Fluorinated gases Hydrofluorocarbons, perfluorocarbons, and sulfur hexfluoride are synthetic, powerful greenhouse gases that are emitted from a variety of industrial processes. Fluorinated gases are sometimes used as substitutes for ozone-depleting substances such as cholorofluorocarbons (CFCs), hydrochlorofluorocarbons (HCFCs), and halons. The fluorinated gases are generally emitted in smaller quantities, but because they are potent greenhouse gases, they are sometimes referred to as high global warming potential gases.

Fluorocarbons Carbon–fluorine compounds that often contain other elements such as hydrogen, chlorine, or bromine. Common fluorocarbons include cholorofluorocarbons (CFCs), hydrochlorofluorocarbons (HCFCs), hydrofluorocarbons (HFCs), and perfluorocarbons (PFCs). Fluorocarbons are classified as ozone-depleting substances. An ecodesign goal is to avoid using these substances.

Flush out Process to remove volatile organic compounds (VOCs) in a building by operating the building's heating, ventilation, and air conditioning (HVAC) system at 100% outside air for a specific period. This is usually performed during the pre-occupancy phase in order to maximize internal air quality (IAQ) in ecodesign.

Fly ash Small, solid particles of ash and soot generated when coal, oil, or waste materials are burned. Fly ash is suspended in the flue gas after combustion and is removed by pollution-control equipment. Its use as an engineering material primarily comes from its pozzolanic nature, spherical shape, and relative uniformity. Its pozzolanic characteristics allow it to react with calcium hydroxide and alkali to form cementitious compounds. Fly ash recycling includes use in Portland cement and grout; embankments and structural fill; waste stabilization and solidification; raw feed for cement clinkers; mine reclamation; stabilization of soft soils; road subbase; aggregate; flowable fill; and mineral filler in asphaltic concrete. *See also: **Pozzolana***

Fly ash cement Fly ash eliminates carbon emissions normally emitted in the production of regular Portland cement. Fly ash is pozzolanic and reacts with calcium hydroxide and alkali to form cementitious compounds. Fly ash cement allows a lower concrete water content, and early strength can be maintained. It reduces vapor transmission in concrete floors and increases resistance to sulfate attack. The use of fly ash cement is more environmentally friendly as it emits far less CO_2 than regular Portland cement, the all-purpose cement commonly used. When fly ash is used to make concrete, less Portland cement is required. Fly ash cement can be recycled as aggregate and other products. *See also: **Fly ash; Portland cement; Pozzolana***

Focusing collector Device that collects solar energy from sunlight which has been focused toward it. *See also: **Photovoltaic (PV)** and associated entries; **Appendix 4: Photovoltaics***

Food chain Feeding relationship between species in an ecological community; the path of food consumption. Species transfer material and energy from one to another within an ecosystem. Organisms are connected to the organisms they consume. It is an important consideration in the study of the ecosystem of a locality in ecodesign. The source of all food is mainly photosynthesis by plants, known as producers because only they can manufacture food from inorganic raw

Table 2 Food chain

Organisms:	Autotrophs	Herbivores	Carnivores	Decomposers
Functions:	Producers	Primary Consumers	Secondary and Tertiary consumers	Waste recycling

materials. This food feeds herbivores, called primary consumers. Carnivores that feed on herbivores are called secondary consumers. Carnivores that feed on other carnivores are tertiary (or higher) consumers. Each level of consumption in a food chain is called a trophic level.
*See also: **Food network; Food web***

Food network   Made up of interrelated trophic levels of food chains; interdependence of organisms, animals and plants for survival. *See also: **Food chain; Food web***

Food web   Interconnected food chain, in which energy and materials circulate within an ecosystem. *See also: **Food chain; Food network***

Footcandle (fc)   Quantitative measurement of the amount of direct light from one candle falling on a square foot of surface one foot away.

Foot lambert (fL)   Quantitative measurement of luminance due to reflection, transmission, or emission of one footcandle from a surface.

Forb   Any herbaceous plant that is not a grass or is not grasslike.

Forced oxidation   Chemical process in which pollutants in an exhaust or emission are forced into contact with air or pure oxygen to change them into a stable form.

Forcing mechanism   Process that changes the energy balance of the climate system. Changes the balance between incoming solar radiation and outgoing infrared radiation. Such mechanisms include changes in solar irradiance, volcanic eruptions, and the greenhouse effect.

Forest fragmentation   Division of formerly healthy vegetated or forest land and ecosystems into patches, usually as a result of conversion to agricultural or residential land. Ecodesign site-planning goals are to avoid fragmentation, rehabilitate existing fragmented ecosystems, and create new green linkages in fragmented land as new ecological corridors or eco-infrastructures.

Formaldehyde (H_2CO)   Intermediate gas in the oxidation or combustion of methane (CH_4) and other carbon compounds. It is present in the smoke from forest fires, automobile exhaust, and tobacco smoke. In the atmosphere, formaldehyde is produced by the action of sunlight and oxygen on atmospheric methane and other hydrocarbons. It thus becomes part of smog pollution. An ecodesign goal is to avoid the use of this substance. *See also: **Urea formaldehyde; Phenol formaldehyde***

Fossil fuel   Any naturally occurring organic fuel formed in the Earth's crust, including petroleum, coal, natural gas, peat, and other hydrocarbons. Fossil fuels are the remains of ancient plants and animals. They are considered nonrenewable energy resources because they cannot be replaced after their removal. The biological, chemical, and physical processes needed to produce them take eons. When combusted, fossil fuels emit carbon dioxide (CO_2), a major greenhouse gas.

Framework Convention on Climate Change (FCCC)   *See: **United Nations Framework Convention on Climate Change***

Francis turbine   A type of water-powered turbine, developed by James B. Francis, used to transform water falling vertically into mechanical (rotating) energy. It is used to power electrical generators, and is the most commonly used water turbine. It can operate in a wide range of heads, from 10 to 700 meters (32.8–2,296 feet), and can produce electrical output ranging from a few kilowatts to 1000 megawatts. Francis turbines can also be used for pumped storage, where a reservoir is filled by the turbine acting as a pump during low power demand, and reversed and used to generate power during high peak demand. Water turbines replaced the water wheel in the 19th century, and can compete with steam engines. *See also: Water turbine; Kaplan turbine; Pelton turbine*

Free-jet turbine   *See: Pelton turbine*

Freon   Family of compounds containing carbon, chlorine, and fluorine. They are used in aerosol cans, as foaming agents and solvents, and as heat-transfer gas in refrigerators and air conditioners. As part of the Montreal Protocol and other international agreements, freon production is being phased out. This substance should be avoided in ecodesign. *See also: Hydrochlorofluorocarbons (HCFCs)*

Freshwater systems   Include rivers and streams, lakes, ponds, and reservoirs; groundwater connected to rivers, streams, lakes, and wetlands; freshwater wetlands, including forested, shrub, and emergent wetlands (marshes) and open water ponds; riparian areas.

Fresnel lens   Type of concentrating solar collector. It is a flat, optical lens that focuses light like a magnifying glass, using concentric rings faced at slightly different angles so that light falling on any ring will be focused to the same point. *See also: Concentrating solar collector*

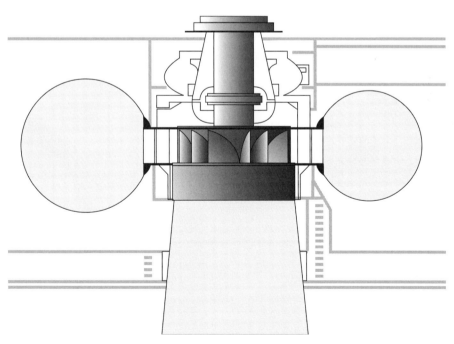

Figure 28 A Francis Turbine
Source: Voith-Siemens

Fuel Material used to create heat or power through conversion in processes such as combustion or electrochemistry.

Fuel cells Electromechanical "engines" that convert the chemical energy of hydrogen and oxygen into electricity without combustion; the only by-product is water. Fuel cells are simple devices. They have no moving parts and contain only four functional component elements: two catalytically activated electrodes for the fuel (anode) and the oxidant (cathode); an electrolyte to conduct ions between the two electrodes; and an interconnect. The fuel cell converts chemical energy directly into electricity and heat. Electrons are removed from fuel elements (catalytic reaction) in the fuel cell to create electric current. The absence of the combustion process eliminates the formation of pollutants including nitrogen oxides NO_x, sulfur oxide (SO_x), hydrocarbons, and particulates, and significantly improves electrical power-generation efficiency. Input fuels pass over the anode and oxygen passes over the cathode, where it splits catalytically into ions and electrons. The electrons go through an external circuit to serve an electric load, while the ions move through the electrolyte toward the oppositely charged electrode. At the electrode, ions combine to create by-products, mainly water and carbon dioxide (CO_2). Used for electrical generation in stationary application and provision of motor force for transportation vehicles.

There are a variety of fuel cell types: alkaline (AFC), phosphoric acid (PAFC), molten carbonate (MCFC), solid oxide (SOFC), proton exchange membrane (PEM), direct methanol (DMFC), and direct carbon.

There is ongoing research on new fuel cells using titanium-crusted carbon nanotubes, which will store hydrogen. Automobile manufacturers are interested in this new fuel cell for future use in cars (see Table 3). *See also: **Alkaline fuel cell; Direct carbon fuel cell; Direct methanol fuel cell; Molten carbonate fuel cell; Phosphoric acid fuel cell; Proton exchange membrane fuel cell; Regenerative fuel cell; Solid oxide fuel cell; Solid oxide hybrid fuel cell power system***

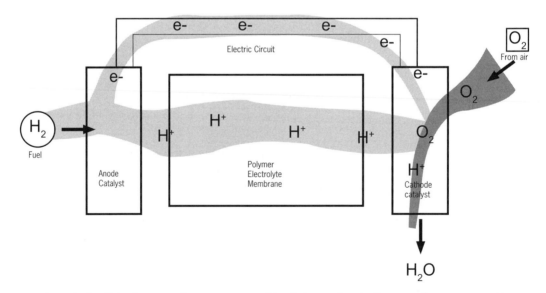

Figure 29 A fuel cell: hydrogen and oxygen are combined electrochemically to produce energy, with water and useful heat as the only by-products
Source: Fuel Cells 2000/US Department of Energy

Table 3 Characteristics of fuel cell types

Technology	Alkaline (AFC)	Polymer electrolyte (PEM)	Direct methanol (DMFC)	Phosphoric acid (PAFC)	Molten carbonate (MCFC)	Solid oxide (SOFC)
Electrolyte	Potassium hydroxide	Polymer	Polymer membrane	Phosphoric acid	Lithium or potassium carbonate	Ceramic composed of calcium or zirconium oxides
Operating temperature (°C)	50–200	50–100	50–200	160–210	800–800	500–1000
Efficiency (%) (HHV)	45–60 (up to 70 with CHP)	35–55	40–50 (up to 80 with CHP)	40–50	50–60 (up to 80 with CHP)	50–65 (up to 75 with CHP)
Power density (kW/m²)	0.7–8.1	3.8–13.5	1–6	0.8–1.9	0.1–1.5	1.5–5.0
Fuel source						
Fuels	H_2	H_2, reformate	Methanol, ethanol, gasoline	H_2, reformate	H_2, CO, reformate	H_2, CO_2, CH_4
Reforming	External	External	Not required	External	External or internal	External or internal
Technology development						
Stage	Mature technology	Prototype	Prototype	Commercially available	Full-scale demonstration	Prototype
Materials	Platinum catalyst	Platinum catalyst	Platinum catalyst	Platinum catalyst	Nickel catalyst	Ceramic
Issues	Requires very little H_2	Small amounts of CO will poison catalyst		Sulfur must be removed if fuel is gasoline	High temperature means more resistance to CO poisoning	
Uses	Space vehicles	Automobiles, buses	Small CHP, transportation, portable	Medium CHP, buses	Large CHP	All sizes of CHP

Fuel economy, automobile The amount of fuel needed to move an automobile over a specific distance. The two most common ways to measure automobile fuel economy are: i) miles per gallon or km per litre; and ii) amount of fuel per unit of distance, such as litres per 100 km (62 miles). *See also: Corporate Average Fuel Economy (CAFE)*

Fuel economy regulations, automobile

Regulations established by state, national, or international jurisdictions that require vehicle manufacturers to comply with the gas mileage or fuel economy standards set by that government or country. Along with fuel economy regulations, many countries have also imposed regulations and targets to decrease the emissions of carbon dioxide (CO_2). The following are examples of the fuel economy and greenhouse gas emissions regulations in the world's major auto markets.

In the European Union, the ACEA agreement goal of 25% reduction in vehicle CO_2 emission levels by 2008, from 1995 levels. Agreement may be extended an additional 10% by 2012. In February 2007 the European Commission published its key proposal (COM 2007 0019) of EC legislation to limit average CO_2 emissions to 120 g CO_2/km by 2012. Some volume manufacturers of smaller cars are already quite close to the target, while smaller-volume manufacturers of higher-emissions cars are a long way from reaching it.

Japan requires 23% reduction in vehicle CO_2 emissions by 2010, from 1995 levels, and an increased average of 23.5% by fiscal year 2015 from 32 to 40 mpg for passenger cars.

Australia has instituted a voluntary commitment to improve fuel economy by 18% by 2010.

Canada has proposed a 25% improvement of fuel economy by 2010.

China introduced new fuel economy standards in 2004, and activated weight-based standards in 2005 and 2008.

The USA has three different sets of fuel economy values: i) the National Highway Traffic Safety Administration (NHTSA)'s Corporate Average Fuel Economy (CAFE) values; ii) USEPA's unadjusted dynamometer values; and iii) USEPA's adjusted on-road values. CAFE values are used to determine manufacturers' compliance with the applicable average fuel economy standard. USEPA's unadjusted dynamometer values are calculated from the emissions generated during testing using a carbon balance equation. USEPA knows the amount of carbon in the fuel, so by measuring the carbon compounds expelled in the exhaust, the fuel economy can be calculated.

See also: **ACEA agreement; Corporate Average Fuel Economy (CAFE)**

Fuel, nuclear   Natural and enriched uranium or other radionuclide that sustains the fission chain reaction in a nuclear reactor. Also refers to the entire fuel element, including structural materials and cladding. Also known as reactor fuel. Nuclear power does not produce greenhouse gas emissions (CO_2, NO_2) directly, but the nuclear fuel cycle produces them indirectly, although at much lower rates than fossil fuels. Nuclear generation does not directly produce sulfur dioxide, nitrogen oxides, mercury or other pollutants associated with the combustion of fossil fuels.

Fugitive emissions   Substances that enter the atmosphere without physical restraints. Examples are dust from soil erosion, strip mining, rock crushing, and building demolition. These particulates enter the atmosphere freely, become airborne, and can remain airborne or settle into bodies of water, seeping into the groundwater if they settle on land. Usually refers to an emission that escapes from a containment system.

Full mode design   Full mode is the conventional full environmental heating, ventilation, and air-conditioning system (HVAC) in buildings, in which mechanical and electrical systems are used for a regular building. Full mode provisions for heating, cooling, lighting, and ventilation are controlled artificially through energy-intensive mechanical systems in addition to the internal environment. Full mode buildings consume more than half the energy used worldwide. Full mode systems should be coordinated with the other mode systems in order to improve energy efficiency.

Ecodesign strategy seeks to reduce or eliminate dependency on nonrenewable fuels in full mode systems through increased efficiency of systems and equipment, the use of building automation systems and combined heating and power systems, and a combined strategy with other modes—passive, mixed, and composite—that specifies improved energy design in relation to the climate of the locality. *See also:* **Mixed-mode design; Passive mode design; Productive mode design**

Functional diversity   One of the three main types of diversity in an ecosystem. Functional diversity is the ecological interactions between species, and includes predation and mutualism as well as ecological functions such as nutrient cycling and episodic natural disturbances. *See also: Species diversity; Structural diversity*

Fungi   Lower plants that lack chlorophyll, and need organic material and moisture to grow. Examples include molds and mildews.

Furans   Toxic chemical. The term "furans" is sometimes used as shorthand for a group of environmental contaminants called the dibenzofurans, a family of toxic chlorinated organic compounds made up of two benzene rings connected by two bridges, one a carbon–carbon link and the other a carbon–oxygen–carbon link. Emitted into the air from hazardous waste incinerators. An ecodesign goal is to avoid this substance. *See also: Toxic chemicals*

Fusion energy   *See: Joint European Torus*

G

Gallium arsenide (GaAs) Crystalline form of gallium and arsenic, which yields high-efficiency solar cells.

Galvanic cell *See: Electrochemical cell*

Gamma radiation Form of radiant energy consisting of high-energy particles of light. *See also: Ionizing radiation*

Gas 1. Fuel gas, such as natural gas, undiluted liquefied petroleum gases (vapor phase only), liquefied petroleum gas–air mixtures, or mixtures of these gases. Combustion of these gases produces CO_2 and H_2O. CO_2 is a major contributor to greenhouse gas.
   2. Biofuel gas is made from biomass feedstock, renewable organic matter. Examples of biofuels are ethanol and methanol. Ethanol is a cleaner-burning fuel than petroleum-based ones, but it still produces greenhouse gas emissions. *See also: Ethanol; Methanol*

Gas control and recovery system Series of vertical wells or horizontal trenches containing permeable materials and perforated piping. The system is designed to collect landfill gases for treatment or for use as an energy source.

Gas sorption Process used to reduce levels of airborne compounds by passing the air containing these compounds through materials that extract the gases.

Gasification Also known as pyrolitic distillation or pyrolisis. It is a commonly used technology for turning biomass and solid waste materials into energy rich fuels by heating these materials under controlled conditions. While incineration converts the waste into energy and ash, gasification limits the conversion so that combustion does not take place directly. Rather, the wastes are converted into a gas. The gasification process takes place as the char reacts with carbon dioxide and steam to produce carbon monoxide and hydrogen ($C + H_2O$ yields $H_2 + CO$), which are utilized in gas turbines of integrated gasification combined cycle systems for power production. By controlling the amount of oxygen present in the gasification process, hydrocarbons can be broken down into syngas. *See also: Biomass gasification; Pyrolysis; Synthesis gas*

Gasifier Device for converting solid fuel to a gaseous fuel. Four types of gasifier are currently available for commercial use: counter-current fixed bed; co-current fixed bed; fluidized bed; and entrained flow.

Gasohol Also known as E10 or unleaded plus. Gasoline that contains 10% ethanol by volume.

Gasoline gallon equivalent (GGE) A GGE is the amount of alternative fuel that contains the same amount of energy as a gallon of gasoline. A GGE equals about 5.7 lb (2.6 kg) of compressed natural gas. *See also: Compressed natural gas*

GBI   *See: Green Building Initiative*

General system theory approach   Term for ecological design which considers the outcome of design as a system, either a designed system or a built system, that exists in a human-made and natural environment.

Generator   Also known as an electrical generator. Changes mechanical kinetic energy into electrical energy. Sources of mechanical energy include wind passing through a turbine, internal combustion engines, turbine steam engines, falling water that passes through either a waterwheel or turbine, or any other source of mechanical energy, including a hand crank. The reverse conversion of electrical energy into mechanical energy is done by a motor. Motors and generators have many similarities.

Genetic assimilation   A situation or environment in which a characteristic that is normally expressed only in certain environmental situations becomes fixed in a population/species so that it no longer requires specific environmental factors to be expressed. This can happen when there are changes to an ecosystem's balance. A species may adapt to those changes, or that species may crossbreed with similar species.

The classic example of genetic assimilation was a 1953 experiment by C.H. Waddington, in which *Drosophila* embryos were exposed to ether, producing a bithorax-like phenotype (a homeotic change). Flies that developed halteres with wing-like characteristics were chosen for breeding for 20 generations, by which point the phenotype could be seen without ether treatment.

The result of genetic assimilation is the extinction of the original species and decreased biodiversity. Both natural and anthropogenic factors may bring about changes in a biome.

Geo-exchange system   *See: Ground-source heat pump*

Geological sequestration   Also known as carbon capture and storage. Capture and storage of carbon dioxide (CO_2) in deep underground geological formations. It is designed to mitigate global warming by capturing CO_2 from large point sources such as fossil fuel power plants and storing it instead of releasing it into the atmosphere. Although CO_2 has been injected into geological formations for various purposes, the long-term storage of CO_2 is a relatively untried concept and, as of 2007, no large-scale power plant operates with a full carbon capture and storage system.

Geomorphologic factors   Planning and design considerations to protect the ecosystem and to restore disturbed or degraded ecosystems.

Geopressurized brines   These brines are hot (300–400 °F) (149–204 °C), pressurized waters that contain dissolved methane and lie at depths of 10,000 ft (3048 m) to more than 20,000 ft (6096 m) below the Earth's surface. The best known geopressured reservoirs lie along the Texas and Louisiana Gulf Coast. At least three types of energy could be obtained: thermal energy from high-temperature fluids; hydraulic energy from the high pressure; and chemical energy from burning the dissolved methane gas.

Geosphere   Soils, sediments, and rock layers of the Earth's crust, both continental and beneath the ocean floors.

Geothermal energy   Energy produced by the internal heat of the Earth. Geothermal heat sources include: hydrothermal convective systems; pressurized water reservoirs; hot dry rocks; manual gradients; and magma. Geothermal energy can be used directly for heating or to produce electric power. It is an alternative energy source. Geothermal energy is brought to near surface by thermal conduction and by intrusion into the Earth's crust of molten magma. It is clean and sustainable.

Geothermal heat pump   *See: Ground-source heat pump*

Geothermal power technology Geothermal power is produced by using one of three technologies: dry steam, flash steam, and binary cycle systems. Dry steam uses very hot steam (>455 °F; >235 °C) and little water from the geothermal reservoir. Flash steam, using hot water (>360 °F; >182 °C) from the geothermal reservoir, releases the pressure of the pumped water, causing it to vaporize to steam. Binary cycle power uses moderate-temperature water (225 °F; >107 °C). Hot geothermal fluids are passed through one side of a heat exchanger to heat a working fluid in a separate adjacent pipe. The working fluid, usually an organic compound with a low boiling point, is vaporized and passed through a turbine to generate electricity. *See also: **Binary cycle geothermal power; Dry steam geothermal power; Flash steam geothermal power***

GGE   *See: Gasoline gallon equivalent*

Gigawatt (GW)   Unit of power equal to 1 billion watts; 1 million kilowatts, or 1000 megawatts.

Glassphalt Asphalt containing glass cullet as an aggregate. Since the 1960s widely tried as a means to dispose of surplus waste glass. Glassphalt is basically the same as conventional hot-mix asphalt, except that 5–40% of the rock and/or sand aggregate is replaced by crushed glass. The cost-effectiveness of substituting glass for conventional aggregate is highly dependent on the location, quality, and cost of local aggregates, plus any credits available for using recycled materials in beneficial reuse applications. Glassphalt was originally developed as an alternative to landfill disposal of mixed-color waste glass. Mixed-color glass, which is unsuitable for recycling into new containers, is generated by most recycling programs.

Glazed thermal walls Glazing the outer side of an external wall traps solar radiation transmitted through the glazing by suppressing part of the convective and radiative heat losses from the face of the wall.

Glazing Transparent or translucent material (glass or plastic) used to admit light and/or to reduce heat loss; used for building windows, skylights, or greenhouses, or for covering the aperture of a solar collector.

Global warming An average increase in the temperature of the atmosphere near the Earth's surface and in the troposphere, which can contribute to changes in global climate patterns. Global warming can be both natural and human-induced. In common usage, often refers to the warming that can and does occur as a result of increased emissions of greenhouse gases from human activities. Heat flowing away from the troposphere and toward space is absorbed by water vapor, carbon dioxide, ozone, and other gases, and is trapped in the lower atmosphere, adding to the warmth of the Earth's atmosphere. *See also: **Greenhouse effect***

Global warming potential (GWP) Index used to compare the relative radiative forcing of different gases without directly calculating the changes in atmospheric concentrations. GWP is the ratio of radiative force that would result from emission of 1 kg (2.2 lbs) of greenhouse gas to that from the emission of 1 kg of carbon dioxide over a fixed period, such as 100 years.

Graetzel cell New generation of solar cell, which is dye-sensitized. It was developed by Swiss scientists Michael Graetzel and Brian O'Regan. This cell uses dye-adsorbed highly porous nanocrystalline titanium oxide (nc-TiO_2) to produce electrical energy. Based on a semiconductor formed between a photosensitized anode and an electrolyte, the Graetzel cell is made of low-cost materials and can be manufactured inexpensively. The European Union's Photovoltaic Roadmap indicates that the Graetzel cell will be a significant contributor to renewable electrical generation by 2010.

Grassed waterway   Creation of a land area planted or naturally covered with vegetation to allow runoff or effluent to a receiving stream without causing erosion.

Grassland   Biomes dominated by grasses and similar herbaceous plants. Modifications in the diversity of soil biota in grassland ecosystems due to climate change, and the functional impact of these modifications on plant nutrient availability, can change the genetic, morphological, and functional diversity of grasslands and associated species.

Green architecture   *See: Ecodesign*

Green belt   1. Land areas that have been restored after extensive damage caused by deforestation, industrialization, urbanization, or poor agricultural practices. Agricultural practices of overgrazing and extensive use of synthetic fertilizer have disrupted biogeochemical cycles. Poor agricultural practices have also created problems with soil depletion and erosion.

2. Area set aside to preserve natural habitat, vegetation and open space; can also be established as a buffer zone between built-up urban areas and natural ecosystems, and to prevent urban sprawl, as in the United Kingdom.

Green Building Council, US (USGBC)   US nonprofit trade organization that promotes sustainability in how buildings are designed, built, and operated. Best known for the development of the Leadership in Energy and Environmental Design (LEED) rating system and Greenbuild, a green building conference that promotes the green building industry, including environmentally responsible materials, sustainable architecture techniques, and public policy. There are also Green Building Councils in other countries. *See also: Leadership in Energy and Environmental Design*

Green Building Initiative (GBI)   American nonprofit organization that promotes the adoption of building practices that result in energy-efficient, healthy, and environmentally sustainable buildings through the use of practical green building approaches for residential and commercial construction. The GBI uses the Canadian Green Globes green rating system. *See also: Green Globes*

Green building rating systems   Also known as environmental assessment methods and standards for buildings. Standards used to promote sustainability through the use of green building materials, decreased energy use, decreased waste, better land use, and ecologically sustainable practices. The rating systems measure the environmental performance of buildings. Many countries have developed their own standards of energy efficiency for buildings. It is not possible to list all countries and their standards here; some examples of building environmental assessment tools currently in use are listed below.

- Australia: National Australian Built Environment Rating Systems (NABERS); Green Star
- Brazil: AQUA; Leadership in Energy and Environmental Design (LEED) Brasil
- Canada: LEED Canada; Green Globes
- China: Green Building Assessment System (GBAS); Green Olympic Building Assessment System (GOBAS)
- Finland: PromisE
- France: High Environmental Quality (HQE)
- Germany: German Sustainable Building Council
- Hong Kong: Hong Kong Building Environmental Assessment Method (HKBEAM)

- India: LEED India; Terri GRIHA (Green Rating for Integrated Habitat Assessment)
- Italy: Protocollo Itaca
- Japan: Comprehensive Assessment System for Building Environmental Efficiency (CASBEE)
- Mexico: LEED Mexico
- Netherlands: Building Research Establishment Environmental Assessment Method (BREEAM) Netherlands
- New Zealand: Green Star NZ
- Portugal: Lider A
- Singapore: Building Construction Authority Green Mark Scheme
- South Africa: Green Star SA
- Spain: VERDE
- United Arab Emirates: Emirates Green Building Council
- United Kingdom: BREEAM
- USA: LEED; Living Building Challenge; Green Globes

*See also: **Building Research Establishment Environmental Assessment Method (BREEAM); Green Globes; Leadership in Energy and Environmental Design (LEED)***

Green certificates   Also known as green tags, renewable energy certificates, or tradable renewable certificates. Represent the environmental value of power produced from renewable resources. Generally, one certificate represents generation of 1 megawatt hour of electricity. It is a tradable commodity, certifying that certain electricity is generated using renewable energy sources (including biomass, geothermal, solar, wave, and wind). The certificates can be traded separately from the energy produced. Several countries use green certificates as a way to bring green electricity generation closer to the market economy. National trading in green certificates are currently being used in Poland, Sweden, the UK, Italy, Belgium, and some US states. By separating the environmental value from the power value, clean power generators are able to sell the electricity they produce to power providers at a competitive market value. The additional revenue generated by the sale of green certificates covers the above-market costs associated with producing power made from renewable energy sources.

Green design   *See: Ecodesign*

Green façade   External wall that results in energy savings by permitting permeability to light, heat, and air to be controllable and capable of modification so the building can react to changing local climatic conditions. Variables include solar screening, glare protection, temporary thermal protection, and adjustable natural ventilation options. It must be multifunctional.

Green Globes   The Canadian environmental assessment and rating system, researched and developed by a wide range of international organizations and experts. The genesis of the system was the Building Research Establishment Environmental Assessment Method (BREEAM), which was brought to Canada in 1996 in cooperation with the company ECD Energy and Environment. Since that time, Canada has continued to refine and expand its assessment methods and standards. Green Globes is also used in the USA, where it is managed through the Green Building Initiative. *See also: **Building Research Establishment Environmental Assessment Method (BREEAM); Green Building Initiative; Green building rating systems***

Green manure   Cut or still growing green vegetation that is plowed into the soil to increase organic matter and humus available to support crop growth.

Green power   A popular term for energy produced from clean, renewable energy resources.

Green pricing   A practice used by some regulated utilities, in which electricity produced from clean, renewable resources is sold at a higher cost than that produced from fossil fuel or nuclear power plants. It is based on the premise that some buyers are willing to pay a premium for clean power.

Green Revolution Refers primarily to genetic improvement of crop varieties and the major production increases in cereal grain that resulted in many developing countries from the late 1960s. The term was first used in 1968 by former USAID director William Gaud, who noted the spread of the new technologies and said, "These and other developments in the field of agriculture contain the makings of a new revolution." Beginning in the mid-1940s, research in crop genetics, funded by the Rockefeller Foundation, Ford Foundation, and other agencies, resulted in a worldwide change in agriculture and a sizeable increase in agricultural production. Plant geneticist Norman Borlaug was instrumental in helping to develop disease-resistant wheat varieties, which improved yields in Mexico and helped avert famine in India and Pakistan. Dr Borlaug was awarded the 1970 Nobel Peace Prize for his efforts. Significant improvements were also made in corn and rice production. By 1992 the research network included 18 centers, mostly in developing countries, staffed by scientists from around the world, supported by a consortium of foundations, national governments, and international agencies.

Recent research responds to criticism that the Green Revolution depends on fertilizers, irrigation, and other factors that poor farmers cannot afford and that may be ecologically harmful; and that it promotes monoculture and loss of genetic diversity. While production yields have improved substantially in less-developed countries to meet the needs of growing populations, there have been adverse effects on the environment. Organizations such as the International Food Policy Research Institute have monitored the progress of increased crop yields. It notes

that yields are not increasing as they have in the past, and there is still not enough food for an ever-growing world population. Intensive farming has caused soil degradation and erosion; and has increased the use of pesticides such as DDT and dieldrin, which do not break down in the environment, instead accumulating in the food chain and spreading throughout ecosystems. Pesticides are toxic when inhaled by farm workers and contaminate water through runoff. In addition, the creation of a monoculture of crops decreases the biodiversity of ecosystems; water depletion becomes a problem; and monocrops may be susceptible to new pathogens that have the potential to wipe out genetic traits that were indigenous to those crops.

Green roof Also known as a rooftop garden. An alternative to traditional roofing materials, green roofs reduce rooftop and building temperatures, filter pollution, decrease pressure on sewer systems, and reduce the heat island effect. The aim is to achieve a self-sustaining plant community. Installation of an extensive green roof consists of a waterproof, root-safe membrane covered by a drainage system, a lightweight growing medium, a soil layer of 6 inches (15 cm) or less, and plants that require no irrigation system (such as turf, grass, and other ground cover).

Green roofs may be either intensive or extensive (see Figure 30). *See also:* **Extensive green roof; Intensive green roof**

Green tags *See:* **Green certificates**

Green wall system *See:* **Breathing wall**

Greenfield site Site that has not previously been used as a site for a built structure. *See also:* **Brownfield site**

Greenhouse effect The trapping and build-up of heat in the troposphere, the lower part of the

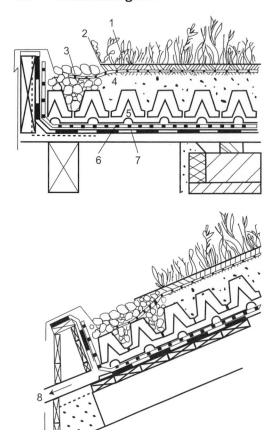

1. Vegetable
2. Layer of organic material
3. Anti-erosion sheet in open mesh
   jute, for roof slopes above 15 or
   very windy sites
4. Zincolit substrate
5. Profiled drainage element
6. Moisture tetention/protection mat
7. Root-resistant waterproofing
8. Water outlet

Figure 30 Example of roof-edge greening details

atmosphere. Some of the heat flowing away from the Earth and back toward space is absorbed by water vapor, carbon dioxide (CO_2), ozone, and several other gases in the atmosphere. The downward-directed heat emitted by these gases is known as the greenhouse effect. The absorbed

heat is re-radiated back toward the Earth's surface and trapped. Re-radiation of some of this energy keeps surface temperatures higher than would occur if the gases were absent. If the atmospheric concentrations of these greenhouse gases rise, the average temperature of the lower atmosphere will gradually increase. Atmospheric concentrations of greenhouse gases are affected by the total amount of greenhouse gases emitted to, and removed from, the atmosphere around the world over time. Figure 31 shows a breakdown of global greenhouse gas emissions by each gas.

Figure 32 shows data on the major global sources of CO_2 emissions by country, from the beginning of the Industrial Revolution to 2002.

The World Resources Institute's Climate Analysis Indicators Tool (CAIT) provides existing greenhouse gas data on global emissions by year, country, source, and greenhouse gas. In addition, the Intergovernmental Panel on Climate Change synthesizes existing scientific data on global fluxes of greenhouse gas emissions and removals in its assessment reports. These reports provide global data by gas and by type of emission pathway, such as general type of source or sink, and include both human and natural emissions.

Figure 33 shows a projection of future greenhouse gas emissions of developed and developing countries. Total emissions from the developing world are expected to exceed those from the developed world by 2015.

See also: **Global warming; Greenhouse gases**

Greenhouse gases   Gases that trap heat in the lower atmosphere (troposphere). Some greenhouse gases, such as carbon dioxide (CO_2) and water vapor, occur naturally and are emitted to the atmosphere through natural processes and human activities. The principal greenhouse gases that enter the atmosphere solely through human activities are CO_2, methane (CH_4), nitrous oxide (N_2O), and fluorinated gases. Other human

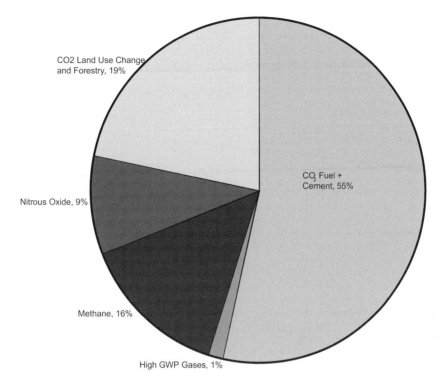

Figure 31 Global greenhouse gas emissions 2000
Source: US Environmental Protection Agency

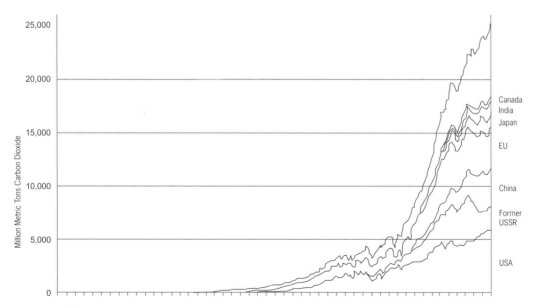

Figure 32 Global CO₂ emissions 1751–2002
Source: Carbon Dioxide Information Analysis Center

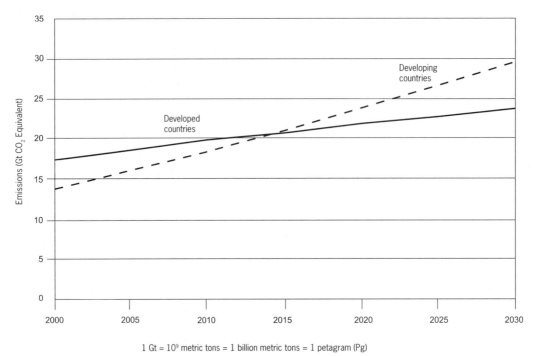

1 Gt = 10^9 metric tons = 1 billion metric tons = 1 petagram (Pg)

Figure 33 USEPA's global anthropogenic emissions of non CO_2
Source: SGM Energy Modeling Forum EMF-21 Projections, *Energy Journal* Special

activities that add to greenhouse gas levels include use of fossil fuels, deforestation, livestock and paddy rice farming, changes in land use and wetlands, landfill emissions, pipeline losses, use of chlorofluorocarbons (CFCs) in refrigeration, fire suppression and manufacturing, and use of fertilizers. Gases such as water vapor, CO_2, CH_4, N_2O, ozone, hydrofluorocarbons, perfluorocarbons, and sulfur hexafluoride are transparent to solar, short-wave radiation but opaque to long-wave infrared radiation, thus preventing long-wave radiant energy from leaving the Earth's atmosphere. The net effect is trapping of absorbed radiation and a tendency to warm the planet's surface.

Greenhouse gas score   Reflects the vehicle exhaust emissions of carbon dioxide. The score is from 0 to 10, where 10 is best. The score is determined by analyzing the vehicle's estimated

fuel economy and its fuel type. The lower the fuel economy, the more carbon dioxide (CO_2) is emitted as a by-product of combustion. The amount of CO_2 emitted per liter or gallon burned varies by fuel type, as each type of fuel contains a different amount of carbon per gallon or liter.

Gray water   Wastewater produced from baths and showers, clothes washers, lavatories, and dishwashing. The primary method of gray water irrigation is through subsurface distribution. The use of gray water for irrigation requires separate black water and gray water waste lines in the house (see Figure 34). *See also: **Black water***

Grid-connected system   Solar electric or photovoltaic (PV) system in which the PV array becomes a distributed generating plant, supplying power to the grid. A grid-connected system

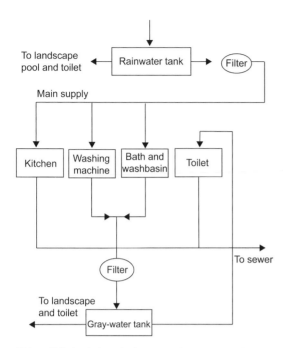

To landscape
pool and toilet ← Rainwater tank → Filter

Main supply

Kitchen | Washing machine | Bath and washbasin | Toilet

To sewer

Filter

To landscape
and toilet ← Gray-water tank

Figure 34 An integrated gray water reuse system

provides power for a home or small business with renewable energy during those periods—diurnal as well as seasonal—when the Sun is shining, the water is running, or the wind is blowing. Any excess electricity produced is fed back into the grid. When renewable resources are unavailable, electricity from the grid can supply the consumer's needs.

Ground cover   Material over the surface of soil to prevent erosion and leaching of the soil. Material may be organic humus, plants, or synthetic biodegradable sheets.

Ground-level ozone   Ozone (O_3) occurs in two layers of the atmosphere. The layer closest to the Earth's surface is the troposphere. Here, ground-level or "bad" ozone is an air pollutant that is harmful to breathe, and damages crops, trees, and other vegetation. It is a main ingredient of urban smog. The troposphere generally extends to a level about 6 miles (9.7 km) up,

where it meets the second layer, the stratosphere. The stratosphere or "good" ozone layer extends upward from about 6 to 30 miles (9.7–48 km) and protects life on Earth from the Sun's harmful ultraviolet rays. *See also:* **Ozone**

Ground loop   In geothermal (ground-source) heat pump systems, a series of fluid-filled plastic pipes buried in the shallow ground, or placed in a body of water, near a building. The fluid within the pipes is used to transfer heat between the building and the shallow ground (or water) in order to heat and cool the building. *See also:* **Ground-source heat pump**

Ground reflection   Solar radiation reflected from the ground onto a solar collector.

Ground-source heat   Using the natural heat of the ground as the energy source for heat pumps.

Ground-source heat pump (GSHP)   Also called a geothermal heat pump or geo-exchange system. A heat pump in which the refrigerant exchanges heat (in a heat exchanger) with a fluid circulating through an earth connection medium (ground or groundwater). The fluid is contained in a variety of loop (pipe) configurations depending on the temperature of the ground, and the available ground area. Loops may be installed horizontally or vertically in the ground or submersed in a body of water. Higher efficiencies are achieved with geothermal (ground-source or water-source) heat pumps, which transfer heat between the house and the ground or a nearby water source. Although they cost more to install, geothermal heat pumps have low operating costs because they take advantage of relatively constant ground or water temperatures. However, the installation depends on the size of the building lot, the subsoil, and landscape. Ground-source or water-source heat pumps can be used in more extreme climatic conditions than air-source heat pumps, and customer satisfaction with the systems is very high. For example, based on results to date, the US Department of Energy estimates savings of as much as 20–40% of the energy consumption at each site that is retrofitted. *See also: **Air-source heat pump***

Groundwater   Subsurface water that occurs beneath the water table in soils and geological formations that are fully saturated.

GSHP   *See: Ground-source heat pump*

GWP   *See: Global warming potential*

H

Habitat Biotic environment for an organism or community of organisms. The environment includes food, water, space, and shelter. The environment must remain relatively stable for the existing biodiversity of organisms and species to be maintained. Changes in habitat environment may cause disruptions to the ecobalance.

Habitat conservation plans Agreements in which a federal or state governmental conservation agency allows private property owners to harvest resources or develop land as long as the natural habitat is conserved or replaced to benefit endangered or threatened species. Most agreements have an allowance for incidental loss of endangered species.

Habitat patch Areas (habitats) with high local variability in shape and pattern, which can accommodate many species of organism. If the patches decrease in size or are separated by distance, species abundance and composition also decrease.

Halocarbons Compounds containing chlorine, bromine, or fluorine and carbon. These compounds can act as powerful greenhouse gases in the atmosphere. The chlorine- and bromine-containing halocarbons also contribute to depletion of the ozone layer.

Halogens Compounds that contain atoms of chlorine, bromine, or fluorine.

Halon Toxic chemical. Compound consisting of bromine, fluorine, and carbon. Halons are used as fire extinguishing agents. By federal regulation, halon production in the USA ended on December 31, 1993 because they contribute to ozone depletion. They cause ozone depletion because they contain bromine. Bromine is many times more effective at destroying ozone than chlorine. *See also: Toxic chemicals*

HAP *See: Hazardous air pollutant*

Hardwoods Deciduous, slow-growing trees, used for flooring and furniture because of their durability. Typically, hardwoods take from 25 to 80 years to grow to harvestable maturity. They include ash, cherry, elm, hickory, maple, poplar, oak, and teak. Because hardwoods grow at such a slow rate, their depletion dramatically changes the ecosystem of forested areas. Alternatives for flooring and furniture include bamboo, which grows very quickly and is easily replenished; and the faster-growing softwoods. *See also: Bamboo; Deciduous; Softwoods*

Harvested rainwater Rainwater captured and stored in a cistern or other container, and used for irrigating plants (see Figure 35).

Hazardous air pollutant (HAP) Chemical that causes adverse health and environmental problems. Health effects may include birth defects, nervous system problems, and death. HAPs are released by sources such as chemical plants, dry cleaners, printing plants, and motor vehicles. *See also: Air pollutants; Toxic chemicals*

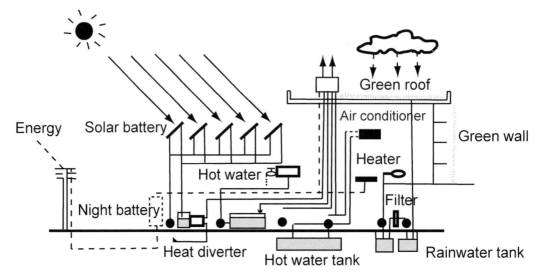

Figure 35 A combined solar collection and rainwater collection system

Hazardous material Chemical or product that affects human health and/or the environment adversely. Characteristics of hazardous materials are toxicity, corrosivity, ignitability, and explosivity. *See also: Air pollutants; Soil contaminants; Water pollutants*

Hazardous waste Waste with properties that make it dangerous or potentially harmful to human health or the environment. These wastes may be liquids, solids, contained gases, or sludges. They can be by-products of manufacturing processes, or discarded commercial products such as cleaning fluids or pesticides. Four characteristics of hazardous waste are: ignitability, corrosivity, reactivity, and toxicity. Ignitable wastes can create fires, are spontaneously combustible, or have a flash point less than 60 °C (140 °F). Corrosive wastes are acids or bases that corrode metal containers. Reactive wastes are unstable and can cause explosions, toxic fumes, gases or vapors when heated, compressed, or mixed with water. Toxic wastes are harmful or fatal when ingested or absorbed. USEPA has also developed a list of more than

500 specific hazardous wastes. Hazardous waste may be solid, semi-solid, or liquid. *See also: Toxic waste*

HDD Heating degree day *See: Degree day*

HDPE *See: High-density polyethylene*

Heat Form of energy resulting from combustion, chemical reaction, friction, or movement of electricity.

Heat-absorbing window glass A type of window glass that contains special tints that allow the window to absorb as much as 45% of incoming solar energy, to reduce heat gain in an interior space. Part of the absorbed heat will continue to be passed through the window by conduction and re-radiation.

Heat balance Thermal energy output from a system that equals thermal energy input.

Heat engine A device that produces mechanical energy directly from two heat reservoirs of different temperatures. A machine that converts thermal energy to mechanical energy, such as a steam engine or turbine.

Heat exchanger   A device that transfers heat from one material to another. Usually constructed to transfer heat from a fluid (liquid or gas) to another fluid where the two are physically separated. In phase-change heat exchangers, heat transfers to or from a solid to a fluid. *See also:* ***Heat recovery ventilator***

Heat gain   In buildings, the amount of heat introduced to a space from all heat-producing sources, such as building occupants, lights, and appliances, and from the environment, mainly solar energy.

Heat gain from bulbs   Electrical light bulbs generate heat according to the wattage consumed by the light bulb (power = current × voltage). As long as the light is absorbed in the space, the light bulb electrical power equals the heat gain in the space. This can be converted to Btu by multiplying the wattage by 3.42 Btu/h (3.42 Btu/h = 1 watt). For example, a 100 W bulb × 3.4 = 340 Btu/h.

Heat island   Urban air and surface temperatures that are 2–10 °F (1–6 °C) higher than nearby rural areas. Elevated temperatures can affect communities by increasing peak energy demand, air-conditioning costs, air pollution levels, and heat-related illness and mortality. Heat islands form as cities replace natural land cover with pavements, buildings, and other infrastructure. These changes contribute to higher urban temperatures by i) displacing trees and vegetation, minimizing the natural cooling effects of shading and evaporation of water from soil and leaves (evapotranspiration); ii) tall buildings and narrow streets heating air trapped between them and reducing air flow; iii) waste heat from vehicles, factories, and air conditioners adding

warmth to their surroundings, further exacerbating the heat island effect. In addition to these factors, heat island intensities depend on an area's weather and climate, proximity to water bodies, and topography. Heat islands can occur year-round during the day or night. Urban–rural temperature differences are often largest on calm, clear evenings, because rural areas cool off more quickly at night, whereas cities retain heat stored in roads, buildings, and other structures. As a result, the largest urban–rural temperature difference, or maximum heat island effect, is often 3–5 hours after sunset. During the winter, some cities in cold climates may benefit from the warming effect of heat islands. Warmer temperatures can reduce heating energy needs and may help melt ice and snow on roads. In the summer, however, the same city will experience the negative effects of heat islands. In general, the harmful impacts from summertime heat islands are greater than the wintertime benefits, and most heat island reduction strategies can reduce summertime heat islands without eliminating wintertime benefits.

While they are distinct phenomena, summertime heat islands may contribute to global warming by increasing demand for air conditioning, which results in additional power plant emissions of heat-trapping greenhouse gases. Strategies to reduce heat islands therefore can also reduce the emissions that contribute to global warming.

Heat island effect   The increased temperatures of urban heat islands have a direct influence on the health of residents, such as heat strokes or respiratory problems from impure air. Other effects of heat islands are an increase in energy use for cooling buildings, changes in local wind patterns, development of clouds, fog, smog, humidity, and precipitation. Heat island effects can be mitigated by using white or reflective materials to build houses, pavements, and roads, thus increasing the overall albedo of the

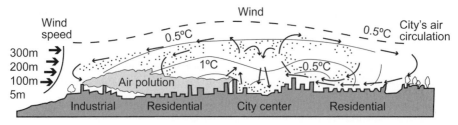

Figure 36 Heat island effect in cities

city. This is a long-established practice in many countries. A second option is to increase the amount of well watered vegetation. These two options can be combined with the implementation of green roofs. For example, the city of New York determined that the largest cooling potential per area was from street trees, followed by living roofs, light colored surfaces, and planting of open spaces. From the standpoint of cost effectiveness, light surfaces, light roofs, and curbside planting have lower costs per temperature reduction. *See also:* **Heat island**

Heat load   Amount of energy needed to heat a space.

Heat loss   Heat lost from a building through its windows, doors, and roof.

Heat pipe   A device that transfers heat by the continuous evaporation and condensation of an internal fluid. Heat pipes have a good heat-transfer capacity and rate, with almost no heat loss.

Heat pump   An electric powered device that extracts available heat from one area (the heat source) and transfers it to another (the heat sink) using a refrigerant. In air-conditioning mode, it cools an interior space by transferring the interior heat to the outside. In heat pump mode, it heats an interior space by transferring outdoor heat to the inside. In the refrigeration cycle, a refrigerant is compressed as a gas and passed through a condenser, which condenses the gas to a liquid

by removing the heat. Next the high-pressure liquid passes through an expansion device, which lowers the pressure. The last part of the cycle involves absorbing heat from a warm fluid in an evaporator by boiling the refrigerant. The resulting gas then begins the cycle again by being compressed. For climates with moderate heating and cooling needs, heat pumps offer an energy-efficient alternative to furnaces and air conditioners. Like a refrigerator, heat pumps use electricity to move heat from a cool space into a warm one, making the cool space cooler and the warm space warmer. Because they move heat rather than generate heat, heat pumps can provide up to four times the amount of energy they consume.

A new type of heat pump for residential systems is the absorption heat pump, also called a gas-fired heat pump. Absorption heat pumps use heat as their energy source, and can be driven with a wide variety of heat sources. Although absorbers have low efficiency—a coefficient of performance (COP) of less than 1 is common—they can use waste heat to improve the overall plant efficiency.

Heat pump, air-source   *See: Air-source heat pump*

Heat pump efficiency   The efficiency of a heat pump—the electrical energy needed to operate it—is directly related to the temperatures between which it operates. Ground-source (geothermal) heat pumps are more efficient than conventional heat pumps or air conditioners that use the outdoor air, as the ground or groundwater a few feet below the Earth's surface remains at a higher temperature in winter and a cooler temperature in summer. It is more efficient in winter to draw heat from the relatively warm ground than from the atmosphere, where the air temperature is much colder; and in summer to transfer waste heat to the relatively cool ground than to the hotter air. Ground-source heat pumps are generally more expensive to install than outside-air heat pumps. However, depending on the location, ground-source heat pumps can reduce energy consumption (operating cost), and thus emissions, by more than 20% compared with high-efficiency outside-air heat pumps. Some ground-source heat pumps also use the waste heat from air conditioning to provide hot water heating in summer.

Heat pump, geothermal   *See: Ground-source heat pump*

Heat pump water heaters   A water heater that uses electricity to move heat from one place to another instead of generating heat directly.

Heat recovery   Use of heat that would otherwise be wasted. Sources of heat include machines, lights, and human warmth.

Heat recovery ventilator (HRV)   Also known as a heat exchanger, air exchanger, or air-to-air exchanger. Device that captures a portion of the heat from the exhaust air from a building, and transfers it to the supply/fresh air entering the building to preheat the air and increase overall heating efficiency. The HRV provides fresh air and improved climate control, while saving energy by reducing the heating (or cooling) requirements. It is closely related to energy recovery ventilators; however, ERVs also transfer the humidity level of the exhaust air to the intake air. *See also: Energy recovery ventilator*

Heat sink   A structure or medium that absorbs heat. *See also: Thermal mass*

Heat storage   *See: Thermal mass*

Heat transfer   Heat flow. There are three methods of heat flow: conduction, convection, and radiation. *See also: Conduction, thermal; Convection; Radiation*

Heat wheel   *See: Thermal wheel*

Heating penalty   *See: Winter penalty*

Heating season   Time of year that requires internal heat in buildings to maintain comfort.

Heavy metals   Toxic chemicals. Metallic elements with high atomic weights; can damage living things at low concentrations, and tend to accumulate in the food chain. Examples of heavy metals include mercury, chromium, cadmium, arsenic, and lead. *See also: Toxic chemicals*

Heliochemical process   The utilization of solar energy through photosynthesis.

Heliodon   Device used to simulate the angle of the Sun for assessing shading potentials of building structures or landscape features.

Heliostat   A device that tracks the movement of the Sun; used to orient solar concentrating systems such as photovoltaic arrays.

Heliostat power plant   *See: Power tower*

Heliothermal   Any process that uses solar radiation to produce useful heat.

Heliothermic planning   Site planning that takes into account natural solar heating and cooling processes and their relationship to building shape, orientation, and siting.

Heliothermometer   An instrument for measuring solar radiation.

Heliotropic Any device (or plant) that follows the Sun's apparent movement across the sky.

Hemispherical bowl technology A solar energy-concentrating technology that uses a linear receiver to track the focal area of a reflector or array of reflectors.

HEPA *See: High-efficiency particulate arrestance*

Herbaceous Plant that has the characteristics of a herb, is not woody, and has a green color and leafy texture.

HERS *See: Home Energy Rating System*

Heterocyclic hydrocarbon Carcinogenic dioxins that occur as impurities in petroleum-derived herbicides.

Heterojunction 1. One of the basic photovoltaic devices.
    2. Region of electrical contact between two different materials. *See also: Photovoltaic device*

Heterotroph Organism that cannot synthesize its own food and must feed on organic compounds produced by other organisms (see Table 2, page 98). *See also: Autotroph; Lithotroph*

Heterotrophic layer Also known as brown belt. Layer in which organisms utilize, rearrange, and decompose complex substances. *See also: Autotrophic layer*

HEV *See: Hybrid electric vehicle*

High-density polyethylene (HDPE) Nonbiodegradable plastic.

High-efficiency particulate arrestance (HEPA) HEPA filters are used in hospital operating rooms, clean rooms, and other specialized areas requiring totally antiseptic conditions.

High global warming-potential gases *See: Fluorinated gases; Greenhouse gases*

High-level radioactive waste Highly radioactive materials produced as a by-product of the reactions that occur inside nuclear reactors. High-level wastes take one of two forms: i) spent (used) reactor fuel when it is accepted for disposal; ii) waste materials remaining after spent fuel is reprocessed. Spent nuclear fuel is used fuel from a reactor that is no longer efficient in creating electricity because its fission process has slowed. However, it is still thermally hot, highly radioactive, and potentially harmful. Until a permanent disposal repository for spent nuclear fuel is built, licensees must store this fuel safely at their reactors. Research estimates indicate that these wastes decay very slowly and remain radioactive for thousands of years.

High-throughput economy Most prevalent in industrialized countries. Maximizes the use of energy and other resources and does little to prevent pollution, or to recycle, reuse, or minimize waste. *See also: Low-throughput economy*

High-voltage disconnect The voltage at which a charge controller will disconnect the photovoltaic array from batteries to prevent overcharging.

HIPPO Acronym for leading causes of extinction: habitat destruction; invasive species; pollution; population (human); overharvesting.

Home Energy Rating System (HERS) Energy rating program in the USA that gives builders, mortgage lenders, secondary lending markets, homeowners, sellers, and buyers an estimation of energy use in homes based on construction plans and onsite inspections. The HERS score is being phased out, and a newer HERS index is now being used. This scale assigns a score of 100 to the reference baseline home and then subtracts 1% for each 1% improvement in efficiency. Builders can use this system to gauge energy quality in a building, and also to qualify for an Energy Star rating to compare with other similarly built homes.

Homojunction 1. One of the basic types of photovoltaic device.

2. Region between an n-layer and a p-layer in a single-material photovoltaic cell. Requires that the band gap be the same for the n-type and p-type semiconductors. *See also: Photovoltaic device*

Horizontal-axis wind turbine Wind power turbine in which the axis of the rotor's rotation is parallel to the wind stream and the ground. There are two types of turbine that use wind as a source of power to generate mechanical power or electricity: the horizontal axis; and the vertical, eggbeater-style Darrieus model. *See also: Darrieus wind turbine*

Horizontal ground loop Type of closed-loop geothermal heat pump installation in which fluid-filled plastic heat exchanger pipes are laid out in a plane parallel to the ground surface. The most common layouts use either two pipes, one buried at 6 feet (1.8 m), the other at 4 feet (1.2 m), or two pipes placed side by side at 5 feet (1.5 m) in the ground in a 2-foot (0.6-m)-wide trench. The trenches must be at least 4 feet deep. Horizontal ground loops are generally most cost-effective for residential installations, particularly for new constructions, where sufficient land is available. *See also: Ground-source heat pump*

Hot dry rock A geothermal energy resource that consists of high-temperature rocks above 300 °F (150 °C) that may be fractured and have little or no water. To extract the heat, the rock must first be fractured, then water is injected into the rock and pumped out to extract the heat. In the western USA, as much as 95,000 square miles (246,050 km^2) have hot dry rock potential.

Human population The human population in the world in 2007 was 6.6 billion. Demand on resources, and the consequences for the environment and biodiversity, are greatly influenced by population density. The regions of the world that have few threatened species and low human population density are usually located at high latitudes, in arid regions, or in wilderness areas, such as northern Canada, the Sahara desert, and the Amazon basin. These regions provide opportunities for preventive conservation measures as there is little human demand at present for resources, and species are currently relatively unthreatened. Regions that have a large number of threatened species but a relatively low human population density, for example Bolivia and the Russian Far East, are uncommon. In some regions, such as Europe and eastern North America, high population densities coincide with low numbers of threatened species. This is partly due to decreasing numbers of species with increasing latitude, but could also be a reflection of species susceptible to habitat loss in these regions having declined a long time ago. In general, these regions are of less concern for the conservation of globally threatened species than most other parts of the world.

The regions where high human population density and high numbers of threatened species overlap are mostly in Asia (in particular, southeast China, the Western Ghats of India, the Himalayas, Sri Lanka, Java (Indonesia), the Philippines, and parts of Japan, as well as the Albertine Rift in Central Africa, and the Ethiopian Highlands. These regions present the greatest conservation challenges, as the needs of billions of humans must be met while also working to prevent the extinction of large numbers of species.

Many developing nations are experiencing high population growth and face conflicting needs between the developed and undeveloped sectors of the population.

Density

The countries that are most densely populated at present are not necessarily those that are currently experiencing a high human population growth rate. In general the highest human population densities are found in Asia while the highest population growth rates are in Africa. Most African countries, however, currently have a relatively low level of population density so the impact of population growth might be more easily absorbed. With the annual rate of population growth declining in almost all countries, it is unpredictable whether these African countries will ever reach the high population density levels of some Asian countries today. Countries with high population growth rates and high numbers of threatened species such as Cameroon, Colombia, Ecuador, India, Madagascar, Malaysia, Peru, Philippines, Tanzania, and Venezuela are areas where conflicts between the needs of threatened species and increasing human populations are anticipated to rapidly intensify. Countries that currently have a low human population density but a high rate of population growth could be opportunistic places for pre-emptive conservation initiatives, for example Bolivia, Papua New Guinea, Namibia, Angola, and the countries of northern Africa. The Amazonian slopes of the Andes are also a region of relatively low human population density at present, and all of the Andean countries have relatively high population growth rates, as well as being extremely important for threatened species.

Conserving biodiversity

Countries with relatively strong economies but a large number of threatened species include Argentina, Australia, Malaysia, Mexico, USA, and Venezuela. However not all of these countries have significant funds available for threatened species conservation. Those countries that have a large number of threatened species but a relatively low per capita income include Brazil, Cameroon, China, Colombia, Ecuador, India, Indonesia, Madagascar, Peru, and the Philippines. These countries share a large responsibility towards conserving globally threatened species but are less likely to have financial resources available for conservation purposes. Other countries, particularly those in Europe, have significant financial resources but generally very few globally threatened species.

The International Union for the Conservation of Nature and Natural Resources, known as the World Conservation Union, has done extensive research on the interaction of population growth and density and its impact on conservation. Some of its research conclusions are listed below.

- People and threatened species are often concentrated in the same areas. At present these areas are mostly in Asia as well as the Albertine Rift in Central Africa and the Ethiopian Highlands.
- Future conflicts between the needs of threatened species and rapidly increasing human populations are predicted to occur in Cameroon, Colombia, Ecuador, India, Madagascar, Malaysia, Peru, Philippines, Tanzania, and Venezuela.
- Countries with low population densities but high rates of population growth, like Bolivia, Papua New Guinea, Namibia, and Angola, can establish conservation measures now in order to preserve their environments for future generations.
- Countries with a large number of threatened species are often not financially able to invest in conservation, such as Brazil, Cameroon, China, Colombia, Ecuador, India, Indonesia, Madagascar, Peru, and the Philippines.

The United Nations projects that there will be 14 megacities in the world in 2015: Tokyo, 28.7 million; Shanghai, 23.3 million; Beijing, 19.4 million; Jakarta, 21.2 million; Calcutta, 17.3 million; Mumbai, 27.4 million; Karachi, 20.6 million; Cairo, 14.4 million; Lagos 24.4, million; New York, 17.6 million; Los Angeles, 14.2 million; Mexico, City, 19 million; Sao Paulo, 19 million, and Buenos Aires, 13.9 million. These projections indicate heightened demands for resources and increased challenges of heat island effects, smog and other pollutants, urban congestion and sprawl development. *See also: Appendix 5: Population by country*

Humic substance   Popularly known as humus or compost, it is an organic material resulting from decay of plant or animal matter. The end product of decayed matter is humus. Humic substances supply growing plants with food, make soil more fertile and productive, and increase the water-holding capacity of soil, leading to improved drainage and increased soil aeration.

Humidity   A measure of the moisture content of air; may be expressed as absolute, mixing ratio, saturation deficit, relative, or specific humidity. The amount of humidity in the air greatly influences the level of human comfort. The higher the heat, the higher the level of discomfort. *See also: Absolute humidity; Relative humidity*

Humidity ratio   *See: Absolute humidity*

HVAC (Heating, ventilation, and air-conditioning)   Technology of indoor environmental and temperature controls.

HVDC   High-voltage DC. *See: Direct current*

Hybrid electric vehicle (HEV)   Vehicle powered by two or more energy sources, one of which is electricity. HEVs may combine the conventional internal combustion engine and fuel with the batteries and electric motor of an electric vehicle in a single drivetrain. The vehicle can run on the battery, or the engine, or both simultaneously, depending on the performance objectives for the vehicle. Hybrid vehicles are being developed as clean-energy alternatives to petroleum gas-powered ones, which emit substantial amounts of CO_2 into the troposphere. Automobile manufacturers design HEVs to focus on one or more of the following features: improved fuel economy, increased power, or additional auxiliary power for electronic devices and power tools.

Some of the advanced technologies typically used by hybrids are as follows.

- Regenerative braking—the electric motor applies resistance to the drivetrain, causing the wheels to slow down. In return, the energy from the wheels turns the motor, which functions as a generator, converting energy normally wasted during coasting and braking into electricity, which is stored in a battery until needed by the electric motor.
- Electric motor drive/assist—the electric motor provides additional power to assist the engine in accelerating, passing, or hill climbing. This allows a smaller, more efficient engine to be used. In some vehicles, the motor alone provides power for low-speed driving conditions where internal combustion engines are least efficient.
- Automatic start/shutoff—automatically shuts off the engine when the vehicle comes to a stop, and restarts it when the accelerator is pressed. This prevents wasted energy from idling.

(See Figure 37). *See also: Hybrid engine; Smart fortwo car; Solar electric-powered vehicle*

Hybrid electricity system   A renewable energy system that includes two different types of

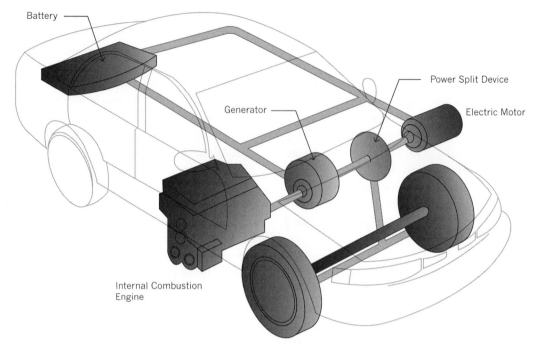

Battery

Power Split Device

Generator

Electric Motor

Internal Combustion
Engine

Figure 37 A hybrid electric vehicle
Source: US Department of Energy

technologies that produce the same type of energy. For example, a wind turbine and a solar photovoltaic array can be used together to meet a power demand.

Hybrid engine   The general definition of a hybrid car is that it contains a gasoline engine, an electric engine, a generator (mostly on series hybrids), fuel storage container, batteries, and a transmission. There are basically two different types of hybrid engine. i) Parallel hybrid—contains both a gasoline and electric motor that both operate independently to propel the car forward. ii) Series hybrid—the gas- or diesel-powered engine does not connect to the transmission directly, so does not propel the car by itself. It works indirectly by powering a generator, controlled by computer monitoring systems, that either feeds power to the batteries or feeds power directly to an electric motor that connects to the transmission. *See also: Battery electric vehicle*

(BEV); Dual-fuel vehicle; Hybrid electric vehicle (HEV); Hybrid vehicle; Hydraulic hybrid; Plug-in hybrid electric vehicle (PHEV); Tribrid vehicle

Hybrid vehicle   Term currently used to describe any vehicle that uses two or more distinct power sources to propel the vehicle. Such vehicles generally have higher fuel efficiency, lower emissions, and decreased operating costs. Among the power sources are: i) on-board rechargeable energy storage system and a fuel power source such as an internal combustion engine or fuel cell; ii) air and internal combustion engines. The term usually refers to hybrid electric vehicles; other vehicles that fall into this general category include a bicycle that combines human power with an electric motor or gas engine assist; and a human-powered sailboat with electric power. These two types do not necessarily have fuel efficiency or lower emissions. There are different levels of hybrid.

- Strong or full hybrid—a vehicle that can run on just the engine, just the batteries, or a combination of both. The Toyota Prius, Ford Escape, and Mercury Mariner hybrids are examples of cars that can be moved forward on battery power alone. A large, high-capacity battery pack is needed for battery-only operation. These vehicles have a split power path that allows more flexibility in the drivetrain by interconverting mechanical and electrical power. To balance the forces from each portion, the vehicles use a differential-style linkage between the engine and motor connected to the head end of the transmission.

- Power assist hybrid—uses the engine for primary power, with a torque-boosting electric motor also connected to a largely conventional powertrain. The electric motor, mounted between the engine and transmission, is essentially a very large starter motor, which operates not only when the engine needs to be turned over, but also when the driver "steps on the gas" and requires extra power. The electric motor may also be used to restart the combustion engine, deriving the same benefits from shutting down the main engine at idle, while the enhanced battery system is used to power accessories. Honda's hybrids, including the Insight, use this design; their system is dubbed integrated motor assist (IMA). Assist hybrids differ fundamentally from full hybrids in that they cannot run on electric power alone.

- Mild hybrid—essentially a conventional vehicles with an oversized starter motor, allowing the engine to be turned off whenever the car is coasting, braking, or stopped, yet restart quickly and cleanly. Accessories can continue to run on electrical power while the engine is off, and, as in other hybrid designs, the motor is used for regenerative braking to recapture energy. The larger motor is used to spin up the engine to operating rpm speeds before injecting any fuel.

Many do not consider these to be hybrids at all, and these vehicles do not achieve the fuel economy of full hybrid models.

- Plug-in hybrid electric vehicle (PHEV), gas-optional, or griddable hybrid—can be plugged in to an electrical outlet to be charged; and has a certain range that can be traveled on the energy stored while plugged in. This is a full hybrid, able to run in electric-only mode, with a larger battery and the ability to recharge from the electric power grid. Can be parallel or series hybrid design. Their main benefit is that they can be gasoline-independent for daily commuting, but also have the extended range of a hybrid for long trips. They can also be multi-fuel, with the electric power supplemented by diesel, bio-diesel, or hydrogen. The Electric Power Research Institute indicates a lower total cost of ownership for PHEVs due to reduced service costs and gradually improving batteries. The "well-to-wheel" efficiency and emissions of PHEVs compared with gasoline hybrids depend on the energy sources of the grid (the US grid is 50% coal; California's grid is primarily natural gas, hydroelectric power, and wind power). There is particular interest in PHEVs in California, where a "million solar homes" initiative is under way, and global warming legislation has been enacted. Researchers believe PHEVs will become standard in a few years. *See also: Hybrid electric vehicle (HEV); Hybrid engine*

Hydraulic hybrid Hybrid engine, developed by USEPA, which can charge a pressure accumulator to drive the wheels by way of hydraulic drive units. It can recover almost all the energy that is usually lost during vehicle braking, and uses it to propel the vehicle the next time it needs to accelerate. This makes the system more efficient than battery-charged hybrids. Tested in a mid-sized sedan, the hydraulic hybrid triples fuel economy, allows acceleration from 0 to 60 mph in 8 seconds, and has higher fuel efficiency. USEPA has formalized partnerships with a number of private companies. It is estimated that it will be manufactured before long. *See also: Hybrid engine*

Hydrocarbon   Organic chemical compound of hydrogen and carbon in gas, liquid, or solid phase. Hydrocarbons can vary from simple methane to very heavy, complex compounds. Fossil fuels are made up of hydrdocarbons. In vehicle emissions, these are usually vapors created from incomplete combustion or from vaporization of liquid gasoline. Another source of hydrocarbon pollution is fuel evaporation, which occurs when gasoline vapors are forced out of the fuel tank (as during refueling) or when gasoline spills and evaporates. Emissions of hydrocarbons contribute to ground-level ozone.

Hydrochlorofluorocarbons (HCFCs)   Air pollutant. Compounds that contain hydrogen, fluorine, chlorine, and carbon atoms. Introduced as replacements for the more potent chlorofluorocarbons (CFCs), they also are greenhouse gases. The effect of HCFCs on metabolism and toxicity have not been studied in detail, according to studies available to the US National Institutes of Health. Research to date indicates that HCFCs show a low acute toxicity, but are listed as toxic chemicals by USEPA pending further research. HCFC-22, also known as Freon 22, is in wide use in air conditioners, but in compliance with the Montreal Protocol, HCFC-22 can no longer be used in new air conditioners, beginning in 2010. *See also: Air pollutants; Montreal Protocol on Substances that Deplete the Ozone Layer; Toxic chemicals*

Hydroelectric power plant   Power plant that produces electricity by transforming the potential energy of water into kinetic energy by changing the height of the water level, then using the kinetic energy to power a hydrogenerator to produce electricity. Water constantly moves through a natural cycle: evaporation, cloud formation, rain or snow, deposition in bodies of water. Hydropower uses a fuel—water—that is not reduced or depleted in the process, and thus is a renewable energy source. Most hydroelectric power comes from the potential energy of dammed water driving a water turbine and generator, although less common variations use water's kinetic energy, or dammed sources such as tidal power. The energy extracted from water depends not only on the volume, but also on the difference in height between the source and the water's outflow. This height difference is called the head. The amount of potential energy in water is proportional to the head. To obtain very high head, water for a hydraulic turbine may be run through a large pipe called a penstock.

There are three types of hydropower facility: impoundment, diversion, and pumped storage. Some hydropower plants use dams, others do not. The plants vary in size from small systems for homes or villages to large projects producing electricity for utilities.

An impoundment plant is usually a large hydropower system. It uses a dam to store river water in a reservoir. Water released from the reservoir flows through a turbine, spinning it, which in turn activates a generator to produce electricity.

A diversion facility, sometimes called run-off-river, channels a portion of a river through a canal or penstock. It may not require the use of a dam.

Pumped storage stores energy by pumping water from a lower reservoir to an upper reservoir. During periods of high demand, the water is released back to the lower reservoir to generate electricity. *See also: Diversion power plant; Impoundment power plant; Pumped storage plant*

Hydrofluorocarbons (HFCs)   Compounds containing only hydrogen, fluorine, and carbon atoms. Introduced as an alternative to ozone-depleting substances, HFCs are emitted as by-products of industrial processes and are also used in manufacturing. They do not significantly deplete the stratospheric ozone layer, but they are potent greenhouse gases with global warming potential.

Hydrogen economy   A hypothetical model of an economy in which energy is stored and transported as hydrogen. Term coined by John Bockris during a talk given in 1970 at General Motors Technical Center. The goals are to eliminate the use of carbon and carbon dioxide (CO_2), and to replace the use of petroleum with hydrogen. Proponents of a hydrogen economy suggest that hydrogen is an environmentally cleaner source of energy; does not release pollutants, such as greenhouse gases; and does not contribute to global warming. Countries without oil, but with renewable energy resources, could use a combination of renewable energy and hydrogen instead of fuels derived from petroleum to achieve energy independence. Opponents contend that alternate means of storage, such as chemical batteries, fuel plus fuel cells, or production of liquid synthetic fuels from CO_2 might accomplish many of the same net goals of a hydrogen economy, while requiring only a small fraction of the investment in new infrastructure.

Hydrogen energy   Hydrogen is the simplest element known to man. Each atom of hydrogen has only one proton. It is the most plentiful gas in the universe. Stars are made primarily of hydrogen. Hydrogen gas is lighter than air and thus rises in the atmosphere, so hydrogen as a gas (H_2) is not found by itself on Earth; it is found only in compound form with other elements. Hydrogen combined with oxygen is water (H_2O); hydrogen combined with carbon forms different compounds including methane (CH_4), coal, and petroleum. Hydrogen is also found in all growing things—biomass. It is also an abundant element in the Earth's crust.

Hydrogen has the highest energy content of any common fuel by weight (about three times more than gasoline), but the lowest energy content by volume (about four times less than gasoline). It is the lightest element, and is a gas at normal temperature and pressure. Like electricity, hydrogen is an energy carrier and must be produced from another substance. Hydrogen is not widely used at present, but it has great potential as an energy carrier in the future. Hydrogen can be produced from a variety of resources (water, fossil fuels, biomass) and is a by-product of other chemical processes. Currently, there is research on producing hydrogen through artificial photosynthesis. Unlike electricity, large quantities of hydrogen can easily be stored to be used in the future. Hydrogen can also be used in places where it is difficult to use electricity. Hydrogen can store the energy until it is needed, and can be moved to where it is needed. *See also: Artificial photosynthesis; Hydrogen economy*

Hydrogen fusion   The Sun is a fusion reactor, held together by its own gravity. In the future, a fusion nuclear reactor may be able to sustain nuclear fusion by combining two hydrogen nuclei to form a helium nucleus. To date, a fusion reaction has been achieved with a net positive energy flow out. Major engineering problems need to be resolved to overcome the problems associated with fusion power. The reactor containment vessel has major corrosion challenges, with neutrons impinging in the interior vessel wall and causing the material to erode quickly. Fusion reactors also produce large quantities of deuterium and tritium, among other radioactive waste material, which will be very difficult to isolate.

Hydrogen-powered vehicle   An automobile or any other vehicle that uses hydrogen as its principal fuel. The power mechanisms of hydrogen-powered vehicles convert the chemical energy of hydrogen to mechanical energy (torque) by one of two methods: combustion; or electrochemical conversion in a fuel cell. In combustion, the hydrogen is burned in engines using fundamentally the same method as traditional gasoline (petrol) cars. In fuel-cell conversion, the hydrogen is reacted with oxygen to produce water and electricity, the latter being used to power an electric traction motor.

The hydrogen internal combustion car is a modified version of the traditional gasoline internal combustion engine car. These hydrogen engines burn fuel in the same manner as gasoline engines. The first hydrogen internal combustion engine was designed by François Isaac de Rivaz in 1807.

Some car manufacturers, such as Daimler Chrysler and General Motors, are investing in the efficient hydrogen fuel cells; others, such as Mazda, have developed Wankel engines that burn hydrogen.

While hydrogen fuel cells themselves are potentially very energy efficient, there are four technical obstacles to the development and use of a fuel cell-powered hydrogen car.

- Fuel cell cost—hydrogen fuel cells are currently costly to produce, and are fragile. There is ongoing development of inexpensive fuel cells that are hardy enough to survive automobile vibrations. Also, many designs require rare and costly substances such as platinum as a catalyst in order to work properly. Such a catalyst can also become contaminated by impurities in the hydrogen supply. In the past few years, however, a nickel–tin catalyst has been under development, which may lower the cost of cells.
- Temperature sensitivity—temperatures below freezing (32 °F or 0 °C) are a major concern with fuel-cell operations. Operational fuel cells have an internal vaporous water environment that could solidify if the fuel cell and contents are not kept above freezing. Most fuel cell designs are not yet robust enough to survive in below-freezing environments. This makes startup of the fuel cell a major concern in cold weather operation. Places where temperatures can reach –40 °C (–40 °F) at startup would not be able to use early model fuel cells. Ballard Power Systems has announced that it has already hit the US Department of Energy's 2010 target for cold-weather starting, which was 50% power achieved in 30 seconds at –20 °C.

- Life span of the fuel cell—although service life is coupled to cost, fuel cells have to be compared with existing machines with a service life in excess of 5000 hours for stationary and light duty. Marine proton-exchange membrane (PEM) fuel cells reached the target in 2004. Research is being carried out on heavy-duty cells for use in buses. The goal is to have a service life of 30,000 hours.
- Hydrogen production and environmental concerns—the molecular hydrogen needed as an on-board fuel for hydrogen vehicles can be produced through many thermochemical methods, using natural gas, coal (coal gasification), liquefied petroleum gas, or biomass (biomass gasification); by a process called thermolysis; or as a microbial waste product called biohydrogen or biological hydrogen production. Hydrogen can also be produced from water by electrolysis, or by chemical reduction using chemical hydrides or aluminum. Current technologies for manufacturing hydrogen use energy in various forms, totalling between 25 and 50% of the higher heating value of the hydrogen fuel, to produce, compress or liquefy, and transmit the hydrogen by pipeline or truck. Electrolysis, currently the most inefficient method of producing hydrogen, uses 65–112% of the higher heating value on a well-to-tank basis.

Concerns about environmental effects of the production of hydrogen from fossil energy resources include the emission of greenhouse gases, a consequence that would also proceed from the on-board re-forming of methanol into hydrogen. Studies comparing the environmental consequences of hydrogen production and use in fuel-cell vehicles with the refining of petroleum and combustion in conventional automobile engines have found a net reduction of ozone and greenhouse gases in favor of hydrogen. Hydrogen production using renewable energy resources would not create such emissions or, in the case of biomass, would create near-zero net emissions.

In addition to the inherent losses of energy in the conversion of feedstock to produce hydrogen, which makes hydrogen less advantageous as an energy carrier, there are economic and energy penalties associated with packaging, distribution, storage, and transfer of hydrogen.

Researchers in the area of artificial photosynthesis are trying to replicate the process of splitting water into hydrogen and oxygen using sunlight energy. If successful, this process could provide a source of hydrogen as a clean, non-polluting fuel. The attraction of hydrogen is that it produces no pollution or greenhouse gases at the tailpipe. Current methods of producing hydrogen from oil and coal produce substantial carbon dioxide. Unless and until this carbon can be captured and stored, renewable (wind or solar) and nuclear power, with their attendant problems of supply and waste, are the only means of producing hydrogen without also producing greenhouse gases.

In addition, setting up a completely new infrastructure to distribute hydrogen would cost at least US$5,000 per vehicle. Transporting, storing, and distributing a gaseous fuel, as opposed to a liquid, raises many new problems.

It has been estimated that a substantial investment of many billion dollars will be needed to develop hydrogen fuel cells that can match the performance of today's gasoline engines. Researchers indicate that improvements to current cars and current environmental rules are more than 100 times cheaper than hydrogen cars at reducing air pollution. And for several decades, the most cost-effective method to reduce oil imports and CO_2 emissions from cars will be to increase fuel efficiency.

Buses, trains, PHB© bicycles, cargo bikes, golf carts, motorcycles, wheelchairs, ships, airplanes, submarines, high-speed cars, and rockets already can run on hydrogen, in various forms and sometimes at great expense. NASA uses hydrogen to launch space shuttles. Some airplane manufacturers are pursuing hydrogen as fuel for airplanes. Unmanned hydrogen planes have been tested, and in February 2008 Boeing tested a manned flight of a small aircraft powered by a hydrogen fuel cell. Boeing reported that hydrogen fuel cells were unlikely to power the engines of larger passenger jets, but could be used as backup or auxiliary power units onboard. Rockets use hydrogen because it gives the highest exhaust velocity as well as providing a lower net weight of propellant than other fuels. It is very effective in upper stages, although it has also been used on lower stages, usually in conjunction with a dense fuel booster.

The main disadvantage of hydrogen in this application is its low density and deeply cryogenic nature, requiring insulation—this makes the hydrogen tankage relatively heavy, which greatly offsets many of the otherwise overwhelming advantages for this application. *See also: Artificial photosynthesis*

Hydrogen-rich fuel Fuel that contains a significant amount of hydrogen, such as gasoline, diesel fuel, methanol, ethanol, natural gas, and coal.

Hydrological cycle Process of evaporation and transport of vapor, condensation, precipitation, and the flow of water from continents to oceans. It is a major factor in determining climate through its influence on surface vegetation, clouds, snow and ice, and soil moisture. The hydrological cycle is believed to be responsible for 25–30% of the mid-latitudes' heat transport from the equatorial to polar regions.

Hydrology   Science of water, its properties, distribution, and circulation. Geology of groundwater, with emphasis on the chemistry and movement of water.

Hydronic heating system   A type of heating system in which water is heated in a boiler and either moves by natural convection or is pumped to heat exchangers or radiators in rooms; radiant floor systems have a grid of tubing laid out in the floor for distributing heat. The temperature in each room is controlled by regulating the flow of hot water through the radiators or tubing.

Hydronic system   System of heating or cooling using forced circulation of liquids or vapors in pipes.

Hydroponic   Method of growing plants in a nutrient-rich liquid medium rather than soil. It is an important component of vertical farming. *See also: Vertical farming*

Hydropower   *See: Hydroelectric power plant*

Hydrosphere   All the water on Earth; includes lakes, oceans, seas, glaciers, other liquid surfaces, subterranean water, and clouds and water vapor.

Hydrothermal fluids   These fluids can be either water or steam trapped in fractured or porous rocks; they are found from several hundred feet to several miles below the Earth's surface. Temperatures vary from about 90 to 680 °F (32 to 360 °C), but roughly two-thirds range in temperature from 150 to 250 °F (66 to 121 °C). The latter are the easiest to access, and therefore the only forms being used commercially.

Hypocaust   Radiating heat into a room through the floor; open space below a floor that is heated by gases from a fire or furnace below, which allows the passage of hot air to heat the room above. This type of heating was developed by the Romans. *See also: Murocaust*

Hypolimnion   The bottom and densest layer of a stratified lake. Usually the coldest layer in summer and warmest in winter. Is isolated from wind mixing, and too dark for much plant photosynthesis to occur.

Hypoxia   Condition in which the levels of oxygen in water are too low to sustain most animal life. It occurs when high concentrations of nutrients enter the water. Nutrients used in fertilizer, including nitrogen and phosphorus, stimulate plant growth in water. The predominant plants in water, algae, thrive on nitrogen and phosphorus and consume huge quantities of oxygen, depriving many aquatic organisms, including fish, of the oxygen they need to survive. The result is massive fish kills and threats to commercial fisheries. Landscape changes through the loss of coastal and freshwater wetlands can also contribute to hypoxia.

I

IAEA *See: International Atomic Energy Agency*

IAQ *See: Internal air quality*

Ice stores Conservation technology that makes use of off-peak refrigeration energy to charge an ice store for release of cooling energy during the day.

ICS Integral collector/storage system. *See: Batch heater*

Impact Environmentally, the effect on either the environment or people of a specific action. *See also: Environmental impact statement*

Impervious surface Hard surface that either prevents or retards the entry of water into the soil, causing water to run off the surface in greater quantities or at an increased rate of flow. Common impervious surfaces include rooftops, walkways, patios, driveways, parking lots, storage areas, concrete or asphalt paving, and gravel roads. High concentrations of impervious surfaces increase the probability of flooding from heavy rains and storms.

Impoundment Body of water confined by a dam, dike, floodgate, or other artificial barrier.

Impoundment power plant One of three types of hydropower plant. The others are diversion and pumped storage plants. *See also: Diversion power plant; Hydroelectric power plant; Pumped storage plant*

Impulse turbine Turbine that is driven by high-velocity jets of water or steam from a nozzle directed to vanes or buckets attached to a wheel. A Pelton turbine or Pelton wheel is an impulse hydroturbine. *See also: Pelton turbine*

Inbreeding depression Accumulation of harmful genetic traits through mutations or natural selection in a species that lowers the viability and reproductive success of enough individual members to affect the entire species. Pollutants in the air, soil, and water can result in genetic mutations and alter the ability of a species to survive.

Incident angle Angle between a ray of light striking a surface (incident ray) and the normal (line perpendicular) to that surface. For a mirror, it is equal to the angle of reflection.

Incident light Light that shines on the face of a solar cell or module.

Incident solar radiation The amount of solar radiation striking a surface per unit of time and area.

Incineration Process of burning at high temperature. Properly operated incineration projects can provide energy in the form of electricity or processed steam, while reducing the volume of landfill waste. Managed incineration also uses processes that minimize emissions of airborne particulate and smoke.

Solid waste incineration is widely used in Denmark, France, Germany, Japan, Luxembourg, the Netherlands, Sweden, and the USA. Incineration can emit various levels of arsenic, nickel, mercury, lead, and calcium, all of which can be toxic even at low levels.

An alternative to incineration is anaerobic decomposition, also known as anaerobic digestion. *See also:* ***Anaerobic decomposition; Solid waste***

Indicator species An organism, often a microorganism or plant, that serves as a measure of the environmental conditions that exist in a specific locality.

Indigenous Native to a specific geographical area.

Indirect heat gain Result of interception and storage of the Sun's energy in proximal storage before it enters a space. Solar masonry walls and water wall collectors are examples of indirect gain systems. Trombe walls are thermal collectors that store the Sun's heat during the day and emit that heat through conduction at night. *See also:* ***Indirect solar gain system; Trombe wall***

Indirect solar gain system A passive solar heating system in which the Sun warms a heat-storage element, and the heat is distributed to the interior space by convection, conduction, and radiation.

Indirect solar water heater These systems circulate fluids, which can be different from water (such as diluted antifreeze), through the collector. The heat collected is used to heat the household water supply using a heat exchanger.

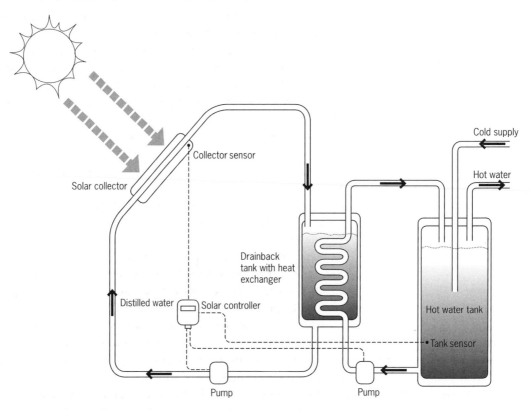

Figure 38 Indirect solar water heater

Also known as closed-loop systems. An indirect system that exhibits effectiveness, reliability, and low maintenance is the drainback system, which uses distilled water as the collector circulating fluid. *See also: **Closed-loop active system; Drainback system; Heat exchanger***

Indoor air pollution   Pollutants that adversely affect internal air quality (IAQ). Pollutants and sources include asbestos, biological pollutants, carbon monoxide, formaldehyde, pressed wood products, household cleaning and maintenance, lead, nitrogen dioxide, pesticides, radon, respirable particles, secondhand smoke, tobacco smoke, stoves, heaters, fireplaces and chimneys. *See also: **Internal air quality***

Indoor air quality   *See: Internal air quality*

Indoor environmental quality (IEQ)   Quality of the air and environment inside buildings, based on pollutant concentrations and conditions that can affect the health, comfort, and performance of occupants—including temperature, relative humidity, light, sound, odors, noise, static electricity, and other factors. Good IEQ is an essential component of any building, especially a green building.

Induction generator   A device that converts the mechanical energy of rotation into electricity based on electromagnetic induction. An electric voltage (electromotive force) is induced in a conducting loop (or coil) when there is a change in the number of magnetic field lines (or magnetic flux) passing through the loop. When the loop is closed by connecting the ends through an external load, the induced voltage will cause an electric current to flow through the loop and load. Thus, rotational energy is converted into electrical energy.

Industrial ecology   Based on the principle of dematerialization, industrial ecology focuses on particular characteristics of raw materials rather than resources per se with the objective of using fewer raw materials and less energy per unit of output.

Transforms production and consumption from a linear process to a circular energy efficient one by inventing, exploring, substituting, and conserving technologies to expand the potential resource base.

Industrial sludge   Semi liquid residue or slurry remaining from treatment of industrial water and wastewater.

Industrial waste   Residue material from construction, industrial or manufacturing operations. Industrial solid waste may be solid, sludge, liquid, or gas held in container and is classified as either hazardous or nonhazardous waste. Hazardous wastes may result from manufacturing or other industrial processes. Certain commercial products such as cleaning fluids, paints, or pesticides that are discarded by commercial establishments or individuals also can be defined as hazardous wastes. Wastes determined to be hazardous are regulated by hazardous waste rules regulated by USEPA's Resource Conservation Recovery Act's Subtitle C requirements.

Non hazardous industrial wastes are those that do not meet the USEPA's definition of hazardous waste—and are not municipal wastes. These nonhazardous wastes fall under USEPA's solid waste management requirements. *See: **toxic waste***

Inert gas   A gas that does not react with other substances, such as argon or krypton; sealed between two sheets of glazing to decrease the *U* value (increase the *R* value) of windows.

Inert solids or inert waste   Category of solid waste that includes soil and concrete that do not have as hazardous an effect on the environment as pollutants.

Infill development   Term used to describe building and developing in vacant lots and areas in urban neighborhoods and city centers. This type of development was originally designed to build new homes in coveted older neighborhoods. As the practice increased, it has benefited neighborhoods and downtown areas of cities. City centers have been revitalized, traffic congestion has been reduced, more liveable and vital downtown communities have resurged, and more rural areas and open spaces are saved. Infill development is closely related in principle to smart growth. One possible negative effect of infill development may be the increased cost of upgrading and increasing utilities and energy. *See: urban renewal*

Infiltration   Uncontrolled air leakage through cracks and holes in any building element, especially windows and doors.

Infrared radiation (IR)   Heat energy emitted from a material. The term refers to energy in the region of the electromagnetic radiation spectrum at wavelengths longer than those of visible light but shorter than those of radio waves. The electromagnetic spectrum includes all types of radiation, from x-rays to radio waves to the microwaves used in cooking. IR radiation is invisible to the eye, but it can be detected as a sensation of warmth on the skin. Radiant heat felt from an oven or fire is IR radiation. Everything emits IR radiation, although some of the emissions cannot be felt because they are too weak.

Greenhouse gases in the atmosphere, especially water vapor, trap some of this IR radiation, and keep the earth habitable for life. Clouds also trap some of this radiation. The reason why the air cools so quickly on a clear, dry evening is because the lack of humidity and clouds allows large amounts of IR radiation to escape rapidly to outer space.

Infrastructure   Large structures of a society which members of the society cannot provide for themselves and on which society depends to link members to each other. Infrastructure includes public utilities, roads, water systems, communication networks, airports, schools, and hospitals.

Inherently low emission vehicle (ILEV)
Inherently low-emission vehicle is a government designation that includes limits on both exhaust pollution and the fuel-cycle (fuel manufacture, distribution, and dispensing) emissions. Unlike other (non-zero) emissions standards like low emission vehicles (LEV), this one can't be met by gasoline vehicles because of the fuel-cycle emission limits. At present, the US standard only indicates that the vehicle meets environmental protection exhaust emissions standards and produces very few or no evaporative emissions.

USEPA manages overall emissions standards unless state restrictions are more stringent, like California. The California Air Resources Board initiated the designations for low emission vehicles in 1990.

Injection well   Constructed well into which treated water is injected directly into the ground. The well is generally drilled into aquifers that do not supply drinking water, are unused aquifers, or below freshwater levels. Wastewater is pumped into the well for dispersal or storage into a designated aquifer.

Inland wetlands   Wetlands that include marshes, wet meadows, and swamps. These areas are often dry during one or more seasons every year.

Inorganic   Term to describe minerals and non-carbon based compounds.

Inorganic compound   Noncarbon-based chemical compound. *See also: Organic compound*

Inorganic cyanides   Toxic chemicals found in gas hydrogen cyanide. Cyanide salts are mainly used in electroplating, metallurgy, the production of organic chemicals (acrylonitrile, methyl methacrylate, adiponitrile), photographic development, the extraction of gold and silver from ores, tanning leather and in the making of plastics and fibers. They are also used to manufacture fumigation chemicals, insecticides, and rodenticides. They are released into the water and soil during the production of the above products.

Cyanide in surface water will form hydrogen cyanide and evaporate. It takes years for cyanide to break down from the air. They settle into the soil and can contaminate groundwater. Cyanides have high acute (short-term) toxicity to aquatic life, birds, and animals. Cyanides have high chronic (long-term) toxicity to aquatic life. Insufficient data are available to evaluate the chronic toxicity to plants, birds, or land animals. Cyanides are not expected to bioaccumulate. *See also: Toxic chemicals*

Insecticide   Chemical to kill insects.

In situ leach mining   Use of chemical leaching to extract valuable mineral deposits rather than physically extracting the minerals from the ground. Also known as solution mining.

Insolation   Amount of solar power that strikes a surface area at a given orientation. It is usually expressed as watts per square meter or Btu per square foot per hour.

Instantaneous efficiency (of a solar collector) The amount of energy absorbed (or converted) by a solar collector (or photovoltaic cell or module) over a 15-minute period.

Insulation   A thermally nonconducting construction material insulation used in walls, floors, and ceilings to achieve high energy efficiency by preventing leakage of electricity, heat, sound, or radioactive particles. These materials prevent or slow down the movement of heat.

Various insulation materials include 1) cellulose insulation made from recycled newspaper and treated with fire retardants and insect protection; 2) CFC and HCFC blowing agents that contain chlorofluorocarbons; 3) cotton mill waste fiber insulation; 4) cementitious magnesium foam insulation made from seawater; 5) volcanic perlite; 6) rockwool made from recycled steel slag.

Health concerns about the use of asbestos and urea formaldehyde based insulation led to their being banned. The health concerns have spread to fiberglass and cellulose insulation. Fiberglass is considered a risk by some because of the insulation fibers' ability to become airborne and be inhaled similar to asbestos.

Insulation blanket   A pre-cut layer of insulation applied around a water heater storage tank to reduce stand-by heat loss from the tank.

Insulator   A device or material with a high resistance to electricity flow.

Integral collector storage system (ICS)   *See: Batch heater*

Integrated heating systems   A type of heating appliance that performs more than one function, for example space and water heating.

Integrated waste management   Waste-management system that uses multiple waste control and disposal methods to minimize the environmental effects of waste. Some of the methods used are source reduction, recycling, reuse, incineration, and land fills.

Intensive green roof   Has thick layers of soil, 6 to 12 inches or more, that can support a broad variety of plant and even tree species, which require more management and artificial irrigation systems. Plants are heavier than those in an extensive roof garden and require more structural support. *See also: Cool roof; Green roof; and Extensive green roof*

Interactions matrix   Interaction framework that informs the designer of all the aspects that a design must take into consideration in order to be comprehensive in its approach to ecodesign. Considerations include the environment of the designed system; the designed system itself and all its activities and processes; inputs of energy and materials to the designed system; outputs of energy and materials from the designed system and all those interactions of the components over the entire life cycle of the designed system.

Interconnect   A conductor within a connector, module, or other means of connection that provides an electrical interconnection. In a fuel cell, it is one of four components—anode, cathode, electrolyte, and interconnect. The interconnect is the mechanism for collection of electrical current. It functions as the electrical contact to the cathode while protecting it from the reducing atmosphere of the anode.

Interconnects must have high electrical conductivity, no porosity, thermal expansion compatibility and inertness with respect to the other fuel cell components. (See Figure 29). *See also: Anode; Cathode; Electrolyte; Solid oxide fuel cell*

Inter ecosystem migration   Migration of fauna and flora across various environments despite barriers that separate the green areas. The migration is a gradual one and may take 30–60 years or more for species to relocate.

Intergovernmental Panel on Climate Change (IPCC)   Established in 1988 by the World Meteorological Organization and the United Nations Environment Programme to assess the scientific information relating to climate change to formulate realistic response strategies. It was awarded the 2007 Nobel Peace Prize, along with former US Vice President Al Gore.

Integrated waste-management   System of practices that minimize solid waste, such as recycling, incineration, landfills, and source reduction.

Internal air quality (IAQ)   Quality of air inside buildings based on conditions that can affect the health and comfort of those who live or work in those buildings. Factors that affect IAQ include ventilation, humidity, pollutants, gases and particulates in the air, and humidity. *See also: Indoor air pollution; Internal environmental quality*

Internal combustion engine   Also known as a reciprocating engine. Combustion of fuel and an oxidizer (typically air) occurs in a confined space called a combustion chamber. The operation of a reciprocating (internal combustion) engine results in work performed by the expanding hot gases acting directly to cause movement of solid parts of the engine, by acting on pistons or rotors, or even by pressing on and moving the entire engine itself. These engines convert energy contained in the fuel into mechanical power. They use natural gas, diesel, landfill gas, and digester gas. They produce pollution, which is caused by incomplete combustion of carbonaceous fuel, leading to carbon monoxide and some soot, along with oxides of nitrogen and sulfur and some unburned hydrocarbons, depending on the operating conditions and the fuel/air ratio. Diesel engines produce a wide range of pollutants, including aerosols of many small particles (PM10) that are believed to penetrate human lungs. Engines running on liquefied petroleum gas (LPG) are very low in emissions, as LPG burns very cleanly and does not contain sulfur or lead.

Other exhaust emissions include sulfur oxides (SO_x), which cause acid rain; nitrogen oxides (NO_x), which have very adverse effects on plants and animals; and carbon dioxide (CO_2), which contributes to greenhouse gases. If biofuel is used, there is no net CO_2 produced from the combustion because plants can absorb the volume of CO_2 emitted from the engine. Some researchers believe that biofuels are "no net" CO_2 generators because their "fuel" is acquired from plants that have processed the carbon and nitrogen from the air and soil within one growing season.

Internal environmental quality (IEQ) Quality of the environment inside buildings based on internal air quality factors and other aspects of the environment that contribute to the health and comfort of those who live or work in those buildings. Other aspects include furnishings and color schemes, maintenance, cleaning, building use, lighting, and noise. *See also: Indoor air pollution; Internal air quality*

Internal heat gain Heat generated within a building from three sources: occupants, lights, and equipment. Internal heat gains tend to be very regular and follow occupancy patterns.

Internal mass Materials with high thermal energy storage capacity contained in or part of a building's walls, floors, or freestanding elements.

International Atomic Energy Agency (IAEA) International organization that seeks to promote the peaceful use of nuclear energy and to inhibit its use for military purposes. Although established independently of the United Nations under its own international treaty (the IAEA Statute), the IAEA reports to both the UN General Assembly and the UN Security Council. It was established as an autonomous organization on July 29, 1957. In 1953, US President Dwight D. Eisenhower envisioned the creation of this international body to control and develop the use of atomic energy, in his "Atoms for Peace" speech before the UN General Assembly. Most UN members are also members of the IAEA; notable exceptions are North Korea, Cambodia, and Nepal.

Inversion Condition that occurs when warm air is trapped near the ground and normal temperature gradients do not permit air to flow into the atmosphere.

Ion Atom or molecule that carries a positive or negative charge because of the loss or gain of electrons.

Ion rocket An alternative method to produce thrust for spacecraft other than through the combustion of flammable fuel. Through the process of ionizing gases such as hydrogen or helium, and by accelerating nuclei (ions) to high speeds, the ion rocket engine produces thrust. The accelerated atomic nuclei are ejected out of the rear of the spaceship, which results in moving the ship forward.

Ionic solution *See: Electrolyte*

Ionizing radiation Radiation with sufficient energy so that, during an interaction with an atom, it can remove tightly bound electrons from the orbit of an atom, causing the atom to become charged or ionized. The most common types are alpha radiation, made up of helium nuclei; beta radiation, made up of electrons; and gamma and X radiation, consisting of high-energy particles of light (photons). Ionizing radiation has always been a part of the human environment. Along with natural radioactive sources present in the Earth's crust and cosmic radiation, human-made sources also contribute to our continuous exposure to ionizing radiation. Environmental radioactive pollution has resulted from past nuclear weapons testing, nuclear waste disposal, and accidents at nuclear power plants, as well as from transportation, storage, loss, and misuse of radioactive sources.

The World Health Organization's Radiation and Environmental Health Program seeks solutions to protect human health from ionizing radiation hazards by raising public awareness of the potential health risks associated with ionizing radiation, and the importance of its safe and rational management. Through promoting research and providing recommendations for emergency medical and public health responses to radiation accidents and terrorist acts, and providing advice to national authorities, national and local public health authorities try to deal with radiation exposure issues effectively, facilitating key research programs and providing sound advice. Sources of ionizing radiation may be found in a wide range of occupational settings, including healthcare facilities, research institutions, nuclear reactors and their support facilities, nuclear weapons production facilities, and other manufacturing settings. These radiation sources can pose a considerable health risk to affected workers if not properly controlled. The US Department of Labor Occupational Safety and Hazards Agency has developed regulatory information regarding the recognition, evaluation, and control of occupational health hazards associated with ionizing radiation.

IPCC   *See: Intergovernmental Panel on Climate Change*

IR   *See: Infrared radiation*

Irradiance   Direct, diffuse, and reflected solar radiation that strikes a surface. It is usually expressed in watts per m². Irradiance × time = insolation.

Isolated gain   Occurs when solar collection and thermal storage are separate from habited space. This relationship allows the system to function independently of the building, with heat drawn from the system only when needed.

ISPRA Guidelines   Published by the Istituto Superiore per la Protezione e la Ricerca Ambientale (ISPRA: Higher Institute for Protection and Environmental Research, Joint Research Centre of the Commission of the European Communities); guidelines used to assess photovoltaic power plants.

Island habitats   Fragmentation and decrease of large, continuous, natural habitats of many species into isolated pocket habitats, when urban development encroaches on a formerly wild area.

Isocyanurate   Volatile organic component; carbon-based chemical used to make plywood.

Isothermal   (Adj.) Constant in temperature.

J

J curve Graphical representation of exponential population growth. This assumes no limit or limitations to population size. Almost all populations tend to grow exponentially as long as the resources they need are available. If population growth becomes limited by its ecosystem's carrying capacity, the growth pattern is an S curve, also known as logistic growth.

In medicine, J curves also chart population groups based on their risks of cardiovascular disease (CVD). Blood pressure or blood cholesterol levels of large groups of people are plotted on a graph against CVD mortality, often resulting in a J-shaped curve—those with higher blood pressure and/or cholesterol levels, closer to the top of the curve, are more likely to die from CVD; those at the lowest end of the curve (with very low blood pressure and/or low cholesterol levels) also have higher CVD mortality. J curves are also used in economic/democracy models, and balance-of-trade models. *See also: S curve*

Jatropha South American plant that grows in tropical and subtropical regions on nonarable

(a) Exponential (unrestricted) growth

(b) Logistic (restricted) growth

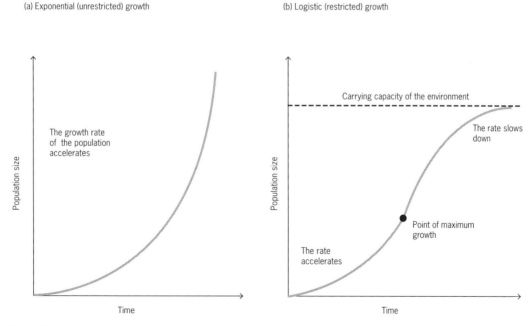

Figure 39 J curves
Source: W. K. Purves *et al.* (1998) *Life: The Science of Biology*, 4th edn, Sinauer Associates/WH Freeman

and waste land. It can be crushed to produce oil that is used to make biodiesel.

Jet fuel   Kerosene- and naphtha-type fuels for jet engines. Kerosene-type jet fuel is a kerosene-quality product used primarily for commercial turbojet and turboprop aircraft engines. Naphtha-type jet fuel is a fuel in the heavy naphtha range used primarily for military turbojet and turboprop aircraft engines.

Joint Implementation Agreement   Agreement between two or more nations under the auspices of the United Nations Framework Convention on Climate Change. The agreement allows one developed country to receive "emissions reduction units" when it helps finance projects that reduce net emissions in another developed country, including countries with economies in transition. *See also: United Nations Framework Convention on Climate Change*

Joint European Torus (JET)   The JET Joint Undertaking was established in June 1978 to construct and operate the JET, the largest the European nuclear fusion program. Coordinated by the European Atomic Energy Community (Euratom), the JET project became the flagship of the Community's Fusion Program. It started operating in 1983, and was the first fusion facility in the world to achieve a significant production of controlled fusion power (nearly 2 MW) with a deuterium–tritium experiment in 1991.

Joule   Metric unit of energy or work; 1 joule per second equals 1 watt or 0.737 foot-pounds; 1 Btu equals 1055 joules.

K

K-adapted species Organisms with population growth influenced by internal and external factors. Large animals (such as whales and elephants) and large predators fall into this category. These species have few offspring and stabilize their population size based on the carrying capacity—the maximum number of individuals of any species that can be supported by a particular ecosystem on a long-term basis. When the population exceeds the carrying capacity, it dies back with a fast decrease in the population

Kaplan turbine A propeller-type water turbine that has adjustable blades, developed in 1913 Viktor Kaplan of Austria. The Kaplan turbine

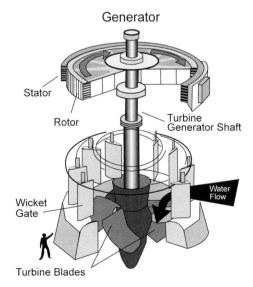

Figure 40 A vertical Kaplan turbine
Source: Voith-Siemens

was an evolution of the Francis turbine. Its invention allowed efficient power production in low-head applications that was not possible with Francis turbines. Kaplan turbines are widely used in high-flow, low-head electrical power production. They cover the lowest-head hydrosites and are especially suited for high-flow conditions. *See also: Francis turbine; Water turbine*

Kerosene-type jet fuel Kerosene-based product having a maximum distillation temperature of 400 °F (204 °C) at the 10% recovery point and a final maximum boiling point of 572 °F (302 °C), meeting American Society for Testing and Materials (ASTM) specification D 1655 and US Military specifications MIL-T-5624P and MIL-T-83133D. It is used for commercial and military turbojet and turboprop aircraft engines. *See also: Jet fuel*

Ketones Toxic chemical. 1. Ketones are water clear, highly mobile liquids with a characteristic odor. They are chemically very stable. Due to the carbonyl group, ketones are hydrogen acceptors and have very good solvency. Petroleum companies produce many ketones from propylene and butylene, covering the whole range of volatilities. Examples are acetone, methyl ethyl ketone (MEK), methyl isobutyl ketone (MIBK), and di-isobutyl ketone (DIBK). Ketones are used in surface coatings, adhesives, thinners, printing inks and cleaning agents. Other industrial uses are in pharmaceuticals, extraction, dewaxing, and as chemical intermediates (methyl methacrylate (MMA), bisphenol A, isophorone).

2. (Medical) Ketones are also a by-product/or waste product when the human body burns stored fat for energy; in this case they are not considered toxic chemicals. *See also: Toxic chemicals*

Keystone species   Species or group of species whose impact on its community or ecosystem is much larger and more influential than would be expected from mere abundance. Because of the interactions, the removal of this species or group of species can cause widespread changes to the community structure.

Kilowatt hour   Unit of electrical energy, or work equal to power supplied by 1 kilowatt for 1 hour.

Kinetic energy   Energy available as a result of motion that varies directly in proportion to an object's mass and the square of its velocity.

Kneewall   A wall usually about 3 to 4 feet (0.9–1.2 m) high that is placed in the attic of a home, anchored with plates between the attic floor joists and the roof joist. Sheathing can be attached to these walls to enclose an attic space.

Kyoto Protocol   The Kyoto Protocol to the United Nations Framework Convention on Climate Change (FCCC), signed in 1997 by 160 nations, is an international treaty designed to limit global greenhouse gas emissions. The Protocol became effective on February 16, 2005, and is legally binding for countries that have ratified it. The binding greenhouse emissions targets include the following gases: carbon dioxide, methane, nitrous oxide, hydrofluorocarbons, perfluorocarbons, and sulfur hexafluoride. The agreement expires in 2012, and signatories agreed to reduce greenhouse gas emissions below the levels recorded in 1990. The European Union agreed to decrease greenhouse gas emissions 8% below the benchmark 1990 levels, and Japan to 6%. Developing nations' reduction is voluntary. Some countries that have ratified the protocol, including India and China, are not required to reduce carbon emissions under the present agreement. As of December 2006, a total of 169 countries and other governmental entities had ratified the agreement. Notable exceptions include the USA and Australia.

L

Lagoon   1. Shallow pond where sunlight, bacterial action, and oxygen work to purify wastewater. Also used for storage of wastewater or spent nuclear fuel rods.

2. Shallow pond of seawater separated from the open sea or ocean by a sandbar or reef.

Land bridge   Linear spatially continuous interconnected parks or open spaces in a green infrastructure. *See also: Ecological corridor*

Land farming   Process to speed up biodegradation and disposal of organic waste. Waste sludge and soil are mixed together so that microorganisms in the soil decompose the organic wastes.

Landfill   Waste-disposal site in which waste is generally spread in thin layers, compacted, and covered with a fresh layer of soil on a regular basis, for decomposition of organic waste and biodegradable materials. Landfills are presently the repositories of throughput materials: resources and raw materials are extracted from the land, manufactured into products, consumed, and finally dumped as waste and garbage into landfills. One of the goals of ecodesign is to close the loop, and reuse and recycle materials and products within the built environment so that the residue and waste products can be reintegrated into the natural environment seamlessly. *See also: Area fill*

Landfill gas   Mixture of gases, primarily methane and carbon dioxide (CO_2), that is generated in landfills by the anaerobic decomposition of organic wastes. Both are greenhouse gases, which contribute to global warming. Methane from landfills contributes to local smog, and as gas accumulates within a landfill there are risks of methane explosions, which affect local vegetation and wildlife. If there is vegetation covering part of a landfill site, the formation and presence of methane and CO_2 could be harmful to that vegetation. *See also: Methane; Carbon dioxide*

Landfill gas collection   *See: Biomass electricity*

Large quantity generator   Person or facility generating more than 2200 pounds (1000 kg) of hazardous waste per month. Such generators produce about 90% of the USA's hazardous waste. *See also: Small quantity generator*

Latent heat   Heat resulting from, or input to, changes of state of all substances from vapor to liquid, liquid to solid, solid to liquid, or liquid to vapor without a corresponding change of temperature. For example, solids can become liquids (ice to water), or liquids can become solids (water to ice), with the addition or removal of heat. In the building industry, latent heat nominally refers to the energy content of water vapor mixed in with dry air, that is, heat of vaporization. *See also: Sensible heat*

Latent heat of vaporization   The quantity of heat produced to change a given amount of liquid to vapor with no change in temperature.

Lateritic soil   Soil that is rich in iron and aluminum compounds. The presence of these minerals makes it unsuitable for agriculture.

Latitude   In geography, distance measured in degrees north or south from the equator.

Law of the minimum   *See: Liebig's law*

Laws of ecology   Based on *The Closing Circle: Nature, Man, and Technology* (1971) by Barry Commoner. Often used as axioms for environmental protection: everything is connected to everything else; everything must go somewhere; nature knows best; there is no such thing as a free lunch.

Layer-cake model   Technique of ecological site mapping begun in the 1960s. Analysis should include not only the fauna and flora species, but also the interactions that operate within an ecosystem, and changes that take place within the system. Assessment should also include a determination of the species most crucial to maintain the ecosystem. The resulting design minimizes changes to biotic communities and changes to terrain (see Figure 41).

LCA   *See: Life-cycle assessment*

LDPE   *See: Low-density polyethylene*

Leachate   Liquids in landfill sites, including rainwater and the material that is leached from the wastes as the infiltrating liquids percolate downwards through the waste. Landfill design and management are required to minimize adverse environmental impacts during the stages of leachate, from aerobic and pH neutrality, to anaerobic and high acidity and ammonia concentrate, to an eventual return to neutral conditions. Depending on the toxicity and ability to decompose, landfill materials and chemicals may contaminate the surrounding soils and groundwater. *See also: Landfill*

Leaching   Process by which water removes chemicals from soil through chemical reactions and the downward movement of water.

Lead (Pb)   1. Major air and water pollutant and soil contaminant. Heavy metal. There are two major sources of lead contamination: i) lead-based paint—contamination may occur when paint chips from old buildings mix with the soil; ii) lead from auto emissions. Studies conducted in urban areas have shown that soil lead levels are highest around building foundations and within a few feet of busy streets. Once lead has been deposited, it moves very slowly through the soil and can persist for a long time. At high concentrations, lead is potentially toxic to humans and other forms of life. Lead particularly affects children six years old and under through air pollution, as well as lead-contaminated waste and dust, residential soil, and food and paint chips. It is still found at high levels in urban and industrial areas. Deposits in soil and water harm animals and fish. Lead tends to accumulate in the food chain. Because of its toxicity, lead is regulated in the USA by the Clean Air Act, Clean Water Act, Safe Drinking Water Act, Food, Drug and Cosmetic Act, and other environmental laws. *See also: Air pollutants; Heavy metals; Soil contaminants; Water pollutants*

2. An octane enhancer in fuels. *See: Tetraethyl lead*

Leadership in Energy and Environmental Design (LEED)   A widely accepted benchmark for the design, construction, and operation of high-performance green buildings, established by the US Green Building Council in 1996. LEED emphasizes performance in six areas: sustainable site development; water savings; energy efficiency; materials selection; indoor environmental quality; and innovation. It provides a measure of sustainability for buildings and sites. *See also: Building Research Establishment Environmental Assessment Method (BREEAM);*

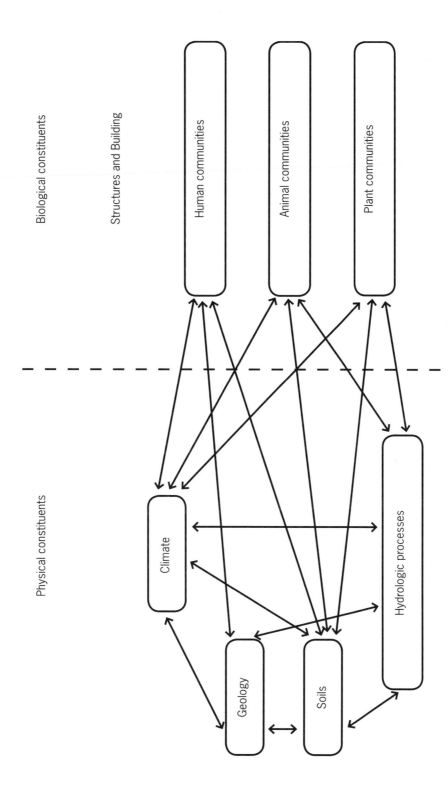

Biological constituents

Structures and Building

Human communities

Animal communities

Plant communities

Physical constituents

Climate

Geology

Soils

Hydrologic processes

Figure 41 Interactions between the layers within the ecosystem (the physical and biological constituents) in the layer-cake model

Comprehensive Assessment System for Building Environmental Efficiency (CASBEE); Green building rating systems; Green Globes

Lemna gibba   Popularly known as duck weed. Species of small, free-floating plant used to determine the toxicity of pollutants to aquatic plant life. Duck weed is normally found in waters contaminated with sewage.

Lentic waters   Ponds or lakes.

Lethe   A measure of air purity that is equal to one complete air change (in an interior space).

Levee   Natural or human-made earthen barrier along the edge of a stream, lake, or river. Used as a protection against flooding.

Liebig's law   Also known as the law of the minimum. Proposed by German chemist Justus von Liebig in the 1800s, this principle asserts that the existence, abundance, or distribution of a population is limited by the physical or chemical factor that is in shortest supply relative to the level required by those organisms. That short supply limits the growth of a species' population. Liebig is commonly known as the "father of the fertilizer industry", and his research was carried out primarily on plants. He found that any deficiency of a nutrient, no matter how small an amount is needed, will hold back plant development. If the deficient element is supplied, growth will be increased up to the point where the supply of that element is no longer the limiting factor. Increasing the supply beyond this point is not helpful, as some other element would then be in a minimum supply and become the limiting factor. The concept of the law of the minimum has been modified as additional elements have proved to be essential in plant nutrition. It has been extended to include other factors such as moisture, temperature, insect control, light, plant population, and genetic capacities of plant varieties.

Life cycle   (Architecture) The total life of a project: design, development, construction or production, marketing, transportation, use, and disposal.

Life-cycle assessment (LCA)   Also known as life-cycle analysis, life-cycle inventory, cradle-to-grave-analysis, or dust-to-dust energy cost. The assessment of the environmental impact of a given product or service throughout its life-span. The goal of LCA is to compare the environmental performance of products and services and to select the one that does the least amount of damage. The concept also can be used to get the best environmental performance of a single product. *See also:* **Life cycle**

Life-cycle cost   Total recurring and nonrecurring dollar cost of a product, structure, system, or service during its life span or specified time period.

Light beam radiation   *See: Direct radiation*

Light nonaqueous-phase liquid (LNAPL)
Contaminant of groundwater. LNAPL is a non-aqueous-phase liquid with a specific gravity less than 1.0. Most LNAPLs float on top of the water table. The most common are petroleum hydrocarbon fuels and lubricating oils. Contamination of groundwater by nonaqueous-phase liquids (NAPL) is a major environmental problem in the USA and worldwide. Common organic contaminants include trichloroethylene, tetrachloroethylene, trichloroethane, carbon tetrachloride, and gasoline. Generally, organic-phase contaminants are categorized as either LNAPLs or dense nonaqueous-phase liquids (DNAPLs), depending on their density relative to that of water. Petroleum hydrocarbons, which have a density lighter than water, are classified as LNAPLs, while chlorinated solvents, which have a density heavier than water, are classified as DNAPLs.

LNAPL contaminants usually migrate downward through unsaturated zones in the Earth's subsurface, and pool when they reach the water table. Once in the subsurface, an LNAPL source can either spread due to advection, be trapped in pores, or dissolve to form a downstream plume of contaminant in the aqueous phase. Light contaminants tend to remain at the capillary fringe, which benefits remediation because the contamination source can often be effectively targeted using techniques such as vapor extraction, vacuum extraction, and various pump-and-treat methods. *See also: Dense nonaqueous-phase liquid; Nonaqueous-phase liquid*

Light pipe A passive mode daylight system, a horizontal pipe using highly reflective material at the external wall of a building and diffusing film along the pipe. This allows the pipe to transmit adequate ambient daylight to areas that are quite distant from windows. The light pipe has been shown to perform more efficiently throughout the year than the light shelf. *See also: Light shelf*

Light pollution Caused by the upward and outward distribution of light directly from artificial lighting fixtures or from reflection off the ground or other surfaces of the built environment. The effects are light glare, light trespasses, sky glow, and wasted energy. Light pollution disrupts ecosystems, can cause adverse health effects, obscures the stars for city dwellers, and interferes with astronomical observatories. It falls into two main categories: i) annoying light that intrudes on an otherwise natural or low light setting; ii) excessive light, generally indoors, that leads to worker discomfort and adverse health effects. Since the early 1980s, a global dark-sky movement has emerged, with people campaigning to reduce the amount of light pollution. Light pollution is a side effect of industrial civilization. Its sources include building exterior and interior lighting, advertising, commercial properties, offices, factories, streetlights, and illuminated sporting venues. It is most severe in

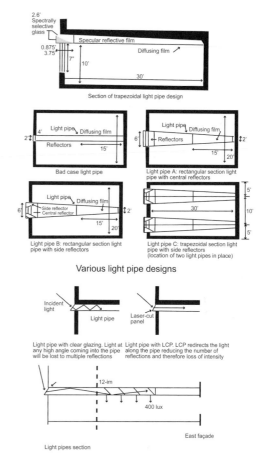

Passive-mode daylight systems: light pipe

Light pipe building integration

Figure 42 A light pipe (passive mode daylight system

highly industrialized, densely populated areas of North America, Europe, and Japan, but even relatively small amounts of light can be noticed and create problems. *See also:* **Sky glow**

Light quality   In an architectural context, a description of how well people in a lighted space can see to do visual tasks and how visually comfortable they feel in that space.

Light shelf   A passive mode daylight system, a light shelf is a horizontal light-reflecting overhang placed above eye level with a transom window placed above it. This design, which is most effective in southern orientations, improves daylight penetration, creates shading near the window, and helps reduce window glare. Exterior light shelves are more effective shading devices than interior shelves. A combination of exterior and interior will work best in providing an even illumination gradient. *See also:* **Light pipe**

Linear low-density polyethylene (LLPE)
Nonbiodegradable plastic used for packaging and trash bags.

Liquefied natural gas (LNG)   Natural gas that has been converted to liquid form so that it can be stored on board a vehicle in a smaller volume. To produce LNG, natural gas is purified and condensed into liquid by cooling to –260 °F (–162 °C). At atmospheric pressure, LNG occupies only 1/600 the volume of natural gas in vapor form. A gasoline gallon equivalent (GGE) equals about 1.5 gallons of LNG. Because it must be kept at such cold temperatures, LNG is stored in double-wall, vacuum-insulated pressure vessels. LNG fuel systems typically are only used with heavy-duty vehicles. The cooling process and cryogenic tanks make LNG expensive. Use of LPN in place of petroleum fuel produces fewer polluting emissions. According to research by the US Department of Energy, vehicles that use LNG (like its counterpart compressed natural gas, CNG) emit 50–75% less nonmethane hydrocarbons, 25% less carbon dioxide, 90–97% less carbon monoxide, and 35–60% less nitrogen oxide. CNG has a lower cost of production and storage compared with LNG, but CNG requires a much larger volume to store the same mass of natural gas, and the use of very high pressures. *See also:* **Compressed natural gas; Gasoline gallon equivalent**

Liquefied petroleum gas   *See:* **Propane**

Lithic   Associated with stones and rock.

Lithosphere   The solid, outermost part of the Earth, including the crust and uppermost mantle. The lithosphere is about 100 km (62 miles) thick, although its thickness is age-dependent (older lithosphere is thicker). The lithosphere below the crust is brittle enough at some locations to produce earthquakes by faulting, such as within a subducted oceanic plate. There are two types of lithosphere: oceanic lithosphere, associated with oceanic crust; and continental lithosphere, associated with continental crust.

Lithotroph   Type of bacteria that can obtain metabolically useful energy from the oxidation

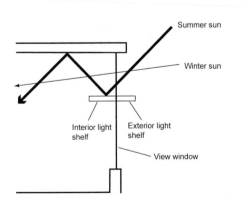

Figure 43 A light shelf preventing glare close to the window and reflecting light deep into the room

of inorganic chemicals, including ammonium, nitrite, iron, and sulfur. *See also:* **Autotroph; Heterotroph**

Living machine   Refers to natural biological sewage treatment plants that mimic the processes found in wetland environments. Botanic purifying systems that use plants, fish, bacteria and snails to purify water on site to potable standards. These systems can be integrated into water-reuse systems that minimize energy, provide nitrification and good nitrogen removal, eliminate most of the residual biosolids, eliminate clarifiers, and allow tertiary treatment for water reuse. They can be used in industrial facilities, resorts, and communities, and for agricultural operations.

LLPE   *See: Linear low-density polyethylene*

LNAPL   *See: Light nonaqueous-phase liquid*

LNG   *See: Liquefied natural gas*

Load   The power required to run a defined circuit or system, such as a refrigerator, a building, or an entire electricity distribution system.

Load shedding   Turning off or disconnecting loads to limit peak demand.

Locally unwanted land uses (LULU)   Position of residents who oppose land uses such as toxic waste dumps, landfills, incinerators, airports, or freeways close to their homes. Also known as "not in my back yard" (NIMBY).

London Agreement   1990 amendment to the 1987 Montreal Protocol, an international agreement to regulate and decrease ozone depleting sources. The London Agreement of 1990 stipulated that the production and consumption of compounds that deplete ozone in the stratosphere—chlorofluorocarbons (CFCs), halon (bromofluorocarbons), carbon tetrachloride, and methyl chloroform—were to be phased out by 2000 (2005 for methyl chloroform). *See also:* **Montreal Protocol on Substances that Deplete the Ozone Layer**

Longitude   Distance east or west on the Earth's surface measured as an arc of the equator in degrees up to 180.

Loose-fill insulation   Insulation made from rockwool fibers, fiberglass, cellulose fiber, vermiculite or perlite minerals, and composed of loose fibers or granules; can be applied by pouring directly from the bag or with a blower.

Lotic waters   Flowing waters, as in streams and rivers.

Low-carbon design   *See: Zero-carbon design*

Low-density polyethylene (LDPE) Nonbiodegradable plastic used for bottles, bags, films, and plastic wrapping.

Low-emissivity windows and (window) films Commonly called "low-e windows". These energy-efficient windows have a coating or film applied to the surface of the glass to reduce heat transfer through the window. This film is normally positioned on the inside surface of a double-pane window, as the low-e surface material can easily be scratched or degraded. The low-e coated glass side should be placed on the "warm" side of the window. In hot climates, the low-e side should be oriented to the outside of the structure; in cold climates, the low-e side should be on the glass pane in the interior space. Double-low-e windows have a low-e surface coating on both panes and can be effective in both cold and warm conditions.

Low-flush toilet   A toilet that uses less water than a standard one during flushing, for the purpose of conserving water resources.

Low-impact development Sustainable landscaping that can be used to replicate or restore natural watershed functions and/or address targeted watershed goals.

Low-slope roof Roof surface with a maximum slope of 2 inches rise for 12 inches (5/30.5 cm) run.

Low-throughput economy Economy based on working with nature by recycling and reusing materials and resources, preventing pollution, conserving resources and matter, living within a population's capacity to carry itself in an environment while maintaining biodiversity. *See also: High-throughput economy*

Lower atmosphere Also known as the troposphere layer, which affects most of the people on Earth; extends roughly 5 miles (8km) above the poles and 10 miles (16 km) above the equator, and contains about 75% of the total mass of the atmosphere. Because of its closeness to the Earth's surface, nearly all water vapor and solid particles (from forest fires, volcanoes, and the burning of fossil fuel, for example) are found in this sphere. All of Earth's plant and animal life exists within the troposphere or the waters beneath it.

LPG Liquefied petroleum gas. *See: Propane*

LULU *See: Locally unwanted land uses*

Lumen One lumen equals one candela across one steradian, and is a measure of luminous flux, which is adjusted to the human eye's perception of the light's power. Lighting efficiency or efficacy is measured in lumens per watt. Incandescents typically have an efficacy in the range 15–20 lm/watt. Ultra-high efficacy lighting can achieve over 120 lm/watt.

Lumen method Most common method of daylighting analysis in the USA. Variables are sky conditions, position of the Sun, room size, glazing area, and transmission characteristics such as overhangs, shades, and blinds. This calculation is limited to predicting the amount of illumination on a centerline five feet (1.5 m) from the window, five feet from the back wall, and at a point midway between.

M

Maglev *See: Magnetic levitation*

Magnesium oxide (MgO) cement A cement-like material that produces much lower carbon dioxide (CO_2) emissions than Portland cement. It uses MgO rather than calcium oxide, together with a lower-carbon method of obtaining the MgO. As CO_2 is a major greenhouse gas, it is beneficial to the environment to reduce its emission whenever possible. MgO cement is also a good industrial binder.

Magnetic levitation Also known as maglev or magnetic suspension. Alternative propulsion system for transportation, particularly trains. A method by which an object is suspended above another object with no support other than magnetic fields. The electromagnetic force is used to counteract the effects of the gravitational force. Maglev suspends, guides, and propels vehicles via electromagnetic force. This method can be faster than wheeled mass transit systems, potentially reaching velocities comparable with turboprop and jet aircraft (500 km/h; 310 mph). The maximum recorded speed of a maglev train is 581km/h (360 mph), achieved in Japan in 2003. The first commercial Maglev was opened in 1984 in Birmingham, UK, covering some 600 meters (1968 feet) between its airport and rail hub, but was closed in 1995 because of technical problems. The only currently operating high-speed maglev line of note is the initial operating segment demonstration line of the German-built Transrapid train in Shanghai, China, which transports people 30 km (18.6 miles) to the airport in just 7 minutes 20 seconds, achieving a top velocity of 431 km/h (268 mph), averaging 250 km/h (150 mph).

There are two primary types of maglev technology: i) electromagnetic suspension (EMS), which uses the attractive magnetic force of a magnet beneath a rail to lift the train up; and ii) electrodynamic suspension (EDS), which uses a repulsive force between two magnetic fields to push the train away from the rail. In current EMS systems, the train levitates above a steel rail while electromagnets, attached to the train, are oriented toward the rail from below. The electromagnets use feedback control to maintain a train at a constant distance from the track, at approximately 15 mm (0.6 inches).

In EDS, both rail and train exert a magnetic field and the train is levitated by the repulsive force between these magnetic fields. The magnetic field in the train is produced by either electromagnets (as in JR-Maglev) or by an array of permanent magnets (as in Inductrack). The repulsive force in the track is created by an induced magnetic field in wires or other conducting strips in the track. At slow speeds, the current induced in these coils and the resultant magnetic flux is not large enough to support the weight of the train. For this reason, the train must have wheels or some other form of landing gear to support it until it reaches a speed that can sustain levitation. Propulsion coils on the guideway are used to exert a force on the magnets in the train and make it move forward. The

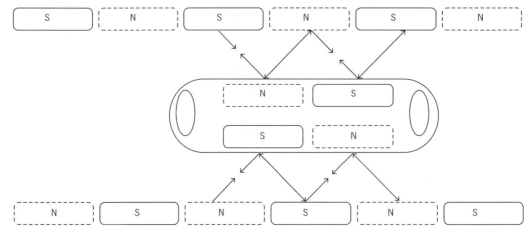

Figure 44 Electrodynamic suspension
Source: Wikipedia

propulsion coils that exert a force on the train are effectively a linear motor: an alternating current flowing through the coils generates a continuously varying magnetic field that moves forward along the track. The frequency of the alternating current is synchronized to match the speed of the train. The offset between the field exerted by magnets on the train and the applied field creates a force, moving the train forward.

Maize   *See: Corn*

Make-up air   Air brought into a building from outside to replace exhaust air.

Management of outputs   Design strategies to manage materials and energy in the built form and its servicing systems. There are four design strategies: one-through, open-circuit, closed-circuit, and combined open-circuit. *See also: Closed-circuit system design strategy; Combined open-circuit system design strategy; Once-through system design strategy; Open-circuit system design strategy*

Manual D   Manual developed by the Air Conditioning Contractors of America (ACCA) which covers designing and sizing duct systems for residential and commercial space.

Manual J   The standard method for calculating residential cooling loads developed by the Air Conditioning Contractors of America (ACCA).

Manual N   Standard method for calculating commercial cooling loads developed by the Air Conditioning Contractors of America (ACCA).

Mariculture   Cultivation of marine organisms for use as a food resource.

Marsh   *See: Wetlands*

Masonry stove   A type of heating appliance similar to a fireplace, but much more efficient and clean-burning. Made of masonry and has long channels through which combustion gases give up their heat to the heavy mass of the stove, which releases the heat slowly into a room. Often called a Russian or Finnish fireplace.

Mass mixing ratio   (Chemical engineering) Mass of water vapor per unit mass of dry air. *See also: Absolute humidity*

Materials cycle Natural cycle in which materials are used, decomposed, and returned to the ecosystem to be used again. In humanmade materials cycles, materials are used, recycled, and reused. In both systems, waste is minimized or eliminated. *See also: Aerated static pile*

Materials flow analysis Calculation of the transfer of natural and manufactured materials, resources, and capital out of a built system compared with those flowing in. Also examines the stocks, flows, and transformation of energy and materials within the systems. Assesses sustainability, cost savings, improved regulations, and infrastructure and economic activity.

Matter-recycling economy Economy based on recycling as many materials and resources as possible, to allow economic growth to continue without depleting resources or producing excessive pollution of the environment.

MCFC *See: Molten carbonate fuel cell*

Mechanical and electrical systems *See: HVAC Heating, ventilation, and air-conditioning*

Mechanical waste separator Device that separates waste by category for recycling.

Mechanical recovery system More complex version of the mechanical waste separator (see Figure 46).

Mechanically stabilized earth Combination of soil, soil reinforcement, and facing panels that increase the strength of soil in order to support built structures such as roadways, bridges, retaining walls and noise barriers. The soil reinforcement consists of horizontal layers of metallic or geosynthetic materials.

Mechanically ventilated crawlspace system System designed to increase ventilation within a

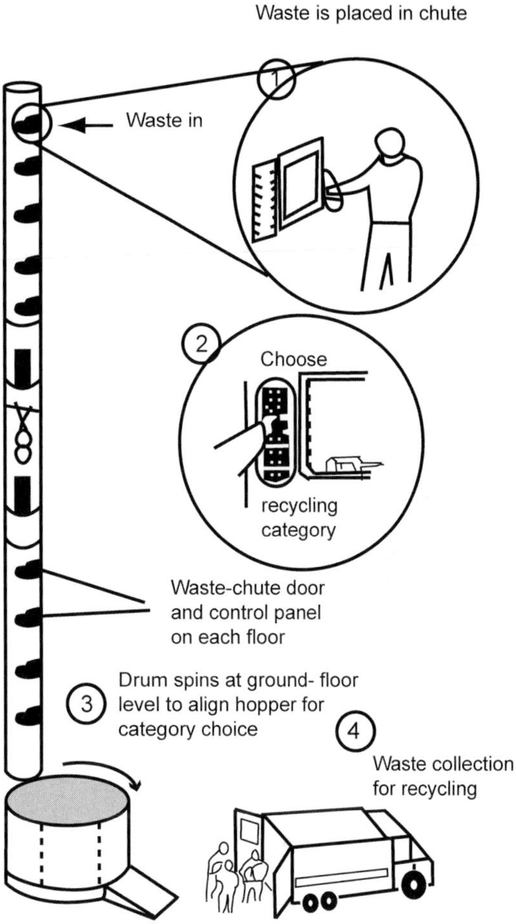

Waste is placed in chute

Waste in

①

② Choose
recycling category

Waste-chute door and control panel on each floor

③ Drum spins at ground-floor level to align hopper for category choice

④ Waste collection for recycling

Figure 45 A mechanical waste separator

crawlspace, achieve higher air pressure in the crawlspace relative to air pressure in the soil beneath the crawlspace, or achieve lower air pressure in the crawlspace relative to air pressure in the living spaces, by use of a fan.

Medium-temperature solar collector Functions like an indirect solar water heating system, but is used for heating built space. It has a larger collector array area, larger storage units, and a more complex control system. It can also be adapted to provide solar water heating, and can supply 30–70% of residential heating requirements.

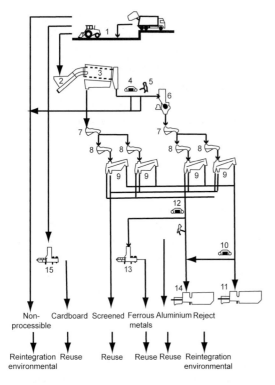

1. Tipping floor
2. Feeder
3. Rotary screen
4. Magnet
5. Visual control
6. Shredder
7. Flow divider
8. Flow spreader
9. Ballistic classifier
10. Magnet
11. Static packer
12. Magnet
13. Bailer
14. Static compacter
15. Bailer

Figure 46 A mechanical recovery system

This type of solar collector will raise the heat transfer fluid to 20–150 °F (–6.7 to +66 °C) above ambient. Applications can include domestic hot water and space heating. *See also: **Indirect solar water heater***

Megawatt (MW)   1000 kilowatts or 1 million watts. Standard measure of electric power plant power-generating capacity.

Membrane   A permeable layer in a fuel cell that acts as an electrolyte as well as a barrier film separating the gases in the anode and cathode compartments of the fuel cell. *See also: **Fuel cells***

MEPS   *See: Molded expanded polystyrene*

Mercury (Hg)   Air pollutant and soil contaminant. Heavy metal. A naturally occurring element in the Earth's crust. Commonly found in air, water, and soil, and exists in several forms: elemental or metallic mercury, inorganic mercury compounds, and organic mercury compounds. When coal is burned, mercury is released into the environment. Fossil fuel power plants, especially coal-fired plants, generate the greatest mercury emissions to the air in the USA, accounting for over 40% of all domestic human-caused mercury emissions. Municipal waste incinerators are also a large source of mercury emissions. Burning hazardous wastes, producing chlorine, breaking mercury products, and spilling mercury, as well as the improper treatment and disposal of products or wastes containing mercury, can also release it into the environment. Mercury tends to accumulate in the food chain. Mercury exposure at high levels can harm the brain, heart, kidneys, lungs, and immune system of people of all ages. *See also: **Air pollution; Heavy metals; Soil contaminants***

Mesophyte   Plants that require only moderate amounts of water for growth.

Mesosphere   Atmospheric layer above the stratosphere and below the thermosphere. It is the middle layer and lies 31–50 miles (17–80 km) above the Earth's surface. Temperatures are usually very low. *See also: **Mesosphere; Stratosphere; Troposphere***

Mesotrophic   Pertaining to a lake or other body of water characterized by moderate nutrient concentrations and moderate productivity in terms of aquatic animal and plant life. *See also: Eutrophic; Oligotrophic*

Metabolite   Compound produced from human digestion of contaminants; serves as biomarker of exposure.

Metal   Natural mineral resource with the characteristic of good conductivity of electricity and heat.

Metal-insulator-semiconductor   (MIS)   New generation of solar cell in which the inner electrical field is produced by the junction of a thin oxide layer to a semiconductor.

Methane (CH$_4$)   Air pollutant and toxic chemical. A hydrocarbon that is a greenhouse gas with global warming impact estimated to be 20 times greater than that of carbon dioxide (CO$_2$). It reacts with the Sun's radiation and other chemical compounds to form ozone (O$_3$). Methane is produced through anaerobic decomposition of waste in landfill, animal digestion, decomposition of animal wastes, production and distribution of natural gas and petroleum, coal production, and incomplete fossil fuel combustion.

Methane and CO$_2$ are the main constituents of landfill gas, which is the greatest contributor of atmospheric methane. Consequently, it has a significant impact on global warming and climate change.

Methane is also a primary constituent of natural gas and an important energy source. As a result, efforts to utilize methane emissions can provide significant energy, economic, and environmental benefits. *See also: Air pollutants; Landfill gas; Ozone precursors; Toxic chemicals*

Methane hydrates   A natural gas located below marine hydrate deposits. It is being researched to allow commercial production of methane from hydrate deposits. As it is believed to have the potential to provide clean energy, new technology is being developed to ensure safe drilling and to minimize the impact on seafloor stability and deep-sea life. More research is needed to understand the role hydrate plays in climate change and the carbon cycle.

A methane hydrate is a cage-like lattice of ice, inside which are trapped molecules of methane (the chief constituent of natural gas). (The name for its parent class of compounds, "clathrates", comes from the Latin word meaning "to enclose with bars".)

Methane hydrates generally form in two types of geological setting: i) on land in permafrost regions where cold temperatures persist in shallow sediments; ii) beneath the ocean floor at water depths greater than about 500 m (about 1640 feet), where high pressures dominate. The hydrate deposits themselves may be several hundred meters thick.

Today, methane hydrate has been detected around most continental margins. Around the USA, large deposits have been identified and studied in Alaska, the west coast of California to Washington, the east coast offshore of the Carolinas and in the Gulf of Mexico. Worldwide estimates of the natural gas potential of methane hydrate approach 400 million trillion cubic feet. If just 1% of the methane hydrate could be recoverable, the USA could more than double its domestic natural gas resource base. It is a viewed as a feasible alternative to fossil fuels. Natural gas requires relatively low capital costs to build new natural gas-fired equipment.

Methanol (CH$_3$OH)   Also known as methyl alcohol or wood alcohol. Liquid fuel formed by catalytically combining carbon monoxide (CO) with hydrogen in a 1:2 ratio under high temperature and pressure. Methanol is an alternative fuel. Commercially, it is usually manufactured by steam reforming natural gas. It is also formed in the distillation of wood. It is usually combined with gasoline to form M85 (85% methanol and 15% gasoline), and is used in dual-fuel vehicles. Methanol can also be used to make methyl tertiary butyl ether (MTBE), an oxygenate that is blended with gasoline to enhance octane and create cleaner-burning fuel.

Methanotrophs   Bacteria that use methane as food and oxidize it into carbon dioxide.

Methyl alcohol   *See: Methanol*

Methyl bromide (MeBr)   Toxic chemical. A class I ozone-depleting substance. It is an odorless, colorless gas used as an agricultural soil and structural fumigant to control a wide variety of pests. *See also: **Toxic chemicals***

Methyl chloride (CH_3Cl)   Toxic chemical. Combining methanol and hydrochloric acid gives methyl chloride and water: $CH_3OH + HCl \rightarrow CH_3Cl + H_2O$. USEPA has classified methyl chloride as a group D carcinogen. Low levels of methyl chloride occur naturally in the environment. Higher levels may occur at chemical plants where it is made or used. It has been found to have adverse health affects in humans. *See also: **Toxic chemicals***

Methyl tertiary butyl ether (MTBE)   Toxic carcinogenic chemical. Fuel oxygenate used as an additive to gasoline to increase octane and reduce engine knock. According to USEPA, MTBE has been detected in groundwater in the USA, sometimes contaminating drinking water. *See also: **Toxic chemicals***

Metropolitan area   A core with a large population nucleus, together with adjacent communities that have a high degree of economic and social integration with that core.

MFC   *See: Microbial fuel cell*

Micro-compact automobile   Micro-compact car designed primarily for urban use in European cities, where parking is scarce and fuel economy is of great importance. For example, the Smart fortwo's length of only 8 ft (2.4 m) allows as many as three of the vehicles to be parked in the space normally taken by one standard-length car. *See also: **Smart fortwo car***

Micro-irrigation   *See: Drip irrigation*

Microbial   Refers to microorganisms including bacteria, protozoa, yeasts, molds, viruses, and algae.

Microbial fuel cell (MFC)   Fuel cell that uses the catalytic reaction of microorganisms such as bacteria to convert virtually any organic material into fuel. Some common compounds include glucose, acetate, and wastewater. Enclosed in oxygen-free anodes, the organic compounds are consumed (oxidized) by the bacteria or other microbes. As part of the digestive process, electrons are pulled from the compound and conducted into a circuit with the help of an inorganic mediator. MFCs operate well in mild conditions relative to other types of fuel cell (such as 20–40 °C (68–104 °F)), and could be capable of producing over 50% efficiency. These cells are suitable for small-scale applications such as potential medical devices fueled by glucose in the blood, or larger applications such as water treatment plants or breweries producing organic waste that could then be used to fuel the MFCs.

Microbial pathogen   Any disease-producing agent or microorganism. Listed by USEPA as major water pollutants, microbial pathogens include certain types of bacteria, viruses, protozoa, and other organisms. Some pathogens are often found in water, frequently as a result of fecal matter from sewage discharges, leaking septic tanks, or runoff from animal feedlots into bodies of water. *See also:* **Water pollutants**

Microbiologicals   *See: Biological contaminants*

Microclimate   The local climate of specific place or habitat, as influenced by landscape features.

Microturbine   Low-emission power generators used in hybrid electric vehicles, distributed generation and micro-cogeneration.

Mill tailings   Sand-like material residue obtained when separating uranium from its ore. More than 99% of the ore becomes tailings. Tailings typically contain about 85% of the radioactivity present in unprocessed ore.

Mineral wool   *See: Rock wool*

MIS   *See: Metal-insulator-semiconductor*

Mitigation   Reduction of adverse effects. Environmentally, decreasing harmful impacts on the environment.

Mixed artificial ecosystem   Type of ecodesign site type. Mixed ecosystems that are artificially maintained by humans through crop rotation, agroforestry, parks, and gardens. These are compromised areas—where the natural ecosystem components are out of balance and the ecosystem requires artificial means to keep functioning—with a combination of productive and protective areas. *See also:* **Ecodesign site types**

Mixed-mode design   Ecodesign strategy that specifies low-energy design. Requires an understanding of the climate of the building site in order to design the most effective energy-efficient system. Dependent on benign interaction between the structure's interior and exterior ambient forces. Strategies include natural lighting, passive solar systems, ventilation, secondary glass skin, active and interactive walls (see Figure 47). *See also:* **Full mode design; Passive mode design; Productive mode design**

Mixing layer   Area near the surface where air is well mixed from turbulence caused by the interaction of the Earth's surface and atmosphere. The mixing layer is usually located at the base of a temperature inversion.

Modular systems   *See: Biomass electricity*

Modular construction   Prefabricated construction using standardized units.

Molded expanded polystyrene (MEPS) Fabricated foam core panel used as structural wall panel.

Molten carbonate fuel cell (MCFC)   Fuel cell that uses a molten carbonate salt mixture, usually lithium carbonate and potassium carbonate, as its electrolyte. The electrolyte is suspended in a ceramic matrix. The anode is a nickel–chromium alloy; the cathode is a lithium-doped nickel oxide. MCFCs operate at very high temperatures, 600–800 °C (1112–1472 °F). These high temperatures allow MCFCs to convert more energy-dense fuels to hydrogen within the fuel cell itself. It does not need an external reformer, thereby reducing costs. This characteristic separates it from alkaline, phosphoric acid, and polymer electrolyte membrane fuel cells. High-temperature MCFCs can extract hydrogen from a variety of fuels using either an internal or an external reformer. They are also less prone to carbon monoxide "poisoning" than lower-temperature fuel cells, which makes coal-based fuels more attractive for this type of fuel cell. MCFCs work

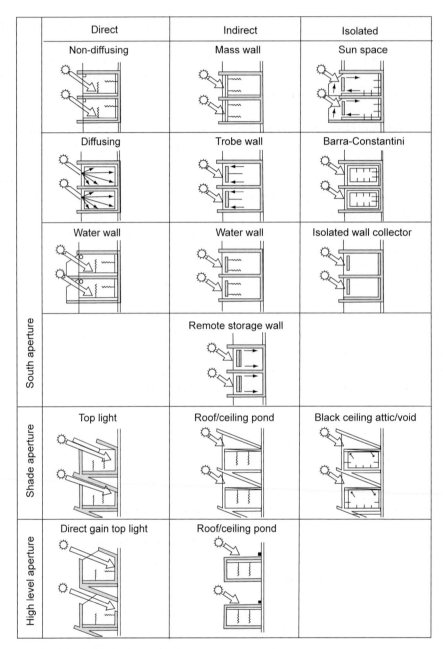

Figure 47 Mixed-mode design using various generic passive solar systems

well with catalysts made of nickel, which is much less expensive than platinum. MCFCs exhibit up to 60% efficiency, and this can rise to 80% if the waste heat is utilized for cogeneration.

Two major difficulties with molten carbonate technology put it at a disadvantage compared with solid oxide cells: one is the complexity of working with a liquid electrolyte rather than a solid; the other stems from the chemical reaction inside a molten carbonate cell. Carbonate ions from the electrolyte are used up in the reactions at the anode, making it necessary to compensate by injecting carbon dioxide at the cathode. In addition, the electrolyte used in MCFCs is highly corrosive, limiting some of its potential applications. MCFCs are used for natural gas- and coal-based power plants for electrical utility, industrial, and military applications. *See also: Fuel cells*

Monitoring   Regulatory surveillance to determine compliance with legal or code requirements. For example, USEPA monitors toxic levels in air, water, and soil.

Monoculture   Agricultural cultivation of one crop rather than diverse types of crop. This often results in crop vulnerability to insect pests, requiring an increase in the use of pesticides, pollution from which seeps into the groundwater.

Monoculture ecosystem   Design site classification measured by the condition of ecosystem characteristics and features. Ecosystems used for agricultural purposes, but whose ecological succession is limited by human controls to maintain high levels of productivity. *See also: Ecodesign site types*

Montmorillonite   Main constituent of the volcanic ash product bentonite. It is used in oil drilling as a soil additive to hold water because of its clay-like water-swelling properties.

Montreal Protocol on Substances that Deplete the Ozone Layer   International agreement designed to protect the stratospheric ozone layer by phasing out production of substances that cause ozone depletion. The Montreal Protocol, which supplemented the Vienna Convention for the Protection of the Ozone Layer (Vienna, 1985), was originally signed in 1987 and became effective on January 1, 1989. It was signed by 29 countries in Montreal. The Protocol is designed to regulate the production and consumption of ozone-depleting substances. The signatories agreed to reduce production and consumption of CFCs by half by 1998 and to freeze production and consumption of halons by 1992. Developing countries were granted a 10-year grace period to meet their obligations.

The Protocol has been substantially amended five times, in 1990 (London), 1992 (Copenhagen), 1995 (Vienna), 1997 (Montreal), and 1999 (Beijing). The London Agreement of 1990 stipulated that the production and consumption of compounds that deplete ozone in the stratosphere—chlorofluorocarbons (CFCs), halon (bromofluorocarbons), carbon tetrachloride, and methyl chloroform—were to be phased out by 2000 (2005 for methyl chloroform). *See also: Ozone-depleting substance*

Movable insulation   A device that reduces heat loss at night and during cloudy periods, and reduces heat gain during the day in warm weather. A movable insulator could be an insulating shade, shutter panel, or curtain.

MTBE   *See: Methyl tertiary butyl ether*

Mulch   Layer of material, such as wood chips, straw, or leaves, placed around plants to hold moisture, prevent weed growth, and enrich the soil.

Muellerian mimicry   Evolution of two species, both of which are unpalatable and have defensive mechanisms, to resemble each other. *See: Batesian mimicry*

Multijunction   One of the basic types of photovoltaic device. *See also: Photovoltaic device*

Murocaust   Similar to a hypocaust, except that a massive wall with air channels is used, and the air flow is vertical instead of horizontal. *See also: Hypocaust*

Mutualism   Type of symbiosis in which both members of the partnership benefit. *See also: Amensalism; Commensalism; Parasitism; Symbiosis*

MW   *See: Megawatt*

Mycorrhizal fungi   Inhabit the root systems of trees, and pump soil nutrients into the roots. These fungi also protect plants from other harmful fungi; they knit the soil together to prevent erosion; and they influence which plants will grow in a particular area.

N

Nanocrystal solar cell   A third-generation solar cell, developed in 2005 at the US Department of Energy's Lawrence Berkeley National Laboratory in conjunction with University of California at Berkeley. It is the first ultra-thin solar cell comprised entirely of inorganic nanocrystals, and spin-cast from solution. The cost and manufacture are comparable with solar cells made from organic polymers. They are more stable in air because they contain no organic materials. They combine the properties of organics with the ability to retain the broadband absorption and superior transport properties of traditional photovoltaic semiconductors. They have the cost-reduction potential that has made organic cells a viable alternative to conventional semiconductor counterparts. Rod-shaped nanometer-sized crystals of two semiconductors, cadmium–selenide (CdSe) and cadmium–telluride (CdTe), are synthesized separately and then dissolved in solution and spin-cast onto a conductive glass substrate. The resulting films, which are about 1000 times thinner than a human hair, have comparable conversion efficiencies as the best organic solar cells. It is still substantially lower than conventional silicon solar cell thin film.

Unlike conventional semiconductor solar cells, in which an electrical current flows between layers of n-type and p-type semiconductor films, with these new inorganic nanocrystal solar cells, current flows due to a pair of molecules that serve as donors and receptors of electrical charges, also known as a donor–acceptor heterojunction. This is the same mechanism by which current flows in plastic solar cells. The two semiconductor films are electrical insulators in the dark, but when exposed to sunlight they undergo a rise in electrical conductivity, as much as three times more. Sintering the nanocrystals was found to significantly enhance the performance of these films. Unlike plastic solar cells, performance of which deteriorates over time, aging seems to improve the performance of these inorganic nanocrystal solar cells. According to the Energy Foundation, if the available residential and commercial rooftops in the USA were to be coated with solar cell thin films, they could furnish an estimated 710,000 MW of electricity across the country, which is more than three-quarters of all the electricity that the USA is currently able to generate.

Nanoenergy   Use of nanomaterials—typically on the scale of billionths of a meter, or 10,000 times smaller than a human hair—to design materials with properties tailored to specific needs, such as strong, lightweight materials, new lubricants, and more efficient solar energy cells. By building structures one atom at a time, the materials may have enhanced mechanical, optical, electrical, or catalytic properties. *See also: Nanotechnology*

Nanometer   Distance measure equivalent to one billionth of 1 meter.

Nanotechnology   Field of applied science that deals with the control of matter on an atomic and molecular scale. Generally, nanotechnology deals with materials or devices approximately 100 nanometers or smaller. Nanotechnology is a multidisciplinary field, including applied physics, materials science, interface and colloid science, device physics, supramolecular chemistry (referring to the area of chemistry that focuses on the noncovalent bonding interactions of molecules), self-replicating machines and robotics, chemical engineering, mechanical engineering, biological engineering, and electrical engineering. Grouping of the sciences under the umbrella of "nanotechnology" has been questioned on the basis that there is little actual boundary-crossing between the sciences that operate on the nano-scale. Instrumentation is the only area of technology common to all disciplines. There is ongoing research to determine future applications of various fields of nanotechnology, as well as the health safety of nanoproducts. *See also: Nanocrystal solar cell*

Naphtha jet fuel   Common jet fuel used in civilian aviation. Fuel in naphtha–kerosene is used to enhance cold-weather performance. It is known as JET B and has a lighter composition than an unleaded/paraffin oil-based fuel classified as JET A-1, which is produced to international specifications. JET B's lighter composition makes it more dangerous to handle, so it is restricted only to areas where its cold-weather characteristics are absolutely necessary. *See also: Kerosene-type jet fuel; Jet fuel*

NAPL   *See: Nonaqueous-phase liquid*

National Electrical Code (NEC)   Guidelines for all types of electrical installation. From 1984, the NEC has contained Article 690, "Solar Photovoltaic Systems", which provides instructions on installing photovoltaic systems.

National Energy Modeling System   Computer-based model created by the Energy Information Administration division of the US Department of Energy. The system is a model of energy markets through 2025, and projects energy, economic, environmental, and security impacts of US energy policies and energy markets. This model is particularly helpful for long-range planning, public policy implementation, and energy legislation.

National Energy Policy   Developed in 2001 in the USA, its three principles are: provide a long-term, comprehensive energy strategy; advance new, environmentally friendly technologies to increase energy supplies and encourage cleaner, more efficient energy use; and integrate energy, environmental, and economic policies.

National Environmental Policy Act   Passed by US Congress in 1970, the Act seeks to protect the environment, and requires that environmental factors are considered when federal agencies make decisions.

Native   Indigenous to a specific area or region.

Natural   Indigenous or untouched by civilization.

Natural cooling   Space cooling achieved by shading, natural (unassisted, as opposed to forced) ventilation, conduction control, radiation, and evaporation. *See also: Passive cooling systems*

Natural draft   Draft (air movement) caused by temperature differences in the air.

Natural gas   Underground deposits of gases. Mixture of hydrocarbons and small quantities of various nonhydrocarbons in the gaseous phase or in solution with crude oil in natural underground reservoirs. Natural gas consists of 50–90% methane (CH_4) and small amounts of heavier gaseous hydrocarbon compounds such as propane (C_3H_8) and butane (C_4H_{10}). Natural gas is clean-burning and produces fewer harmful emissions than reformulated gasoline or diesel. *See also: Compressed natural gas; Liquefied natural gas*

Natural gas car   Automobile powered by natural gas or propane; does not emit carcinogenic particles and produces fewer emissions that are harmful to the environment. *See also: Compressed natural gas; Liquefied natural gas*

Natural resource   Resource that occurs in nature, which can be used to meet human needs.

Natural ventilation   Ventilation that is created by the differences in the distribution of air pressures around a building. Air moves from areas of high pressure to areas of low pressure, with gravity and wind pressure affecting the airflow. The placement and control of doors and windows alters natural ventilation patterns.

Near-neat fuel   Fuel that is virtually free from admixture or dilution. The usual additives to fuel include detergents and corrosion inhibitors.

Neat alcohol fuel   Straight or 100% alcohol, usually in the form of ethanol or methanol.

Neat fuel   Fuel that is free from admixture or dilution with other fuels.

NEC   *See: National Electrical Code*

Neritic   1. Pertains to the shallow area around a lake or ocean that border the land.
    2. Also used to describe the species that live along the water's border.

Net building load   Energy required to satisfy needs of a specific building and its occupants.

New town   Planning model that combines developed urban living and a natural environment. Most of the planned communities create cluster residential and commercial development and extensive green areas.

New urbanism   Movement, begun in the USA, that opposes suburban sprawl, advocating instead the reintroduction of the concept of community in urban planning.

Niche   In ecology, the effect an environment has on an organism, and the effect an organism has on the ecosystem.

Niche diversity   Relates to both species and habitat diversity. Relationships between organisms and their habitat.

NIMBY   *See: Not in my back yard*

Nitric acid (HNO$_3$)   A highly corrosive and toxic strong acid. It is a source of nitrous oxide (N$_2$O), a powerful greenhouse gas.

Nitrogen cycle   Nitrogen circulation through plants and animals and back to the atmosphere. A disruption of the cycle may alter the ecobalance.

Nitrogen dioxide (NO$_2$)   Poisonous gas used in making nitric acid and as a rocket-fuel oxidizer. Also formed from automobile exhausts.

Nitrogen dioxide-absorbing cement   *See: Pollution-absorbing cement*

Nitrogen fixation   Conversion by bacteria of biologically unusable nitrogen gas (N$_2$) into biologically usable ammonia (NH$_3$) and nitrates (NO$_3$).

Nitrogen oxides (NO$_x$)   Major air pollutants and toxic chemicals. Group of highly reactive gases that contain nitrogen and oxygen in varying amounts. Most of the nitrogen oxides are colorless and odorless, but nitrogen dioxide (NO$_2$) is reddish brown. Fossil fuels such as coal and gasoline release NO_x into the atmosphere when burned. NO_x can also be formed naturally. NO_x reacts with the Sun's radiation and other chemical compounds, such as hydrocarbons, to form ground-level ozone. It contributes to the formation of acid rain and smog; eutrophication of lakes, streams, coastal waters, and rivers; and global warming. NO_x and the pollutants formed from them can be transported over long distances, following the pattern of prevailing winds. This means that problems associated with NO_x are not confined to areas where NO_x are emitted. *See also: Air pollutants; Toxic chemicals*

Nitrous oxide (N₂O)   Powerful greenhouse gas with global warming potential 296 times more than that of carbon dioxide (CO_2). It has an atmospheric lifetime of approximately 120 years. It is 310 times more effective in trapping heat in the atmosphere than CO_2 over a 100-year period. Major sources of N_2O include chemically altered agricultural soil, agricultural residue, animal manure, sewage treatment, fuel combustion, adipic acid production, and nitric acid production. N_2O is also emitted naturally from a wide variety of biological sources. *See also: Adipic acid; Nitric acid*

Nocturnal cooling   The effect of cooling by the radiation of heat from a building to the night sky.

Noise pollution   Ambient noise at high levels from various sources; can have adverse effects on human health and other fauna. *See also: Decibel*

Nonaqueous-phase liquid (NAPL)   Contaminants that remain undiluted as the original bulk liquid in the subsurface, such as spilled oil. *See also: Dense nonaqueous-phase liquid; Light nonaqueous-phase liquid*

Nonattainment area   Geographical area in which the level of criteria air pollutant is higher than the level allowed by government standards. *See also: Attainment area*

Nonbiodegradable   Matter that will not decompose under normal atmospheric conditions.

Nonimaging optics   In solar thermal energy, energy collection can be improved by using reflectors designed to be nonimaging in order to concentrate the radiation over an area uniformly. Imaging optics focus the radiation and create "hot spots" on the collectors.

Nonpoint-source pollution   Pollution discharged over a wide area. This diffused pollution is caused by sediment, nutrients, and organic and toxic substances resulting from land-use activities, and is carried to and deposited into rivers, lakes, streams, coastal waters, or groundwater. Includes sediments, nutrients, pesticides, pathogens (bacteria and viruses), toxic chemicals, and heavy metals that run off from agricultural land, urban development, or roads. *See also: Point-source pollution*

Nonrecyclable   Not able to be recycled and used again.

Nonrenewable energy   Irreplaceable sources of energy: coal, oil, and natural gas. These sources are considered nonrenewable because it takes eons to produce them, and they cannot be replaced once they have been consumed. *See also: Renewable energy*

Nonrenewable resource   Resource that cannot be replaced as it is used. Fossil fuels, such as coal and oil, form at such a slow rate that they are considered nonrenewable.

North   True north is a navigational term referring to the direction of the north pole relative to the navigator's position. Magnetic north refers to the direction of the magnetic north pole.

Not in my back yard (NIMBY)   Position of residents who oppose local unwanted land uses, such as toxic waste dumps, landfills, incinerators, airports, or freeways close to their homes. *See also: Locally unwanted land uses*

Nuclear energy   Energy produced from splitting atoms of radioactive materials, such as uranium, which produces radioactive wastes. It should be noted that fusion also provides energy from lighter element nuclides.

Nuclear fusion plant   Because a fusion reactor releases far less radioactive pollution than an ordinary fission nuclear plant, active research is being conducted to determine its feasibility. According to the International Thermonuclear Experimental Rector consortium, fusion power offers the potential of "environmentally benign, widely applicable and essentially inexhaustible" electricity, properties that will be needed as world energy demands increase while simultaneously greenhouse gas emissions must be reduced; but a fusion power plant is still decades away despite US$20 billion of extensive research done so far. Researchers remain skeptical about results that will lead to anything practical or useful in producing electricity through fusion power. Engineering problems still exist, along with prohibitive costs of building and difficulties of repairing and maintaining the reaction vessel. In addition, a massive "blanket" of lithium and rare metals—which must surround the fusion-generating plasma in order to absorb its emitted neutrons—will degrade and become radioactive over time, requiring regular dismantling and replacement. *See also: Nuclear power plant*

Nuclear power plant   Power plant that relies on the process of nuclear fission. In this process, the nucleus of a heavy element, such as uranium, splits when bombarded by a free neutron in a nuclear reactor. The fission process for uranium atoms yields two smaller atoms, one to three free neutrons, plus an amount of energy. Because more free neutrons are released from a uranium fission event than are required to initiate the event, the reaction can become self-sustaining—a chain reaction—under controlled conditions, thus producing a tremendous amount of energy.

In most of the world's nuclear power plants, heat energy generated by burning uranium fuel is collected in ordinary water and carried away from the reactor's core either as steam in boiling-water reactors, or as superheated water in pressurized-water reactors. In a pressurized-water reactor, the superheated water in the primary cooling loop is used to transfer heat energy to a secondary loop for the creation of steam. In either a boiling-water or pressurized-water installation, steam under high pressure is the medium used to transfer the nuclear reactor's heat energy to a turbine that mechanically turns a dynamo-electric machine, or electric generator. Boiling-water and pressurized-water reactors are called light-water reactors, because they use ordinary water to transfer the heat energy from reactor to turbine in the electricity generation process. In other reactor designs, the heat energy is transferred by pressurized heavy water, gas, or another cooling substance.

A current concern in the nuclear power field is the safe disposal and isolation of either spent fuel from reactors or, if the reprocessing option is used, wastes from reprocessing plants. These materials must be isolated from the biosphere until the radioactivity contained in them has diminished to a safe level. Under the Nuclear Waste Policy Act of 1982, as amended, the US Department of Energy has responsibility for development of the waste disposal system for spent nuclear fuel and high-level radioactive waste. Current plans call for the ultimate disposal of the wastes in solid form in licensed deep, stable geological structures.

Nuclear waste facility   Facility to dispose of nuclear waste in which the waste is sealed in a ceramic material. The ceramic material is then placed in corrosion-resistant containers and buried in deep earth chambers. The facility must last up to 10,000 years or longer.

Nutrient   Substance that an organism gets from the environment to use as a source of energy or growth. Usually associated with substances used for plant growth.

Nutrient cycling   Natural process of cycles and recycles of decomposition of plant and organic matter to provide soil nutrients for new generations of plants and animals.

Nylon   Generic designation for a family of synthetic polymers first produced in 1935. Plastic is made from petrol, and petrol cannot degrade very easily. Nylon can also be made from plastic. Most nylon products take a long time to degrade and are classified as nonbiodegradable. Research continues to develop biodegradable nylon.

Nylon 6   One of the newly developed biodegradable nylons. It is a recyclable polymer; used for textiles.

O

Occupational Safety and Health Administration (OSHA) Division of the US Department of Labor. Enforces safety and protection of employees in their workplace.

Occupied space The space within a building or structure that is normally occupied by people and that may be conditioned (heated, cooled, and/or ventilated).

Ocean energy systems Energy-conversion technologies that harness the energy in tides, waves, and thermal gradients in the oceans.

Ocean thermal energy conversion (OTEC) Process or technologies for producing energy by harnessing the temperature differences (thermal gradients) between ocean surface waters and ocean depths. Warm surface water is pumped through an evaporator containing a working fluid in a closed Rankine-cycle system. The vaporized fluid drives a turbine/generator. Cold water from deep below the surface is used to condense the working fluid. Open-cycle OTEC technologies use ocean water itself as the working fluid. Closed-cycle OTEC systems circulate a working fluid in a closed loop. A working 10 kilowatt, closed-cycle prototype was developed by the Pacific International Center for High Technology Research in Hawaii with US Department of Energy funding, but was not commercialized.

Octane An alkane with the chemical formula $CH_3(CH_2)_6CH_3$. It has 18 isomers. Flammable liquid hydrocarbon found in petroleum. Used as a standard to measure the anti-knock properties of motor fuel.

Octane rating Indicates how much fuel can be compressed before it spontaneously ignites. If gas ignites by compression, rather than because of the spark from the spark plug, it causes knocking in the engine, which can damage an engine.

Offgassing Release of gas or vapor into the air.

Off peak The period (time of day) of low energy system demand, as opposed to maximum, or peak, demand. *See also: On-peak energy*

Offset allowances *See: Emissions trading*

Ohm Measure of the electrical resistance of a material, equal to the resistance of a circuit in which the potential difference of 1 volt produces a current of 1 ampere.

Ohm's law In an electrical circuit, a current (I) through a resistor (R) produces a voltage (V) drop according to the following equation: $V = I \times R$.

Oligotrophic Pertaining to a lake or other body of water characterized by extremely low nutrient concentrations, often with very limited plant growth, but with high dissolved oxygen levels. *See also: Eutrophic; Mesotrophic*

One-hundred-year floodplain Area that has a 1% chance of being flooded in a given year.

Urban and suburban developments and their accompanying paved roads and surfaces have increased the probabilities of flooding.

On-peak energy   Energy supplied during periods of relatively high system demand as specified by the supplier. *See also: Off peak*

Once-through system design strategy   One of four design strategies to manage materials and energy in the built form and its servicing systems. Resources are consumed with the belief that they are unlimited. Once they have fulfilled their usefulness, they are discarded as waste. Uses the environment as its ultimate sink. *See also: Closed-circuit system design strategy; Combined open-circuit system design strategy; Open-circuit system design strategy*

Open access   The ability to send or wheel electric power to a customer over a transmission and distribution system that is not owned by the power generator (seller).

Open access system   Also known as the "tragedy of the commons". Commonly held resource for which there are no management rules. Experience has shown that common resources are often exploited or degraded by some of the owners.

Open-circuit system design strategy   One of four design strategies to manage materials and energy in buildings and their servicing systems. Like the once-through system, it uses the environment as a sink to receive waste products, but in this system the emissions do not exceed the ability of the ecosystem to absorb them. The wastes are pretreated before they are discharged. *See also: Closed-circuit system design strategy; Combined open-circuit system design strategy; Once-through system design strategy*

Open-loop active system   Solar water heating system. Pumps circulate water through the solar collectors. These systems are most effective in geographical areas that do not freeze for long periods and do not have hard or acidic water.

Open-loop geothermal heat pump system   Also known as a direct system. Circulates water drawn from a ground or surface water source. Once the heat has been transferred into or out of the water, the water is returned to a well or surface discharge (instead of being recirculated through the system). This option is practical where there is an adequate supply of relatively clean water, and all local codes and regulations regarding groundwater discharge are met.

Open system   Area in which there is a supply of chemical elements used to support plant and animal communities in one ecosystem and a simultaneous loss of biomass and chemical elements from the area outside of that ecosystem.

Operational costs   Direct monetary costs of operating a business or facility.

Organic   Contains carbon, and is composed of living or previously living matter.

Organic agriculture   Concept and practice of agricultural production without the use of synthetic inputs and without allowing the use of transgenic organisms.

Organic compound   Compound containing carbon chains or rings and hydrogen with or without oxygen, nitrogen and other elements; foundation of modern polymer chemistry. *See also: Inorganic compound; Volatile organic compound*

Organic cyanides   Toxic chemicals. Any chemical compound containing the combining group CN. Cyanide is highly toxic and fast-acting: it inhibits cells' oxidative processes. Cyanides occur naturally in certain seeds, such as apple seeds and wild cherry pits. Cyanides, including hydrogen cyanide (HCN or hydrocyanic acid), are used industrially in the production of acrylic fibers, synthetic rubbers, and plastics as well as in electroplating, case-hardening of iron and steel, fumigation, and concentration of ores. *See also: Toxic chemicals*

Organic waste Materials that decompose naturally.

Organically grown Agricultural crops grown without the use of synthetic fertilizers or pesticides.

Organism Anything that is living, from bacteria to plants to animals.

Orientation Orientation of a surface in degrees away from solar south, towards either east or west. Solar or true south is distinct from magnetic south.

Oriented-strand board (OSB) An engineered, reconstituted mat-formed building material panel made of strands, flakes, or wafers sliced from small-diameter, round wood logs and bonded with an exterior-type binder under heat and pressure. Exterior or surface layers are composed of strands aligned in the long panel direction; inner layers consist of cross-aligned or randomly aligned strands.

Osmotroph Organism that obtains nutrients through its cell membrane. Examples are fungi and bacteria, which can't use particulate matter as nutrients. *See also: Phagotroph*

OTEC *See: Ocean thermal energy conversion*

Outage A discontinuance of electric power supply.

Outfall Site where effluent is discharged into receiving waters.

Outgassing The process by which materials expel or release gases.

Overhang Building element that shades windows, walls, and doors from direct solar radiation and protects these elements from precipitation.

Overload To exceed the design capacity of a device.

Ovonic This word, invented by Standford Ovshinsky, is composed of OVshinsky and electrONIC. Refers to amorphous glassy semiconductors (germanium, tellurium, arsenic) that change reversibly from an electrically nonconducting state to a conducting state under application of an electric field of the order of 10.5 V/cm.

Oxidant Also known as an oxidizer agent. Chemical, such as oxygen, that consumes electrons in an electrochemical reaction.

Oxidation 1. Mixture of a substance with oxygen; rust or burning may result.
2. Process in which electrons are removed from atoms or ions.

Oxidation pond Human-made body of water in which waste is consumed by bacteria. Used most frequently with other waste-treatment processes. Could be a sewage lagoon.

Oxidize 1. Chemically transform a substance by combining it with oxygen.
2. Remove electrons from atoms or ions.

Oxidizer agent *See: Oxidant*

Oxygen cycle Circulation of oxygen through environmental compartments. It is closely linked to the carbon cycle.

Oxygenated fuel (oxyfuel) Special type of gasoline that burns more completely than regular gasoline in cold-start conditions. It produces reduced carbon dioxide compared with regular gas.

Oxygenate   To treat, combine, or infuse with oxygen.

Oxygenates   Substances which, when added to gasoline, increase the amount of oxygen in the gasoline blend. Ethanol, methyl tertiary butyl ether (MTBE), ethyl tertiary butyl ether (ETBE), and methanol are common oxygenates. Additives to gasoline reduce its carbon dioxide emissions.

Ozone (O_3)   A major air pollutant, ozone gas is a triatomic form of oxygen. It is not usually emitted directly into the air, but at ground level it is created by a chemical reaction between oxides of nitrogen (NO_x) and volatile organic compounds (VOC) in the presence of sunlight.

Ozone has the same chemical structure whether it occurs miles above the Earth or at ground level. It is produced in two layers: the troposphere or ground-layer ozone, known as "bad" ozone; and the stratosphere or upper ozone, known as "good" ozone.

Ozone is a primary constituent of smog. Motor vehicle exhaust and industrial emissions, gasoline vapors, and chemical solvents, as well as natural sources, emit NO_x and VOC that help form ozone. Sunlight and hot weather cause ground-level ozone to form in harmful concentrations in the air. As a result, it is known as a summertime air pollutant. Ozone occurs in both urban and rural areas. It is considered a significant health risk, particularly for children with asthma. It also damages crops, trees, and other vegetation.

Ozone is produced naturally in the stratosphere. "Good" ozone occurs naturally in the stratosphere approximately 10–30 miles (16–48 km) above the Earth's surface, and forms a layer that protects life on Earth from the Sun's harmful ultraviolet (UV) rays. This natural shield has gradually been damaged or depleted by human-made chemicals including chlorofluorocarbons (CFCs), hydrochlorofluorocarbons (HCFCs), halons, methyl bromide, carbon tetrachloride, and methyl chloroform, all known as ozone-depleting substances.

Even though there has been a reduction in the use of many ozone-depleting substances, their use in the past can still affect the protective ozone layer. Research indicates that depletion of the "good" ozone layer is being reduced worldwide. Thinning of the protective ozone layer can be observed using satellite measurements, particularly over the polar regions.

Ozone depletion can cause increased amounts of UV radiation to reach the Earth, which can lead to more cases of skin cancer, cataracts, and impaired immune systems. Measures are being taken to reduce ozone emissions in the USA through the Clean Air Act, and also in other countries. *See also: **Air pollutants; ozone-depleting substance***

Ozone-depleting substance (ODS)   Family of human-made compounds that have been shown to deplete stratospheric ozone. ODS include chlorofluorocarbons (CFCs), bromofluorocarbons (halons), methyl chloroform, carbon tetrachloride, methyl bromide, and hydrochlorofluorocarbons (HCFCs). Once released into the air, these ozone-depleting substances degrade very slowly. They can remain intact for years as they move through the troposphere until they reach the stratosphere. There they are broken down by the intensity of the Sun's ultraviolet rays and release chlorine and bromine molecules, which destroy the "good" ozone. Scientists estimate that one chlorine atom can destroy 100,000 "good" ozone molecules. *See also: **Ozone***

Ozone hole   Thin place in the ozone layer in the stratosphere. Thinning of the stratospheric ozone has been linked to the destruction of stratospheric ozone by chlorofluorocarbons (CFCs) and related chemicals. Reductions in ozone levels will lead to higher levels of ultraviolet B (UVB) reaching the Earth's surface. The Sun's output of UVB does not change; rather, less ozone means less protection, and hence more UVB reaches the Earth. Studies have shown that in the Antarctic, the amount of UVB measured at the surface can double during the annual ozone hole. Another study confirmed the relationship between reduced ozone and increased UVB levels in Canada during the past several years.

Ozone layer   The layer of ozone that begins approximately 15 km (9.3 miles) above Earth and thins to an almost negligible amount at about 50 km (31 miles), and shields the Earth from harmful ultraviolet radiation from the Sun. The highest natural concentration of ozone (approximately 10 parts per million by volume) occurs in the stratosphere at approximately 25 km (15.5miles) above Earth. The stratospheric ozone concentration changes throughout the year as stratospheric circulation changes with the seasons. Natural events such as volcanoes and solar flares can produce changes in ozone concentration, but human-made changes are of the greatest concern. The ozone layer protects the Earth against most ultraviolet (UV) radiation coming from the Sun. UVB is a type of ultraviolet light from the Sun (and sunlamps) that has several harmful effects, particularly in damaging DNA. It is a cause of melanoma and other types of skin cancer. Studies have found adverse effects on plants, materials, and marine organisms from excessive exposure to UV. Solar UVB radiation has been found to cause damage to early developmental stages of fish, shrimp, crab, amphibians, and other animals. The most severe effects are decreased reproductive capacity and impaired larval development. Even at current levels, solar UVB radiation is a limiting factor, and small increases in UVB exposure could result in significant reduction in the size of the population of animals that eat these smaller creatures. *See also: **Stratosphere**, **Ultraviolet radiation***

Ozone precursors   Chemical compounds, such as carbon monoxide, methane, nonmethane hydrocarbons, and nitrogen oxides, which react with the Sun's radiation and other chemical compounds to form ozone. *See also: **Troposphere***

P

Packaging Wrappers for products; wrappers may be made of a variety of materials: plastic, cardboard, paper, metal, glass, wood, and ceramics.

Packed tower Also known as packer tower scrubber. Air pollution control device. Contaminated air is circulated through a tower containing materials that have a large surface area. The contaminants are absorbed into a liquid flowing over the tower materials. The liquid falls downward and the air is forced upward through the tower. The vapors or particulates contained in the air go up through the surface area. The fumes come into contact with the surface and take up the material releasing the air and cleaning it. *See also: Absorption process; Scrubbers; Ventury scrubber*

Packed tower aeration Process to remove organic contaminants from groundwater. Groundwater flows downward in a tower filled with material over a large surface. Air is introduced at the bottom of the tower and is forced upward past the falling groundwater. Organic contaminants are transferred from the water to the air.

Packer tower scrubber *See: Packed tower*

PAFC *See: Phosphoric acid fuel cell*

Panemone A type of vertical-axis wind turbine. It has a rotating axis positioned at 90° to the direction of the wind, while the wind-catching blades move parallel to the wind. By contrast, the shaft of a horizontal-axis wind turbine points into the wind while its blades move at right-angles to the wind's thrust. A panemone primarily uses drag, whereas the blades of a horizontal-axis wind turbine use lift. The panemone windmill dates from ancient Persia, where it was used as a power source to grind wheat. It is drag-type wind machine that can react to wind from any direction.

Paper Product made from tree pulp in a process that produces acid rain and dioxin.

Parabolic aluminized reflector lamp A type of lamp with a lens of heavy, durable glass that focuses the light. They have longer lifetimes with less lumen depreciation than standard incandescent lamps.

Parabolic dish solar collector A solar energy conversion device that has a bowl-shaped dish covered with a highly reflective surface that tracks the Sun and concentrates sunlight on a fixed absorber, thereby achieving high temperatures: for process heating, or to operate a heat (Stirling) engine to produce power or electricity. *See also: Stirling engine*

Parabolic trough A type of solar thermal collector. A solar energy conversion device that uses a trough covered with a highly reflective surface of either coated silver or polished aluminum to focus sunlight onto a linear absorber, usually a Dewar tube, containing a working fluid that absorbs the concentrated sunlight. The

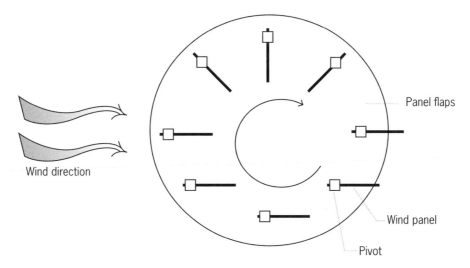

Figure 48 A panemone—wind-catching panels turn edge-on to the wind when moving against the wind's thrust and side-on when moving downwind

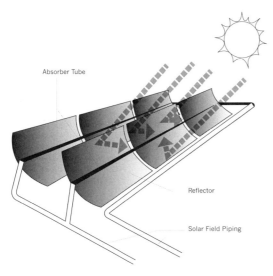

Figure 49 A parabolic trough collector
Source: US Department of Energy

heat-transfer fluid, usually oil, is used to heat steam in a standard turbine generator. Estimates of its economic and thermal efficiency range from 60 to 80%. *See also: **Solar thermal electric systems***

At present, all parabolic troughs are hybrids. They include a fossil fuel system to supplement the solar energy at night or when it is cloudy. The fossil fuel is usually natural gas.

Parasitism   Form of symbiosis in which one species benefits and the other is harmed. *See also: **Amensalism; Commensalism; Mutualism; Symbiosis***

Partial zero-emission vehicle (PZEV)
Designation by the California Air Resources Board for a vehicle that has zero evaporative emissions from its fuel system, has a 15 year (or at least 150,000 mile) warranty, and meets super-ultra-low-emission vehicle (SULEV) tailpipe emissions standards. A PZEV falls into the SULEV category. *See also: **Emissions standards, designations***

Particulate matter   Also known as particle pollution or PM. Common air pollutant, toxic chemical, and health threat. A complex mixture of extremely small particles and liquid droplets. Particle pollution is made up of a number of components, including acids (such as nitrates and sulfates), organic chemicals, metals, and soil or dust particles. Particulate pollution can cause health problems, especially to the respiratory system. *See also: **Air pollutants;** **Toxic chemicals***

Particulates   Small particles that are suspended in air, such as soot, ash, dust, or other air emissions. *See also: **Air emissions***

Partitioned matrix (LP)   Developed by ecodesigners to depict the interactions between a designed system and the environment. Using 1 for the designed system, 2 for the environment, and L for the interdependencies within a given framework, the matrix is:

L_{11} = processes that occur within the system (internal interdependencies); L_{22} = activities in the environment (external interdependencies); L_{12} and L_{21} = system/environment and environment system exchanges.

$$LP = \frac{L_{11}}{L_{21}} \Bigg|\ \frac{L_{12}}{L_{22}}$$

Passive cooling systems   Various simple cooling techniques designed to lower indoor temperature through the use of natural energy sources. Design considerations include layout of building, orientation, number, size, location, and details of windows, shading devices, thermal resistance, and heat capacity of the building envelope. The designs involve minimizing heat gain by the building, minimizing solar heat build-up of the building envelope and solar penetration through windows, and providing natural ventilation. Minimizing heat gain has not traditionally been regarded as a cooling technology. Passive cooling systems typically involve deep sky cooling or other cooling without using motors to move a fluid to transport the heat (or cool) liquids. *See also: **Passive solar cooling***

Passive daylight device   Nonmechanical device used to project daylight into the interior of a structure. *See also: **Light pipe; Light shelf; Tubular skylight***

Passive diffuser   Air supply outlet, without a fan, that relies on pressurized plenum or duct air to deliver air into the conditioned space of a building.

Passive mode design   Also known as bioclimatic design. An ecodesign strategy that specifies low-energy consumption systems by taking advantage of the ambient climate of the locality. Passive mode ecodesign emphasizes three main design considerations: i) low-energy design; ii) the climate of the locality and the site's natural features; iii) the appropriate shape of a building and its ratio of volume to surface. In design terms, passive mode design strategies include appropriate built form configuration and orientation, internal spatial disposition, façade design, such as solid to glass ratio, insulation, and color, use of building mass, use of vegetation, natural ventilation, and even color. Passive mode design as low-energy design seeks to maximize natural and ambient energy sources and minimize the use of nonrenewable energy resources. This can be achieved through the use of radiation, conduction, and convection instead of electromechanical heating and cooling systems that require external sources of energy.

The climate and locality and the site's natural features influence the kind of design for the built form, but do not determine the design. The design is a response to the prevailing climate and seasons over the year. Designs for temperate and cold climates are necessarily different, for example, just as the specific site's topography and neighbors influence the design. The appropriate shaping of the building and its orientation are determined by the locality's Sun path, use of natural ventilation, use of vegetation, appropriate façade design, and Sun shading and other similar considerations. Passive mode design relates to the climatic conditions of the locality and results in built forms that are more adapted to a specific region.

Passive solar cooling   Use of natural ventilation is a primary strategy for cooling buildings without mechanical assistance in hot humid climates. Methods to increase the effectiveness of natural ventilation include the following:

- operable windows—should be placed on the south exposure
- wing walls—vertical solid panels placed alongside windows perpendicular to the wall on the windward side of the house
- thermal chimneys
- sunrooms.

Sunrooms can be designed to perform this function by venting at the top any excessive heat generated in a south-facing sunroom during the summer. With the connecting lower vents to the living space open along with windows on the north side, air is drawn through the living space to be exhausted through the sunroom upper vents. (The upper vents from the sunroom to the living space and any side operable windows must be closed and the thermal mass wall in the sunroom must be shaded.) Thermal mass indirect gain walls can be made to function similarly, except that the mass wall should be insulated on the inside when performing this function. Thermal chimneys can be constructed in a narrow configuration (like a chimney) with an easily heated black metal absorber on the inside behind a glazed front that can reach high temperatures and be insulated from the house. The chimney must terminate above the roof level. A rotating metal scoop at the top, which opens opposite the wind, will allow heated air to exhaust without being overcome by the prevailing wind. Thermal chimney effects can be integrated into houses with open stairwells and atria.

Other ventilation strategies include making the outlet openings slightly larger than the inlet

openings; and placing inlets at low-to-medium heights to provide airflow at occupant levels in the room. Inlets close to a wall result in air "washing" along the wall; it is important to have centrally located inlets for air movement in the center areas of the room. Window insect screens decrease the velocity of slow breezes more than stronger breezes (60% decrease at 1.5 mph (2.4 km/ph), 28% decrease at 6 mph (9.6 km/ph)). Screening a porch will not reduce air speeds as much as screening the windows. Night ventilation of a home should be done at a

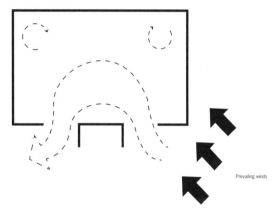

Figure 50a Passive solar cooling

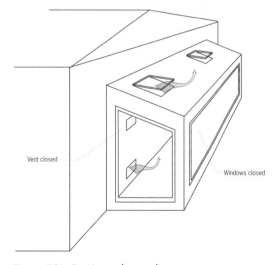

Figure 50b Passive solar cooling

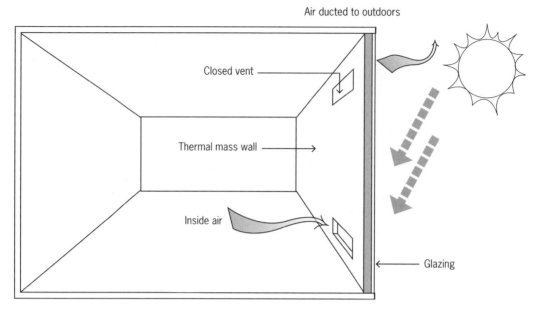

Air ducted to outdoors

Closed vent

Thermal mass wall

Inside air

Glazing

Day

Figure 50c Passive solar cooling

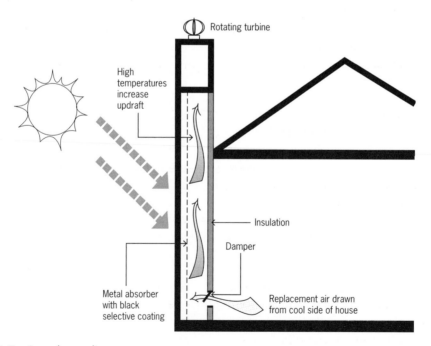

Rotating turbine

High
temperatures
increase
updraft

Insulation

Damper

Metal absorber
with black
selective coating

Replacement air drawn
from cool side of house

Figure 50d Passive solar cooling

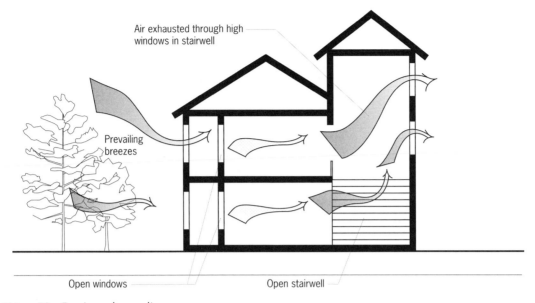

Air exhausted through high windows in stairwell

Prevailing breezes

Open windows

Open stairwell

Figure 50e Passive solar cooling

ventilation rate of 30 air changes per hour or greater. Mechanical ventilation will be required to achieve this. High-mass houses can be cooled with night ventilation provided fabric furnishings are minimized in the house. Keep a high-mass house closed during the day and opened at night. *See also: Passive cooling systems; Thermal chimney; Wing wall*

Passive solar design   Design that uses the Sun's energy for heating and cooling of living spaces. In this approach, the building itself or some element of it takes advantage of natural energy characteristics in materials and air created by exposure to the Sun to heat and cool the building without use of mechanical equipment. Passive systems are simple, have few moving parts, and require no mechanical systems and minimal maintenance.

Principal design elements include proper building orientation, window sizing, placement and design of window overhangs to reduce summer heat gain and ensure winter heat gain, and proper sizing of thermal energy storage mass such as a Trombe wall or masonry tiles. The heat is distributed primarily by natural convection and radiation, although fans can also be used to circulate room air or ensure proper ventilation. Operable windows, thermal mass, thermal chimneys, and wing walls are common elements found in passive design. Wing walls are vertical exterior wall partitions placed perpendicular to adjoining windows to enhance ventilation through windows. *See also: Thermal chimney; Thermal mass; Trombe wall; Wing wall*

Passive solar energy system   General term used to designate solar heating or cooling that uses natural energy flows to transfer heat.

Passive solar heater   A solar water or space-heating system in which solar energy is collected, and/or moved by natural convection without using pumps or fans. Passive systems are usually integral collector/storage or batch collectors, or thermosiphon systems. These systems do not use controls, pumps, sensors, or other mechanical parts, so little or no maintenance is required over the lifetime of the system. *See also: Batch heater; Thermosiphon*

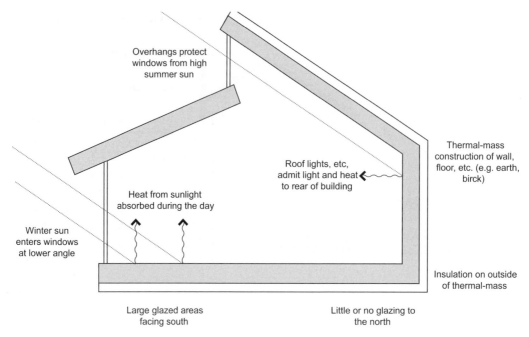

Overhangs protect
windows from high
summer sun

Thermal-mass
construction of wall,
floor, etc. (e.g. earth,
birck)

Roof lights, etc,
admit light and heat
to rear of building

Heat from sunlight
absorbed during the day

Winter sun
enters windows
at lower angle

Insulation on outside
of thermal-mass

Large glazed areas
facing south

Little or no glazing to
the north

Figure 51 Basic passive solardesign principles (temperate zone)

Passive solar heating   Requires two primary elements: south facing glass, and thermal mass to absorb, store, and distribute heat. There are three approaches to passive systems: i) direct gain; ii) indirect gain; iii) isolated gain. The goal of all passive solar heating systems is to capture the Sun's heat within the building's elements and release that heat during periods when the Sun is not shining. At the same time as the building's elements (or materials) are absorbing heat for later use, solar heat is available for keeping the space comfortable but not overheated. In this system, the actual living space is a solar collector, heat absorber, and distribution system. South-facing glass admits solar energy into the house, where it strikes thermal mass materials in the house such as masonry floors and walls. The direct gain system will utilize 60—75% of the Sun's energy striking the windows.

In a direct gain system, the thermal mass floors and walls are functional parts of the house. It is also possible to use water containers inside the house to store heat. However, it is more difficult to integrate water storage containers in the design of a house. The thermal mass will temper the intensity of the heat during the day by absorbing the heat. At night, the thermal mass radiates heat into the living space. *See also: Direct solar gain; Indirect solar gain system; Isolated gain*

Passive system   Uses nonmechanical means to satisfy space loads. Passive system design is part of the ecodesign process and is carried out according to the local environment and prevailing biota. Passive systems do not rely on electromechanical systems for energy. An example is a passive solar system. *See also: Active system; Solar energy*

Passive treatment walls   Technology in which a chemical reaction takes place when contaminated groundwater comes into contact with a barrier such as limestone or a wall containing iron filings.

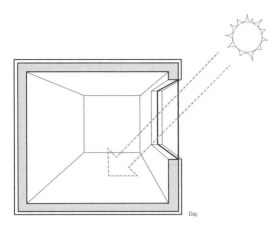

Figure 52a Passive solar heating: thermal mass in the interior absorbs the sunlight in the daytime

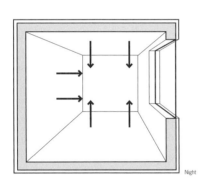

Figure 52b Passive solar heating: radiates the heat at night

Pathogens   Disease-causing microorganisms. Pathogens can cause diseases in humans, plants, and animals.

Pay as you throw   System in which residents pay for municipal waste management by weight and volume collected, rather than by a fixed fee.

PBTs   *See: Persistent bioaccumulatic toxic pollutants*

PCBs   *See: Polychlorinated biphenyls*

PCE   *See: Perchloroethylene*

PCFC   *See: Protonic ceramic fuel cell*

Peak oil   Also known as "end of oil". Refers to the point in time when the maximum rate of global petroleum extraction is reached, after which the rate of production enters terminal decline. The concept is based on the observed production rates of individual oil wells and the combined production rate of a field of related oil wells. The aggregate production rate from an oil field over time appears to grow exponentially until the rate peaks, and then declines until the field is depleted. It has been shown to be applicable to the sum of a nation's domestic production rate, and is similarly applied to the global rate of petroleum production. Peak oil is not about running out of oil, but concerns the peaking and subsequent decline of the production rate of oil.

Peak power current   (Electrical) Amperes produced by a photovoltaic module or array operating at the voltage of the current–voltage (I–V) curve that will produce maximum power from the module.

PECs   *See: Photoelectrochemical cells*

Pellet stove   A space-heating device that burns compressed wood or biomass pellets, usually used in homes. It is more efficient, cleaner-burning, and easier to operate than conventional cord wood-burning appliances. Most pellet stoves are cast iron with stainless steel to encase circuitry and exhaust areas.

Peltier effect   Conversion of heat from the flow of an electric current, often implemented as a thermoelectric cooler. When two dissimilar metals or semiconductors form a junction with a current flowing through the circuit, heat moves from one side of the junction to the other. The thermoelectric cooler construction uses heavily doped p-type and n-type semiconductors to transfer heat from the cooled surface to a hot surface. *See also:* **Seebeck effect; Thomson effect**

Pelton turbine   Also known as a free-jet turbine. Invented in 1880 by L. A. Pelton. A type of impulse hydropower turbine in which water passes through nozzles and strikes cups arranged on the periphery of a runner, or wheel, which causes the runner to rotate, producing mechanical energy. The runner is fixed on a shaft, and the rotational motion of the turbine is transmitted by the shaft to a generator.

Generally used for high-head, low-flow applications. Used in storage power stations with downward gradients up to 2000 meters (6,561 ft) and can contain up to six nozzles. *See also:* **Water turbine**

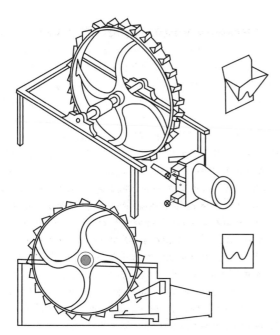

Figure 53 The diagram from Pelton's original patent (October 1880)

PEM   *See:* ***Proton exchange membrane fuel cell***

Perched water   Zone of unpressurized water held above the water table by impermeable rock or sediment.

Perchloroethylene (perc, PCE)   Also known as tetrachloroethylene or tetrachloroethene. Soil contaminant. $Cl_2C = CCl_2$ is a manufactured chemical used in dry cleaning and degreasing. It is regulated by the US Safe Drinking Water Act of 1974, which determines safe levels of chemicals in drinking water. Ingestion may increase risks of cancer and liver damage. *See also:* **Soil contaminants; Toxic chemicals**

Percolation   1. Movement of water downward and radially through subsurface soil layers, usually continuing downward to groundwater. It can also involve upward movement of water.

2. Slow seepage of water through a filter.

Perfluorocarbons (PFCs)   Group of human-made chemicals composed of carbon and fluorine only. These chemicals, predominantly CF_4 and C_2F_6, were introduced as alternatives, along with hydrofluocarbons, to ozone-depleting substances. PFCs are emitted as by-products of industrial processes and are also used in manufacturing. PFCs do not harm the stratospheric ozone layer, but they are powerful greenhouse gases: CF_4 and C_2F_6 have global warming effects.

Perimeter zone   Area adjacent to and within about 15 feet (5 meters) of an exterior wall. These spaces have heating and cooling loads that are significantly different from internal/core zone areas because of factors such solar gain and heat loss through the building envelope.

Peripheral service core   Placement of the service core along the periphery of a building. Its features include no need for fire protection pressurization ducts, provision of natural ventilation to the elevators, provision of natural sunlight to the elevator and stair lobbies, and more natural light in the building in the event of power failure.

Perlite   Chemically inert natural volcanic material; used as insulation either in loose form or as an aggregate in concrete.

Permaculture   From "permanent agriculture". Represents a whole-systems approach to agriculture through the conscious design and maintenance of agriculturally productive ecosystems that have the diversity, stability, and resilience of natural ecosystems. The design assembles conceptual, material, and strategic components in a biological pattern that focuses on benefiting all life forms.

Permeable   Materials that can be penetrated or passed through, usually by liquids.

Persistent bioaccumulatic toxic pollutants (PBTs)   Chemicals that are toxic, persist in the environment and bioaccumulate in food chains, and pose risks to human health and ecosystems. The biggest concerns about PBTs are that they transfer easily among air, water, and land, and span boundaries of programs, geography, and generations.

Persistent organic pollutants (POPs)   Toxic chemicals that adversely affect human health and the environment around the world. Because they can be transported by wind and water, most POPs generated in one country can affect people and wildlife far from where they are used and released. They persist for long periods in the environment, and can accumulate and pass from one species to the next through the food chain. They include organochlorine pesticides, polycholorinated biphenyls, dioxins, and furans. *See also: Stockholm Convention on Persistent Organic Pollution*

Pervious materials   Materials that permit water to pass through with little restriction because of their porous nature or large spaces in the material. Examples include gravel, crushed stone, open paving blocks, or pervious paving blocks, which are used for driveways, parking areas, walkways, and patios. Their use reduces runoff from those areas, as well as increasing infiltration.

Pesticides   Any substance or mixture of substances intended to prevent, destroy, repel, or mitigate any pests. Pests can be insects, mice, other animals, unwanted plants, fungi, or microorganisms. Applies to herbicides, fungicides, and other substances used to control pests. In the USA, a pesticide is also any substance used as a plant regulator, defoliant, or desiccant.

PET   *See: Polyethylene terephthalate*

Petrochemical   Also known as petroleum chemical. Chemical made from petroleum or natural gas feedstock, such as ethylene, butadiene, most major plastics, and resins.

Petroleum   A nonrenewable fossil fuel, petroleum means "rock oil" or "oil from the earth". Hydrocarbon mixtures, including crude oil, lease condensate, natural gas, products of natural gas processing plants, refined products, semifinished products, and blending materials. The five countries producing the most crude oil are Saudi Arabia, Russia, USA, Iran, and China. Because modern society uses so many petroleum-based products—including gasoline, kerosene, fuel oil, mineral oil, and asphalt—contamination of the environment is potentially widespread. They are released to the environment through accidents, as releases from industries, or as by-products from commercial or private uses. When released directly to water through spills or leaks, certain petroleum fractions will float in water, whereas others will accumulate in the sediment at the bottom of the water, affecting bottom-feeding fish and organisms. When released to the soil, petroleum compound emissions move through the soil to the groundwater. Depending on the compound, some emissions will evaporate, others will dissolve in the water, and still others will remain for a long time. Exposure to petroleum compounds can also affect human health adversely. The effects will depend on the toxicity of the compounds, and can range from respiratory problems to death.

PFCs   *See: Perfluorocarbons*

pH   Scale denoting the level of acidity in a substance. Water, for example, is neutral with a pH of 7. pH values from 0 to 7 indicate acidity; values from 7 to 14 indicate alkalinity.

Phagotroph   Organism that obtains nutrients through ingestion of organic matter or other organisms. This class of organism includes all animals, from single-celled amoeba to larger animals. *See also: Osmotroph*

Phantom load   Any appliance that consumes power even when it is turned off. Examples of phantom loads include appliances with electronic clocks or timers, appliances with remote controls, and appliances with wall cubes (a small box that plugs into an AC outlet to power appliances). Phantom loads add to the total consumption of power.

Phenol   By-product of petroleum refining, tanning, and textile, dye, and resin manufacturing. *See also: Phenol formaldehyde*

Phenol formaldehyde   One of two types of formaldehyde resin (the other is urea formaldehyde). An industrial chemical, it is also used to make composite wood products, but these products emit lower levels of gas than similar products made with urea formaldehyde. The most widely used completely formaldehyde-free alternative resins are methylene diphenyl isocyanate (MDI) and polyvinyl acetate (PVA). (Despite its name, PVA is not closely related to PVC; without chlorine in its molecule, it avoids many of the worst problems that PVC has in its life cycle.) *See also: Formaldehyde; Urea formaldehyde*

Phenotype   Visible and/or measurable characteristics of an organism. As ecobalances change, organisms may mutate.

Phosphoric acid fuel cell (PAFC)   One type of fuel cell. PAFC, developed in the 1980s, has the most mature fuel cell technology in terms of system development and commercialization activities. The phosphoric acid fuel cell uses liquid phosphoric acid (H_3PO_4) as the electrolyte. The phosphoric acid is contained in a Teflon-bonded silicone carbide matrix. The small pore structure of this matrix preferentially keeps the acid in place through capillary action. Some acid may be entrained in the fuel or oxidant streams, and addition of acid may be required after many hours of operation. Platinum-catalyzed, porous carbon electrodes are used on both the fuel (anode) and oxidant (cathode) sides of the electrolyte. PAFC power plant designs show electrical efficiencies in the range 36–42% (HHV2). The higher-efficiency designs operate with pressurized reactants, require more components,

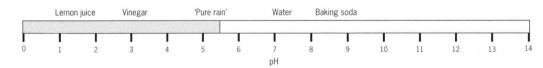

Figure 54 pH levels of some common substances

and could have a higher cost. A portion of the thermal energy can be supplied at temperatures of approximately 250–300 °F (121–149 °C); however, the majority of the thermal energy is supplied at about 150 °F (65 °C). A PAFC has a power density of 160–175 W/ft^2 (929 cm^2) of active cell area.

PAFCs are less powerful than other fuel cells, given the same weight and volume. As a result, they are usually large and heavy, and expensive as they use platinum catalysts. In 2007, it was estimated that a typical PAFC costs between US$4000 and US$4500 per kilowatt to operate. They are 85% efficient when used for cogeneration of electricity and heat, but less efficient at generating electricity alone (37–42%). This is only slightly more efficient than combustion-based power plants. If the source of hydrogen fuel is reformed gasoline, sulfur must be removed from the fuel entering the PACF cell, or it will damage the electrode catalyst. *See also: Fuel cells*

Phosphorus (P)   Chemical element used as a dopant in making n-type semiconductor layers.

Photochemical cycle   Also known as the photolytic cycle. A series of chemical reactions that result in accumulation of ozone or other oxidants in the troposphere. The cycle includes the absorption of sunlight by NO_2, causing conversion of the dioxide into NO and O (atomic oxygen). The atomic oxygen combines with O_2 to form ozone (O_3).

Photochemical modeling   Computer modeling of reactions in the atmosphere that produce ozone from nitrogen oxides and volatile organic compounds. It can be used to evaluate the air quality impacts of heat island reduction strategies.

Photochemical oxidants   The products of reactions between NO_x and a wide variety of volatile organic compounds. The best known

oxidants are ozone (O_3), peroxyacetyle nitrate and hydrogen peroxide (H_2O_2). The main impact on the natural environment is caused by elevated ozone. Excessive concentrations of tropospheric ozone have toxic effects on both plants and human health.

Photodecomposition   *See: Photolysis*

Photodissociation   *See: Photolysis*

Photoelectric effect   *See: Appendix 4: Photovoltaics*

Photoelectrochemical cells (PECs)   1. Generic name for solar cells that extract electrical energy from light, including visible light. Each cell consists of a semiconducting photoanode and a metal cathode immersed in an electrolyte. Some PECs simply produce electrical energy; others produce hydrogen in a process similar to the electrolysis of water.

2. Type of photovoltaic device in which the electricity induced in the cell is used immediately within the cell to produce a chemical, such as hydrogen, which can then be withdrawn for use.

Photolysis   Also known as photodissociation or photodecomposition. Photolysis is the process of chemical decomposition of a substance or material when it is subjected to light. Light includes both visible light and ultraviolet radiation.

1. The formation of the ozone layer in the stratosphere is the result of photolysis. Ozone in the stratosphere is created by ultraviolet light striking oxygen molecules containing two oxygen atoms (O_2), splitting them into individual oxygen atoms (atomic oxygen). The atomic oxygen then combines with the unbroken O_2 to create ozone (O_3). This ozone is known as "good" ozone because it serves as a filter of the middle and far ultraviolet radiation. Photolysis is also the process by which toxic chlorofluorocarbons

(CFCs) are broken down in the upper atmosphere to form ozone-destroying chlorine free radicals.

2. Photolysis can degrade air pollutants and contaminants in the water and on the land. Two toxic pesticides that are decomposed through photolysis are chlorophenol and diazinon.

3. Photolysis is an important component of the light-dependent phase of photosynthesis. It uses light energy (sunlight) to break water molecules or some other electron donor, to obtain electrons for photosynthesis. The function of these electrons is to replace electrons lost by the photosystems to the electron transport systems. Water serves as a substrate for photolysis, resulting in the generation of free oxygen (O_2). Water (H_2O) serves as a substrate for photolysis, resulting in the generation of free oxygen (O_2). Photolysis of water occurs in the thylakoids of cyanobacteria and the chloroplasts of green algae and plants.

The effectiveness of photons of different wavelengths depends on the absorption spectra of the photosynthetic pigments in the organism. Chlorophylls absorb light in the violet–blue and red parts of the spectrum, while accessory pigments capture other wavelengths as well. The phycobilins of red algae absorb blue-green light, which penetrates more deeply into water than red light, enabling them to photosynthesize in deep waters. Each absorbed photon causes the formation of an exciton (an electron excited to a higher energy state) in the pigment molecule. The energy of the exciton is transferred to a chlorophyll molecule (P_{680}, where P stands for pigment and 680 for its absorption maximum at 680 nm) in the reaction center of photosystem II via resonance energy transfer. P_{680} can also directly absorb a photon at a suitable wavelength. Photolysis during photosynthesis occurs in a series of light-driven oxidation events. The energized electron (exciton) of P_{680} is captured by a primary electron acceptor of the photosynthetic electron transfer chain and thus exits photosystem II. In order to repeat the reaction, the electron in the reaction center needs to be replenished. This occurs by oxidation of water in the case of oxygenic photosynthesis. The electron-deficient reaction center of photosystem II ($P_{680}*$) is the strongest biological oxidizing agent known on Earth, which allows it to break apart molecules as stable as water.

Photolytic cycle   *See: Photochemical cycle*

Photon   Under the photon theory of light, a photon is a discrete bundle (or quantum) of electromagnetic (or light) energy. Photons are always in motion and, in a vacuum, have a constant speed of light to all observers, at the vacuum speed of light (more commonly just called the speed of light) of $c = 2.998 \times 10^8$ m/s.

Photoperiod response   Relates plant and tree response to frequencies and intensities of light that regulate the development and flowering of plants and trees.

Photosynthesis   The process of acquiring and using light energy to produce food. It provides the energy and reduced carbon essential for the survival of almost all life on Earth. It also provides molecular oxygen needed by oxygen-consuming organisms. Plants take in CO_2 from the air or from bicarbonate in water to build carbohydrates, releasing O_2 in the process. The key initial step in the growth of biomass, its equation is: $CO_2 + H_2O$ + light + chlorophyll $\rightarrow (CH_2O) + O_2$. The various pathways of photosynthesis produce different responses to atmospheric CO_2 concentrations. Photosynthesis is the basis for food production in plants, algae, and certain bacteria, and thus the beginning of the food chain. *See also: Artificial photosynthesis; Food chain; Sun*

Photovoltaic (PV)   Pertaining to the direct conversion of light into electricity. *See: Appendix 4: Photovoltaics*

Photovoltaic (PV) array A linked collection of PV modules, which in turn are made of interconnected solar cells. The cells convert solar energy into direct current (DC) electricity via the PV effect. The power that one module can produce is usually not sufficient to meet requirements of a home or a business, so the modules are linked together to form an array. Most PV arrays use an inverter to convert the DC power produced by the modules into alternating current (AC) that can plug into the existing infrastructure to power lights, motors, and other loads. The modules in a PV array are usually first connected in series to obtain the desired voltage; the individual strings are then connected in parallel to allow the system to produce more current. Solar arrays are typically measured by the electrical power they produce in watts, kilowatts, or megawatts. Interconnected systems of PV modules function as a single electricity-producing unit. The modules are assembled as a discrete structure, with common support or mounting. In smaller systems, an array can consist of a single module. Individual PV modules can be connected in series, in parallel, or both, to increase either output voltage or current. This also increases the output power. *See: Appendix 4: Photovoltaics; Photovoltaic module*

Photovoltaic automobile Automobile that is powered by photovoltaic cells. *See also: Solar electric-powered vehicle*

Photovoltaic cell Treated semiconductor material that converts solar irradiance to electricity. Also known as a solar cell, as it converts sunlight directly into electricity. Smallest semiconductor element within a photovoltaic (PV) module to perform the immediate conversion of light into electrical energy. PV is a specialized form of semiconductor anode that converts visible light, or infrared or ultraviolet radiation, directly into electricity. The conversion process is based on the photoelectric effect discovered by Alexander Bequerel in 1839. The photoelectric effect describes the release of positive and negative charge carriers in a solid state when light strikes its surface.

Solar cells are composed of various semiconducting materials, about 95% of which are made of silicon. One side of the semiconductor material has a positive charge; the other side is negatively charged. Sunlight hitting the positive side will activate the electrons on the negative side and produce an electrical current.

There are three types of PV cell: monocrystalline, polycrystalline, and amorphous. i) Monocrystalline rods are extracted from melted silicon and then sawn into thin plates. This production process guarantees a relatively high level of efficiency. ii) Polycrystalline cells are more cost-efficient to produce, but less efficient than the monocrystalline cell. iii) Amorphous or thin-layer cells form a silicon film which adheres to glass or another material. This is the least expensive and least efficient of the three types of cell. Because of this, they are primarily used in low-power equipment (watches, pocket calculators) or as façade elements. Their efficiency is half that of crystalline cells, and they degrade with use. *See: Appendix 4: Photovoltaics*

Photovoltaic device Solid-state electrical device that converts light directly into direct current electricity. The electricity produced has voltage-current characteristics that are determined by the light source, and the materials and design of the device. Solar PV devices are made of various semiconductor materials, including silicon, cadmium, sulfide, cadmium telluride, and gallium arsenide; and may be in single crystalline, multicrystalline, or amorphous form. The structure of a PV device depends on the limitations of the material used in the PV cells. There are four basic device designs: i) homojunction, ii) heterojunction, iii) p-i-n/n-i-p, and iv) multijunction. *See: Appendix 4: Photovoltaics*

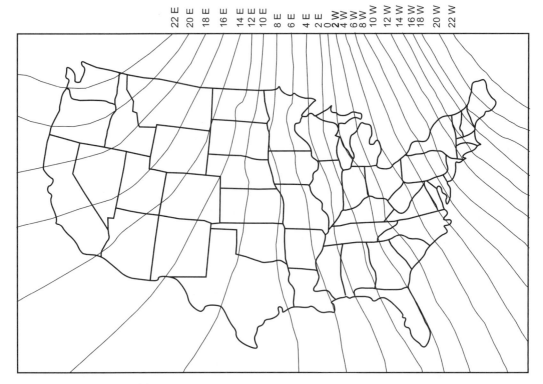

22 E 20 E 18 E 16 E 14 E 12 E 10 E 8 E 6 E 4 E 2 E 0 2 W 4 W 6 W 8 W 10 W 12 W 14 W 16 W 18 W 20 W 22 W

Figure 55 Isogonic map of the USA

Photovoltaic generator   All PV strings of a PV power supply system, which are electrically connected. *See: Appendix 4: Photovoltaics*

Photovoltaic module   Single solar cells are interconnected to form larger units to generate electricity for different uses. Cells connected in series have a higher voltage, while those connected in parallel produce more electric current. The interconnected solar cells are usually embedded in transparent ethyl vinyl acetate, fitted with an aluminum or stainless steel frame and covered with transparent glass on the front. A junction box on the underside of the module is used to allow for connecting the module circuit conductors to external conductors.

Photovoltaic module tilt angle   For proper operation, PV modules must be oriented as closely as possible toward the equator. In the

Table 4 Photovoltaic module tilt angles

When system most used	Recommended tilt angle
All year	Latitude
Mostly winter	Latitude +15°
Mostly summer	Latitude -15°
Mostly autumn or spring	Latitude

northern hemisphere, the direction is true south: in most areas this varies from the magnetic south given by a compass. A simple connection must be made. First, find the magnetic variation from the isogonic map. This is given in degrees east or west from magnetic south.

The modules should be installed within 200° of true south. In areas with morning fog, the array can be oriented up to 200° toward the west to compensate. Conversely, arrays in areas with a high incidence of afternoon storms can be oriented toward the east.

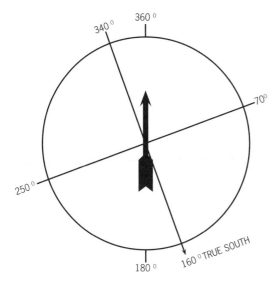

Figure 56 Directions on a compass at 20° east magnetic variation

If the array is located in the Southern Hemisphere, the array must face true north. Small, portable arrays are usually just pointed at the Sun, and moved every hour or so to follow the Sun across the sky. *See: Appendix 4: Photovoltaics*

Photovoltaic productive mode system   Use of photovoltaic cells to convert sunlight directly into electricity. *See: Appendix 4: Photovoltaics*

Photovoltaic Roadmap   Industry-led effort to help countries guide their domestic PV research, technology, manufacturing, applications and standards. The goal of the European Union's PV Roadmap is for the EU to be one of the top three in the development of PV systems; to achieve energy independence from fossil fuels; and to multiply the use of PV by 30 times by 2010. Members of the EU share research results. Other countries, including the USA, Japan, and Australia, also have a PV Roadmap.

Photovoltaic system   Complete set of components for converting sunlight into electricity by the photovoltaic (PV) process, including the array

and balance of system components. A complete PV energy system is composed of three subsystems.

- On the power-generation side, a subsystem of PV devices (cells, modules, arrays) converts sunlight to direct-current (DC) electricity.
- On the power-use side, the subsystem consists mainly of the load, which is the application of the PV electricity.
- Between these two, a third subsystem enables the PV-generated electricity to be properly applied to the load. This third subsystem is often called the balance of system (BOS).

Figure 57 shows the elements needed to get the power created by a PV system to the load (in this example, a house). The stand-alone PV system (a) uses battery storage to provide dependable DC electricity day and night. Even for a home connected to the utility grid (b), PV can produce electricity (converted to AC by a power conditioner) during the day. The extra electricity can then be sold to the utility during the day, and the utility can in turn provide electricity at night or during poor weather. *See: Appendix 4: Photovoltaics; Balance of system*

Photovoltaic tracking array   Photovoltaic (PV) array that follows the path of the Sun to maximize the solar radiation incident on the PV surface. The ability to follow the Sun produces significantly greater amounts of energy when the Sun's energy is predominantly direct. Two common orientations are i) one-axis tracking, where the array tracks the Sun east to west; and ii) two-axis tracking, where the array points directly at the Sun at all times. Tracking arrays use both direct and diffuse sunlight. Two-axis tracking captures the maximum possible daily energy from the Sun. *See: Appendix 4: Photovoltaics*

Phthalates   Toxic chemicals. Also known as phthalate esters. Group of chemical compounds that are mainly added to plastics to increase

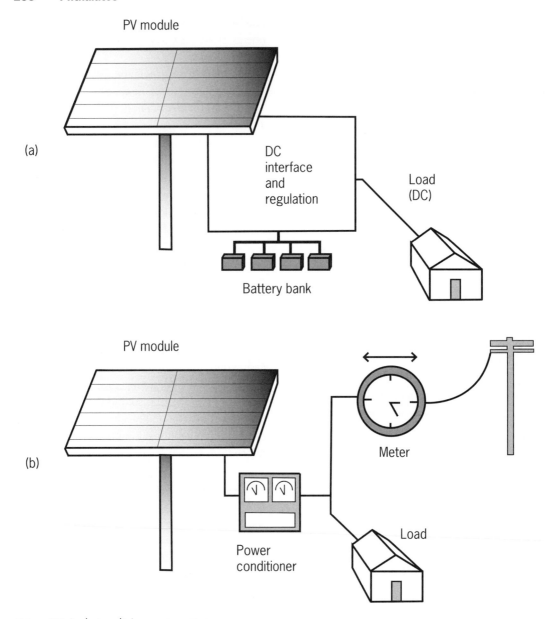

Figure 57 A photovoltaic energy system

their flexibility. They are chiefly used to turn polyvinyl chloride from a hard plastic into a flexible plastic. Phthalate esters are the dialkyl or alkyl aryl esters of 1,2-benzenedicarboxylic acid; the name phthalate derives from phthalic acid. The most widely used phthalates are di-2-ethyl hexyl phthalate (DEHP), diisodecyl phthalate (DIDP), and diisononyl phthalate (DINP). DEHP is the dominant plasticizer used in PVC, due to its low cost. Benzylbutylphthalate (BBzP) is used in the manufacture of foamed PVC, which is mostly used as a flooring material. Phthalates with small R and R groups are used as solvents in perfumes and pesticides. Phthalates are also used in nail polish, fishing lures, adhesives, caulk, and paint pigments. Because they are used in almost every major category of consumer products, and because they degrade very slowly, phthalates and their toxicity are very widespread. *See also:* ***Toxic chemicals***

Phylogenetic divergence   Evolution and diversity of organisms in a specific environment or site.

Physiographical change   Physical changes in geography and its features. Also known as geomorphology.

Phytochemical   Emissions from biological plants that suppress spores and bacteria.

Phytoplankton   Microscopic plants, such as algae, that live in water. In the ocean, phytoplankton are the foundation of the marine food chain. As they depend on certain conditions for growth, they are a good indicator of changes in their environment. Phytoplankton obtain energy through photosynthesis and must live in the well lit surface layer. Through photosynthesis, phytoplankton are responsible for much of the oxygen present in the Earth's atmosphere—up to 90%. Used in biological wastewater treatment systems to purify sewage.

Phytoremediation   Use of plants to remediate contaminated soil and groundwater. *See also:* ***Bioremediation***

Picocurie (pCi)   Unit for measuring radioactivity, often expressed in pCi per liter of air. Radon gas occurs as a by-product of uranium decay. Levels above 4 pCi/liter are considered harmful.

p-i-n and n-i-p   One of the basic types of photovoltaic (PV) device. A semiconductor PV device structure that layers an intrinsic semiconductor between a p-type and an n-type semiconductor. *See also:* ***Photovoltaic device***

Pioneer species   Plants, lichens, and microbes that first colonize a terrestrial site.

Planned obsolescence   Products that have a predetermined life span.

Plastics   Traditional plastics are synthetic polymers manufactured from nonrenewable resources including as oil, coal, and natural gas. The petrochemicals are combined with a number of toxic chemicals to make plastic. These plastics are not biodegradable, linger in the environment, and become contaminants because of their oil and coal content. Traditional plastics do not biodegrade because their long polymer molecules are too large and too tightly bonded together to be broken apart and assimilated by decomposer organisms. Researchers estimate that it takes 30–40 years for synthetic plastics to biodegrade.

Biochemical researchers and engineers have developed biodegradable plastics that are made from renewable resources, such as plants. Plastics derived from wheat or corn starch are easily broken down by microbes, so they can be decomposed by living organisms and become humus. Humus is recycled in nature when it is used as mulch. Another way of making biodegradable polymers involves getting bacteria to produce granules of a plastic called polyhydroxyalkanoate (PHA) inside their cells. Bacteria are simply grown in culture, and the plastic is then harvested. Researchers have also taken genes from this kind of bacteria and stitched them into corn plants, which then manufacture the plastic in their own cells.

Plastics pyramid   A pyramid of plastic materials based on composition, designed to assist in making material selections. The base of the pyramid (e.g. biobased polymers) damages the environment the least; the top of the pyramid (e.g. polyvinyl chloride, PVC) inflicts the worst environmental damage. The five levels of the plastic pyramid are: i) worst—PVC and other halogenenated plastics; ii) second worst—polyurethane, polystyrene, acrylonitrile butadiene styrene resin, polycarbonate; iii) middle of the pyramid—polyethylene terephthalate; iv) second least polluting—polyolefins (polyethylene, polypropylene, etc.); v) least polluting—biobased polymers.

Playas　Areas at the bottom of undrained desert basins that are sometimes covered with water.

Plug flow digester　A type of anaerobic digester that has a horizontal tank in which a constant volume of material is added, and which forces material in the tank to move through and be digested. This process speeds up the process of waste and material decomposition.

Plug-in hybrid electric vehicle (PHEV)　A type of hybrid engine with batteries that can be charged externally to displace some or all of their internal combustion engine power and gasoline fuel. A pure battery electric vehicle (BEV) during its charge-depleting mode. BEVs include automobiles, light trucks, and neighborhood electric vehicles. *See also: Battery electric vehicle; Hybrid engine*

Plugging　Act or process of stopping the flow of water, oil, or gas into or out of a formation through a borehole or well penetrating that formation.

Plume　Visible or measurable discharge of a contaminant from a given point of origin.

PM　*See: Particulate matter*

Point-source pollution　Pollution coming from a single point, such as a sewage outflow pipe in the case of water pollution. *See also: Nonpoint-source pollution*

Pollutant　Harmful chemical or waste material discharged into the water or atmosphere, which contaminates the environment. Sustained presence of pollutants can alter the species that can live in that environment, thereby changing the balance of that ecosystem.

Pollutants, air　*See: Air pollutants*

Pollutants, water　*See: Water pollutants*

Pollution-absorbing cement　Also called nitrogen dioxide-absorbing cement. An Italian company has begun marketing a cement that is capable of absorbing pollution from vehicles, factories, and household heating and transforming it into nontoxic gases. It uses the chemical process photocatalysis, in which sunlight triggers a chemical reaction when titanium dioxide (TiO_2) on the surface of the cement comes into contact with pollutants in the air and catalyzes NO_x and SO_x, which can then be turned into calcium nitrate and sodium nitrate—gases that occur naturally and are harmless in small doses. Other car exhaust fumes are transformed into carbon dioxide (CO_2).

The cement, known as TX Active (or TX Millennium), was researched by an Italian university and is manufactured by a private company. It works best in bright sunlight. Early tests indicate that the material reduces NO_x and CO_2 by over 40%. Life tests have not been completed. TX Active cement has already been used on a number of buildings, including Air France's new headquarters at Paris's Charles de Gaulle Airport, Rome's Dives in Misericordia church, and Bordeaux's Hotel de Police.

Polycarbonate (PC)　Nonbiodegradable plastic, the production of which emits airborne toxins. A thermal plastic that is easily molded, it is widely used in the chemical industry and for food storage products.

Polychlorinated biphenyls (PCBs)　($C_{12}H_{10-x}Cl_x$) A class of organic compounds. Classified as a persistent organic pollutants, and banned in

1979 after research showed that PCBs cause skin disease and liver damage and are possible carcinogens. Once used in making paint and electrical transformers and a source of industrial waste, PCBs are nonbiodegradable and accumulate in surface and groundwater because they are drawn to sediment. PCBs remain prevalent in the environment because they are not biodegradable. *See also:* **Soil contaminants; Toxic chemicals**

Polycrystalline silicon   Material used to make photovoltaic cells.

Polyesters   Nonbiodegradable plastic commonly used in food containers and wraps, microwave cookware, and bathroom counters. *See also:* **Plastics**

Polyethylene   Nonbiodegradable plastic used for bottles, bags, films, and plastic wrapping. *See also:* **High-density polyethylene; Linear low-density polyethylene; Low-density polyethylene; Polyethylene terephthalate**

Polyethylene terephthalate (PET)
Nonbiodegradable plastic that can be recycled. Used as containers for soft drinks.

Polyisocyanurate   Foam insulation made with chlorofluorocarbons (CFCs) and hydrochlorofluorocarbons (HCFCs), both of which when released into the atmosphere accumulate in the stratosphere, where they harm the ozone layer. Polyisocyanurate is made as a liquid, sprayed foam and a rigid foam board. It can also be made into laminated insulation panels.

Polymer   A macromolecule, a polymer is a large molecular mass composed of repeating structural units, or monomers, connected by covalent chemical bonds. Examples of polymers include plastics, DNA, and proteins. A simple example is polypropylene, the repeating unit structure of which is shown in Figure 58.

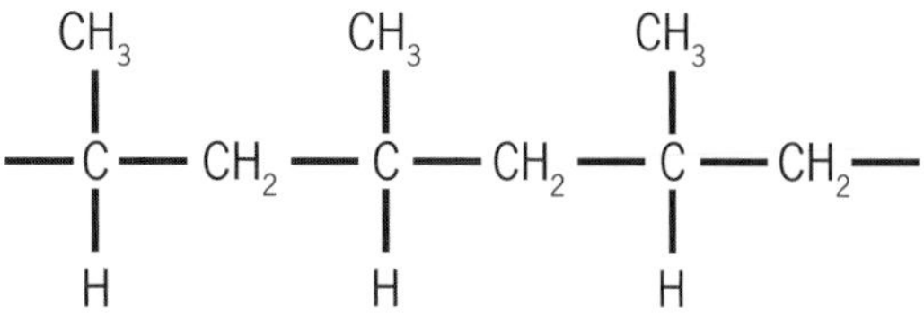

Figure 58 Polypropylene or poly(1-methylethylene)

Polymers make up a large class of natural and synthetic materials with many purposes and characteristics. Natural polymer materials such as shellac and amber have been in use for centuries. Biopolymers such as proteins (e.g. hair, skin, part of the bone structure) and nucleic acids play crucial roles in biological processes. A variety of other natural polymers exist, such as cellulose, the main constituent of wood and paper. Typical synthetic polymers are bakelite, neoprene, nylon, polyvinyl chloride (PVC), polystyrene, polyacrylonitrile, and polyvinyl butyral (PVB). The term is commonly used to indicate plastic.

Polymer electrolyte membrane fuel cell (PEM)
See: **Proton exchange membrane fuel cell**

Polymer solar cell   The unique characteristic of these solar cells is their easy, low-cost processing and good performance. To convert sunlight into electricity, they use a thin photoactive layer consisting of a nanoscale phase-separated blend of two polymer materials with complementary electronic properties. At the interface of these two materials, positive and negative charge carriers are created by the action of light. These charges are then transported and collected at two opposite electrodes. In 2005, a new plastic solar cell was invented at the University of Toronto. Using the infrared spectrum, this solar cell is able to harness the Sun's invisible, infrared rays. It is predicted that plastic solar cells will eventually be five times more efficient than current solar cell technology.

Like paint, the composite can be sprayed onto other materials and used as portable electricity. A sweater coated in the material could power a cell phone or other wireless devices. A hydrogen-powered car painted with the film could potentially convert enough energy into electricity to continually recharge the car's battery. Researchers foresee future "solar farms" consisting of the plastic material that could be rolled across deserts to generate enough clean energy to supply the entire planet's power needs.

Plastic solar cells are not new, but existing materials are only able to harness the Sun's visible light. While half the Sun's power lies in the visible spectrum, the other half lies in the infrared spectrum. Specially designed nano-particles called quantum dots, combined with a polymer, result in the plastic that can detect energy in the infrared. With further advances, researchers believe the new plastic could allow up to 30% of the Sun's radiant energy to be harnessed, compared with 6% in today's best plastic solar cells. Developments released in 2008 indicate that US scientists have created another new technique for fabricating organic polymer solar cells—a step toward producing low-cost, plastic solar cells. Researchers at the University of California, Los Angeles (UCLA) Henry Samuel School of Engineering and Applied Science and UCLA's California Nano-Systems Institute used an electronic, glue-based lamination process, combined with interface modification, to create a one-step method for semitransparent polymer solar cell fabrication. The method eliminates the need for expensive and time-consuming high-vacuum processes now used in fabrication, and the resulting device has the advantage of being low-cost and achieving high transparency for various applications. Other research cautions that polymers act like an amorphous material and could be doped to behave like an amorphous semiconductor. The band gap would be fuzzy, which would enhance the recombination and thus lower the efficiency.

Polyolefins Family of polymer products including polyethylene and polypropylene.

Polypropylene (PP) Nonbiodegradable plastic used in packaging, fibers, and molded parts for cars.

Polystyrene (PS) Nonbiodegradable plastic used for foam insulation, cups, and toys. A polymer made from the monomer styrene, a liquid hydrocarbon that is commercially manufactured from petroleum by the chemical industry. USEPA has estimated that it takes approximately 2000 years for polystyrene to decompose. *See also: Extruded polystyrene*

Polyurethane (PU) Nonbiodegradable plastic used in insulation and products such as carpet underlay.

Polyvinyl chloride (PVC) Nonbiodegradable plastic used in pipes and pipe fittings, floor tiles, house sidings and gutters, packaging, wire insulation, and credit cards.

Polyvinylidene chloride (PVDC) Nonbiodegradable plastic used in household products and plastic wrap, cling film, or cling wrap.

POPs   *See: Persistent organic pollutants*

Population Members of the same species sharing a habitat. *See also: Human population*

Porosity Material with holes that allow air and/or water to pass through it.

Porous block pavement systems Prefabricated lattice structures made of concrete or plastic, designed to support light traffic from cars and pedestrians while allowing water to drain through. The blocks are filled with aggregate or soil planted with vegetation. These systems can be used where traffic is intermittent, such as some parking lots.

Portland cement An all-purpose cement which is made of limestone, some clay minerals, and gypsum. Also known as hydraulic cement (cement that not only hardens by reacting with water but also forms a water-resistant product). Common uses for Portland cement include pavements, foundations, sidewalks, walkways, patios, swimming pool decks, reinforced concrete buildings, bridges, precast and prestressed concrete, railway structures, tanks, reservoirs, culverts, water pipes, and masonry units. Portland cement manufacture emits airborne pollution of dust and gases, particularly carbon dioxide. Workers at cement manufacturing plants may be exposed to sulfur dioxide (SO_2) when fuel containing sulfur is used. Sustained exposure to SO_2 can cause health problems. Other emissions from the manufacture of Portland cement also cause health problems. *See also: Cement; Fly ash cement*

Post-commercial recycled content Production residue solid waste that can be recycled and processed to be used again.

Post-consumer recycled content Materials that can be recycled and processed to be used again, such as making new newsprint from old newspapers.

Potable water Drinkable water.

Powersat *See: Solar power satellite*

Power tower Also known as a central receiver solar power plant, heliostat power plant, or solar power tower. One type of concentrating solar power system. It is composed of a flat array of suntracking mirrors (heliostats) that focus sunlight on a receiver at the top of a tower. Sunlight heats the heat-transfer fluid in the receiver, which is then used to generate steam. The steam is used in a turbine generator to produce electricity. These plants are best used for utility-scale applications in the 30–to 400 MW range.

Since the 1980s, power towers have been constructed in Russia, Italy, Spain, Japan, France, South Africa, and the USA. Heat-transfer fluids have been steam, air, and molten salt. The storage mediums have been sodium, nitrate salt, oil, ceramic, and water. Towers with salt storage allow electricity to be delivered to the grid when the demand for power is highest. This thermal storage also gives the power plant designer greater flexibility to develop plants with a wider range of capacity to meet the needs of the utility grid, thereby increasing efficiency and lowering energy costs.

Pozzolana Powdered volcanic ash used in making hydraulic cement. It contains silicates or aluminosilicates that solidify when combined with cement or lime. One of its uses is to immobilize hazardous waste contaminants and prevent seepage of these contaminants into the ground. Sources of pozzolanic materials are fly ash and slag, which are industrial by-products from blast furnaces.

PP *See: Polypropylene*

Primary production Term used to describe the rate of biomass production. There is higher production of biomass in areas of high temperature, moisture, and nutrient availability.

Primary wastewater treatment First stage of treating wastewater. Filters and scrapers are used to remove pollutants. Solid material in sewage also settles out in this process. *See also: Secondary wastewater treatment; Tertiary wastewater treatment*

Principle of competitive exclusion Natural selection process in which two similar species in an ecosystem occupy different ecological niches to reduce competition for food.

Prior appropriation Primary water-ownership doctrine used in the western USA since the 19th century. It is the practice of giving the first productive user of water the right to that water indefinitely, and was a big incentive to establish the right to use scarce water from rivers and streams, and later groundwater. This doctrine can be summed up as "first in time is first in line". The prior appropriation doctrine is distinguished from the riparian doctrine, under which those who own land next to water have rights to use the water. Prior appropriation severed the tie between land and water rights, so land ownership is not necessary to claim the water rights. The historical requirements for a valid water right under the prior appropriation doctrine are the intent to divert water, the actual diversion of water, and the application of that water to beneficial use.

A corollary of prior appropriation is law of capture or rule of capture, which determines ownership of captured groundwater, oil, and gas. The general rule is that a landowner who extracts or "captures" groundwater, oil, or gas from a well that bottoms within the subsurface of his or her land acquires absolute ownership of the substance, even if it is drained from the subsurface of another's land. In Texas, for example, the law states that wells must be drilled vertically and cannot be slanted to abstract water, oil, or gas from the property of some other land owner. On the other hand, the rule of capture would allow a bottler of spring water to tap water without restraint or regard to a neighbor's needs.

The rule of capture and prior appropriation doctrines and laws threaten water resources for cities, rural areas, farming, and the environment by decreasing local groundwater levels, base flows of rivers, streams, and spring flows, and water supplies. Acute interest in a continued natural ecobalance, along with increases in population, urban growth, and economic development,

require intervention of public policy and laws to govern the use and extraction of water and to ensure proper management, use, and monitoring of water resources. *See also:* ***Riparian rights; Water rights, laws governing***

Producer responsibility laws   *See: Take back laws*

Productive mode design Ecodesign strategy specifying systems that generate their own energy or minimize reliance on nonrenewable sources of energy. Productive mode systems include photovoltaic, solar collectors, wind, and water generators. *See also:* ***Full mode design; Mixed-mode design; Passive mode design***

Propane   Also known as liquefied petroleum gas (LPG). Propane (C_3H_8) is a by-product of natural gas processing and crude oil refining. It is a popular alternative fuel for vehicles because the pipelines, processing facilities, and storage for efficient distribution already exist. LPG produces fewer vehicle emissions than gasoline.

Propellant   Air pollutant; any gas, liquid, or solid the expansion of which can be used to impart motion to another substance or object. In aerosol dispensers, compressed gases such as nitrous oxide, carbon dioxide, and many halogenated hydrocarbons are used as propellants. The propellant may remain in gaseous form (nitrous oxide or carbon dioxide), or it may liquefy under pressure in the container.

Proton exchange membrane fuel cell (PEM)
Also known as a polymer electrolyte membrane fuel cell. One type of fuel cell. A fuel cell converts chemical energy directly into electricity and heat rather than burning a fuel. Electrons are removed from fuel elements (catalytic reaction) in the fuel cell to create electric current. The PEM fuel cell offers higher power density than any other fuel cell system, with the exception of the advanced

aerospace alkaline fuel cell. The proton exchange membrane uses a solid polymer as an electrolyte and porous carbon electrodes containing a platinum catalyst. It needs only hydrogen, oxygen from the air, and water to operate. The use of a solid polymer electrolyte eliminates the corrosion and safety concerns associated with liquid electrolyte fuel cells. It is typically fueled with pure hydrogen supplied from storage tanks or onboard reformers. It can also operate on reformed hydrocarbon fuels, with pretreatment, and on air. The anode and cathode are prepared by applying a small amount of platinum black to one surface of a thin sheet of porous, graphitized paper which has previously been wet-proofed with Teflon.

PEMs operate at relatively low temperatures, around 80 °C (176 °F). This factor allows PEMs to start up instantly, and results in less wear on the system components. However, they require a noble metal catalyst, usually platinum, to separate the hydrogen's electrons and protons, adding to system cost. The platinum catalyst is extremely sensitive to carbon monoxide (CO) poisoning, making it necessary to use an additional reactor to reduce CO in the fuel gas if the hydrogen is derived from an alcohol or hydrocarbon fuel. *See also: Fuel cells*

Protonic ceramic fuel cell (PCFC) This new type of fuel cell is based on a ceramic electrolyte material that exhibits high protonic conductivity at elevated temperatures. PCFCs share the thermal and kinetic advantages of high-temperature operation at 700 °C (1260 °F) with molten carbonate and solid oxide fuel cells, while exhibiting all the intrinsic benefits of proton conduction in proton exchange membrane (PEM) and phosphoric acid fuel cells (PAFCs). The high operating temperature is necessary to achieve very high electrical fuel efficiency with hydrocarbon fuels. PCFCs can operate at high temperatures and electrochemically oxidize fossil fuels directly to the anode. This eliminates the intermediate step of producing hydrogen through

the costly reforming process. Gaseous molecules of the hydrocarbon fuel are absorbed on the surface of the anode in the presence of water vapor, and hydrogen atoms are efficiently stripped off to be absorbed into the electrolyte, with carbon dioxide as the primary reaction product. Additionally, PCFCs have a solid electrolyte so the membrane cannot dry out, as with PEM fuel cells; and liquid cannot leak out, as with PAFCs.

Protist   Single-celled organism.

Proximal energy storage   Storage that is proximal to a space. It can be either coupled with the building structure, or decoupled from the structure but within the building.

P-series   An alternative fuel, P-series is a blend of natural gas liquids (pentanes plus), ethanol, and a biomass derived cosolvent methltetrahydrofuran (MeTHF). P-series fuels are clear, colorless, and have 89–93-octane liquid blends that are formulated for flexible fuel vehicles. P-series fuels can be used alone or freely mixed with gasoline in any proportion inside the flexible fuel vehicle's gas tank.

PS   *See: Polystyrene*

Psychometric   Properties of air, including temperature and water content as they apply to relative humidity.

Psychometric chart   Graph representing the relationship between air temperature and humidity. It is used by designers to understand the factors that affect thermal and internal air quality and human comfort. Dry bulb temperature is measured along the horizontal axis, and absolute humidity, moisture content of the air regardless of the temperature, along the vertical axis. The comfort zone is defined as those temperature and humidity conditions where 50% or more of people feel comfortable. The comfort level is normally 59—80 °F (15–27 °C), with 20–80% relative humidity. Conditions that fall outside the comfort zone indicate the need for some type of intervention.

PU   *See: Polyurethane*

Public trust doctrine   Doctrine dating back to the Roman Empire. It reserves, as a public trust, the right of the public to use certain natural resources, especially oceans, lakes, rivers, and the atmosphere. Implicit in the doctrine is the responsibility of governments to protect those resources held in public trust.

Pull factors   In urban planning, the factors that draw people away from rural areas and toward urban ones: housing, urban utilities, educational institutions, cultural events, employment, medical services. *See also: Push factors*

Pumped storage plant   One of the three types of hydroelectric generating plant; the other two are diversion and impoundment. *See also: Diversion power plant; Hydroelectric power plant; Impoundment power plant*

PUREX   Acronym for plutonium–uranium extraction. The chemical process used to reprocess spent nuclear fuel and irradiated targets.

Push factors   In urban planning, the factors that push rural residents to move to urban areas: unemployment, poverty, lack of medical facilities, poor housing, and isolation. *See also: Pull factors*

PVC   *See: Polyvinyl chloride*

PVDC   *See: Polyvinylidene chloride*

Pyranometer   Instrument used to measure solar reflectance, or albedo, of materials. American Society for Testing and Materials Standard E903–88 provides guidance on performing these measurements.

Pyrolitic distillation   *See: Pyrolysis; Gasification*

Pyrolysis   The process in which biomass is combusted at high temperatures and decomposed in the absence of oxygen. Burning creates pyrolysis oil, char or syngas, which can then be used like petroleum to generate electricity. It transforms the biomass into higher-quality fuel, beginning with a drying process to maximize the burning potential of the biomass. After the burned biomass is cooled, the brown liquid pyrolysis oil can be used as a gasifier. *See also: Biomass electricity; Gasification*

PZEV   *See: Partial zero-emission vehicle*

Q

Quad   One quadrillion British thermal units
(1,000,000,000,000,000 Btu).

R

R2 cement Environmental cement for waste treatment of soluble lead and soil stabilization. Used for treatment of heavy metal-laden waste.

R-adapted species Organisms whose population growth is regulated primarily by external factors. They tend to have both rapid reproduction and high mortality of offspring. They can grow exponentially in a favorable environment. Many pioneer species fit into this category.

R value Measure of resistance to heat flow. Manufacturers measure the R value under controlled conditions. If insulation becomes compacted during the installation, the R value will decrease. The units are Btu/ft^2 °F. It is inversely proportional to the U value. *See also: **U value***

Radiant barrier A layer of metallic foil that blocks radiated heat, assisting in the energy-efficiency performance of a home. Usually placed beneath roofs to block the heat gain radiating from hot roofs. Temperature reductions of 10 °F (-12 °C) or more are typical during peak summer days. The reduction of attic temperatures is considered less important in highly insulated attics (thermal insulation of R-30 and higher), with relation to conduction through the ceiling. Radiant barriers must be installed with the foil side facing the area toward which heat would normally radiate. In an attic, the foil side faces down, and as the emissivity of aluminum foils is approximately 3%, only this portion of the radiant heat is transmitted from the attic roof to other surfaces in the attic. When an engineered wood-oriented strand board surfaces down, the emissivity is in the range of 80%. If air-conditioning ductwork is located in an attic, lowering the attic temperature reduces heat gain on the ductwork.

Radiant floor A type of radiant heating system in which the building floor contains channels or tubes through which hot fluids, such as air or water, are circulated. The entire floor is evenly heated. Thus the room heats from the bottom up. Radiant floor heating eliminates draft and dust problems associated with forced air heating systems.

Radiant heating system A heating system that supplies (radiates) heat into a room by means of heated surfaces, such as electric resistance elements, or hot water (hydronic) radiators.

Radiation Transmission of energy in the form of electromagnetic radiation through space through a material medium such as water. Light (including sunlight), radio waves, and X-rays are all forms of radiation. Energy is transferred in the form of electromagnetic waves of particles that release energy when absorbed by an object. Infrared radiation, often referred to as heat, radiates according to the Stephan–Boltzmann law. The radiation is proportional to the differences between the fourth power of the temperature of two objects multiplied by the emissivity of the warmer object. *See also: **Stephan–Boltzmann law***

Radiative cooling The process of cooling by which a heat-absorbing medium absorbs heat from one source and radiates the heat away.

Radiative forcing   Term used in climate science and by the Intergovernmental Panel on Climate Change (IPCC) to define the difference between solar radiation entering the atmosphere and the Earth's radiation going out. A positive radiative forcing tends to warm the Earth's surface, while a negative forcing tends to cool the surface. It is measured in watts per m², and is a measure of energy. Greenhouse gases, for example, have a positive radiative forcing because they absorb and emit heat. Tropospheric ozone has a relatively small warming effect; stratospheric ozone has a relatively small cooling effect; aerosols can be either positive or negative contributors to heat build up; land-use change can have significant effects on radiative forcing and climate changes.

The radiation balance can be altered by factors such as intensity of solar energy, reflection by clouds or gases, absorption by various gases or surfaces, and emission of heat by various materials. Any such alteration is a radiative forcing, and causes a new balance to be reached. This happens continuously as sunlight hits the surface, clouds and aerosols form, the concentrations of atmospheric gases vary, and seasons alter the ground cover.

The term "radiative forcing" as used in the IPCC Assessments has a specific technical meaning to denote an externally imposed perturbation in

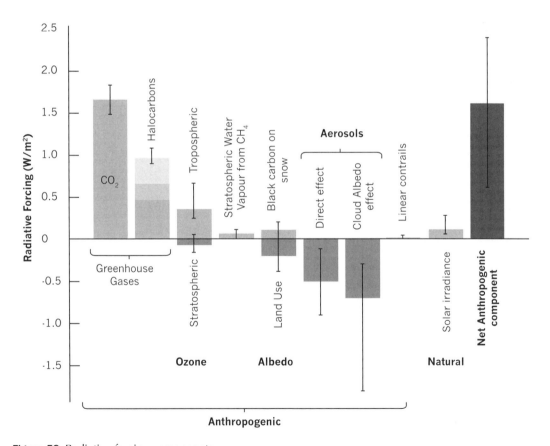

Figure 59 Radiative forcing components

Note: The two main components of radiative forcing are anthropogenic and natural. The chart shows the dominance of anthropogenically produced radiative forcing.

the radiative energy budget of the Earth's climate system, which may lead to changes in climate parameters. In terms of climate change, the term "forcing" is limited to changes in the radiation balance of the surface-troposphere system imposed by external factors, with no changes in stratospheric dynamics, without any surface and tropospheric feedbacks in operation, that is, no secondary effects induced because of changes in tropospheric motions or its thermodynamic state, and with no dynamically-induced changes in the amount and distribution of atmospheric water (vapor, liquid, and solid forms). Radiative forcing can be used to estimate a subsequent equilibrium surface temperature change arising from that forcing via the equation:

$$\delta T_s = \lambda RF$$

where λBB; is the climate sensitivity in K/(W/m^2). A typical value is 0.8, which gives a warming of 3 K for a doubling of carbon dioxide.

Figure 60 shows estimates of the globally and annually averaged anthropogenic radiative forcing (in Wm^2) due to changes in concentrations of greenhouse gases and aerosols from pre-industrial times to the year 2000, and to natural changes in solar output from 1750 to the year 2000. The height of the rectangular bar indicates a mid-range estimate of the forcing; error bars show the uncertainty range. Confidence level shows the researcher's confidence that the actual forcing lies within the given error range. Forcing associated with stratospheric aerosols resulting from volcanic eruptions is not shown because it is very variable over this period.

Radioactive substances   Toxic chemicals. The Atomic Energy Act designates the following as radioactive substances: nuclear fuels such as plutonium 239 and plutonium 241; uranium enriched with isotopes 235 and 233; any substance containing one or several of the above substances; other substances that spontaneously

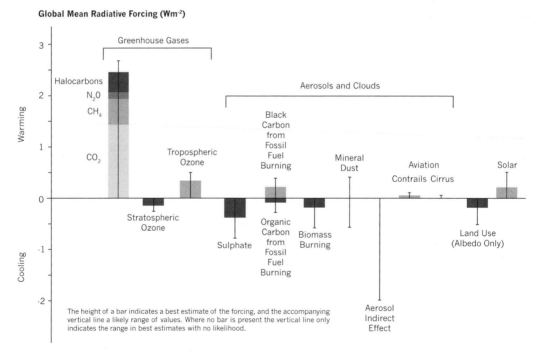

Global Mean Radiative Forcing (Wm^{-2})

The height of a bar indicates a best estimate of the forcing, and the accompanying vertical line a likely range of values. Where no bar is present the vertical line only indicates the range in best estimates with no likelihood.

Figure 60 Changes in radiative forcing between 1750 and 2005 as estimated by the IPCC

emit ionizing rays, contain one of the pluto-niums or uraniums mentioned above, or are contaminated by those substances. *See also: Toxic chemicals*

Radioactivity   Energy is released when a nucleus decays by breaking apart, either spontaneously or from another subatomic particle hitting the nucleus. This results in the formation of multiple new atoms of smaller atomic number and the release of high-energy particles, which can be ionizing radiation. The resulting nuclei may themselves be unstable and undergo radioactive decay. The process stops only when the decay product is stable. The radiative half-life varies for different radionuclides from a few micro-seconds to thousands of years. For example, plutonium has a half-life of over 24,000 years. *See also: Ionizing radiation*

Radioisotope thermoelectric generators
Devices using radionuclides that produce heat as they decay to generate electricity. They are used to supply electricity for nuclear weapons, spacecraft, and medical devices. The efficiency of converting the heat directly to electricity is generally a few per cent. Disposal of the fuel is problematic.

Radionuclide   Radioactive species of an atom. May also be a toxic chemical. *See also: Toxic chemicals*

Radon   Air pollutant. Radioactive gas formed in the decay of uranium. Radon typically enters a building through cracks in the foundation. Radon decay products can be inhaled where they continue to release radiation as they decay further, thereby damaging lungs. An indoor air pollutant that can accumulate in buildings; carcinogenic. *See also: Air pollutants*

Rain forest   Also known as tropical rain forest. Rich in biomass and species. Found primarily in equatorial regions of South and Central America, Central Africa, and Southeast Asia.

Rainwater, harvested   *See: Harvested rainwater*

Rammed earth   A construction material made by compressing earth in a form; used tradition-ally in many areas of the world and widely throughout North Africa and the Middle East.

Rankine-cycle engine   A Rankine-cycle heat engine provides cooling by vapor compression. It uses solar thermal energy or solar electricity to power a cooling appliance, so is known as a solar cooling device. The vapor power consists of four processes: i) expansion using the steam turbine; ii) heat rejection using the condenser; iii) compression using the pump; iv) heat supply using the boiler.

The Rankine-cycle system uses a liquid that evaporates when heated and expands to produce work, such as turning a turbine, which, when connected to a generator, produces electricity. The exhaust vapor expelled from the turbine condenses and the liquid is pumped back to the boiler to repeat the cycle. The working fluid most commonly used is water, although other liquids can also be used. Rankine cycle design is used by most commercial electric power plants. The traditional steam locomotive is also a common form of the Rankine cycle engine. The Rankine engine itself can be either a piston engine or a turbine. *See also: Solar cooling*

RCRA   *See: Resource Conservation and Recovery Act*

RDF   *See: Refuse-derived fuel*

REA   *See: Rural Electrification Administration*

Recapture clause   Statutory term that applies to agricultural land which adjoins urban devel-opment. Many states in the USA have enacted

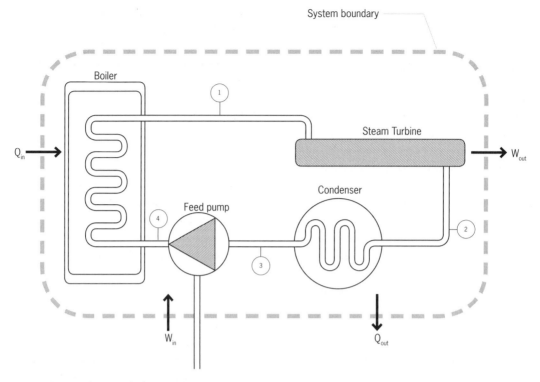

Figure 61 A Rankine-cycle heat engine

laws that allow farmers to continue farming their land in close proximity to urban development lands. The increased market value of these agricultural lands and the accompanying property taxes imposed on the increased value create financial hardship for working farms. State legislatures have enacted laws that continue an agricultural designation and the pre-urban surge value of the farm land for active working farms. However, when farmers sell their land at market value, they must pay back (recapture) the fair market value taxes that would have been imposed on their land had they not continued farming. State recapture clauses average seven to eight years' back taxes at market assessed value. These laws help prevent financial duress selling by farmers and limit ever-growing urban sprawl.

Reciprocating engine   *See: Internal combustion engine*

Reclamation   1. Conversion of unusable land into land suitable for agriculture or other uses.

2. Extraction of useful materials/substances from waste or refuse.

Recover   To salvage material embedded in waste.

Recoverable waste heat   Quantity of waste heat that is directly or indirectly available for use in some other purpose. *See also: Cascading energy; Waste heat*

Recovered materials   Materials or by-products salvaged or diverted from solid waste. These are different from materials reused in a manufacturing process.

Recovery rate   All recovered waste materials plus those returned via deposit divided by the total designated materials available. Waste materials and by-products are those that have been diverted or salvaged from various areas, such as garden waste, composting, and reused.

Recyclables   Materials that are still useful after their original use. They can be recycled or remanufactured into other products.

Recycle   To salvage useable materials from waste products and use them again in a form similar to their original use.

Recycled content   Portion of a new product that is made from recycled materials.

Recycling loop   Process of converting waste materials into new products.

Red tide   Common name for certain phytoplankton species that "bloom" so that the water appears to be colored red. These algae contain reddish pigments.

Reduction strategy   Conservation design strategy to reduce the amount of materials used in construction, particularly scarce or nonrecyclable materials. Also includes specification of materials that can be reused or recycled to minimize waste (see Figure 62).

Reflectance   Ratio of the amount of light reflected by a surface to the total amount of light striking that surface.

Reflective window film   A material, applied to window panes, that controls heat gain and loss, reduces glare, minimizes fabric fading, and provides privacy. These films can be retrofitted on existing windows.

Reflective glass   A window glass that has been coated with a reflective film and is useful in controlling solar heat gain during the summer.

Reflectivity   Ratio of reflected sunlight to received sunlight. If the reflective sunlight (albedo) is captured, more than 100% of the direct solar energy on a surface is available. *See also: Albedo*

Reforestation   Planting of forests on lands that previously contained forest but have been converted to some other use.

Reformate   Hydrocarbon fuel that has been processed into hydrogen and other products for use in fuel cells.

Reformer   Device used to generate hydrogen from fuels such as natural gas, propane, gasoline, methanol, and ethanol for use in fuel cells.

Reformulated gasoline (RFG)   Gasolines that have had their compositions or characteristics altered to reduce vehicular emissions of pollutants—low levels of smog-forming volatile organic compounds and low levels of hazardous air pollutants—particularly pursuant to USEPA regulations.

Refrigerants   Compounds used in heat cycles that reversibly undergo a phase change from a gas to a liquid. Traditionally fluorocarbons (especially chlorofluorocarbons) were used as refrigerants, but they are being phased out because of their ozone-depleting effects. *See also: Air pollutants*

Refuse-derived fuel (RDF)   Solid fuel produced by shredding municipal solid waste. Noncombustible materials such as glass and metals are generally removed prior to making RDF. The residual material is sold as-is, or compressed into pellets, bricks, or logs. RDF processing facilities are typically located near a source of municipal solid waste, while the RDF combustion facility can be located elsewhere. Existing RDF facilities process between 100 and 3000 tons per day.

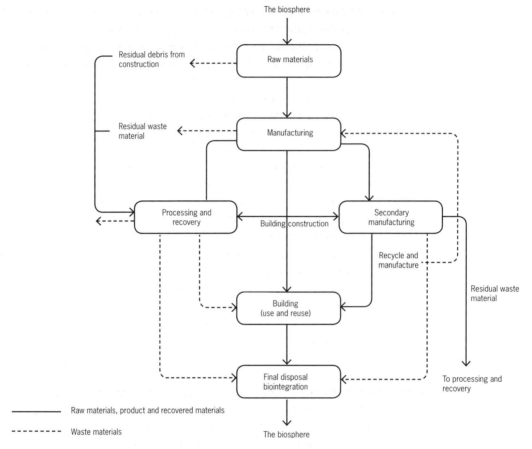

The biosphere

Raw materials

Residual debris from construction

Manufacturing

Residual waste material

Processing and recovery

Building construction

Secondary manufacturing

Recycle and manufacture

Residual waste material

Building (use and reuse)

Final disposal biointegration

To processing and recovery

———— Raw materials, product and recovered materials

- - - - - - - Waste materials

The biosphere

Figure 62 A model of use, reuse, and recovery

Regeneration   Reclamation or repair of something that was lost or damaged, for example, restoration of forests and mine sites.

Regenerative cooling   A type of cooling system that absorbs or rejects heat during the charging and discharging cycle to perform the specified process, often using a thermal latent heat storage subsystem.

Regenerative farming   Land and farming practices that maintain productivity and health of the soil by rotating crops, planting ground cover, protecting uncultivated surfaces with crop residue, and reducing synthetic chemical inputs and mechanical compaction.

Regenerative fuel cell (RFC)   Also known as a reversible fuel cell. Produces electricity from hydrogen and oxygen and generates heat and water as by-products, like other fuel cells. RFCs can also create hydrogen during the day with solar electric power, then use the hydrogen fuel at night to power a hybrid solar/hydrogen fuel cell for high-altitude unmanned reconnaissance airplanes. The ability to use electricity from solar power to divide the excess water into oxygen and hydrogen fuel is called electrolysis. This is comparatively young fuel cell technology, and is being developed by NASA.

Regenerative heating   The process of using heat that is rejected in one part of a cycle for another function or in another part of the cycle. May be referred to as combined heat and power.

Relative humidity   Percentage of water in the air compared with the maximum amount of water it can hold at any given temperature. Warmer air can hold more moisture than colder air. In technical terms, relative humidity (RH) is the ratio of the mole fraction of the water vapor in a volume of air to the largest mole fraction possible in that same volume at the same temperature and pressure. It indicates the probability of precipitation. A reading of 100% RH means the air is totally saturated with water vapor at that temperature and pressure. When an air volume has 100% RH and experiences the temperature lowered or the pressure raised, condensation will occur. For condensation to occur within a volume that has sorbent materials, the materials will need to be at a state where additional water vapor cannot be absorbed before condensation will occur. The diffusivity of the material as a function of time affects this process. *See also: Absolute humidity*

REC   *See: Renewable energy credits*

Recommended Exposure Limits
Recommendations made by the National Institute for Occupational Safety and Health for the maximum exposure to specific chemicals, inhalants, and other materials.

Release   Any spilling, leaking, pumping, pouring, emitting, emptying, discharging, leaching, dumping, or disposing into the environment of a hazardous or toxic chemical or extremely hazardous substance.

Remedial action   *See: Cleanup*

Remote energy storage   Storage located outside the building and its envelope. Remote storage is designed to improve heating and cooling system efficiency.

Removal action   *See: Cleanup*

Renewable energy   Energy resources that are virtually inexhaustible in duration, but limited in the amount of energy that is available per unit of time. These resources include: biomass, hydrogen, geothermal, solar, wind, ocean thermal, wave action, and tidal action.

Renewable energy certificates   *See: Green certificates*

Renewable energy credits (REC)   Energy credits that competitive electricity retailers can purchase or trade among each other to meet their individual renewable energy requirements. One REC is equal to 1 megawatt hour of qualified renewable energy generated from a renewable energy resource.

Renewable materials and products   Products and materials made from plants that are typically harvested within a 10-year cycle or shorter. *See also: Bamboo*

Repairability   Damaged or old product that can be repaired or restored at a cost that is less than the cost of replacing that product with a new one.

Residual fuel oil   Oils left over after distillate fuel oils and lighter hydrocarbons have been distilled. These are heavier oils and include: No. 5 medium viscosity oil; Navy Special for use in steam-powered vessels and in shore power plants; and No. 6 used for commercial and industrial heating, electricity generation, and to power ships.

Residue   Remnants or salvage materials that remain after processing, incineration, composting, or recycling has been completed.

Resin-modified emulsion pavement   Pavement that contains a binder made primarily from tree resins. The construction process is similar to those for asphalt pavements. The resin binder is translucent, so the pavement keeps the color of the aggregate. Research results show that pavements that are light gray or tan decrease pavement surface temperatures by 20–40 °F (11–22 °C) and may also increase pavement life. Increased use of this type of pavement could substantially reduce the heat island effect.

Resource Conservation and Recovery Act, US (RCRA)   Protects human health and environment from the potential hazards of waste disposal, conserves energy and natural resources, reduces the amount of waste generated, and ensures wastes are managed in an environmentally sound manner. Has legal enforcement authority.

Resource partitioning   Species adaptation in a shared ecosystem to reduce direct competition for the same food or resources. It is a self-selected ecological niche, and helps maintain the natural biodiversity of a specific biome.

Resources   In ecodesign, refers to the nature components of an ecosystem.

Response action   *See: Cleanup*

Respiration   Process in which living organisms convert organic matter to carbon dioxide, releasing energy and consuming oxygen.

Restriction of Hazardous Substances directive   *See: Take back laws*

Retention basin   Area designed to return precipitation runoff and prevent erosion and pollution.

Retrofit   1. Addition of a pollution-control device to an existing facility without making major changes to the generating plant. Also called backfit.

2. Addition of new technology or features to older systems or products.

3. Modification of existing structure to make it more modern or more resistant to acts of nature.

Return irrigation   Irrigation water that is applied to an area, but is neither evaporated nor transpired, and returns to a surface stream or aquifer.

Reusability   Ability of a product to be used again in the same form.

Reuse   Using a product again without reprocessing it.

Reverse osmosis   Water or wastewater cleansing or purifying treatment that uses a semi-permeable membrane to separate waters from pollutants. An external force is used to reverse the normal osmotic process, resulting in the solvent moving from a solution of higher concentration to one of lower concentration.

Reverse thermosiphoning   Process in which heat flows from a warm area to a cooler area, such as a solar air collector at night without a reverse-flow damper. *See also: Thermosiphon*

Reversible fuel cell   *See: Regenerative fuel cell*

RFC   *See: Regenerative fuel cell*

RFG   *See: Reformulated gasoline*

Ribbon sprawl   In urban planning, description of residential and commercial development along major highways that carry traffic into a city.

Ridge-and-soffit venting   A venting system composed of a continuous, weather-shielded opening at the peak of the roof in combination with continuous screened openings along the eaves of the house. This system provides air movement under the roof, which washes the underside of the roof with air that is exhausted out the top of the roof through the ridge vent. A continuous ridge-and-soffit vent system is an effective method to ventilate an attic. It is a passive system (no fans) and is reported to out-perform fans. The effect of pulling air from the eaves and out at the ridge is an example of the thermal chimney effect.

Rigid insulation board   An insulation product made of a fibrous material or plastic foams, pressed or extruded into board-like forms. It provides thermal and acoustic insulation strength with low weight, and coverage with few heat-loss paths.

Rill   Channel made by a small stream.

Rio Declaration   United Nations Conference on Environment and Development, 1992, in Rio de Janeiro. It reaffirmed the Declaration of the United Nations Conference on the Human Environment, adopted in Stockholm on 16 June 1972, and sought to expand it. Set forth in 18 principles, the goal was to establish a new and equitable global partnership through the creation of new levels of cooperation among states, key sectors of societies, and people, and to have effective international agreements that respect the interests of all and protect the integrity of the global environmental and developmental system.

Riparian area   Area adjacent to streams and rivers, important as buffers to runoff. Many riparian areas include wetlands.

Riparian rights   Common practice in England and USA's New England since the 19th century; allow landowners adjacent to a stream to have the right to use the water in the stream. The rights to adjacent water were considered part of

the right of ownership of land. In law, riparian rights were recognized as the qualified privilege of a landowner to use the water adjacent to or flowing through his or her property. The privilege may be modified or even denied because of the competing needs of other private property-holders, or of the community at large. There is no private ownership of such water in most cases, and it cannot ordinarily be impounded and sold. The owner, however, may use the water for private purposes, such as stock watering or irrigation, and then return the unused residue. Most uses of water affect its purity to some degree, and recent environmental legislation has greatly restricted the amount of permissible water-use pollution. Water projects such as dams that threaten the survival of rare species can be blocked under the US Endangered Species Act.

The essential nature of water in maintaining the balance of natural ecosystems, as well as meeting the increased needs of growing populations, cities, and economies, creates a need for public policy and laws to govern the appropriate water abstraction, use, and management. *See also: **Prior appropriation; Water rights, laws governing***

Riparian zone   A buffer, commonly 30 m (98 feet), on each side of a stream or river.

Riprap   Broken stones placed in areas to prevent erosion, especially along banks of rivers and streams.

Rock bed   Also known as a rock bin. A container that holds rock used as the thermal mass to store solar energy in a solar heating system.

Rock bed storage   Remote thermal storage system using uniform sized rocks that can load and unload heat by thermosiphoning. Thermosiphoning relies on the gravity principle of denser cold air falling and hot air rising.

Rock wool Also known as mineral wool, vitreous fibers made from minerals or metal oxides, synthetic or natural. Stone wool and rock wool are synthetic materials and are used for insulation and filtering. Made from molten stone, rock wool is used in spray fireproofing, stud cavities in drywall assemblies with fire-resistance requirements, and packing materials in firestops. Long-term exposure to airborne rock wool has an adverse effect on human health.

Roof garden   *See: Green roof*

Roof pond   Heat storage collector mass placed on a roof, that contains water and is exposed directly to the Sun. The collector absorbs and stores the solar gained heat. Thermal storage in the ceiling will radiate uniform, low-temperature heat to the entire building in both sunny and cloudy conditions and at night. It can cool a building by evaporation at night.

Roof ventilator   A stationary or rotating vent used to ventilate attics or cathedral ceilings, usually made of galvanized steel or polypropylene. May also use ridge ventilators.

Rotary kiln incinerator   Incinerator with rotating combustion chamber that keeps waste moving, thereby allowing it to vaporize for easier burning.

Run-of-river hydropower A type of hydro-electric facility that uses the river flow with very little alteration and little or no impoundment of the water.

Runoff Water that flows across the ground surface rather than soaking into the ground. It can be the result of natural rain and storms, industrial effluent, or flooding. Stormwater runoff occurs when precipitation from rain or snowmelt flows over the ground. Impervious surfaces such as driveways, sidewalks, and streets prevent stormwater runoff from naturally soaking into the ground. Stormwater can pick up debris, chemicals, dirt, and other pollutants, and flow into a storm sewer system or directly to a lake, stream, river, wetland, or coastal water. Anything that enters a storm sewer system is discharged untreated into the water bodies used for swimming, fishing, and drinking water.

Rural Electrification Administration (REA)   An agency of the US Department of Agriculture that makes loans to states and territories in the USA for rural electrification, and provides electrical energy to rural areas that do not receive central station service. It also furnishes and improves electricity and telephone service in rural areas, assists electricity borrowers to implement energy conservation programs and on-grid and off-grid renewable energy systems, and studies the condition and progress of rural electrification.

S

S curve Graphic representation of population growth that levels out once the population reaches its carrying capacity. *See also: J curve*

Salt gradient solar pond An efficient, low-cost solar energy collection and long-range storage system for low-temperature heat. Although current research is primarily geared to space heating (which varies seasonally) and industrial process heating (which poses a constant demand), crop-drying, water desalination, cooling, and electricity production are possible applications of the solar pond. In a constructed salt gradient solar pond, there are three main layers. The top layer is near ambient temperature and has low salt content. The bottom layer is hot, typically 160–212 °F (71–100 °C), and is very salty. The important gradient zone separates these zones. This zone acts as a transparent insulator, permitting sunlight to be trapped in the hot bottom layer from which useful heat is withdrawn. This is because the salt gradient, which increases the brine density with depth, counteracts the buoyancy effect of the warmer water below, which would otherwise rise to the surface and lose its heat to the air. A Rankine cycle engine is used to convert the thermal energy to electricity.

Saltcake Cake of dry crystals of radionuclides, found in high-level waste tanks.

Salvage Reclamation or recovery of damaged or discarded material.

Sand filters Devices that remove suspended solids from sewage. Aerobic decomposition of the remaining wastes cleans the water further.

Saprotroph Organism able to absorb soluble organic nutrients from dead plant or animal matter; assists in the decomposition process.

Satellite power systems Systems that provide large amounts of electricity for use on Earth from one or more satellites in geosynchronous Earth orbit. Researched by Arthur D. Little Corporation in the 1970s, probably for military applications. A large array of solar cells on each satellite would provide electricity, which would be converted to microwave energy and beamed to a receiving antenna on the ground. There it would be reconverted into electricity and distributed in the same way as any other centrally generated power, through a grid. Currently, the systems are very inefficient and expensive. *See also: Solar power satellite*

Schottky diode Electronic barrier used as an interface between a semiconductor, such as silicon, and a sheet of metal, creating a diode. The largest differences between a Schottky diode or barrier and a p–n junction are its typically lower junction voltage, and decreased (almost nonexistent) depletion width in the metal. It is used in photovoltaic cells. *See also: Avalanche diode; Diode; Zener diode; Appendix 4: Photovoltaics*

SCR *See: Selective catalytic reduction*

Scrubbers Air pollution control devices that remove industrially produced pollutant gases—particularly acid gases, carbon dioxide, and mercury—and particulates from exhaust streams, or neutralize those substances to minimize their harmful effects on the environment. Many pollutants come from burning fossil fuels, such as coal, natural gas, and oil. Pollutants such as sulfur dioxide (SO_2) and nitrogen oxides (NO_x) result from burning fossil fuels. Other pollutants result from burning medical or municipal waste, or are by-products of industrial production. Scrubbers are devices that chemically remove SO_2 from gases leaving the smokestack. In other industrial processes, carbon dioxide (CO_2) is produced and emitted into the environment unless it is chemically removed. There are two main categories of scrubber.

- Wet scrubbers use a wet solution to bond with compounds and particulates. Water can be used as a scrubber for simple particles such as dust.
- Dry scrubbers or semidry scrubbers are used to remove acid gases, such as SO_2 and hydrochloric acid (HCl), from combustion sources. Dry sorbent scrubbers use an alkaline material such as hydrated lime or soda ash to react with acid gases to form solid salts, which can be removed through a particulate control device; these are used in medical waste incinerators and some municipal incinerators. Another type of dry scrubber uses a fine alkaline slurry to absorb the acid gases and transform the gases into solid salts, which are removed by a particulate control device.

Mercury removal produces a waste product that requires extraction of raw mercury, or its burial in a special hazardous wastes landfill to prevent mercury contamination of the environment and groundwater. Catalytic converters on automobiles serve as a kind of scrubber that reduces NO_x emissions: these devices have been required in the USA since the 1980s. *See also: Absorption process; Packed tower; Ventury scrubber*

Seasonal energy efficiency ratio (SEER) Measure of the efficiency of air conditioners with the cooling output during its normal annual usage (in Btu) divided by the total electric energy input (in watt-hours) during the same period. The higher the number, the more efficient the device.

Secondary wastewater treatment Following primary wastewater treatment, it reduces suspended, colloidal, and dissolved organic matter in effluent from primary treatment systems. Activated sludge and truckling filters are two most common means of secondary treatment. The treatment removes the solid wastes, oxygen-demanding substances, and suspended solids. The final process is disinfection. *See also: Primary wastewater treatment; Tertiary wastewater treatment*

Sedimentary rock Type of rock that is part of the Earth's crust. Usually composed of geological deposits of material that has been buried, compacted, and fused with stone.

Sedimentation basin Excavated land used to allow solid particles in water to settle out.

Sedimentation tank Wastewater tanks in which floating wastes are skimmed off and settled solids are removed for disposal.

Seebeck effect Predicts the conversion of temperature differences into a small voltage difference using a circuit made from two dissimilar metals. A temperature difference between the two junctions produces an electrical current between the metals, with the voltage being proportional to the temperature difference (the

Seebeck coefficient). The Seebeck voltage does not depend on the distribution of temperature along the metals between the junctions. This is the physical basis for a thermocouple, which is often used for temperature measurement. Thermopiles, which contain thousands of dissimilar metal junctions, can be used to generate electricity using the Seebeck effect.

Although inefficient, scientists and researchers have noted that the Seebeck effect could be used as an environmentally clean way of producing electricity, although to date, the process is too inefficient for practical commercial applications. Current research at the University of California's Lawrence Berkeley Laboratory focuses on using the Seebeck effect to produce clean electricity. *See also: Peltier effect; Thomson effect*

SEER   *See: Seasonal energy efficiency ratio*

Selective catalytic reduction (SCR)   A method of controlling and removing nitrogen oxides (NO_x), a major environmental pollutant and primary ingredient of ground-level ozone. SCR systems inject ammonia into boiler flue gas and pass it through a catalyst bed, where the ammonia and NO_x react to form nitrogen and water vapor. Selective catalytic reducers are a post-combustion technology used in coal burning and petrochemical processing applications to reduce NO_x emissions. In the USA, SCRs are often the technology of choice for meeting USEPA regulations governing the amount of NO_x emissions that can be released into the atmosphere. Other technologies for NO_x reduction include low-NO_x burners, staged combustion, gas recirculation, low-excess-air firing, and selective noncatalytic reduction.

SCRs work in a manner similar to the way a catalytic converter works to reduce automobile emissions. A gaseous or liquid reductant (generally ammonia or urea) is added to the exhaust gases before they exit a smokestack. The mixed gases travel through several catalytic layers, causing a reaction between the NO_x emissions and the ammonia injection. The reaction converts the NO_x emissions into pure nitrogen and water vapors. The benign elements are then released into the air. One common problem with selective catalytic reducers, however, is that they operate well only within narrow temperature bands. Consequently, control units are required to ensure the exhaust gas temperatures are within the range that will allow the catalytic reaction to occur.

Selective noncatalytic reduction (SNCR)   Like selective catalytic reducers (SCR), SNCR controls nitrogen oxides (NO_x) emissions using urea or ammonia; but unlike SCR, SNCR does not require a catalyst.

Semiconductor   A material that is separated by a narrow band gap, usually around 0.3–1 electron-volt. Semiconductors make up the basis for the computer industry, almost all modern electronics, and energy conversion devices such as photovoltaic cells. They include silicon, gallium arsenide, copper indium diselenide, and cadmium telluride, and can be suited to the photovoltaic conversion process. As a semiconductor, silicon conducts electricity better than an electrical insulator, but not as well as silver or copper. To produce a solar cell, the semiconductor is contaminated or doped using boron or other materials to alter the internal structure and change the electronic properties. *See also: Doping*

Sensible heat   The change in temperature of an object as heat (thermal energy) is added to it. The thermal body must have a temperature higher than its surroundings. Sensible heat is heat that, when added to a substance, changes only its temperature and not its state. The heat can be conveyed by conduction, convection, and radiation. Similarly, when heat is removed from an object and its temperature falls, the heat removed is also called sensible heat.

Sensible heat ratio (SHR)   Ratio of sensible heat load to total heat load. It can be expressed as:

$$SHR = q_s/q_t$$

where q_s = sensible heat (kW, Btu/h) and q_t = total heat (kW, Btu/h) (includes sensible and latent heat).

Sensible load   Heating or cooling load needed to meet the comfort level of the air temperature.

Septic system   Onsite system used to treat and dispose of domestic sewage. Typically used where municipal sewers are unavailable. Waste goes directly from the home or structure into a septic tank (see Figure 63).

Sequestration   In energy and environmental terms, indicates capturing carbon dioxide emissions from large commercial facilities such as coal-fired electricity plants and injecting the emissions underground for permanent storage.

Settling pond   Open lagoon into which wastewater, contaminated with solid pollutants, is placed and allowed to stand. Solid pollutants sink to the bottom of the lagoon, and the liquid is allowed to overflow out of the enclosure. Pollutants such as chemical pesticides or

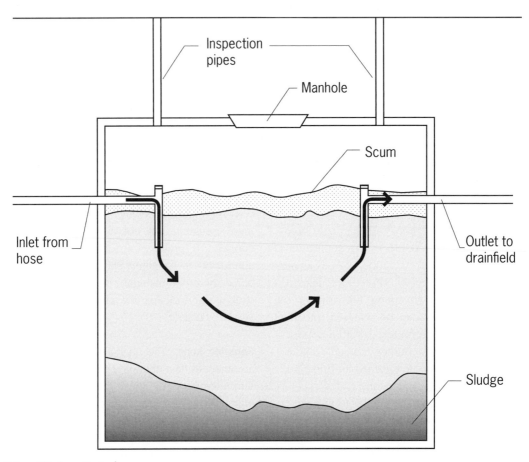

Figure 63 A septic tank

fertilizers, coal mining, and dredging could have adverse environmental and health effects if they seep into the groundwater or if their components are evaporated by the Sun and return as acid rain. The high nutrients in chemical fertilizers can cause eutrophication of rivers, lakes, and streams, resulting in fish kills.

Sewage Waste and wastewater from homes and buildings that is discharged into sewers.

Shading coefficient Ratio of solar energy transmitted through a window to that transmitted through a 1/8 inch (3/10 cm) clear glass. Note that the 1/8 inch clear glass has a shading coefficient of 1.0. This definition is different from a solar heat gain coefficient. *See also: Solar heat gain coefficient*

Shallow mound gray water system System that reuses gray water for irrigation. The shallow

mound uses an elevated absorption field for disposal of wastewater. For irrigation, a shallow layer of sand fill and top soil is placed over existing soil. This technique is used when existing soil is unsuitable for wastewater disposal. Pipes are placed near the root zone to provide irrigation. This system will require pumping of the gray water to function properly. *See also: Gray water*

Shallow trench gray water system System that reuses gray water for irrigation. Gray water flows from the house through pretreatment and is piped into shallow trenches (pipes placed 8 inches/20 cm deep). These pipes are placed close enough to the surface to feed the plant roots. The distinction between a conventional septic tank system and a shallow trench subsurface landscape irrigation system occurs in the absorption field design. Conventional septic tank systems are designed for disposal only, so

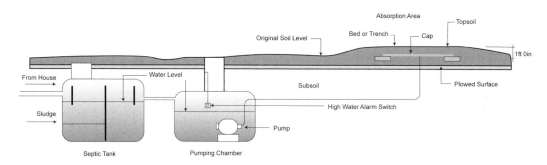

Figure 64 Shallow mound (section view)

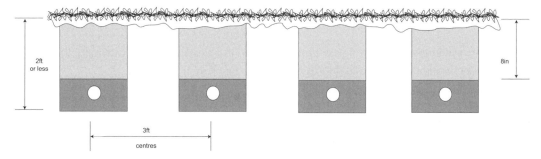

Figure 65 Shallow trench (section view)

the distribution pipes are usually placed too deep for efficient irrigation and the spacing of the trenches is sometimes too wide. Consequently, irrigation gaps may occur, which will need additional watering to prevent a lawn from having a striped effect. Mulched plant beds would pose less of a problem as the wicking effect of the mulch will even out the water concentration.

The shallow-trench gray water system can provide irrigation through shallow placement of distribution pipes and the optimum spacing of trenches. In shallow trench systems, the distribution pipes need to be installed so that they remain buried at the specified depth. *See also: Gray water*

Sheet Metal and Air Conditioning Contractors' National Association (SMACNA)   International association of union contractors, publishes guides and standards for energy conservation, energy recovery equipment and systems, installation standards for heating, air conditioning, and solar systems, and retrofit of building energy systems and processes.

Shelterwood cutting   Systematic harvesting of mature tress from a forest area over a period of decades. This method eliminates shading by older trees and provides more sunlight to encourage growth of immature, younger trees.

SHGC   *See: Solar heat gain coefficient*

SHR   *See: Sensible heat ratio*

Sick building syndrome   Various illness symptoms that affect building occupants during the time they spend in a building, and diminish or go away when they leave the building. Cannot be traced to specific pollutants or sources within the building, but researchers have identified various possible contributing factors that may include combinations of indoor air pollution, artificial fragrance, thermal discomfort, poor lighting, poor acoustics, poor ergonomics, and chemical and biological contaminants.

Sidehill construction   Term used in passive solar design, in which the structure is built into the earth on the south face of a hill. Windows on the south side admit sunshine during the day, and curtains cover these windows at night. Thermal masses in the attic floor, as well as in the north wall and floor, facilitate heat retention.

Sieve mapping   Mapping of the ecosystem in terms of its natural physical features in a way that produces a plan showing land areas suitable for different intensities of development and building types in relation to the carrying capacities of the natural systems.

Silica gel   Dehumidifying and dehydrating agent.

Silicon (Si)   Semi metallic chemical element that is a very good semiconductor material for photovoltaic devices. It crystallizes in a face-centered cubic lattice like a diamond. Commonly found in sand and quartz as the oxide.

Silviculture   Cultivation of a forest.

Sink   1. Any process, activity, or mechanism that removes a greenhouse gas, aerosol, or precursor of a greenhouse gas or aerosol from the atmosphere.

2. Natural reservoir that can absorb or receive matter or energy without undergoing change.

3. In internal air quality, material that absorbs chemicals or pollutants.

Sinkhole   Depression in the ground surface caused by dissolving underlying limestone, salt, or gypsum. Drainage is provided through underground channels that may be enlarged by the collapse of a cavern roof.

Sky court Recessed balcony area with full-height glazed doors that open out from internal areas to the terrace spaces.

Sky glow Describes the light pollution that occurs when too much artificial illumination and unmanaged glare, emitted from unshielded light fixtures, enters the night sky and reflects off airborne water droplets and dust particles.

Sky vault Term used to describe the influence of overall climate on an area's available daylight. In a predominantly cloudy climate, for example, there may be 500–510,000 footcandles of light available for most of the year. To take advantage of these conditions, a designer

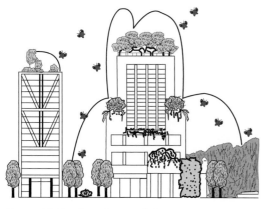

Figure 66 Roof gardens and sky courts create new urban habitats

may designate larger windows or skylight, monitors, or clerestories. As overcast skies are brighter overhead than at the horizon, the designer can use lighting source direction, such as top lighting or high windows. On the other hand, a clear sky is brighter at the horizon except near the Sun, and the designer may want to use side lighting. There are many planning methodologies and formulae available to improve the quality of the built environment based on controlling of solar radiation and the view of the sky vault.

Sky vault temperature The radiative temperature of the sky, which can be as much as 20–40 °C (70–104 °F) below the ambient air temperature. This "deep sky" temperature varies considerably with cloud cover and incident solar.

Slag By-product formed in smelting, welding, and other metallurgical and combustion processes from impurities in the metals or ores being treated. Slag consists mostly of mixed oxides of elements such as silicon, sulfur, phosphorus, and aluminum; ash; and products formed in their reactions with furnace linings and fluxing substances such as limestone. During smelting or refining, slag floats on the surface of the molten metal, protecting it from oxidation by the atmosphere and keeping it clean. Slag cools into a coarse aggregate used in certain concretes; it is used as a road-building material, as ballast, and as a source of available phosphate fertilizer. In architecture, a grayish aggregate, left as a residue of blast furnaces, is used as surfacing on built-up roofing and in manufactured products such as slag cement and slag wool.

Slash Debris left over from felling trees.

Slash and burn Destruction of forest lands for short-term use. Method of clearing natural forests and burning of residue to clear land for agricultural purposes. When the fertility of the soil is depleted, the process is repeated in a new area. The initial land is abandoned.

Slash windrows   Rows of slash or cut vegetation placed on the side of an access road to control erosion.

Sloped roof   *See: Steep-slope roof*

Sludge   Solid, semisolid, or liquid waste generated from a municipal, commercial, or industrial wastewater facility.

Slurry wall   In-ground physical containment device designed to isolate contaminant source zones and groundwater plumes from the surrounding environment. Contaminated soil, wastes, and groundwater can be physically isolated within surrounding low-permeability barriers by constructing a vertical trench excavated down to and keyed into a deeper confining layer, such as low-permeability clay or shale, and filling the trench with a slurry. Slurry walls usually consist of a soil, bentonite, or cement mixture. The slurry mix shores the trench to prevent collapse and forms a permeation barrier to prevent escape of contaminants from the contained area. Slurry walls are commonly used as subsurface barriers to reduce groundwater flow in unconsolidated earth material. Cement and bentonite in the wall can adsorb and retard the escape of heavy metals and larger organic molecules, but cannot completely stop water movement. As a result, slurry walls either are stop-gap measures, or are accompanied by pump-and-treat systems.

SMACNA   *See: Sheet Metal and Air Conditioning Contractors' National Association*

Small quantity generator   Sometimes referred to as "squeegee". Persons or enterprises that produce 220–2200 lb (90–1000 kg) per month of hazardous waste. The largest producers are automotive shops, dry cleaners, and photographic developers. *See also: **Large quantity generator***

Smart fortwo car   Micro-compact car; also called a supermini. Three-cylinder, five-speed manual transmission, German-made automobile made as both a turbodiesel and an electric car by Smart GmbH (formerly MCC Smart GmbH).

Smart fortwo seats two. It is 8 ft 2.5 in long, 5 ft wide, and 5 ft tall, allowing it to back up to the curb to park rather than parallel parking.

Figure 67 The smart fortwo cabriolet
Source: Mercedes Benz

One model has a 50 horsepower engine and three models have 61 horsepower engines. Although it is a manual transmission, the clutch is not required. Both the 50-hp and 61-hp engines are three-cylinder engines, have manual transmissions, and have turbochargers. Cars this small and light become very unstable at high speeds.

The name SMART is an acronym for Swatch Mercedes.

An electric, rechargeable version was released in the UK in 2007. The electric version has a 41-hp electric motor, which is able to reach speeds up to 69 mph and has a range of 70 miles. Charging time for the electric smart car is about 8 hours, and it will only go from 0–60 in about 19.8 seconds. *See also: Hybrid electric vehicle*

Smart growth   Term used to describe management of urbanization that seeks to serve the economy, community, and the environment. Smart growth seeks to foster healthy communities, a clean environment, economic development and jobs, strong neighborhoods with a range of housing options, and the involvement of local residents to develop decisions about their communities. Planning and development decisions to preserve natural lands and critical environmental areas, protect water and air quality, and reuse already developed land. It includes conservation of resources, such as reinvesting in existing infrastructure and reclaiming historical buildings through adaptive reuse. By designing neighborhoods that have shops, offices, schools, churches, parks, and other amenities near homes, communities provide their residents and visitors with the options of walking, bicycling, taking public transportation, or driving as they go about their business.

Smart growth principles   Based on the smart growth approach to develop and maintain communities, the Smart Growth Network developed a set of ten basic principles:

- mix land uses
- use compact building design
- create a range of housing opportunities and choices
- create walkable neighborhoods
- foster distinctive communities with a strong sense of place
- preserve open space, farmland, natural beauty, and critical environmental areas
- strengthen, and direct development towards, existing communities
- provide a variety of transportation choices
- make development decisions predictable, fair, and cost-effective
- encourage community and stakeholder collaboration in development decisions.

Smart window   Term used to describe a glazed window system that can change or switch its optical qualities when an electrical voltage is applied to it, or in response to changes in heat or light. *See also: Electrochromic windows*

SMES   *See: Superconducting magnetic energy storage*

Smog   Mixture of pollutants, especially ground-level ozone, produced by chemical reaction in the air involving smog-forming chemicals. Major source smog-formers are petroleum-based fuels and volatile organic compounds. Can have adverse health and environmental effects.

SNCR   *See: Selective noncatalytic reduction*

Sod busting   Originally used to describe tilling and cultivation of the soil. Currently used to describe both the destruction of the native ground cover and negative effects of plowing, which increases the rate of soil erosion, both by wind and water, where soil is moved elsewhere on land or deposited in bodies of water, such as the oceans.

SOFC   *See: Solid oxide fuel cell*

Softwoods   Wood from evergreen coniferous trees. They are used primarily for construction. Softwoods include cedar, fir, hemlock, pine, redwood, and spruce. They grow to maturity more quickly than hardwoods, but more slowly than bamboo. *See also: Bamboo; Hardwoods*

Soil   Top layer of the Earth's surface in which plant life can grow.

Soil carbon   Major component of the terrestrial biosphere pool in the carbon cycle. The amount of carbon in the soil is a function of the historical vegetative cover and productivity, which in turn is dependent in part on climatic variables. It is necessary to maintain a stable carbon content in the soil in order to have continued agricultural crop cultivation. If there is too little carbon in the soil, crop production becomes inefficient. This condition also influences climate change. There is evidence of carbon depletion in the soil in sub-Saharan Africa, south and central Asia, the Caribbean, and the Andean region of South America.

Methods to maintain and increase carbon in the soil include: no-till farming, leaving residue from previous crops on the field; agroforestry to increase the quality of the soil; crop covers to decrease erosion; and using compost and biosolids to fertilize crops.

Soil contaminants   USEPA lists the following as major soil contaminants: acetone, arsenic, barium, benzene, cadmium, chloroform, cyanide, lead, mercury, polychlorinated biphenyls (PCBs), tetrachloroethylene, toluene, and trichloroethylene (TCE).

Soil cut-and-fill balances   Technique used in earthmoving. Used widely in mining operations, railway, road, or canal construction, the amount of soil cut away roughly matches the amount of earthfill needed to fill a specified land area or to make nearby embankments. This method was designed to minimize the amount of earthwork and construction costs.

Soil flushing   Method of cleaning soil contaminated with hazardous wastes. The soil is flooded with a flushing solution, and leachate is removed through shallow wells or subsurface drains. The recovered leachate is then purified.

Soil stabilization   Environmentally, soil stabilization can be achieved through erosion and sediment control, storm water management, revegetation, wetland restoration, remediation, hydrocarbon removal, and detoxification of the land. *See also: Soil carbon*

Sol-air effect   Combined effects of solar radiation and air temperature on a surface. The sol-air effect is determined by solar radiation on all building surfaces, outside air temperature relative to time of day and solar position, building orientation, exterior materials relative to thermal mass, conductivity, color, textures and movable insulations, shading on surfaces, and window placement. Calculations indicate the net heat gain into a building during cooling periods and net heat loss during heating periods:

$$T_{\text{sol-air}} = T_{\text{amb}} = (I\text{-}q_{\text{ir}})/h_0$$

where: T_{amb} is the ambient temperature; I is the global solar irradiance on a surface; α is the absorbance of the material; Δq_{ir} is a correction factor to the infrared radiation transfer q_{ir}; h_0 is the heat transfer coefficient.

Solar air systems   There are six primary types of solar air heating/ventilation system.

- Type 1—a very simple construction: ambient air passes from a glazed or unglazed collector directly into the room to provide ventilation and heating. Applications include vacation cottages (dehumidification) and large industrial buildings requiring adequate ventilation.

- Type 2—circulates room air to the collector. Heated air rises to a thermal storage ceiling, from which it is conveyed back into the room. This system uses natural convection and is well suited for apartment buildings.

- Type 3—particularly suited for retrofitting poorly insulated buildings. Collector-heated air passes through a cavity between an outer, insulated wall and an inner façade. This creates a buffer, which considerably reduces heat loss via the façade of the building.

- Type 4—the classical solar air heating system, commonly used. Collector-heated air is circulated through channels in the floor or

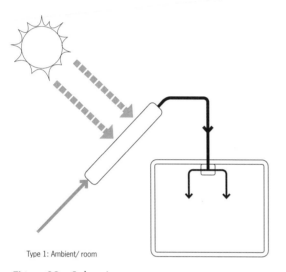

Type 1: Ambient/ room

Figure 68a Solar air systems

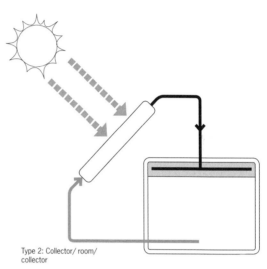

Type 2: Collector/ room/ collector

Figure 68b Solar air systems

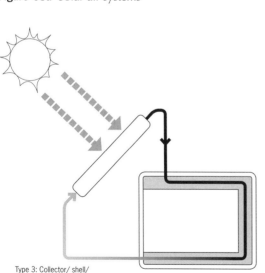

Type 3: Collector/ shell/ collector

Figure 68c Solar air systems

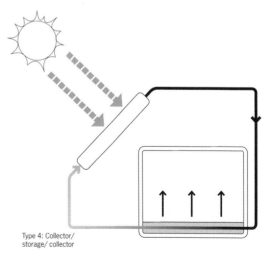

Type 4: Collector/ storage/ collector

Figure 68d Solar air systems

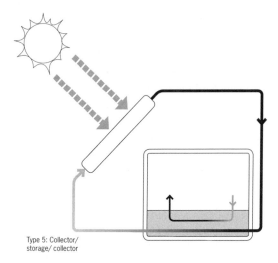

Type 5: Collector/
storage/ collector

Figure 68e Solar air systems

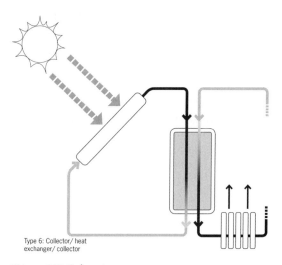

Type 6: Collector/ heat
exchanger/ collector

Figure 68f Solar air systems

in the wall. Heat is radiated into the room with a time delay of 4–6 hours. Large radiating surfaces provide a comfortable climate. Systems with forced ventilation (fans) provide the best efficiency and thermal output. They may be used in buildings with large surfaces, which serve as radiation sources.

- Type 5—an advanced version of type 4; room air is circulated through separate channels of the storage. Thus heat can be stored for a longer period and released when needed. Rarely used because investment costs are high.
- Type 6—combines a solar air collector and, via a heat exchanger, a conventional heating system. Thus common radiators and floor or wall heating components may be used. Can also provide domestic hot water; is particularly suited for retrofitting and for buildings in which heat has to be transported over long distances.

Solar cell   A semiconductor-based cell that converts sunlight into electricity. The most common solar cell is a photovoltaic cell. *See also: Nanocrystal solar cell; Polymer solar cell; Appendix 4: Photovoltaics*

Solar chimney   *See: Thermal chimney*

Solar collector   In an active solar system, usually a flat plate that absorbs light, made of a dark colored material such as metal, rubber, or plastic that is covered with glass. The absorber plate collects radiant energy from the Sun and then transfers that heat to the tubing, usually copper, and heats the fluid in the tubing, usually air or water, circulating above or below it. The fluid is used for immediate heating or stored for later use. Flat-plate collectors are the most common type used for solar water- or pool-heating systems. In the case of a photovoltaic system, the solar collector could be crystalline silicon panels or thin-film roof shingles.

Solar collector, residential use   Three types of solar collector are used for residential applications: i) flat-plate collectors; ii) integral collector-storage systems or batch heaters; iii) evacuated-tube solar collectors. *See: Batch heater; Evacuated-tube collector; Flat-plate solar thermal/heating collector*

Solar cooling   The use of solar thermal energy or solar electricity to power a cooling appliance.

The basic types of solar cooling technology are: i) absorption cooling, which can use solar thermal energy to vaporize the refrigerant; ii) desiccant cooling, which can use solar thermal energy to regenerate (dry) the desiccant; iii) vapor compression cooling, which can use solar thermal energy to operate a Rankine-cycle heat engine; and iv) evaporative coolers ("swamp" coolers), and heat-pumps and air conditioners that can by powered by solar photovoltaic systems. *See also: Desiccant cooling; Rankine-cycle engine*

Solar electric-powered vehicle Powered by photovoltaic cells. The first solar-electric hybrid car, Venturi Astrolab, made in France, is a full production zero-emission vehicle and was made available in 2008. The solar vehicle is covered with 3.6 meters of photovoltaic cells (nanoprisms) with a 21% yield, and has a top speed around 74 mph. *See also: Hybrid electric vehicle; Tribrid vehicle*

Solar energy Also known as solar power. There are two types: passive and active. Passive solar systems use nonmechanical means of capturing, converting, and distributing sunlight into usable heating, lighting, or ventilation. Examples include passive solar water heaters, Trombe walls, clerestory windows, light shelves, skylights, and light tubes. Active solar systems use electrical and mechanical components such as photovoltaic panels, pumps, and fans to process sunlight into usable outputs.

Solar energy systems Includes all types of solar power to provide energy for use in lighting, water heating, heating, cooling, and desalination of water. The solar energy may be either passive or active. *See also: Concentrating solar power system; Photovoltaic; Solar energy*

Solar envelope The largest hypothetical volume that can be constructed on a lot without overshadowing neighboring properties during critical energy-receiving hours and seasons. It is both a temporal and a spatial calculation. As buildings become taller and densities increase, access of sunlight to buildings decreases and the maximum buildable volume of the site approximates a pyramid. Researchers indicate that they will be able to do specific calculations of the solar envelope in the future.

Solar heat gain coefficient (SHGC)
Measurement of a window's capacity to block heat from sunlight. The SHGC is the fraction of the heat from the Sun that enters through fenestration, and ranges from 0 to 1. The lower the SHGC, the less solar heat the window transmits.

Solar insolation   *See: Insolation*

Solar irradiance   *See: Irradiance*

Solar pond A body of water containing brackish (highly saline) water that forms layers of differing salinity (stratifies), which absorb and trap solar energy. This density gradient inhibits heat exchange by natural convection in the salt water. Solar ponds can be used to provide heat for industrial or agricultural processes, for building heating and cooling, and to generate electricity. *See also: Salt gradient solar pond*

Solar power satellite (SPS) Also known as Powersat. A solar power station installed by NASA that is a satellite in geosynchronous orbit. The power station consists of a very large array of solar photovoltaic (PV) modules that convert solar-generated electricity to microwaves and beam them to a fixed point on the Earth. An SPS has three parts: a solar collector, usually PV modules; a microwave antenna on the satellite aimed toward the Earth; and receiving antennae on the Earth. The idea of using microwaves over long distances to transmit power was conceived by Peter Glaser in 1968 and patented in 1974. Both NASA and the US Department of Energy have been researching its feasibility since then. Current research indicates that in its present state, this satellite's PV lifespan is limited by ionizing radiation from the radiation belts and the Sun, and degrades 1–2% per year. In addition, the SPS is currently very expensive to launch, requires very large apertures required by the microwaves' power beaming, is inefficient, is hard to maintain in orbit, and cannot compete economically with more traditional sources of energy. *See also: Satellite power systems*

Solar power tower   *See: Power tower*

Solar radiation   Radiant energy emitted by the Sun from a nuclear fusion reaction that releases high-energy particles and a wide spectrum of electromagnetic energy. Of the energy that arrives at the Earth's surface, about half the electromagnetic radiation is in the visible short-wave part of the electromagnetic spectrum. Most of the other half is the near-infrared part, and the smallest portion is the ultraviolet part of the spectrum. If the radiation reaches the Earth without any interference, it is called direct solar radiation. If the radiation is scattered by the atmosphere, it is called diffuse solar radiation. A combination of direct and diffuse is called global solar radiation.

Solar sail   Alternative energy source for propulsion systems of spaceships. Using the photons from the Sun, the sail reflects incoming photons and thus a force forward propels the sail. The sail works only for travel away from the Sun. It still requires energy to maneuver and to slow down. A solar sail craft requires no fuel and emits no radiation or waste products. It is still in an experimental stage.

Solar shading   Passive mode solar control devices, including louvers, tinted and reflective glass.

Solar spectrum   Total distribution of electromagnetic radiation from the Sun. The different regions of the solar spectrum are described by their wavelength range. The visible range is about 390–780 nanometers. (A nanometer is 1 billionth of 1 meter.) Approximately 99% of the Sun's energy is contained in a wavelength region from 280 nm (ultraviolet) to 3000 nm (near infrared). Combined radiation in the wavelength region from 280 to 4000nm is called the broadband, or total solar radiation.

Solar thermal electric systems   Solar energy-conversion technologies that convert solar energy to electricity by heating a working fluid to power a turbine that drives a generator. Examples include central receiver systems (concentrating solar collectors) and parabolic troughs. It should be noted that the Seebeck effect is also being used to convert thermal to electrical energy. *See also: Concentrating solar collector; Parabolic trough; Seebeck effect*

Solar thermal parabolic dish   *See: Parabolic dish solar collector*

Solar thermal system   System that collects or absorbs solar energy. The energy collected can be used to generate high-temperature heat for electricity production and/or to process heat; medium-temperature heat to process space/water heating and electricity generation; and low-temperature heat for water and space heating and cooling.

Solar trough system   *See also: Parabolic trough*

Solar water heater   Water heater that obtains its heat from solar collectors. Heat is then transferred by pumps to a storage unit. Solar water heating systems include storage tanks and solar collectors. There are two types of solar water heating system: active systems have circulating pumps and controls; passive systems do not. Most solar water heaters require a well insulated storage tank. Solar storage tanks have an additional outlet and inlet connected to and from the collector. In two-tank systems, the solar water heater preheats water before it enters the conventional water heater. In one-tank systems, the back-up heater is combined with the solar storage in one tank.

Solar water heating systems almost always require a backup system for cloudy days and times of increased demand. Conventional storage water heaters usually provide backup and may already be part of the solar system package. A backup system may also be part of the solar collector, such as rooftop tanks with thermosiphon systems. As an integral collector storage system already stores hot water in addition to collecting solar heat, it may be packaged with a demand (tankless or instantaneous) water heater for backup. *See also: Solar water heater, active; Solar water heater, passive*

Solar water heater, active   There are two types of active solar water heating systems.

- Direct circulation system—pumps circulate household water through the collectors and into the home. They work well in climates where it rarely freezes.
- Indirect circulation system—pumps circulate a nonfreezing heat-transfer fluid through the collectors and a heat exchanger. This heats the water that then flows into the home. They are popular in climates prone to freezing temperatures.

Solar water heater, passive   Passive solar water heating systems are usually less expensive than active systems, but are usually not as efficient. However, passive systems can be more reliable and may last longer. There are two basic types of passive system.

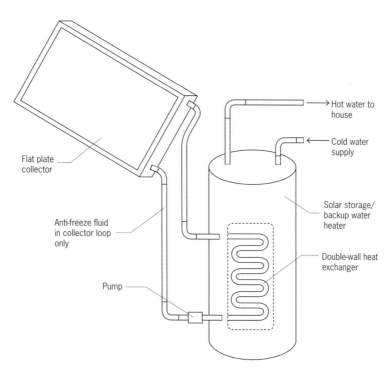

Figure 69 Active: closed loop solar water heater
Source: US Department of Energy

- Integral collector-storage passive system—works best in areas where temperatures rarely fall below freezing; also works well in households with significant daytime and evening hot-water needs.
- Thermosiphon system—water flows through the system when warm water rises as cooler water sinks. The collector must be installed below the storage tank so that warm water will rise into the tank. These systems are reliable, but contractors must pay careful attention to the roof design because of the heavy storage tank. They are usually more expensive than integral collector-storage passive systems.

Solar wind A fast outflow of hot gas in all directions from the upper atmosphere of the Sun (solar corona), which is too hot to allow the Sun's gravity to hold onto its gas. Its composition matches that of the Sun's atmosphere (mostly hydrogen) and its typical velocity is 400 km/s, or 1 million miles per hour, covering the distance from Sun to Earth in 4–5 days. The solar wind confines the Earth's magnetic field inside a cavity known as the magnetosphere and supplies energy to phenomena in the magnetosphere such as polar aurora (northern lights) and magnetic storms. It is responsible for the anti-sunward tails of comets and the shape of the magnetic fields around the planets. Solar wind can also have a measurable effect on the flight paths of spacecraft. The solar wind varies routinely through the 27-day rotation of the Sun, as well as sporadically in response to violent eruptions in the corona. These eruptions can result in geomagnetic storms on Earth.

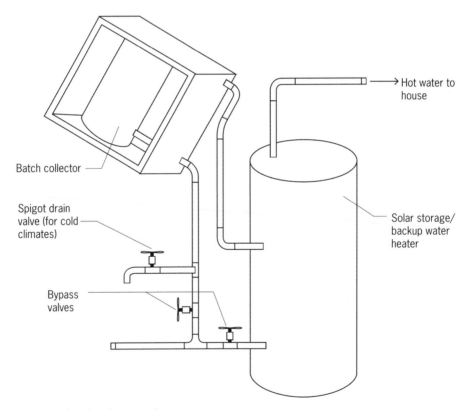

Batch collector

Spigot drain valve (for cold climates)

Bypass valves

Hot water to house

Solar storage/ backup water heater

Figure 70 Passive: batch solar water heater
Source: US Department of Energy

Solid fuel   Any fuel in solid form, such as wood, peat, lignite, coal, and manufactured fuels such as pulverized coal, coke, charcoal, briquettes, or pellets.

Solid fueled rockets   Rockets that burn a solid mixture of fuel and oxidizer and have no separation between the combustion chamber and fuel reservoir. Gunpowder is such a mixture, and was the earliest rocket fuel. They are less efficient than the best liquid fuel rockets, but are preferred for military use because they need no lengthy preparation and are easily stored in ready-to-fly condition. They are also used in auxiliary rockets that help heavily loaded liquid-fuel rockets, like the space shuttle, lift off and go through the first stage of their flight.

Solid oxide fuel cell (SOFC)   One type of fuel cell. A fuel cell converts chemical energy directly into electricity and heat rather than burning a fuel. It is done without combustion, and the only by-product is water. SOFCs use a hard, nonporous ceramic compound as the electrolyte. As the electrolyte is a solid, the cells do not have to be constructed in the plate-like configuration typical of other fuel cell types. SOFCs are expected to be around 50–60% efficient at converting fuel to electricity. In applications designed to capture and utilize the system's waste heat (cogeneration), overall fuel-use efficiencies could top 80–85%.

SOFCs operate at very high temperatures— around 1000 °C (1830 °F). High-temperature operation removes the need for a precious metal catalyst, thereby reducing cost. It also allows SOFCs to reform fuels internally, which enables the use of a variety of fuels and reduces the cost associated with adding a reformer to the system. SOFCs are also the most sulfur-resistant fuel cell type. In addition, they are not poisoned by carbon monoxide, which can even be used as fuel. This allows SOFCs to use gases made from coal.

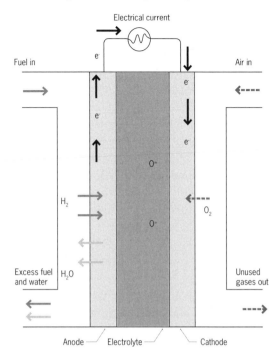

Figure 71 A solid oxide fuel cell
Source: US Department of Energy

High-temperature operation has disadvantages. It results in a slow startup and requires significant thermal shielding to retain heat and protect personnel, which may be acceptable for utility applications but not for transportation and small, portable applications. The high operating temperatures also place stringent durability requirements on materials. The development of low-cost materials with high durability at cell operating temperatures is the key technical challenge facing this technology. Scientists are currently exploring the potential for developing lower-temperature SOFCs operating at or below 800 °C (1472 °F) that have fewer durability problems and cost less. Lower-temperature SOFCs produce less electrical power, however, and stack materials that will function in this lower temperature range have not been identified. *See also: Fuel cells*

Solid oxide hybrid fuel cell power system   A recent development in high-temperature stationary fuel cell power plants is the coupling of a micro-turbine generator with a high-pressure, natural gas-fueled solid oxide fuel cell (SOFC). High-pressure waste heat from the SOFC is routed into a microturbine, generating 10% or more additional power than if the exhaust gas energy had not been recaptured. These systems are 55–60% efficient in converting the energy in natural gas into power, better than the current 50% efficiency of natural gas turbines. Research indicates that hybrid SOFCs may have the potential to reach 70% efficiency as hybrid technology improves. *See also: **Fuel cells***

Solid waste   Any garbage sludge from waste-water treatment plants, water supply treatment plants or air pollution control facilities. Includes solid, liquid, semi-solid or contained gaseous material wastes from industrial, commercial, mining, and agricultural operations. Because proper disposal of solid waste is environmentally important, states and national governments have established waste management regulations and standards. Many municipalities and states are establishing integrated solid waste management programs, as no single waste management option can handle the enormous volume of waste by itself. A typical municipal solid waste facility contains glass (4–16%), cardboard (3–15%), plastic (2–18%), dirt, ashes, and brick (0–10%), paper (25–45%), food waste (6–25%), yard and garden waste (0–20%), ferrous metals (2–10%), textiles (0–4%), rubber (0–2%), leather (0–2%), wood (1–45%), and nonferrous metals (2–10%). Hazardous waste programs regulate commercial businesses as well as federal, state, and local government facilities that generate, transport, treat, store, or dispose of hazardous waste. Each of these entities is regulated to ensure proper management of hazardous waste from the moment it is generated until its ultimate disposal or destruction.

Other ways to deal with solid waste include source reduction, which means consuming and throwing away less; composting, the degrading of organic material by microorganisms in aerobic conditions; and incineration, the burning of waste to produce energy. *See also: **Composting; Incineration; Source reduction***

Sorbent   Material that can adsorb or absorb solids, liquids, gases or vapors within a place or environment, such as a workplace respirator that can remove gases as air passes through it.

Source reduction   Reducing the amount of materials entering the waste stream by redesigning products, or production or consumption patterns. Includes purchasing durable, longlasting goods and seeking products and packaging that are as free of toxics as possible. It can be as complex as redesigning a product to use less raw material in production, have a longer life, or be used again after its original use is completed. Because source reduction actually prevents the generation of waste in the first place, it is the preferred method of waste management.

Source back to source   Concept of designing to ensure reuse, recycling, and reintegration of a structure's physical components after its designated lifespan is completed.

Source to sink   Concept covering the entire flow of the built system's components during its life cycle.

Southern Oscillation   *See: El Niño—Southern Oscillation*

Space charge   *See: Cell barrier*

Sparge   *See: Air sparging*

Species diversity   One of the three main types of diversity in an ecosystem. The diversity of the compositional element in an ecosystem includes a wide range of species of organisms, and includes genetic diversity and diversity of communities within the ecosystem. *See also: Functional diversity; Structural diversity*

Spent nuclear fuel Nuclear reactor fuel that has been used to the extent that it can no longer effectively sustain a chain reaction. There are current concerns about the safe disposal and isolation of either spent fuel from reactors or, if reprocessed, wastes from reprocessing plants.

Split spectrum cell Compound photovoltaic (PV) device in which sunlight is first divided into spectral regions by optical means. Each region is then directed to a different PV cell optimized for converting that portion of the spectrum into electricity. Such a device achieves significantly greater overall conversion of incident sunlight into electricity. Efficiencies as high as 27% have been reported, but costs remain a serious problem with this approach.

Spoil Dirt or rock removed from its original location, as in strip mining, dredging, or construction.

Spray tower scrubber This is the simplest type of particulate wet scrubber in commercial service. Sets of spray nozzles located near the top of the scrubber vessel generate water droplets that impact with particles in the gas stream as the gas stream moves upwards.

SPS *See: Solar power satellite*

Stabilization lagoon Shallow artificial pond used for treatment of wastewater. Treatment includes removal of solid material through sedimentation, decomposition of organic material by bacteria, and removal of nutrients by algae.

Stack effect Also known as chimney effect. Movement of buoyant air into and out of buildings via chimneys, flue gas stacks, or other containers. Buoyancy results from temperature

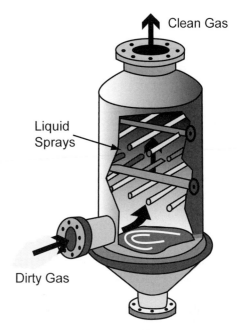

Figure 72 A spray tower scrubber
Source: US Environmental Protection Agency

and moisture differences. Overall upward movement of air inside a building results from heated air rising and escaping through openings in the building's upper structure, resulting in lower indoor pressure than that in the soil beneath or surrounding the building foundation. The greater the thermal difference and height of the structure, the greater the buoyancy force, and thus the stack effect. The stack effect assists natural ventilation and infiltration of air; it does not require the use of electromechanical systems to be effective and thereby saves energy (see Figure 73).

Stacked solar cell *See: Tandem solar cell*

Stagnant zone Area of low air velocity and potential for increased stratification and low air quality.

Stand-alone system Autonomous or hybrid photovoltaic system not connected to a grid.

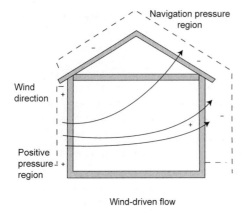

Wind-driven flow

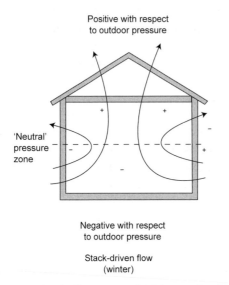

Negative with respect
to outdoor pressure

Stack-driven flow
(winter)

Figure 73 Stack effect—natural driving mechanisms

May or may not have storage, but most stand-alone systems require batteries or some other form of storage.

Steady state economics   1. In macroeconomics, a condition of the economy in which output productivity per worker and capital intensity per worker do not change over time. This is the result of the rate of new capital production from invested savings being exactly equal to the rate of existing capital depreciation. The steady state is generally associated with the Nobel Prize-winning economist Robert Solow, who created the Solow model in 1956. In an economy without technological advances, the steady state is where output and capital per worker stay the same.

2. In ecosystems, refers to production and consumption that take the surrounding ecosystems into account and try to achieve a state of equilibrium (see Figure 74).

Steam   Water in vapor form; used as the working fluid in steam turbines and heating systems.

Steam boiler   A type of furnace in which fuel is burned and the heat is used to produce steam.

Steam stripping   Removal of volatile organic compounds from contaminated groundwater or wastewater. Steam is forced through the liquid, and the higher wastewater temperature results in the evaporation of volatile contaminants. Steam stripping is more effective in removing contaminants than air stripping. *See also:* ***Air stripping***.

Steam turbine   Device that converts high-pressure steam, produced in a boiler, into mechanical energy that can then be used to produce electricity by forcing the turbine shaft to rotate and turn a generator shaft.

Steep-slope roof   Also known as a sloped roof. Roof surface with a slope greater than 2 inches (5 cm) rise for 12 inches (31 cm) run.

Stephan–Boltzmann law   The amount of electromagnetic radiation emitted by a body is directly related to its temperature. If the body is a perfect emitter (black body), the amount of radiation given off is proportional to the fourth power of its temperature as measured in Kelvin.

Standard economics

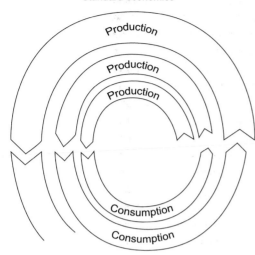

Standard economics considers ever growing cycles of production and consumption but does not consider the role of the supporting ecosystems. Such a view encourages an economy that ultimately strains the surrounding natural environment

Steady-state economics

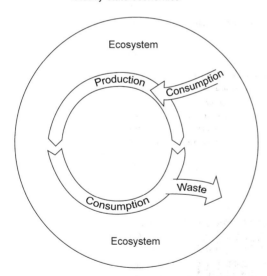

Steady-state economics considers cycles of production and consumption that take the surrounding ecosystems into account and try to achieve a state of equilibrium

Figure 74 (a) Standard economics, (b) steady-state economics

This natural phenomenon is described by the Stephan–Boltzmann law. The equation below describes this law mathematically:

$$E^* = \sigma T^4$$

where $\sigma = 5.67 \times 10^{-8}$ Wm^{-2} K^{-4} and T is the temperature in Kelvin. According to the Stephan–Boltzmann equation, a small increase in the temperature of a radiating body results in a large amount of additional radiation being emitted. In general, good emitters of radiation are also good absorbers of radiation at specific wavelength bands. This is especially true of gases and is responsible for the Earth's greenhouse effect. Similarly, weak emitters of radiation are also weak absorbers of radiation at specific wavelength bands. *See also:* **Radiation**

Stirling engine   Closed-cycle regenerative hot engine. Operates through an external heat source and an external heat sink. It is classified as an external combustion engine, but heat from solar and nuclear energy can be used. The working fluid is permanently contained within the system compared, with open-cycle engines such as internal combustion engines and some steam engines. There is an internal heat exchanger—regenerator—that improves the engine's potential efficiency. *See also:* **Parabolic dish solar collector**

Stockholm Convention on Persistent Organic Pollution   To address global concern about persistent organic pollutants (POPs), 91 countries including the USA and the European Community signed a United Nations treaty in Stockholm, Sweden, in May 2001. Under the treaty, known as the Stockholm Convention, countries agreed to reduce or eliminate the production, use, and/or release of 12 key POPs: aldrin, chlordane, dichlorodiphenyl trichloroethane (DDT), dieldrin, endrin, heptachlor, hexachlorobenzene, mirex, toxaphene, polychlorinated biphenyls

(PCBs), polychlorinated dibenzo-*p*-dioxins (dioxins), and polychlorinated dibenzofurans (furans). The Convention included special provisions to eliminate PCBs and DDT, and specifies a scientific review process that could lead to the addition of other POPs chemicals of global concern.

Many of the POPs included in the Stockholm Convention are no longer produced in the USA. None of the intentionally produced pesticides, for example, are manufactured or registered for use in the USA. However, US citizens and habitats can still be at risk from POPs that have persisted in the environment, from unintentionally produced POPs that are released in the USA, and from POPs that are released elsewhere and then transported here (by wind or water, for example). Although most developed nations have taken strong action to control the 12 POPs, a great number of developing nations have only recently begun to restrict their production, use, and release.

Storage battery   Device that can transform energy from electrical to chemical form and can be reversed. During discharge, chemical energy is converted to electrical energy and is consumed in an external circuit or apparatus. The major battery types sold are lead–acid, lithium-ion, metal hydride, and nickel–cadmium.

Stratosphere   Region of the atmosphere between the troposphere and mesosphere, the layer of the atmosphere 10–30 miles (15–50 kilometers) above the Earth. Ozone in the stratosphere filters out harmful rays from the Sun, including ultraviolet B, which has been linked to health and environmental damage. *See also: Mesosphere; Troposphere*

Straw bale construction   Use of baled straw from wheat, oats, barley, rye, rice, and others in walls. The walls are covered by stucco. Straw bale is traditionally a waste product that farmers do not till under the soil, but do sell as animal bedding or landscape supply due to its durable nature. Hay bales are made from short species of livestock feed grass that is green/alive, and are not suitable for this application. The use of straw bales for constructing walls has been recently revived as a low-cost alternative for building highly insulating walls. The technique was practiced in the plains states of the USA in the latter 1800s and early 1900s. Many of the early structures are still standing and being used. The technique has been applied to homes, farm buildings, schools, commercial buildings, churches, community centers, government buildings, airplane hangars, and well houses. Straw is also used as a building material in sheet materials such as sheathing and wall panels.

Two basic styles of straw bale construction have been used: post-and-beam construction with straw bale infill; and structural straw bale construction or "Nebraska" style, in which the weight of the roof is supported by the bales.

Strawboard   Construction material used for partitions, manufactured from rice or wheat straw.

String   Number of photovoltaic modules or panels interconnected electrically in series to produce the operating voltage required by the load.

Strip cutting   Conservation practice of harvesting trees in strips narrow enough to minimize edge effects and to allow natural regeneration of a forest.

Strip farming   Conservation practice of planting different types of crops in alternative strips along land contours. When one crop is harvested, the other crop remains to prevent erosion or excessive runoff. The practice dates back to manorial farming in the 9th century in Europe.

Structural diversity   One of the three types of diversity in an ecosystem. Plants and animals occupy space efficiently, which allows a variety of size, shape, and distribution of species, habitats, and communities across the landscape. *See also: Functional diversity; Species diversity*

Structural wall panels Fabricated panels that use molded expanded polystyrene (MEPS), extruded polystyrene (XEPS), and urethane as foam cores. The outer facings can be made of plywood, waferboard, oriented strand board, sheetrock, and metal. Structural panels serve as an alternative to the standard stud/insulation/sheathing wall system. XEPS and urethane foam use chlorofluorocarbons (CFCs) or hydrochlorofluorocarbons (HCFCs), which contain greenhouse gases, as blowing agents. MEPS does not use any ozone-depleting chemicals.

Styrene Colorless, toxic liquid with a strong aroma. Insoluble in water, soluble in alcohol and ether; can become explosive. Used in polymers and copolymers, polystyrene plastics, and rubbers. It may cause health problems if found in amounts greater than the health standard set by USEPA. *See also: Toxic chemicals*

Subsidence Drop of the land surface resulting from groundwater being pumped. Cracks and fissures can appear in the land. Subsidence is virtually an irreversible process.

Subslab depressurization system An active system uses a fan-powered vent drawing air from beneath the slab; a passive system uses a vent pipe routed through the conditioned space of the building and connecting the subslab area with the outdoor air.

Subsoiling Breaking up compacted soils, without inverting them, using a plow or blade.

Substrate Physical material upon which a photovoltaic cell is applied.

Succession Changes in an ecosystem that eventually result in the establishment of a stable community.

SUDS *See: Sustainable urban drainage system*

SULEV *See: Super-ultra-low-emission vehicle*

Sulfur-based cement Also known as sulfur-solidified concrete. A thermoplastic composite of mineral aggregates bound together with chemically modified sulfur. Research results indicate that it is more durable than Portland cement, and is a good solidifying agent for waste management practices such as solidification/stabilization of hazardous waste; barrier systems for hazardous waste landfills; and wastewater treatment plants.

Sulfur dioxide (SO₂) Gas that causes acid rain. Air pollutant. When burned, fossil fuels such as coal release SO_2 into the atmosphere. Belongs to the family of sulfur oxide gases (SO_x). The gas is produced by burning coal, mostly in power plants. Other industrial processes, such as paper production and metal smelting, also produce SO_2. Closely related to sulfuric acid (H_2SO_4), SO_2 is a strong acid.

Sulfur is prevalent in all raw materials, including crude oil, coal, and ores that contain common metals such as aluminum, copper, zinc, lead, and iron. SO_x gases are formed when fuels containing sulfur, such as coal and oil, are burned, and when gasoline is extracted from oil, or metals are extracted from ore. SO_2 dissolves in water vapor to form acid, and interacts with other gases and particles in the air to form sulfates and other products that can be harmful to people and their environment. These gases dissolve easily in water. SO_2 contributes to respiratory illness, and aggravates existing heart and lung diseases. SO_2 is a major contributor to the production of acid rain, which damages trees, crops, and buildings, and makes soils, lakes, and streams acidic. It contributes to the formation of atmospheric particles that cause visibility impairment, most noticeably in national parks. SO$_2$ and the pollutants formed from it, such as sulfate particles, can be transported over long distances and deposited far from the point of origin. This means that problems with SO$_2$ are not confined to areas where it is emitted. *See also:* **Air pollutants**

Sulfur hexafluoride (SF$_6$)   Toxic chemical. Although it is a colorless, odorless, nontoxic, and nonflammable gas (at standard conditions), the Intergovernmental Panel on Climate Change, a United Nations agency, has declared that SF$_6$ is the most potent greenhouse gas it has evaluated, with a global warming potential of 22,200 times that of CO$_2$ over a 100-year period. *See also:* **Toxic chemicals**

Sulfur oxide (SO$_x$)   Toxic chemical. Refers to any of the following: sulfur monoxide (SO), sulfur dioxide (SO$_2$), or sulfur trioxide (SO$_3$). *See also:* **Toxic chemicals**

Sulfur-solidified concrete   *See:* **Sulfur-based cement**

Sulfates   Occur as microscopic particles (aerosols) resulting from fossil fuel and biomass combustion. They increase the acidity of the atmosphere and form acid rain.

Sump   Pit or tank that catches liquid runoff from drainage or disposal.

Sun   The energy it transmits make life possible on Earth through two critical properties. i) Heat energy captured and stored as warmth in the troposphere is essential to sustain life on Earth. This heat energy both warms the Earth through its natural heat, and cools it through natural ventilation. ii) The energy of sunlight is essential to establish life on Earth through autotrophs using photochemical energy to produce and provide the food for other trophic levels. This process is photosynthesis.

Using the Sun's energy to provide heat can be either passive or active. Passive solar design has been used by organisms, insects, aquatic life, and vertebrates for thousands of years. Human structures designed specifically to utilize the Sun's energy for heating and cooling are collectively called passive solar designs. In this approach, the building itself, or some element of it, takes advantage of natural energy characteristics in materials and air created by exposure to the Sun to heat and cool that structure. Passive systems are simple, have few moving parts, and require minimal maintenance and no mechanical systems. The passive capture of heat can be through absorption, conduction, and transfer of heat through the use of siting, design, and structural materials. The Sun's heat is actively captured and converted into usable electricity through devices such as photovoltaic solar collectors, which can track the path of the Sun; or Graetzel cells, which perform the same function.

Similarly, the winds generated by changes in the intensity of the Sun's heat create a natural cooling effect. Passive solar cooling includes both natural ventilation in the form of wind-driven air movement through structures; and thermal flow ventilation, which is temperature-induced. Both natural and thermal flow ventilations are used in insect and animal habitats, as well as in human structures.

Light energy provides the energy to produce life on Earth through the process of photosynthesis. *See also:* **Graetzel cell; Passive solar cooling; Passive solar design; Passive solar heater; Passive solar heating; Photosynthesis; Photovoltaic** (and related terms); **Solar air systems; Solar cell; Solar collector; Solar cooling; Solar energy; Solar envelope; Solar thermal system; Solar water heater, active; Solar water heater, passive; Appendix 4: Photovoltaics**

Sun space   A well glazed, enclosed space that collects heat and supplies some of that heat to another space, usually an adjoining space. Temperatures in a Sun space fluctuate daily and seasonally, as they are controlled only by the Sun's heat.

Sun-tempered building   A passive solar designed structure with the aim of decreasing the amount of nonrenewable energy to heat and cool a building by collecting solar heat gain, mitigating unwanted solar heat gain, and promoting natural ventilation. A solar-tempered building is elongated in the east–west direction, with the majority of the windows on the south side. The area of the windows is generally limited to about 7% of the total floor area. A Sun-tempered design has no added thermal mass beyond that which is already in the framing, wall board, and other components. Insulation levels are generally high.

Super-ultra-low-emission vehicle (SULEV)   Designation by the California Air Resources Board for conventionally powered or gas–electric hybrid vehicles designed to produce minimal air pollution at their point of use, typically less than 10% of that of an equivalent ordinary vehicle. *See also: See also: Emissions standards, designations*

Super window   Popular term for a highly insulating window with a heat loss so low that it performs better than an insulated wall in winter, as the sunlight it admits is greater than its heat loss over a 24-hour period.

Superconducting magnetic energy storage (SMES)   Technology using the superconducting characteristics of low-temperature materials to produce intense magnetic fields to store energy. SMES has been proposed as a storage option to support large-scale use of photovoltaics and wind as a means to smooth out fluctuations in

power generation. Researchers believe it will take many years before this technology can be implemented practically.

Superfund   US government's program to contain, clean up, or remedy the country's hazardous waste sites. The fund is financed by fees paid by toxic waste generators and by cost recovery from cleanup projects. *See also: Comprehensive Environmental Response Compensation and Liability Act*

Superheat   Additional heat contained in a vapor at a temperature higher than the saturation (boiling) temperature corresponding to the pressure of the vapor.

Superstrate   The covering on the sunny side of a photovoltaic (PV) module, providing protection for the PV materials from impact and environmental degradation while allowing maximum transmission of the appropriate wavelengths of the solar spectrum.

Surface area-to-volume ratio   Indicator of a building's energy efficiency. Surface area can be useful if it increases the potential for passive solar heating, natural ventilation, or daylighting of buildings.

Surface impoundment   Treatment, storage, or disposal of liquid hazardous wastes in ponds.

Surface runoff   Water from rain, flooding, or irrigation that exceeds the ability of the adjoining soil to absorb it. Surface runoff carries pollutants from many sources into rivers, streams, and lakes.

Surface-structured solar cell   New generation of solar cell. Cell has a pyramid structure so that incoming light hits the surface several times. New materials include gallium arsenide (GaAs), cadmium telluride (CdTe), or copper indium selenide ($CuInSe_2$).

Surface water   All bodies of water on the surface and open to the atmosphere, such as rivers, lakes, reservoirs, ponds, seas, and estuaries.

Surface water management system   System designed to prevent surface water from flowing into waste-filled areas.

Sustainable   1. Ability to keep up or support.
2. An ecosystem condition in which biodiversity, renewability, and resource productivity are maintained over time.

Sustainable design   *See: Ecodesign*

Sustainable development   *See: Sustainability*

Sustainable urban drainage system (SUDS)
System designed to reduce the potential impact of new and existing developments with respect to surface water drainage discharges. SUDS are designed to be easy to manage, require little energy input, are resilient, and seek to minimize harmful impacts of drainage on the environment. Examples are reed beds and other wetland habitats that collect, store, and filter dirty water, along with providing a habitat for wildlife. The goal of SUDS is to replicate natural systems that have low environmental impact to drain away surface water runoff through collection, storage, and cleaning before allowing it to be released slowly back into the environment, such as into water courses. Conventional drainage systems often result in flooding, pollution of the environment—with resultant harm to wildlife—and contamination of groundwater sources used to provide drinking water. Originally the term described the UK approach to sustainable urban drainage systems. Other countries have similar approaches in place, using different terminology such as best management practice or low-impact development.
SUDS may use the following techniques: source control, permeable paving, storm water

detention, storm water infiltration, or evapotranspiration. For example, sewer flooding happens when flows entering a sewer exceed its capacity, and it overflows. SUDS aim to minimize or eliminate discharges from the site, thus reducing the impact. The premise is that if all development sites incorporated SUDS, urban sewer flooding would be less of a problem. Unlike traditional urban stormwater drainage systems, SUDS can also help to protect and enhance groundwater quality.

Sustainable yield concept   Ecodesign strategy for the ecomimetic designer to ensure all materials used in a structure are renewable or reusable, and all discharges and emissions are recycled or reused within the built environment itself or within the larger overall urban system. It is the concept of self-sustainability and reintegration.

Sustainability   The basic principles and concepts are balancing a growing economy, protection for the environment, and social responsibility. Common use of the term in the context of modern environmentalism began with the publication of the World Commission on Environment and Development report *Our Common Future*, in 1987. Also known as the Brundtland Report, this document characterized sustainable development as "development that meets the needs of the present without compromising the ability of future generations to meet their own needs." This concept of sustainability encompasses ideas and values that encourage public and private organizations to become better stewards of the environment and promote positive economic growth and social objectives. The principles of sustainability can stimulate technological innovation, advance competitiveness, and improve our quality of life. *See also: Brundtland Report*

SW-846   The official compendium of USEPA's Office of Solid Waste: *Test Methods for*

Evaluating Solid Waste, Physical/Chemical Methods. It provides analytical and sampling methods that have been evaluated and approved for use in complying with the Resource Conservation and Recovery Act (RCRA) regulations. SW-846 functions primarily as a guidance document setting forth acceptable, although not required, methods for the regulated and regulatory communities to use in responding to RCRA-related sampling and analysis requirements. SW-846 was first issued by USEPA in 1980. There have been a number of changes since then as new information and data have been developed.

Swale Elongated trench used to collect and direct the flow of surface water runoff.

Swamp cooler Popular name for evaporative cooling devices. *See also:* **Solar cooling**

Switch grass Energy crop that is cheap to grow and provides a high-yield crop that can make ethanol at low cost. It has fewer nutrient runoff and erosion problems than corn as a component of ethanol.

Symbiosis Relationship of members of two species. *See also:* **Amensalism; Commensalism; Mutualism; Parasitism**

Synfuel Gas or liquid hydrocarbon fuel made from coal or shale and sometimes waste plastic. Fuel made from coal creates many environmental problems, from mine damage to emissions of sulfur oxides, hydrocarbons, and heavy metals. Fuel made from shale requires a large quantity of water during processing, and a large volume of solid waste is produced.

Syngas *See: Synthesis gas*

Synthesis gas (Syngas) Produced by the conversion of solid biomass into gaseous form. Syngas consists primarily of carbon monoxide, carbon dioxide, and hydrogen, and has less than half the energy density of natural gas. It is combustible and is often used as a fuel source or an intermediate for the production of other chemicals. The gas can run through combined-cycle gas turbines or another power-conversion technology such as a coal power plant. Syngas can also be burned directly in internal combustion engines, used to produce methanol and hydrogen, or converted via the Fischer–Tropsch process into synthetic fuel. *See also:* **Biomass electricity; Pyrolysis**

System boundary Natural extent of the ecosystem or boundary conditions within which the ecodesigned system is located. This is not a boundary of separation but a boundary of identity, recognizing the importance of ecotones and the boundaries between discrete ecological communities in terms of nutrient transfer zones, sediments, energy, and ecological processes. The designed human-made boundary should be integrated with the composite ecosystem.

Systemic integration Ecodesign strategy to reduce the use of ecosystem and biospheric services and impacts on the shared global environment. Designing for systemic integration includes assimilation of anthropogenic emissions and waste without contamination, biodegradation of emissions over short periods, and reducing inputs and outputs in general to reduce or eliminate burdening the natural environment to absorb the human-made wastes.

T

Taiga Northernmost edge of boreal forest; includes species-poor woodland and peat deposits, intergrading with the artic tundra.

Tailings Residue of raw material or waste separated out during the processing of crops or mineral ores.

Take back laws Also called producer responsibility laws. Require companies that make or import items to be involved in the "end-of-life" phase of their products' life cycles. In almost all cases there is a requirement to meet minimal recycling or reuse rates. Approximately 28–30 countries have such laws, covering a wide array of products including appliances, computers, telecommunications equipment and, in some cases, cars. The European Union has adopted Waste Electrical and Electronic Equipment (WEEE) and Restriction of Hazardous Substances directives. By the end of 2005, 20 of the 25 members of the EU enacted the WEEE directive into their national laws. They are: Austria, Belgium, Cyprus, Czech Republic, Denmark, Finland, France, Germany, Greece, Hungary, Ireland, Lithuania, Luxembourg, the Netherlands, Poland, Portugal, Slovakia, Slovenia, Spain, and Sweden. The EU reached an agreement in 2000 on a law to have automobile makers bear the cost of recycling scrap cars. Manufacturers must cover most of the cost of taking back all cars sold after January 1, 2001, when they reach the end of their lives and are scrapped. From 2007, they have had to take back without charge any scrap car, regardless of when it was built, and 85% of the car weight must be reused or recycled.

Tackifier Water-based agent used to bind soil particles together to provide erosion protection.

Tandem solar cell Also known as a stacked solar cell. New generation of solar cell. A single-crystal, monolithic, tandem photovoltaic solar cell includes i) an indium phosphide (InP) substrate with upper and lower surfaces; ii) a first photoactive subcell on the upper surface of the InP substrate; and iii) a second photoactive subcell on the first subcell. The first photoactive subcell is gallium indium arsenide phosphide (GaInAsP) of defined composition; the second is InP. The two subcells are lattice matched. The solar cell can be provided as a two-terminal or a three-terminal device. The different semiconductor materials, with different spectral ranges, are arranged on top of one another. This enables a wide spectrum of radiation and different materials to be used. The tandem cell can achieve higher total conversion efficiency by capturing a larger portion of the solar spectrum. In the typical multijunction cell, individual cells with different bandgaps are stacked on top of one another. The individual cells are stacked in such a way that sunlight falls first on the material having the largest bandgap. Photons not absorbed in the first cell are transmitted to the second cell, which then absorbs the higher-energy portion of the remaining solar radiation while remaining transparent to the lower-energy photons. *See also: Multijunction; Photovoltaic cell; Photovoltaic device; Appendix 4: Photovoltaics*

Tankless water heater   A demand water heater that heats water just before it is distributed for end use.

Task lighting   Light that is focused on, and used for, a predetermined activity.

TCE   *See: Trichloroethylene*

TDS   *See: Total dissolved solids*

Temperature inversion   Weather conditions that are often associated with smog, when air does not rise because it is trapped near the ground by a layer of warmer air above it. Pollutants, especially smog and smog-forming chemicals, including volatile organic compounds, are trapped close to the ground.

Tennessee Valley Authority   A US federal agency established in 1933 to develop the Tennessee river valley region of the southeastern USA. It is now the nation's largest power producer.

Tertiary wastewater treatment   Following primary and secondary wastewater treatment processes. This process includes flocculation basins, clarifiers, filters, and chlorine basins, or ozone or ultraviolet radiation process. It is used on substances that were not removed during the first two treatment processes. *See also: Primary wastewater treatment; Secondary wastewater treatment*

Tetrachloroethylene   (or tetrachloroethene) *See: Perchloroethylene*

Tetraethyl lead   An octane enhancer in fuels. Determined to be a health hazard, lead has been prohibited in highway vehicle gasoline since 1996.

Thermal balance analysis   Sum of simultaneously occurring heat gains and heat losses to determine whether there is an overall loss or gain. Thermal balance calculations can be done for rooms, zones, orientations, or entire buildings.

Thermal chimney   Also known as a solar chimney. Method of improving natural ventilation of buildings by using convection of air heated by passive solar energy. *See also: Passive solar cooling*

Thermal conductance   Measure of a material's ability to conduct heat; a function of the material's thermal conductivity (the reciprocal of thermal resistivity) and thickness given a temperature difference between both sides of the material. Used primarily in Fourier's law for heat conduction:

Thermal conductivity = heat flow rate × distance / (area × temperature difference)

$$k = \frac{Q}{t} \times \frac{L}{(A \times \Delta T)}$$

Q = quantity of heat transmitted in time, t, through a thickness, L, toward a surface area, A, due to a temperature difference, ΔT, all under steady-state conditions and when heat transfer is dependent only on the temperature gradient.

Alternatively, it can be thought of as a flux of heat (energy per unit area per unit time) divided by a temperature gradient (temperature difference per unit length):

$$k = \frac{Q}{(A \times t)} \times \frac{L}{\Delta T}$$

In ecodesign, the use of thermal mass in a building's structure achieves decreased reliance on nonrenewable fossil fuels for heat and cooling through thermal conductance. Heat is conducted from the warmer surface of the mass to the cooler interior of the mass, effectively "storing" heat in the mass. Conversely, heat from the warmer interior of the mass is conducted to the surface of the mass as the mass cools.

Thermal envelope house An architectural design (also known as a double envelope house), sometimes called a "house-within-a-house", that employs a double envelope with a continuous airspace of at least 6–12 inches (15–31 cm) on the north wall, south wall, roof, and floor, achieved by building inner and outer walls, a crawl space or subbasement below the floor, and a shallow attic space below the weather roof. The east and west walls are single, conventional walls. A buffer zone of solar-heated, circulating air warms the inner envelope of the house. The south-facing airspace may double as a sunspace or greenhouse. *See also: Double envelope*

Thermal flywheel effect Also known as thermal momentum. The property of a material to remain at a given temperature; related to the building's mass and the thermal conductivity of the materials connecting the mass to the interior space. It is generally applied to buildings or construction materials. This is distinct from a material's insulative value. A building's average internal temperature can remain stable much longer due to this effect. For example, the thermal mass of a house is a measure of its capacity to store and regulate internal heat. Buildings with a high thermal mass take a long time to heat up, but also take a long time to cool down. As a result they have a very steady internal temperature. Like a flywheel, the thermal mass

can store and even out fluctuations in temperature. Buildings with a low thermal mass are very responsive to changes in internal temperature—they heat up very quickly, but they also cool down quickly. They are often subject to wide variation in internal temperature. Materials with a higher to lower flywheel effect include: packed earth, brick, water, hardwood lumber, softwoods, steel, insulation, air, and aluminum.

Thermal inertia Tendency of a massive material to remain at a certain temperature.

Thermal mass Material that stores heat. It can be a liquid or solid substance, and is characterized by a charge-up or dissipation time. Heat storage and heat sink describe the same concept. Liquid thermal mass tends to stratify. A solid thermal mass's ability to store and transfer heat depends on the material's specific heat capacity, thermal conductivity, and convective heat transfer. Architecturally, thermal mass heats up slowly when the surface conditions are warmer than the interior of the mass, and discharges heat when the surface conditions become cooler than the interior of the mass. Solar energy can be used to heat the surface of a thermal mass to increase the energy being stored. The thermal mass averages the temperature and, in effect, reduces the hot and cold peaks a room would otherwise experience. Heating a thermal mass with solar energy during the winter heats

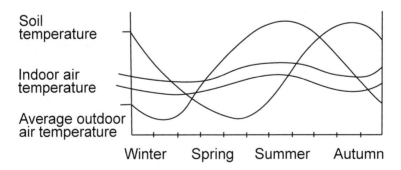

Figure 75 The thermal flywheel effect

the mass that will radiate energy over a longer period through the cooler night to maintain warmer conditions in a room. Conversely, exposing a thermal mass to cool nighttime conditions during a warmer summer can lower the daytime temperature in a room.

The use of thermal mass does not increase or decrease the total energy available, nor does it change the long-term heat loss or gain of the building. However, it does help to reduce energy demands in a home under mild heating and cooling climate conditions. It also helps reduce extreme temperatures within the home, maintaining moderate temperatures inside the home year-round.

Heat flows from warm objects to cool objects by way of conduction, convection, and radiation. Conduction is transfer of heat through physical contact, such as a thermometer under your tongue, or the transfer of heat to the ground. Convection is transfer of heat through a fluid, such as an ice cube cooling a glass of water. Radiation is the transfer of heat through free space, such as warming your hands on an open fire, or feeling the heat from the Sun's rays. Thermal masses use these three types of heat transfer in a four-step process.

i) Heat is radiated to the surface of the mass by a warmer object (such as the Sun, lights, people, or equipment), and heat can be convected to the surface via air circulation.

ii) Heat is then conducted from the warmer surface of the mass to the cooler interior of the mass, effectively "storing" heat in the mass.

iii) When the mass surface becomes warmer than other objects surrounding it, the mass radiates heat to these objects (meaning the mass radiates heat back into the house) and transfers heat to the room by convection using the room air.

iv) Heat from the warmer interior of the mass is conducted to the surface of the mass as the mass cools, a reversal of step ii.

Thermal momentum *See: Thermal flywheel effect*

Thermal pollution Increased temperature of water resulting from the disposal of waste heat from industrial or power-generation processes. Thermally polluted water can harm plants and animals that cannot adapt to the increased temperature.

Thermal power plant Generic term for a facility that generates electricity by using some energy source to convert water to steam. The steam is used to turn turbine generators.

Thermal storage Term used to describe various technologies that store heat, usually from active solar collectors in an insulated repository, for use later to heat space or hot water, or to generate electricity. The thermal reservoir can be kept at temperatures above or below that of the ambient environment. Currently, there are experiments to use molten salt as a medium to retain a high-temperature thermal store for later use in electricity generation. In a passive solar building, thermal storage meets two needs: to absorb solar heat quickly for use over the diurnal cycle; and to avoid overheating. There are two basic thermal storage strategies using thermal mass. i) Direct thermal storage materials, such as concrete masonry or tiles, are placed directly in sunlight so that intense solar energy enters them quickly. ii) Diffuse thermal storage materials are placed throughout the building. They can absorb heat by radiation, through the reflectance of sunlight as it bounces around a room, and via air heated elsewhere in the building, such as sunspaces and atria. Concrete and masonry floors and walls exposed to direct sunlight are probably the most common form of thermal storage used in passive solar buildings. Masonry materials have high thermal capacity; their natural dark color aids in the absorption of sunlight.

As water has high thermal capacity (about twice that of common masonry materials), passive solar designers have experimented with a variety of water-storage containers, primarily built into walls. Solutions include enclosing water containers in seating boxes under south-facing windows, or using water as an indoor feature such as a large tropical aquarium, pond, or pool. Trombe walls are also used for thermal storage in passive solar structures. The wall is a south-facing masonry covered with glass spaced a few inches away. Sunlight passes through the glass and is absorbed and stored by the wall. The glass and airspace keep the heat from radiating back to the outside. Heat is transferred by conduction as the masonry surface warms up, and is slowly delivered to the building some hours later. *See also: Thermal mass; Trombe wall*

Thermal wheel   Also called a heat wheel. Heat exchanger rotating between two air flows to transfer heat from one to the other. It is usually packed with heat-absorbing material such as aluminum or stainless steel wool. The wheels transfer energy from one air stream to another or, for large boiler plants, from flue gas to combustion air. Thermal wheels can be installed only when the hot and cold airstreams are immediately adjacent and parallel. There are two types of thermal wheel: one that transfers sensible heat only; and one that transfers both sensible and latent heat.

Thermodynamic cycle   Process in which a working fluid (water, air, ammonia) successively changes its state (from a liquid to a gas, and back to a liquid) for the purpose of producing useful work or energy, or of transferring energy.

Thermodynamics   Description of heat movement.

Thermodynamics, first law   Energy can be neither created nor destroyed.

Thermodynamics, second law   When free interchange of heat takes place, it is always the hotter of the two bodies that loses energy and the colder that gains energy.

Thermophotovoltaic cell (TPV)   Device in which sunlight concentrated onto an absorber heats it to a high temperature; the thermal radiation emitted by the absorber is used as the energy source for a photovoltaic cell that is designed to maximize conversion efficiency at the wavelength of the thermal radiation. Researchers currently have reservations about its practicability and efficiency.

Thermosiphon   1. Natural convective movement of air or water due to differences in density caused by differences in temperature. In passive solar design, a thermosiphon collector can be constructed or attached to a house to deliver heat by a continuous convective loop.

2. Common type of solar water heater that uses collectors and circulating water, but is still a passive system as no pumps are involved. The storage tank is installed above the collector. As water in the collector is heated and becomes less dense, it rises into the tank by convection. At the same time, cooler water in the tank sinks into the collector, causing circulation throughout the system. The storage tank is attached to the top of the collector so that thermosiphoning can take place.

Thixotropy   Characteristic of a material that allows it to stiffen or thicken in a short time. When the material is shaken or manipulated, it changes to a very soft consistency or a high-viscosity fluid. The materials are gel-like at rest but fluid when agitated, and have high static shear strength and low dynamic shear strength at the same time. *See also: Bentonite*

Thomson effect   Predicts the generation of heat along a current-carrying wire that also has a temperature gradient along it. Thomson's equation contains two terms: the nominal joule heating or I^2R loss; and the Thomson effect, which quantifies the amount of heat generated by multiplying the current, the Thomson coefficient, and the temperature gradient as a function of the length. *See also: Peltier effect; Seebeck effect*

Tidal electric power Power available from the rise and fall of ocean tides to generate electricity. A tidal power plant works on the principle of a dam or barrage that captures water in a basin at the peak of a tidal flow, then directs the water through a hydroelectric turbine as the tide ebbs. There are two types of generating system: tidal barrage, and tidal turbine. The barrage system uses the water flow on the ocean floor (basin) to turn a turbine connected to an electric generator. The tidal turbine is anchored to the ocean floor and uses the large-scale persistent ocean currents, often rip tides, as its source of power. Both are experimental, expensive to install, and may have adverse effects on water turbidity, sedimentation, and marine life.

Tight building Structure designed to minimize infiltration of air from the outside. This reduces heating and cooling costs.

Tilt angle Degree at which a solar collector or module is set to face the Sun relative to a horizontal position. The tilt angle can be set or adjusted to maximize seasonal or annual energy collection. *See also: Photovoltaic module tilt angle; Figure A.2 in Appendix 4: Photovoltaics*

Time lag Term used in relation to release of heat into a space after solar radiation has heated a building's material. *See also: Thermal storage*

Time-of-use rate (TOU) Variable pricing of electricity based on the time of day when a consumer uses electricity. Variable pricing is designed to encourage customers to shift their heaviest use from peak hours (8 am to 8 pm) to off-peak hours (8 pm to 8 am). Variable pricing is also based on the season. TOU rates are particularly beneficial to residential and small business customers. Pricing is based on the marginal cost to produce electricity. It depends on the total load and generating units to serve that load. The marginal cost of electricity production varies with demand at a particular time of day. The primary purpose of this rate system is to even out the use of electricity to make demand more constant. It is also designed to level the peak-and-trough loads on electrical generation and strain of transmission and distribution across a service grid, as well as to decrease the cost for consumers who decide to use electricity during off-peak times. As most electrical utility companies are franchise monopolies and their generating plants require substantial capital construction costs, they want to maximize the efficiency and generating capacity of each plant before undertaking the construction of additional plants.

Tolerance limits Environmental term designating maximum and minimum levels beyond which a particular species cannot survive or is unable to produce. There are tolerance limits in temperatures, moisture levels, nutrient supply, soil and water chemistry, and living space.

Toluene Soil contaminant and toxic chemical. An organic liquid used in making benzene and urethane. It is regulated through the US Safe Drinking Water Act of 1974, which determines safe levels of chemicals in drinking water. Short-term exposure can result in minor nervous system disorders, such as fatigue, nausea, weakness, or confusion. Long-term exposure can produce nervous disorders such as spasms, tremors, impairment of speech, hearing, vision, memory, coordination, or liver or kidney damage. *See also: Soil contaminants; Toxic chemicals*

Topping-cycle A method to increase the thermal efficiency of a steam electric generating system by increasing temperatures and interposing a device, such as a gas turbine, between the heat source and the conventional steam turbine generator to convert some of the additional heat energy into electricity.

Total dissolved solids (TDS)   Measure of the total amount of all the materials dissolved in water. These materials, both natural and anthropogenic, are mainly inorganic solids with a minor amount of organic material. The principal application of TDS is in the study of water quality for streams, rivers, and lakes, although TDS is generally not considered a primary pollutant. Primary sources for TDS in receiving waters are agricultural runoff, leaching of soil contamination, and point-source water pollution discharge from industrial or sewage treatment plants. The most common chemical constituents are calcium, phosphates, nitrates, sodium, potassium, and chloride, which are found in nutrient runoff, general storm water runoff, and runoff from snowy climates where road de-icing salts are applied. TDS has a significant impact on the environment, not only because of its contaminated pollutant content, but also due to the effect the contaminants have on water quality, plant and animal life, and continued healthy biodiversity. Reduction of human-made wastes would mitigate the potential adverse effects of TDS on the environment and the ecosystem.

TOU   *See: Time-of-use rate*

Toxic chemicals   USEPA lists the following as toxic chemicals: benzene, chlorinated solvents, chlorofluorocarbons (CFCs), dichloroethylene (DCE), dioxins, endocrine disruptors, ether, ethylbenzene, furans, halons, hazardous air pollutants (HAPs), heavy metals, hydrochlorofluorocarbons (HCFCs), inorganic cyanides, ketones, methane, methyl bromide, methyl chloride, methyl tertiary butyl ether (MTBE), nitrogen oxides (NO_x),

organic cyanides, particulate matter (PM), perchloroethylene (PCE), phthalates, polychlorinated biphenyls (PCBs), radioactive substances, radionuclides, styrene, sulfur hexafluoride (SF_6), sulfur oxides (SO_x), toluene, trichloroethylene (TCE), and volatile organic compounds (VOCs).

Toxic waste   Waste material, often in chemical form, that can cause death or injury to living creatures. It usually is the product of industry or commerce, but also comes from residential use, agriculture, the military, medical facilities, radioactive sources, and light industries such as dry cleaning establishments. As with many pollution problems, toxic waste began to be a significant issue during the industrial revolution. Toxins can be released into air, water, or land, and can pollute the natural environment and contaminate groundwater. *See also:* **Hazardous waste**

Toxics   Also known as toxic substances. As defined by the US Clean Air Act Amendments of 1990, toxics include benzene, 1.3 butadiene, formaldehyde, acetaldehyde, and polycyclic organic matter. Substances that are poisonous and/or have an adverse affect on organisms, organ systems, tissues, cells, or the environment. There are generally three types of toxic entity: i) chemical—including lead, hydrofluoric acid, chlorine gas, and organic compounds such as methyl alcohol; ii) biological—including bacteria and viruses; iii) physical—including concussion, electromagnetic radiation, ionizing radiation, direct blows, and vibration. *See also:* **Toxic chemicals**

TPV   *See: Thermophotovoltaic cell*

Trace gas   Gases that make up less than 1% of the Earth's atmosphere: carbon dioxide, water vapor, methane, and oxides of nitrogen, ozone, and ammonia. Nitrogen, oxygen and argon make up more than 99% of the Earth's atmosphere.

Trace gases, although small in absolute volume in the atmosphere, still affect weather and climate.

Tracking array *See: Photovoltaic tracking array*

Tradable renewable certificates *See: Green certificates*

Tragedy of the commons *See: Open access system*

Transesterification Chemical process that reacts an alcohol with the triglycerides contained in vegetable oils and animal fats to produce biodiesel and glycerin.

Transpiration Process in which water is absorbed by plants, usually through the roots, and evaporated into the atmosphere from the plant surface, usually the leaf pores. *See also: Evapotranspiration*

Transpired air collector A type of solar collector. It is made of dark, perforated metal. The metal is heated by the Sun, and a fan pulls ambient air through the holes in the metal, which heats the air. Used for pre-heating ventilation and drying crops. Requires no glazing or insulation and is inexpensive to manufacture. Transpired air collectors are low-cost devices and their potential is good in developing countries, where coffee, grains, fruit, vegetables, and other crops are harvested, and conventional fuels are expensive or unavailable.

Transuranic waste Category of radioactive waste. Contains elements that have an atomic number higher than uranium (92), such as plutonium. Results primarily from past nuclear weapons production and cleanup of nuclear weapons facilities. There is concern about its safe disposal and isolation.

Tribrid vehicle The third generation of alternative propulsion vehicles. The second generation is the bivalent hybrid vehicles with turbines. Tribrids are hybrids that obtain additional energy from the ambient environment (solar panel, windmill, or sail). Examples are a velomobile with an electric power-assist motor and additional on-board solar cells, like the new French photovoltaic car, the Venturi-Astrolab. *See also: Hybrid engine; Solar electric-powered vehicle*

Trichloroethylene (TCE) Soil contaminant and toxic chemical. Used to remove grease from fabricated metal parts and some textiles. It is regulated by the US Safe Drinking Water Act of 1974, which determines safe levels of chemicals in drinking water. Ingestion increases risk of cancer and liver problems. *See also: Soil contaminants; Toxic chemicals*

Trickle collector Type of solar thermal collector in which a heat-transfer fluid drips out of header pipe at the top of the collector, runs down the collector absorber and into a tray at the bottom, where it drains to a storage tank.

Triple-pane window Three layers of glazing in a window with an airspace between the middle glass and the exterior and interior panes. This construction provides more insulation and greater energy efficiency.

Trombe wall A wall with high thermal mass used to store solar energy passively in a solar home. The wall absorbs solar energy and transfers it to the space behind the wall by means of radiation and by convection currents moving through spaces under, in front of, and on top of the wall. Trombe walls can provide carefully controlled solar heat to a space without the use of windows and direct sunlight. The masonry wall is part of the building's structural system, effectively lowering costs. The inside, or discharge, surface of the Trombe wall can be painted white to enhance lighting efficiency within the space (see Figure 76).

Trophic level   Term for each level of energy consumption within a food web. Energy within a food web always flows in only one direction, starting with the producers. *See: Food Chain*

Trophic status   Classification of a lake or body of water. *See also: Eutrophic; Mesotrophic; Oligotrophic*

Tropical rain forest   Forests in the equatorial regions of Central and South America, Central Africa, and Southeast Asia. These forests have five times more tree species than those in more temperate regions. The environment is rich in biomass and biodiversity.

Troposphere   Lowest part of the atmosphere from the surface to about 10 km (6 miles) in altitude in mid-latitudes where clouds and weather phenomena occur. In the troposphere, temperatures generally decrease with height. *See also: Mesosphere; Stratosphere*

Tropospheric ozone (O$_3$)   Scientific designation for what is more widely known as "ozone". *See: Ozone*

True south   The direction, at any point on the Earth that is geographically in the northern hemisphere, facing toward the south pole of the earth. Essentially a line extending from the point on the horizon to the highest point that the Sun reaches on any day (solar noon) in the sky.

Tsunami   From the Japanese word which means "large waves in harbors", a series of ocean waves generated by sudden displacements in the sea floor, landslides, or volcanic activity. In the deep ocean, the tsunami wave may only be a few inches high. It may come gently ashore or may increase in height to become a fast-moving wall of turbulent water several meters high. Although a tsunami cannot be prevented, its impact can be mitigated through community preparedness, timely warnings, and effective response. The height and force of these waves create great damage to coastal areas and the built environment. For example, three years after the December 2004 tsunami hit Southeast Asia, Sri Lanka's coastal drinking water supply was still being affected. Much of the island nation's coastal area relies on wells, usually hand-dug and relatively shallow. Some 40,000 wells, each typically serving several families, were destroyed or contaminated by the tsunami. The continued sustainability of the aquifers that supply such wells is in doubt due to continued saltwater contamination, erosion of beaches, and other human impacts, such as sand mining, increased pumping, and pollution.

Tube-type collector   A type of solar thermal collector that has tubes (pipes) through which the heat transfer fluid flows, connected to a flat absorber plate.

Tubular skylight   Method of using reflectors to divert and direct sunlight into an interior space.

Tundra   The coldest of all the biomes. It is noted for its frost-molded landscapes, extremely low

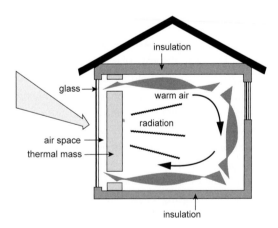

Figure 76 Indirect solar gain system
Source: California Energy Commission

temperatures, little precipitation, poor nutrients, and short growing seasons. Dead organic material functions as a nutrient pool. The two major nutrients are nitrogen and phosphorus. Nitrogen is created by biological fixation, and phosphorus is created by precipitation. Characteristics include extremely cold climate, low biotic diversity, simple vegetation structure, limitation of drainage, short season of growth and reproduction, energy and nutrients in the form of dead organic material, and large population oscillations. *See also: **Alpine tundra; Arctic tundra***

Turbidity   The amount of solid particles suspended in water.

Turbine   Machine for generating rotary mechanical power from the energy in a stream of fluid. The energy, originally in the form of pressure, is converted to rotational energy by passing through a system of stationary and moving blades in the turbine.

Turbocharger   A compressor used for increasing the pressure of a compressible fluid entering an inlet for a combustion engine or a fuel cell. The compressor can be driven by a turbine that extracts energy from the exhaust gas.

Two-axis tracking   A solar array tracking system capable of rotating independently about two axes (e.g. vertical and horizontal). *See also: **Photovoltaic (PV)** and associated entries; **Appendix 4: Photovoltaics***

Two-tank solar system   A solar thermal system that has one tank for storing solar heated water to preheat the water before it enters the second tank, the conventional water heater. Most solar water heaters require a well insulated storage tank. Solar storage tanks have an additional outlet and inlet connected to and from the collector. In one-tank systems, the back-up heater is combined with the solar storage in one tank. *See also: **Solar collector, residential use***

U

U value Also known as *U factor*. Measurement of the thermal conductivity of a material, or how well a product—usually a window, wall, or building envelope component—conducts heat. The *U* value is the inverse of the *R* value. The higher the *R* value, or the lower the *U* value, the better the insulation is to restrict the loss of heat from a building. In a window, this includes the thermal properties of the frame as well as the glazing. Ratings generally fall between 0.20 and 1.20. *See also: R value*

UF *See: Urea formaldehyde*

ULEV *See: Ultra-low-emission vehicle*

Ultra-low-emission vehicle (ULEV) Vehicle that has 50% less polluting emissions than the average for new cars released in that model year. One of a number of designations given by the California Air Resources Board to signify the level of emissions that car-buyers can expect their new vehicle to produce. *See also: Emissions standards, designations*

Ultramembrane New method of water purification; has pores that are so fine they can physically screen individual cells. Considered an environmentally friendly technique for purifying drinking water.

Ultraviolet radiation (UV) Electromagnetic radiation in the wavelength range 4–400 nanometers (1 nanometer is 1 billionth of 1 meter). Energy range just beyond the violet end of the visible spectrum. Although UV radiation constitutes only about 5% of the total energy emitted by the Sun, it is a major energy source for the stratosphere and mesosphere, playing a dominant role in both energy balance and chemical composition. Most UV radiation is blocked by the Earth's atmosphere in the ozone layer, but some solar UV penetrates and aids in plant photosynthesis, and helps produce vitamin D in humans. Excess UV can burn the skin, cause skin cancer and cataracts, and damage vegetation.

Thinning of the ozone layer results in increased UV radiation on Earth. Laboratory and epidemiological studies indicate that UV causes non-melanoma skin cancer and plays a major role in malignant melanoma development. Plant growth, changes in plant form, how nutrients are distributed within a plant, and timing of developmental phases and metabolism are also affected by UV radiation. In addition, aquatic food webs, particularly phytoplankton, have reduced survival rates,

Although the full impact is not known, solar ultraviolet B (UVB) radiation has been found to cause damage to early developmental stages of fish, shrimp, crab, amphibians, and other animals. Increases in solar UV radiation could affect terrestrial and aquatic biogeochemical cycles, altering both sources and sinks of greenhouse and chemically important trace gases such as carbon dioxide, carbon monoxide, carbonyl sulfide, and possibly other gases, including ozone. These potential changes would contribute to biosphere–atmosphere feedbacks that attenuate or reinforce the atmospheric build-up of these gases.

Unconfined aquifer Sometimes referred to as a water table aquifer. An aquifer that is open to the atmosphere and the surface of the land. Its water table goes up and down depending on the rates of discharge and recharge. *See also: Aquifer; Confined aquifer*

Underfloor air distribution System using an underfloor plenum (open space between the structural concrete slab and the underside of a raised floor system) to deliver conditioned air directly into the occupied zone of a building.

Underground home A house built into the ground or slope of a hill, or which has most or all exterior surfaces covered with earth. Because its earth insulation serves as a thermal mass, it retains warmth in winter and remains cool in summer. Utility costs are minimized, and it can be heated with solar panels. Research indicates that underground houses use about half the building materials required for a conventional above-ground house. For the most part they are fire-resistant and impervious to tornado and hurricane winds. Environmentally, they blend in with nature and provide more open space than a regular house. *See also: Earth sheltered design*.

Underground injection Technology of placing fluids underground in porous formation of rocks, through wells or other similar conveyance systems. The fluids may be water, wastewater, or water mixed with chemicals.

Underground injection well A well that has been bored, a drilled or driven shaft, or a dug hole in which the depth is greater than the largest surface dimension that is used to discharge fluids underground. While most of these wells are waste-disposal wells, there are also wells

that inject surface water to replenish depleted aquifers or to prevent salt water infusion. Wells may be as small as septic systems and storm water wells, or as large as several miles below the ground surface.

UNFCCC *See: United Nations Framework Convention on Climate Change*

Uniform Solar Energy Code Developed by the International Association of Plumbing and Mechanical Officials. Provides minimum requirements and standards for active solar systems.

United Nations Framework Convention on Climate Change (FCCC) Agreement at the Earth Summit held in Rio de Janeiro, Brazil, in 1992. Ratified and activated in 1994 by 189 nations, the FCCC sets the overall framework for intergovernmental efforts to deal with climate change in the world. Its goal is the stabilization of greenhouse gas concentrations in the atmosphere at a level that would prevent significant anthropogenically forced climate change. It gathers and shares information about greenhouse gas emissions, national policies, and best practices. It has helped launch national strategies to address greenhouse gas emissions and provisions for financial and technological support to developing countries.

Unsaturated zone Area immediately below the land surface, where the pores contain both water and air but are not totally saturated with water. These zones differ from aquifers, where the pores are saturated with water.

Unvented heater A combustion heating appliance that vents combustion by-products directly into the heated space. The latest models have oxygen sensors that shut off the unit when the oxygen level in the room falls below a safe level. As a safety measure, additional ventilation may be required if the home is tightly sealed.

Upcycling Transforming waste materials into useful products; a practical application of recycling and reuse. The term was made popular by William McDonough and Michael Braungart, authors of *Cradle to Cradle: Remaking the Way We Make Things* (2002). *See also: Downcycling*

Uranium Basic material in the actinide series of the Periodic Table (atomic number 92), used for nuclear technology. Uranium has several isotopes, meaning that the number of neutrons in the nucleus can vary. It is naturally slightly radioactive and can be refined to a metal 70% denser than lead. U-238, also called depleted uranium, comprises over 99% of all uranium on earth. U-235 is about 0.7% and U-234 less than 0.01%. The half-lives of U-238 and U-235 are long: 4,500,000,000 and 700,000,000 years, respectively. U-235 provides power for nuclear reactors and can be used in weapons. As is the case with all radioactive elements, there is concern about its safe storage and isolation.

Urban fabric analysis Method for determining the proportions of vegetative, roofed, and paved surface cover relative to the total urban surface in a city. To analyze the effect of surface cover modifications and simulate realistic estimates of temperature and ozone reductions resulting from such modifications, the baseline urban fabric has to be quantified. Higher percentages of built structures and paved surfaces contribute to the urban heat island effect. Vegetation and open spaces mitigate that effect.

Urban renewal Also known as urban regeneration. Term introduced after World War II to describe public efforts to revitalize aging and decaying inner cities. In the 1940s to 1970s, there was massive demolition of inner-city buildings, slum clearance, and dislocation of the residents. Public housing projects were constructed,

as well as newer, more affluent developments and businesses. It was very controversial politically, and charges of "red lining" and corruption and bribery were common. Since the 1980s, urban renewal has been reformulated with a focus on redevelopment of existing communities, with greater emphasis on renovating and revitalizing central business districts and downtown neighborhoods. The massive demolition and upheavals are all but gone in the USA. Notable cities that have established urban renewal policies and projects include Beijing, China; Melbourne, Australia; Glasgow, Scotland, UK; Boston, MA, USA; San Francisco, CA, USA; Bilbao, Spain; Cardiff, Wales, UK, and Canary Wharf in London, UK.

Urban renewal and revitalization of city centers and urban living decrease commuter traffic congestion from suburbs, make better use of municipal infrastructures, and slow down urban sprawl. However, there remain groups and associations that are still suspicious of the honesty, ethics, and motives of developers and municipal officials. *See also: Infill development*

Urban runoff City street stormwaters that carry municipal pollutants into sewer systems and receiving waters. This class of wastewater can add significant amounts of pollutants to receiving streams because of the material that accumulate on covered surfaces, such as oil and grease, pesticides, sand, sediment, and other detritus.

Urban sprawl Unplanned, unlimited extension of neighborhoods outside a city's limits, usually associated with low-density residential and commercial settlements, dominance of transportation by automobiles, and widespread strip commercial development. Development of open land usually results in decrease of rural areas and decrease in the natural habitat for biota of the region. Significant development may alter the environment and climate suitable for specific species, thereby altering the biodiversity of an area.

Urea formaldehyde (UF)   One of two types of formaldehyde resin; the other is phenol formaldehyde. Industrial chemical used to make other chemicals, building materials, and household products. Building products made with formaldehyde resins—particle board, fiberboard, plywood wall panels, and foamed-in-place UF insulation—can "off-gas" (emit) formaldehyde gas. Exposure to high levels of formaldehyde may adversely affect human health. The most widely used completely formaldehyde-free alternative resins are methylene diphenyl isocyanate (MDI) and polyvinyl acetate (PVA). Despite its name, PVA is not closely related to PVC. Without chlorine in its molecule, it avoids many of the worst problems that PVC has in its life cycle. There are a number of urea-free substitutes for UF. Phenol formaldehyde resin is used in the manufacture of composite wood products, such as softwood plywood and flake or oriented strand board (OSB), produced for exterior construction. Although formaldehyde is present in this type of resin, these composite woods generally emit formaldehyde at considerably lower rates than those containing UF resin. *See also: **Formaldehyde; Phenol formaldehyde***

Urethane   Type of fabricated foam core used as wall panels. Two types of urethane are polyurethane and polyisocyanurate. Neither is biodegradable, and both harm the ozone layer.

US Environmental Protection Agency (USEPA) Established in 1979 to establish, administer, and manage US federal environmental policies and regulations under a single agency.

USA Green Building Council   *See: Green Building Council (US)*

USEPA   *See: US Environmental Protection Agency*

USGBC   *See: Green Building Council, US*

Usage   Total amount of energy used over a given period of time.

UV   *See: Ultraviolet radiation*

Vacuum zero Energy of an electron at rest in empty space; used as a reference level in energy band diagrams. *See also: Zero-point energy*

Vapor barrier Material in a wall that prevents moisture-laden air from condensing on the inner surface of the outer wall of a building.

Vapor-extraction system System in which a vacuum is applied through wells near the source of contamination in the soil. The vacuum vaporizes volatile constituents, and the vapors are drawn toward the extraction wells. Extracted vapor is then treated as necessary (commonly with carbon adsorption) before being released to the atmosphere. The increased air flow through the subsurface can also stimulate bio-degradation of some of the contaminants, especially those that are less volatile. Wells may be either vertical or horizontal. In areas of high groundwater levels, water table depression pumps may be required to offset the effect of upwelling induced by the vacuum.

Variable fuel vehicle (VFV) Vehicle that can burn any combination of gasoline and an alternative fuel. Also known as a flexible fuel vehicle. Vehicles using alternative or variable fuel are being developed by most major automobile manufacturers to decrease reliance on fossil fuels and pollutant emissions into the environment. *See also: Dual-fuel vehicle*

Vehicle, electric *See: Electric vehicle*

Vehicle, fuel cell Like an electric vehicle, except that it uses a fuel cell in place of a storage battery.

Vehicle, hybrid electric *See: Hybrid electric vehicle; Hybrid engine*

Vehicle, hydrogen-fueled *See: Hydrogen-powered vehicle*

Vehicle, solar electric-powered *See: Solar electric-powered vehicle*

Ventilation (Architecture) If too little outdoor air enters a home, pollutants can sometimes accumulate to levels that can pose health and comfort problems. One approach to lowering the concentrations of indoor air pollutants in a home is to increase the amount of outdoor air coming in. Outdoor air enters and leaves a house by both natural and mechanical ventilation. In natural ventilation, air moves through opened windows and doors. Air movement associated with natural ventilation is caused by air temperature differences between indoors and outdoors and by wind. Natural ventilation can be circulated throughout a structure through a passive mode design, through ventilation windows designed with internal shading, through wind tower ventilation, and by a stack effect. There are a number of mechanical ventilation devices, from exhaust fans (vented outdoors) that intermittently remove air from a single room (such as bathrooms and kitchens), to air-handling systems that use fans and duct work to remove indoor air continuously and distribute filtered and conditioned outdoor air to strategic points throughout the house.

Ventury scrubber Pollution-removal device in which polluted fumes are moved through suitably designed "ventury". As the speed of the gas is increased, solutes are sprayed in the stream. The gas becomes fully saturated; solubles and solids are entrenched and thus become separated. *See also: Absorption process; Scrubbers*

Vermiculite A naturally occurring mineral that may contain asbestos, which is an indoor air pollutant. Vermiculite has the unusual property of expanding into worm-like, accordion-shaped pieces when heated. Expanded vermiculite is a light-weight, fire-resistant, absorbent and odorless material. These properties allow it to be used to make numerous products, including attic insulation, packing materials, and garden products.

Vermiculture Composting with worms.

Vertical-axis wind turbine *See: Darrieus wind turbine*

Vertical farming Farming in urban high-rises. Buildings used in this way have been called "farmscrapers". Using greenhouse methods and recycled resources, it is possible to produce fruit, vegetables, fish, and livestock year-round in cities. This proposal might allow cities to become self-sufficient. Combinations of hydroponic, aeroponic, and related growing methods allow most crops to be produced indoors in large quantities. Current building designs plan to use energy from wind power, solar power, and incineration of raw sewage and the inedible portion of harvested crops. Crop success would not be affected by weather, and continuous production of food would occur without regard to seasons. Minimal land use can reduce or

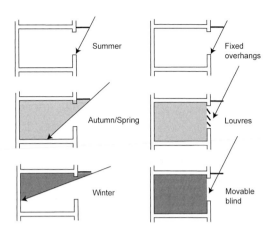

Figure 77a Types of shading device with different effects on view and ventilation

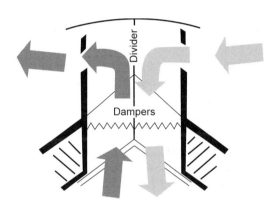

Figure 77b Wind tower ventilation

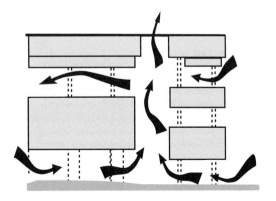

Figure 77c Natural ventilation (passive mode)

prevent further deforestation, desertification, and other consequences of agricultural encroachment on natural biomes. Transportation energy use and pollution are reduced, because the food is produced near the place it is used. Producing food indoors reduces or eliminates conventional plowing, planting, and harvesting by farm machinery, although automation might be used. The controlled growing environment and recycling reduce the need for pesticides, herbicides, and fertilizers. Vertical farms will use less water than conventional land agriculture, and the water can be recycled by condensing the water transpired from the plants. This recycled water is pure, and can be used for crops or drinking.

Vertical integration   Architectural term indicating multilateral integration of the designed system with the ecosystem. *See also: Ecocell*

Vertical landscape   Also known as a green wall system or breathing wall. *See: Breathing wall*

VFV   *See: Variable fuel vehicle*

Vienna Convention for the Protection of the Ozone Layer   Amendment to the Montreal Protocol. In 1985, under the aegis of the United Nations, nations agreed in Vienna to take "appropriate measures" to protect human health and the environment against adverse effects resulting, or likely to result, from human activities that modify or are likely to modify the ozone layer. The goal of the Convention was to encourage research and overall cooperation among countries, and exchange of information. It provided for future protocols and specified procedures for amendments and dispute settlement. The Vienna Convention set an important precedent: for the first time, nations agreed in principle to tackle a global environmental problem before its effects were felt, or even scientifically proven. *See also: Montreal Protocol on Substances that Deplete the Ozone Layer*

Vitrification   Process that stabilizes nuclear waste by mixing it with molten glass. Because there are concerns about the safety and isolation of nuclear wastes, vitrification decreases

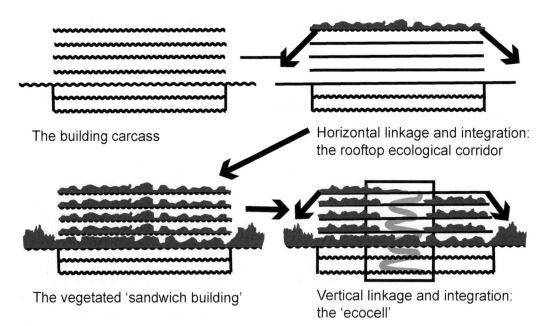

The building carcass

Horizontal linkage and integration: the rooftop ecological corridor

The vegetated 'sandwich building'

Vertical linkage and integration: the 'ecocell'

Figure 78 Designing for horizontal and vertical integration

the probability of nuclear emissions and dangers to the environment by sealing the waste into an amorphous glass structure, which takes thousands of years to decompose.

VOC   *See: Volatile organic compound*

Volatile   Adjective describing any substance that evaporates easily.

Volatile organic compound (VOC)   Compound that vaporizes at room temperature. These are air pollutants and toxic chemicals. Coal, petroleum, and refined petroleum products are all organic chemicals and occur in nature; other organic chemicals are synthesized. Volatile liquid chemicals produce vapors; volatile organic chemicals include gasoline, benzene, solvents such as toluene and xylene, and tetrachloroethylene. Many VOCs are also hazardous air pollutants, such as benzene. Many housekeeping and maintenance products, and building and furnishing materials, are common sources of VOCs in indoor air. *See also:* **Air pollutants; Toxic chemicals**

Volt   Unit of electrical force equal to that amount of electromotive force that will cause a steady current of 1 ampere to flow through a resistance of 1 ohm.

Voltaic cell   *See:* **Electrochemical cell**

Volumetric humidity   *See:* **Absolute humidity**

W

Waste Electrical and Electronic Equipment directive *See: Take back laws*

Waste heat Heat that is not needed at a specific location, or heat that is at too low a temperature or quality to do the work for which it was originally used. *See also: Cascading energy; Recoverable waste heat*

Waste management The collection, transport, processing, recycling, or disposal of waste materials. Usually refers to materials produced anthropogenically; it is generally undertaken to reduce their effect on health, the environment, or aesthetics. Also used as a way to recover resources from waste. May involve solid, liquid, gaseous, or radioactive substances, with different methods and fields of expertise for each. Practices differ in developed and developing nations, in urban and rural areas, and for residential and industrial producers. Management of nonhazardous residential and institutional waste in metropolitan areas is usually the responsibility of local government authorities; management of nonhazardous commercial and industrial waste is usually the responsibility of the generator. *See also: Landfill; Recycle; Waste materials; Waste reduction*

Waste materials Can be classified by their physical, chemical, and biological characteristics. One characteristic is consistency.

- Solid wastes—contain less than 70% water; include household garbage, some industrial wastes, some mining wastes, and oilfield wastes such as drill cuttings.
- Liquid wastes—usually wastewaters that contain less than 1% solids; may contain high concentrations of dissolved salts and metals.
- Sludge—between liquid and solid; usually contains between 3 and 25% solids, while the rest of the material is water dissolved materials.

US federal regulations classify wastes into three categories.

- Nonhazardous wastes—pose no immediate threat to human health and the environment; e.g. household garbage.
- Hazardous wastes—of two types, those with common hazardous properties such as ignitability or reactivity; and those that contain leachable toxic components.
- Special wastes—very specific in nature, and regulated with specific guidelines; e.g. radioactive wastes and medical wastes.

Governments at all levels have established regulations for waste management, both hazardous and nonhazardous. Many governments have set up intergovernment cooperation to manage waste, which has expanded beyond the scope and ability of any one government body to deal with effectively. The goals are to reduce contaminant pollution of the air, ground, and water. Conservationists advocate waste reduction, more reuse and recycling, and composting to cut down on the amount of waste materials generated through anthropogenic activities.

Waste reduction Also known as waste recovery. Broad term that includes all waste management methods, such as source reduction, recycling, and composting, that result in a reduction of the amount of waste going to a combustion facility or landfill.

Waste stream Total flow of solid waste from homes, businesses, and manufacturing plants that must be recycled, burned, or disposed of in landfills, or any segment thereof.

Wastewater Water that has been used in homes, agriculture, industries, and businesses, which cannot be safely reused unless it is treated.

Wastewater treatment Process of removing contaminants from wastewater. Physical, chemical, and biological processes are used to remove physical, chemical, and biological contaminants. The goal is to reuse the treated water (see Figure 79). *See also: **Primary wastewater treatment**; **Secondary wastewater treatment**; **Tertiary wastewater treatment***

Water bars Smooth, shallow ditches excavated at an angle across a road to decrease water velocity and divert water off and away from the road surface.

Water column Conceptual column of water from lake surface to bottom sediments.

Water futures Public policy that ensures management of water supplies to meet the demands of populations, as well as sanitation. *See also: **Water rights, laws governing***

Water management The practices of planning, developing, distribution, and optimum utilization of water resources under defined

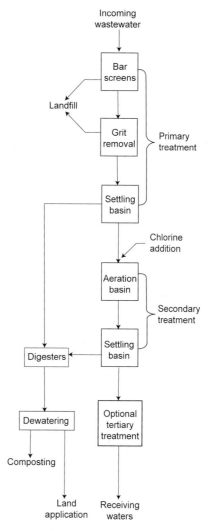

Figure 79 Primary, secondary, and tertiary treatment of wastewater

water polices and regulations. Includes water treatment, sewage or wastewater, management of water resources, flood prevention, and irrigation.

Water pollutants USEPA lists the following as major water pollutants: arsenic, contaminated sediment, disinfection by-products, dredged material, lead, mercury and microbial pathogens. Contaminants and toxins can have adverse effects on the quality and purity of water, and on the organisms that live in water. Left polluted, biota will either change in structure and species, or will perish.

Water-powered car Genepax, a Japanese company, unveiled in 2008 an eco-friendly car prototype that is claimed to run solely on any kind of water—even seawater or tea. With just 1 litre of water, the car is said to be able to run for up to an hour, at a speed of 80 km/h (50 mph). Typical fuel cell vehicles take in hydrogen and emit water, but Genepax's car generates electricity by breaking down water into hydrogen and oxygen. The company reported that this is made possible by a technology called "membrane electrode assembly", which contains a material that is capable of breaking down water into hydrogen and oxygen through a chemical reaction. According to Genepax, it does not require batteries to be recharged, as is the case for most electric cars. Skeptics have questioned the car's legitimacy, claiming that the technology appears to violate the first law of thermodynamics. Genepax is reportedly filing a patent for its new technology.

Water rights, laws governing Modern legal governance of access to water and water use has become a paramount issue because of the exponential increase in demand for water caused by increased populations, climate changes, development of bigger urban areas, rapid economic development worldwide, and more industrialization and commercial manufacturing. All these socioeconomic factors intensify worldwide pressures on water resources and supplies, and require a more orderly management and regulation of water resources and water rights to replace the semi-*laissez-faire* practices established in the 19th century.

Water rights are defined as the legal right to abstract and use water from a natural source, such as a river, stream, or aquifer. The laws governing water rights depend on a country's legal structure, geographical, socioeconomic, and political circumstances. Based on the unique situation of each political jurisdiction and country, it is impossible to have one legal framework for water rights. No one law would fit all the cultural, hydrogeological, economic, and social conditions in the world. In some countries, such as Spain and Chile, water is owned nationally to ensure access by all citizens and to protect the purity of the water. In some states in the USA, water is considered public property and cannot be owned privately. In England, and the New England area of the USA, riparian rights have been the prevailing practice since the 19th century, and the right to abstract and use water from a stream, river, or lake was an integral part of the right of ownership of that parcel of land. In the western USA during the 19th century, the practice of prior appropriation prevailed and severed the link between land and water rights. Prior appropriation was based on the practice and right of "first come, first use". However, The Dublin Principles, established as part of the 1992 United Nations Rio Declaration, declared that water development and management should involve users, planners, and policy-makers at all levels; and water sources, availability, and purity should be safeguarded. To achieve these goals, conservation organizations, government bodies, and international groups such as United Nations agree that the traditional land-based approach to water rights, including the rights to groundwater, is no longer a sound basis for sustainable management and use of water resources. Some groups have proposed state ownership of all water; others have proposed capping the volume abstracted by water rights-holders; all propose regulations to provide equity, transparency, and minimum negative impacts on the environment and third parties. Most agree that water rights-holders should be guaranteed some security, but bear the responsibility of limiting their use and volume abstracted and using water in a beneficial way, which precludes impounding and storing water behind dams or other hydraulic structures. Access to water and possession of water rights has been a primary concern of societies throughout history in all parts of the world. Each society has had its own approach to regulating access to water and water rights. *See also: Prior appropriation; Riparian rights*

Water side economizer Method of reducing energy consumption in cooling mode by turning off the chiller when the cooling tower alone can produce water at the desired chilled water set point. The cooling tower system, rather than the chiller, provides the cold water for cooling.

Water table Level below the Earth's surface at which the ground becomes saturated with water.

Water turbine A turbine that uses water pressure to rotate its blades. The primary types are the Pelton turbine, for high heads (pressure); the Francis turbine, for low to medium heads; and the Kaplan, for a wide range of heads. Primarily used to power an electric generator. The water turbine replaced the water wheel as a generator of power in the 19th century, and was able to compete with the steam engine. *See also: Francis turbine; Kaplan turbine; Pelton turbine*

Water vapor Water in a gaseous form. Water vapor is 99.999% of natural origin and is the Earth's most important greenhouse gas, accounting for about 95% of Earth's natural greenhouse effect, which keeps the planet warm enough to support life. When liquid water evaporates into water vapor, heat is absorbed. This process cools the surface of the Earth. The latent heat of condensation is released again when the water vapor condenses to form cloud water. This source of heat drives the updrafts in clouds and precipitation systems.

Water wall An interior wall made of water-filled containers for absorbing and storing solar energy.

Water wheel A wheel that is designed to use the weight and/or force of moving water to turn it, primarily to operate machinery or to grind grain.

Watershed Also called a drainage basin. Area that drains to a common waterway, such as a stream, lake, reservoir, estuary, wetland, aquifer, or the ocean. North American usage: drainage basin or catchment; the region of land whose water drains into a specific body of water. British and Commonwealth usage: drainage divide, a ridge of land separating two adjacent drainage basins. *See also: Catchment basin*

Watt Rate of energy transfer equivalent to 1 ampere under an electrical pressure of 1 volt. 1 watt equals 1/746 horsepower, or 1 joule per second. It is the product of voltage and amperage (current).

WCED *See: World Commission on Environment and Development*

Weatherization Caulking and weather-stripping to reduce air infiltration and exfiltration into/out of a building. This is an inexpensive and effective method of increasing energy efficiency in a building.

Wet deposition Form of acid rain, fog, sleet, fog water, and snow, contains acid chemicals and falls to the ground when the weather is wet. As acidic water flows over and through the ground, it affects a variety of plans and animals.

Wetlands Land that is partially or totally covered by shallow water, with soil saturated by moisture part or all of the time. Wetlands vary widely because of regional and local differences in soils, topography, climate, hydrology, water chemistry, vegetation, and other factors, including human disturbance. There are four general categories of wetland: i) marshes, which have soft-stemmed vegetation; ii) swamps, which have woody plants; iii) bogs, which have spongy peat deposits, evergreen trees and shrubs, and a floor covered by sphagnum moss; and iv) fens, which are freshwater, peat-forming wetlands covered mostly by grasses, sedges, reeds, and wildflowers. Wetlands serve as natural fish and wildlife habitats, rest stops for migratory birds, natural floodwater storage, water filtration, and erosion control. When functioning properly, wetlands provide water-quality protection. When rivers overflow, wetlands absorb and slow floodwaters, thereby alleviating property damage.

Wetlands can be adversely affected by increased pollution, changes in hydrological conditions that result in saturated soil for certain amounts of time annually, and vegetation damage. Primary pollutants include sediment, fertilizer, human sewage, animal waste, road salts, pesticides, heavy metals, and selenium. The origin of the pollutants can be runoff from urban, agricultural, silvicultural, and mining areas; air pollution from cars, factories, and power plants; old landfills and dumps that leak toxic substances; and marinas, where boats increase turbidity and release pollutants. Hydrological damage to wetlands can include deposits of fill material for development; drainage for development, farming, or mosquito control; dredging and stream channelization for navigation, development, and flood control; diking and damming to form ponds and lakes; diversion of flow to or from wetlands; and addition of impervious surfaces in the watershed. Vegetation damage can occur through domestic animal grazing, introduction of non-native plants that compete with natives, and removal of vegetation for peat mining.

Wetlands, constructed The goal of constructed wetlands is to simulate the ecosystem of the natural wetland. Generally on uplands and outside floodplains or floodways, they are built to prevent damage to natural wetlands and other aquatic resources. After construction, water-control structures are installed to establish the desired hydraulic flow patterns.

White goods Large household appliances such as refrigerators, washers, and dryers.

Whole sustainable building design
Traditionally, commercial building design choices are based on budget or time considerations. Single building components are added or deleted to meet time or budget constraints, often without evaluating their impact on total building performance. Basic design goals such as minimizing energy consumption or maximizing daylight cannot be done without understanding the impact of interrelations between parts of the building, including window glazing systems, thermal envelope, mechanical system integration, orientation, and floor plate proportions. High-performance building design ideally should be completely integrated to achieve optimal building performance. Because these interrelations are very complex, computerized simulation studies are used to analyze the design choices and interrelationships. Tools such as DOE-2 and Energy Plus can help guide the design process by quickly evaluating many design alternatives. Water and resource conservation, along with recycled, reusable, and nontoxic sustainable materials, should also be considered at the design stage (see Figure 80). *See also: DOE-2 computer simulation model; Energy Plus*

Williams alpha diversity index Created by Robert Williams, author of *Rivers: Biology Curriculum Guide,* the diversity index represents the number of species and types of organism present in a biological community. A high diversity index is an indicator of good balance

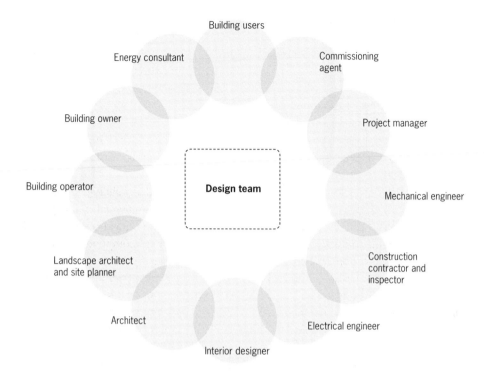

Building users

Energy consultant

Commissioning agent

Building owner

Project manager

Building operator

Design team

Mechanical engineer

Landscape architect and site planner

Construction contractor and inspector

Architect

Electrical engineer

Interior designer

Figure 80 An integrated design team

between stress and natural energy flow. For example, the diversity of a creek will depend on the weather and other resources that run into it. Pollution can affect a creek, resulting in a decrease in the different kinds of bugs and other organisms.

Wind energy Also called wind power. The process by which the wind is used to generate mechanical power or electricity. Wind is a form of solar energy, and wind turbines convert the kinetic energy in the wind into mechanical power. The mechanical power can be used for specific tasks, such as grinding grain or pumping water, or a generator can convert this mechanical power into electricity.

Wind farm Large utility-scale wind turbines grouped together into power plants and connected to an electrical utility grid.

Wind power *See: Wind energy*

Wind turbine Turbines that use the energy in the wind to turn two or three propeller-like blades around a rotor. The rotor is connected to the main shaft, which spins a generator to create electricity. Mounted on a tower to capture the most energy. A typical wind turbine tower measures between 165 and 260 feet (50–80 m). At 100 feet (30 m) or more above ground, they can take advantage of faster and less turbulent wind. The blades of a large wind turbine range from 80 to 130 feet (25–40 m). Most large turbines have three blades. Depending on the velocity of the wind and the size of the blades, a large turbine can generate electricity in a range of a few hundred kilowatts up to several megawatts. Wind turbines can be used to produce electricity for a single home or building, or they can be connected to an electricity grid for more widespread electricity distribution.

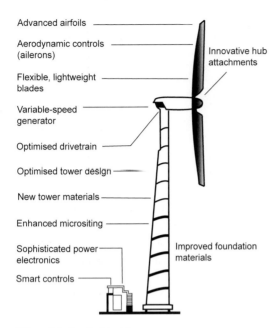

Advanced airfoils ─────────

Aerodynamic controls ─────
(ailerons)

Innovative hub
attachments

Flexible, lightweight ─────
blades

Variable-speed ──────
generator

Optimised drivetrain ─────

Optimised tower design ──────

New tower materials ──────

Enhanced micrositing ──────

Sophisticated power─────
electronics

Improved foundation
materials

Smart controls ──────

Figure 81 A wind turbine

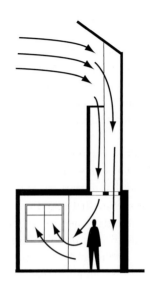

Modern wind turbines fall into two basic groups: the horizontal-axis variety and the vertical-axis design, like the eggbeater-style Darrieus model, named after its French inventor. Horizontal-axis wind turbines typically either have two or three blades. These three-bladed wind turbines are operated "upwind", with the blades facing into the wind (see Figure 81). *See also: **Darrieus wind turbine; Horizontal-axis wind turbine***

Window, electrochromic   *See: Electrochromic windows*

Window-to-wall ratio   Ratio of the glazing area to the gross exterior wall area.

Windscoop   Architectural design of a built form that takes advantage of the ambient energies and maximizes natural ventilation (see Figure 82).

Wing wall   A structural element built onto a building's exterior along the inner edges of all the windows, and extending from the ground to

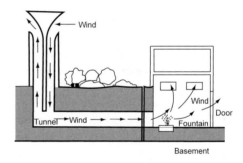

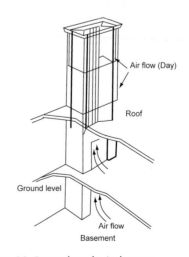

Figure 82 Examples of windscoops

the eaves. Wing walls help ventilate rooms that have only one exterior wall, which leads to poor cross-ventilation. Wing walls cause fluctuations in the natural wind direction to create moderate pressure differences across the windows. They are only effective on the windward side of the building (see Figure 83).

Winter penalty   Potential for increased heating demand in winter due to reflected solar radiation by light-colored roofs. In winter, cool roofs reflect solar energy that could have been used to warm the building, and more heating energy may be required. It is usually offset by cooling energy savings during the summer. Cool roofs usually have a net annual energy savings.

Wood alcohol   *See: Methanol*

Wood, structurally engineered   Structural products made from recycled/reconstituted wood materials that use laminated wood chips or strands and fingerjointing (gluing larger pieces together). These materials fall into the general category of engineered wood.

Wood treatment   Protecting wood from damage caused by insects, moisture, and decay fungi. Methods currently include creosote pressure-treated wood, pentachlorophenol pressure-treated wood, and inorganic arsenical pressure-treated

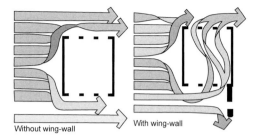

Figure 83 Use of wing wall to increase internal cross-ventilation

wood. Copper napthenate, zinc napthenate, and tributyltin oxide are other wood-treatment options that can be site-applied. All these treatment processes involve dangerous chemicals.

World Commission on Environment and Development (WCED)   Known by the name of its Chair, Gro Harlem Brundtland. Convened by the United Nations in 1983 to address growing concern "about the accelerating deterioration of the human environment and natural resources and the consequences of that deterioration for economic and social development". In establishing the commission, the UN General Assembly recognized that environmental problems are global in nature, and determined that it is in the common interest of all nations to establish policies for sustainable development. A report was published in 1987. *See also: Brundtland Report*

X

Xenobiota Biota displaced from its normal habitat.

XEPS *See: Extruded polystyrene*

Xeriscape Quality landscaping that conserves water and protects the environment. There are seven principles associated with xeriscape landscapes: planning and design, soil improvement, appropriate plant selection, practical turf areas, efficient irrigation, use of mulches, and appropriate maintenance.

Xerophytic plants Plants that are able to survive in an ecosystem with little available water or moisture, usually in environments where potential evapotranspiration exceeds precipitation for all or part of the growing season. Plants such as cacti and other succulents are typically found in deserts where low rainfall amounts are the norm. Plants that live under arctic conditions may also have a need for xerophytic adaptations, as water is unavailable for uptake when the ground is frozen.

X-radiation Form of radiant energy consisting of high-energy particles of radiation. Usually refers to X-rays, which were discovered by Roentgen in 1895. X-rays are ionizing radiation: they can break down molecules by imparting enough energy to bonding electrons to break the valence bonds in molecules. X-rays have useful medical applications and can also cause cancers. *See also: Ionizing radiation*

Y

Yellow water Urine collected separately and used directly on brown land; its nutrient composition suits many types of soil.

Yurt An octagonal-shaped or round shelter that originated in Mongolia, traditionally made from leather or canvas for easy transportation. Central Asian nomads erect their yurts in an hour or less. Modern canvas yurts can be set up in a day. Because they are round, they are more efficient to heat and provide less wind resistance. The roof structure is an architectural design that requires no internal support system, providing an open and spacious interior.

Z

ZEB *See: Zero-energy building*

Zener diode Special kind of diode that permits current to flow in the forward direction as normal, but also allows it to flow in the reverse direction when the voltage is above a certain value—the breakdown voltage, known as the Zener voltage. *See also: Avalanche diode; Diode; Schottky diode*

Zenith angle Angle between the direction of interest, such as the Sun, and the zenith (directly overhead).

Zero-carbon design Also known as low-carbon design. As renewable sources of energy are inexhaustible, clean, and carbon-free, solar, wind, wave, biomass, geothermal, and nuclear are all renewable sources of energy. When used in place of nonrenewable sources of energy, the resulting design is known as zero-carbon design. It is considered one solution to climate change. *See also: Zero-energy building*

Zero-culture ecosystem Design site classification measured by the condition of the existing ecosystem. Totally artificial ecosystem sites with no remaining ecological culture; a total urban site with nothing of the original fauna and flora remaining.

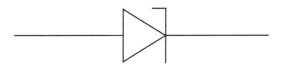

Figure 84 A Zener diode

Zero-emission vehicle (ZEV) Government designation for a vehicle that produces no tail-pipe pollutants, no evaporative emissions, and no onboard emissions-control systems that can deteriorate over time. Vehicles that fall into this category include battery-powered electric vehicles, fuel cell-operated vehicles, compressed air vehicles, plug-in hybrids when in electric mode, and solar-powered cars. *See also: Emissions standards, designations*

Zero-energy building (ZEB) Ability of a residential or commercial building to meet all its energy requirements from low-cost, locally available, nonpolluting, renewable sources. ZEBs usually use traditional energy sources such as electric and natural gas utilities when on-site generation does not meet the loads. When on-site generation is greater than the building's loads, excess electricity is exported to the utility grid. There is a lack of a common definition of this term. ZEB may emphasize demand-side or supply strategies, and whether fuel switching and conversion accounting are appropriate to meet a ZEB goal. There are four well documented definitions.

- Net zero-site energy—ZEB produces at least as much energy as it uses in a year, when accounted for at the site.
- Net zero-source energy—source ZEB produces at least as much energy as it uses in a year, when accounted for at the source. Source energy is the primary energy used to generate and deliver energy to the site. To

calculate a building's total source energy, imported and exported energy is multiplied by the appropriate site-to-source conversion multipliers.

- Net zero energy costs—cost ZEB means that the amount of money the utility pays the building owner for the energy the building exports to the grid is at least equal to the amount the owner pays the utility for the energy services and energy used over the year.
- Net zero energy emissions—a net ZEB building produces at least as much emissions-free renewable energy as it uses from emissions-producing energy sources.

Zero liquid discharge system Process that separates solids and dissolved constituents from plant wastewater and allows the treated water to be recycled or reused in the industrial process, resulting in no discharge of wastewater to the environment.

Zero-point energy In physics, the lowest possible energy level at absolute zero temperature that a quantum mechanical physical system can have; the energy of the ground state of the system. The concept was first proposed by Albert Einstein and Otto Stern in 1913. All quantum mechanical systems have a zero-point energy. Commonly used in reference to the ground state of the quantum harmonic oscillator and its null oscillations. In quantum field theory, a synonym for vacuum energy, an amount of energy associated with the vacuum of empty space. *See also: Vacuum zero*

ZEV   *See: Zero-emission vehicle*

Appendix 1
Conversion tables

English to Metric

English	Metric
1 inch	2.54 centimeters
1 foot	0.30 meters
1 yard	0.90 meters
1 mile	1.60 kilometers
1 square inch	6.50 square centimeters
1 square foot	0.10 square meters
1 square yard	0.80 square meters
1 acre	0.40 hectares
1 cubic foot	0.03 cubic meters
1 cord	3.60 cubic meters
1 quart	0.90 liters
1 gallon (US)	0.9 gallons (imperial)
1 gallon (imperial)	3.79 liters
1 ounce	28.40 grams
1 pound	0.50 kilograms
1 horsepower	0.70 kilowatts

Metric to English

Metric	English
1 centimeter (cm)	0.39 inches
1 meter (m)	3.30 feet; 1.10 yards
1 kilometer (km)	0.60 miles
1 square centimeter (cm^2)	0.20 square inches
1 square meter (m^2)	10.80 square feet; 1.20 square yards
1 hectare (ha)	2.50 acres
1 cubic meter (m^3)	35.30 cubic feet
1 liter (l)	1.10 quarts
1 cubic meter (m^3)	284.20 gallons
1 gram (g)	0.04 ounces

1 kilogram (kg)	2.20 pounds
1 kilowatt (kW)	1.30 horsepower

Temperature conversions

From Fahrenheit to Celsius

To convert from degrees Fahrenheit to degrees Celsius, subtract 32 degrees from the temperature and multiply by 5/9:

Table A1

Fahrenheit	0	10	20	30	40	50	60	70	80	90	100
Centigrade	–18	–12	–7	–1	4	10	16	21	27	32	38

From Celsius to Fahrenheit

To convert from degrees Celsius to degrees Fahrenheit, multiply the temperature by 1.8 and add 32 degrees:

Table A2

Centigrade	–10	–5	0	5	10	15	20	25	30	35	40
Fahrenheit	14	23	32	41	50	59	68	77	86	95	104

Appendix 2

International Environmental Agreements

2007 Bali Roadmap Agreement of 190 participating nations during the United Nations Framework Convention on Climate Change, held in Bali, Indonesia in December, 2007. It sets out a two-year process to finalize a binding agreement in 2009 in Denmark. Affirming scientific evidence of global warming, the convention addressed: i) the need to reduce emissions and the risks of further global warming; ii) policies, incentives, and financial support to halt deforestation and forest degradation and to preserve tropical rainforests; iii) international cooperation to protect poorer nations against climate change impacts; iv) assistance for developing countries to adapt to green technologies to help them reduce or avoid carbon pollution.

Four meetings scheduled for 2008 will develop specific goals and strategies to implement the Bali Roadmap and will be presented for adoption in 2009. It is intended to expand the Kyoto Protocol, the 1997 United Nations treaty on the environment.

2003 Carpathian Convention Framework Convention on the Protection and Sustainable Development of the Carpathians (Coalition of the Czech Republic, Hungary, Poland, Romania, Serbia and Montenegro, Slovak Republic, and Ukraine, 2003) Signed by all members. The Carpathian Convention provides the framework for cooperation and multi-sectoral policy coordination, a platform for joint strategies for sustainable development of the natural resources of the region and preservation of biodiversity of species unique to the area.

2002 Association of Southeast Asian Nations (ASEAN) Agreement on Transboundary Haze Pollution (ASEAN, 2002) Signed by all ASEAN nations. It is an environmental agreement to bring haze pollution under control in Southeast Asia. It was precipitated by land clearing and burning on Sumatra and the haze, assisted by monsoon winds, spread to Borneo, the Malay Peninsula, Malaysia, Singapore, Thailand, and Brunei.

2002 International Treaty on Plant Genetic Resources for Food and Agriculture (International Seed Treaty, 2002) Signed by 102 countries plus the European Union. It became effective in 2004. It complements the Convention on Biological Diversity. Its goals are to develop food security through conservation and sustaining plant genetic resources and biodiversity for food and agriculture.

2001 Stockholm Convention on Persistent Organic Pollution (United Nations, 2001) Signed by 91 countries and the European Union. Signatories agree to eliminate the production, use, and release of 12 key persistent organic pollutants: aldrin, chlordane, dichlorodiphenyl trichloroethane (DDT), dieldrin, endrin, heptachlor, hexachlorobenzene, mirex, toxaphene, polychlorinated biphenyls (PCBs), polychlorinated dibenzo-p-dioxins (dioxins), and polychlorinated dibenzofurans (furans). The Convention included special provisions to eliminate PCBs and DDT. The Convention specifies a scientific review process that could lead to the addition of other persistent organic pollutant chemicals of global concern.

1997 The Kyoto Protocol to the United Nations Framework Convention on Climate Change

(United Nations, 1997) Signed by 160 nations; became effective in 2005. The binding greenhouse gas emission targets include: carbon dioxide, methane, nitrous oxides, hydrofluorocarbons, perfluorocarbons, and sulfur hexafluoride. The agreement expires in 2012.

1994 International Tropical Timber Agreement

Signed by 43 countries; nine countries have signed but not yet ratified. It succeeds the 1983 Agreement.

1994 United Nations Convention to Combat Desertification in those Countries Experiencing Serious Drought and/or Desertification, particularly in Africa

Fifty-six countries signed the convention; 62 others have signed but not yet ratified. Became effective in 1996. Its purpose is to prevent desertification and ease the effects of drought.

1992 United Nations Framework Convention on Climate Change—Rio Declaration

(United Nations Conference on Environment and Development, 1992 in Rio de Janeiro) Signed by over 150 nations; 19 countries signed but not yet ratified. Became effective 1994. It now has 164 signatories and 17 countries that have signed by not yet ratified.

It reaffirmed the Declaration of the United Nations Conference on the Human Environment, adopted in Stockholm on 16 June, 1972, and sought to expand it. Set forth in 18 principles, the goal was to establish a new and equitable global partnership through the creation of new levels of cooperation among states, key sectors of societies and people, and to work towards international agreements that respect the interests of all and protect the integrity of the global environmental and developmental system. A main objective is to stabilize or decrease greenhouse gases in the atmosphere to prevent dangerous impacts on the climate.

1992 Convention on Biological Diversity

(United Nations Environment Programme, 1992) Part of the Rio Earth Summit in 1992; became effective in 1993. The Convention has been signed by 165 countries; 19 countries have signed but not yet ratified. The Convention's objective is to develop national strategies for the conservation and sustainability of biological diversity; ensure the sustainable use of its components; and promote fair and equitable sharing of the benefits arising out of the utilization of genetic resources.

1991 Alpine Convention

(Commission Internationale pour la Protection des Alpes, CIPRA, 1991) Seven member countries signed the agreement in 1991. It became effective in 1995. It is an agreement between various countries for the protection and sustainable development of the Alpine Region. It was signed on November 7, 1991 in Salzburg (Austria) by Austria, France, Germany, Italy, Liechtenstein, Switzerland, and the EU. Slovenia signed the Convention on March 29, 1993. Monaco became a party on the basis of a separate additional protocol.

1989 Basel Convention on Transboundary Movements of Hazardous Wastes and their Disposal

(United Nations Environment Programme, 1989) Signed by 170 nations; became effective in 1992. It strictly regulates the transboundary movements and disposal of hazardous wastes, and obliges its Parties to ensure such wastes are managed and disposed of in an environmentally sound manner. It is the most comprehensive global environmental agreement on hazardous and other wastes.

1987 Montreal Protocol on Substances that Deplete the Ozone Layer   Signed by 161 nations, it became effective in 1989. The Montreal Protocol is the primary international agreement providing for controls on the production and consumption of ozone-depleting substances, including chlorofluorocarbons (CFCs), halons, and methyl bromide. The Montreal Protocol is supplemented by the Vienna Convention of 1985. It has been amended substantially five times: London 1990, Copenhagen 1992, Vienna 1995, Montreal 1997, and Beijing 1999.

1983 International Tropical Timber Agreement
Became effective in 1985 but expired in 1994; succeeded by the 1994 Agreement. It was signed by 54 countries. The goal was to develop cooperation between timber producers and consumers, and to establish sustainable use and conservation of tropical forests.

1982 United Nations Convention on Law of the Sea (**UNCLOS**) (United Nations, 1982) Also called the Convention on the Law of the Sea (LOS); Law of the Sea Convention; or Law of the Sea Treaty. Signatories include 155 countries and the European Union. It became effective in 1994. UNCLOS is the result of the third UN Convention (Conference) on the Law of the Sea, which took place from 1973 to 1982. It defines the rights and responsibilities of nations in their use of the world's oceans, establishing guidelines for businesses, the environment, and the management of marine natural resources. The Convention concluded in 1982 replaced four 1958 treaties. UNCLOS codifies the rules by which nations use the oceans of the world. It includes rules and enforcement of established environmental standards and pollution of the marine environment.

1979 Convention on Long-range Transboundary Air Pollution (United Nations Economic Commission for Europe, 1979) Signed by 40 countries and the European Community; became effective in 1983. The Convention was the first international, legally binding instrument to deal with problems of air pollution on a broad regional basis. Its goals were to reduce and prevent air pollution. There was also an institutional framework established to decrease air pollutant emissions through monitoring and research.

The Convention on Long-range Transboundary Air Pollution now has 51 members, and has been extended by eight specific protocols, including: EMEP (Monitoring and Evaluation of the Long-range Transmission of Air Pollutants in Europe) Protocol, 1988; Nitrogen Oxide Protocol, 1988; Volatile Organic Compounds Protocol, 1991; Sulphur Emissions Reduction Protocols, 1985 and 1994; Heavy Metals Protocol, 1998; Multi-effect (Gothenburg) Protocol, 1999; Persistent Organic Pollutants (POP) Air Pollution Protocol, 2003.

1979 Convention on the Conservation of European Wildlife and Natural Habitats
(Council of Europe, 1979) Also known as the Bern Convention. Signed by 39 members of the Council of Europe together with the European Union, Monaco, Burkina Faso, Morocco, Tunisia, and Senegal. It became effective in 1982. Algeria, Belarus, Bosnia-Herzegovina, Cape Verde, the Holy See, San Marino, and Russia are among nonsignatories that have observer status at meetings of the committee. The goals are to conserve wild flora and fauna and their natural habitats; promote cooperation between states; monitor and control endangered and vulnerable species; and provide assistance concerning legal and scientific issues.

1979 Convention on the Conservation of Migratory Species of Wild Animals (CMS)
(United Nations Environment Programme, 1979) Also known as the Bonn Convention. It became effective in 1983. In 2005, 92 countries were

signatories from Africa, Central and South America, Asia, Europe, and Oceania. The focus of the Convention is the conservation of wildlife and habitats on a global scale, and the protection of terrestrial, marine, and avian migratory species throughout their range. The aim is to protect migratory species on the threatened extinction list, conserving or restoring their natural habitats, mitigating obstacles to migration, and controlling other factors that might endanger them. In addition to establishing obligations for each State joining the Convention, CMS promotes concerted action among the range states of many of these species.

1977 Convention to Combat Desertification (CCD) (United Nations, 1977) The Convention to Combat Desertification in Those Countries Experiencing Serious Drought and/or Desertification, Particularly in Africa was designed to manage both dryland ecosystems and the flow of aid for development. In 1977, the United Nations Conference on Desertification (UNCOD) adopted a Plan of Action to Combat Desertification (PACD). Despite its efforts, the United Nations Environment Programme (UNEP) concluded in 1991 that the problem of land degradation in arid, semi-arid, and dry sub-humid areas had intensified, although there were 'local examples of success'. At the 1992 Rio Earth Summit, a new, integrated approach to the problem was adopted. It emphasized action to promote sustainable development at the community level.

1976 Convention to Prohibit Military or Any Other Hostile Use of Environmental Modifications
Sixty-four member countries signed the agreement; 17 countries have signed but not ratified it. Became effective in 1978. The Convention's objective is to prohibit the military or other hostile use of environmental modification techniques in order to further world peace and trust among nations.

1973 International Convention for the Prevention of Pollution from Ships (United Nations, 1973) Also known as Marpol 73/78 ('Marpol' is short for marine pollution). Did not become effective. A 1978 protocol superseded the original convention and became effective in 1983. Ninety-six countries signed the convention. Its goal is to maintain the marine environment, to eliminate pollution by oil and other hazardous substances, and to minimize pollution through dumping and spills.

1973 Convention on International Trade in Endangered Species (CITES) (World Conservation Union, 1973) Became effective in 1975; 136 countries are signatories. The Convention's objectives are to protect endangered species from overexploitation by establishing worldwide controls on international trade in threatened species of animals and plants. In the case of species threatened with extinction, CITES prohibits all commercial trade in wild specimens. Member countries act by banning commercial international trade in an agreed list of endangered species, and by regulating and monitoring trade in others that might become endangered.

1972 Convention to Prevent Marine Pollution by Dumping Wastes and Other Matter
(International Maritime Organization, 1972) Also known as the London Convention. Became effective in 1975. In 2005, there were 82 country members of the Convention. One of the first global conventions to protect the marine environment from human activities, its objective is to control effectively all sources of marine pollution and to take all practicable steps to prevent pollution of the sea by dumping of wastes and other matter. It prohibits the dumping of certain hazardous materials; requires a prior special permit for dumping of a number of other identified materials; and requires a prior general permit for other wastes or matter.

'Dumping' has been defined as the deliberate disposal at sea of wastes or other matter from vessels, aircraft, platforms, or other manmade structures, as well as the deliberate disposal of these vessels or platforms. Wastes derived from the exploration and exploitation of sea-bed mineral resources are, however, excluded from the definition. The provision of the Convention also does not apply when it is necessary to secure the safety of human life or of vessels in cases of *force majeure*.

Modifications of the Convention include the following. 1978 amendments—incineration; 1978 amendments—disputes; 1980 amendments—list of substances; 1989 amendments—permits; 1993 amendments—banning of dumping of low-level radioactive wastes; phasing out of dumping of industrial wastes; banning of incineration at sea of industrial wastes; 1996 Protocol—revised convention, precautionary approach; prevention of practices that are harmful to sealife or pollute the sea; 1996 Protocol—prohibited dumping of dredged material; sewage sludge, fish waste, vessels and platforms of seagoing vessels, inert, inorganic geological material, organic material, bulky items from construction; 2006 amendments—CO_2 sequestration under the seabed (became effective in 2007).

1971 Convention on Wetlands of International Importance Especially As Waterfowl Habitat

Signed by 94 countries; became effective in 1975. Its objective is to limit encroachment on, and loss of, wetlands because of their importance to ecological balance.

1963 Treaty Banning Nuclear Weapon Tests in the Atmosphere, in Outer Space, and Under Water

Signed by 125 nations. Eleven countries have also signed the treaty but have not ratified it. It became effective in 1963. The objective of the Treaty is to agree on complete disarmament according to the goals outlined by the United Nations. This includes ending the arms race and

production and testing of all weapons, including nuclear ones.

1961 Antarctic Treaty

Coalition of nations active in Antarctic science. Originally drafted in 1959; signed by 12 countries in 1961; became effective in 1961. There are now 43 signatories. The Treaty covers the area south of 60° S latitude. Its objectives are to demilitarize Antarctica, to establish it as a zone free of nuclear tests and the disposal of radioactive waste, and to ensure it is used for peaceful purposes only; to promote international scientific cooperation in Antarctica; and to set aside disputes over territorial sovereignty.

The Treaty remains in force indefinitely. Forty-six countries, comprising around 80% of the world's population, are now members. Consultative (voting) status is open to all countries that have demonstrated their commitment to the Antarctic by conducting significant research. The 1991 Protocol to the Treaty reinforced its basic goals.

Twenty-eight nations, including the UK, have Consultative status. The Treaty parties meet each year at the Antarctic Treaty Consultative Meeting. They have adopted over 300 recommendations and negotiated separate international agreements, of which three are still in use. These, together with the original Treaty, provide the rules that govern activities in Antarctica. Collectively, they are known as the Antarctic Treaty System (ATS). The three international agreements are: Convention for the Conservation of Antarctic Seals (1972); Convention on the Conservation of Antarctic Marine Living Resources (1980); Protocol on Environmental Protection to the Antarctic Treaty (1991).

1958 Convention on Fishing and Conservation of Living Resources of the High Seas

Also known as Marine Life Conservation. Opened for signature in 1958; signed by 37 countries;

became effective in 1966. Twenty-one countries have signed but not yet ratified the agreement. The Convention seeks international cooperation to conserve and preserve living resources of the high seas, and to resolve the overexploitation of marine resources.

1946 International Convention for the Regulation of Whaling Became effective in 1948; signed by 57 countries. The goal of the Convention is to protect whales from overfishing, and to establish international conservation and protection of whales.

Appendix 3
The Periodic Table of elements

Table A3

Chemical element	Symbol	Atomic number	Chemical element	Symbol	Atomic number
Actinium	**Ac**	89	Holmium	**Ho**	67
Aluminum	**Al**	13	Hydrogen	**H**	1
Americium	**Am**	95	Indium	**In**	49
Antimony	**Sb**	51	Iodine	**I**	53
Argon	**Ar**	18	Iridium	**Ir**	77
Arsenic	**As**	33	Iron	**Fe**	26
Astatine	**At**	85	Krypton	**Kr**	36
Barium	**Ba**	56	Lanthanum	**La**	57
Berkelium	**Bk**	97	Lawrencium	**Lr**	103
Beryllium	**Be**	4	Lead	**Pb**	82
Bismuth	**Bi**	83	Lithium	**Li**	3
Bohrium	**Bh**	107	Lutetium	**Lu**	71
Boron	**B**	5	Magnesium	**Mg**	12
Bromine	**Br**	35	Manganese	**Mn**	25
Cadmium	**Cd**	48	Meitnerium	**Mt**	109
Calcium	**Ca**	20	Mendelevium	**Md**	101
Californium	**Cf**	98	Mercury	**Hg**	80
Carbon	**C**	6	Molybdenum	**Mo**	42
Cerium	**Ce**	58	Neodymium	**Nd**	60
Cesium	**Cs**	55	Neon	**Ne**	10
Chlorine	**Cl**	17	Neptunium	**Np**	93
Chromium	**Cr**	24	Nickel	**Ni**	28
Cobalt	**Co**	27	Niobium	**Nb**	41
Copper	**Cu**	29	Nitrogen	**N**	7
Curium	**Cm**	96	Nobelium	**No**	102
Darmstadtium	Ds	110	Osmium	**Os**	76
Dubnium	**Db**	105	Oxygen	**O**	8
Dysprosium	**Dy**	66	Palladium	**Pd**	46
Einsteinium	**Es**	99	Phosphorus	**P**	15
Erbium	**Er**	68	Platinum	**Pt**	78
Europium	**Eu**	63	Plutonium	**Pu**	94
Fermium	**Fm**	100	Polonium	**Po**	84
Fluorine	**F**	9	Potassium	**K**	19
Francium	**Fr**	87	Praseodymium	**Pr**	59
Gadolinium	**Gd**	64	Promethium	**Pm**	61
Gallium	**Ga**	31	Protactinium	**Pa**	91
Germanium	**Ge**	32	Radium	**Ra**	88
Gold	**Au**	79	Radon	**Rn**	86
Hafnium	**Hf**	72	Rhenium	**Re**	75
Hassium	**Hs**	108	Rhodium	**Rh**	45
Helium	**He**	2	Rubidium	**Rb**	37

Table A3 (continued)

Chemical element	Symbol	Atomic number
Ruthenium	**Ru**	44
Rutherfordium	**Rf**	104
Samarium	**Sm**	62
Scandium	**Sc**	21
Seaborgium	**Sg**	106
Selenium	**Se**	34
Silicon	**Si**	14
Silver	**Ag**	47
Sodium	**Na**	11
Strontium	**Sr**	38
Sulfur	**S**	16
Tantalum	**Ta**	73
Technetium	**Tc**	43
Tellurium	**Te**	52
Terbium	**Tb**	65
Thallium	**Tl**	81
Thorium	**Th**	90
Thulium	**Tm**	69
Tin	**Sn**	50
Titanium	**Ti**	22
Tungsten	**W**	74
Ununbium	Uub	112
Ununhexium	Uuh	116
Ununoctium	Uuo	118
Ununpentium	Uup	115
Ununquadium	Uuq	114
Ununseptium	Uus	117
Ununtrium	Uut	113
Ununium	Uuu	111
Uranium	**U**	92
Vanadium	**V**	23
Xenon	**Xe**	54
Ytterbium	**Yb**	70
Yttrium	**Y**	39
Zinc	**Zn**	30
Zirconium	**Zr**	40

Source: Lenntech, the Netherlands

Appendix 4
Photovoltaics

Photoelectric effect In 1839, at the age of 19, French physicist Edmond Becquerel discovered that certain materials would produce small amounts of electric current when exposed to sunlight – but it took scientists almost 75 years to analyze and understand the process. In the 1870s, Heinrich Hertz studied the photoelectric effect in solids such as selenium. This study resulted in the use of selenium photovoltaic (PV) cells to convert light to electricity, and was subsequently adopted for use in light-measuring devices in the infant field of photography.

Continued experimentation and analysis by scientists focused on the photoelectric or PV effect, which causes certain materials to convert light energy into electrical energy at the atomic level. By the 1940s, the Czochralski process was developed for producing highly pure crystalline silicon, and in 1954 scientists at Bell Laboratories used this process to develop the first crystalline silicon PV cell.

The photoelectric effect describes the release of positive and negative charge carriers in a solid state when light strikes a surface—the basic physical process by which a PV cell converts sunlight into electricity. When light shines on a PV cell, it may be reflected, absorbed, or pass right through. However, only the absorbed light generates electricity.

The energy of the absorbed light is transferred to electrons in the atoms of the PV cell. With their additional energy, these electrons escape from their normal positions in the atoms of the semiconductor PV material and become part of the electrical flow, or current, in an electrical circuit. A special electrical property of the PV cell—a "built-in electric field"—provides the force, or voltage, needed to drive the current through an external load, such as a light bulb.

To induce the built-in electric field within a PV cell, two layers of somewhat differing semiconductor materials are placed in contact with one another. One layer is an n-type semiconductor with an abundance of electrons, which have a negative electrical charge. The other layer is a p-type semiconductor with an abundance of "holes," which have a positive electrical charge.

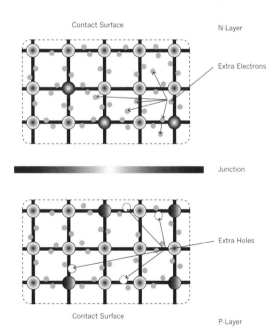

Figure A.1 Photoelectric effect
Source: US Department of Energy

Although both materials are electrically neutral, n-type silicon has excess electrons, and p-type silicon has excess holes. Sandwiching these together creates a p/n junction at their interface, thereby creating an electric field.

When n-type and p-type silicon come into contact with each other, excess electrons move from the n-type side to the p-type side. The result is a buildup of positive charge along the n-type side of the interface, and a buildup of negative charge along the p-type side.

Because of the flow of electrons and holes, the two semiconductors behave like a battery, creating an electric field at the surface where they meet—the p/n junction. The electrical field causes the electrons to move from the semiconductor toward the negative surface, where they become available to the electrical circuit. At the same time, the holes move in the opposite direction, toward the positive surface, where they wait for incoming electrons.

The p-type ("positive") and n-type ("negative") silicon materials become the PV cells that produce solar electricity through the addition of an element that has an extra electron or lacks an electron. This process of adding another element is called doping.

Photovoltaic (PV) Pertaining to the direct conversion of light into electricity.

Photovoltaic array An array is an interconnected system of PV modules, which in turn are made of interconnected solar cells. The cells convert solar energy into direct current (DC) electricity via the PV effect. The power that one module can produce is usually not sufficient to meet a consumer's needs, so the modules are linked together to form an array. Most PV arrays use an inverter to convert the DC power produced by the modules into alternating current (AC) that can plug into the existing infrastructure to power lights, motors, and other loads. The modules in a PV array are usually first connected in series to obtain the needed voltage, but individual strings can be connected in parallel to allow the system to produce more current. Solar arrays are usually measured by the electrical power they produce: watts, kilowatts, or megawatts.

Flat-plate stationary arrays are the most common. Some of the tilts can be adjusted from their horizontal position. These changes can be made any time throughout the year, although they are normally changed only twice a year. The modules in the array do not move throughout the day.

A stationary array does not capture as much energy as a tracking array, which follows the

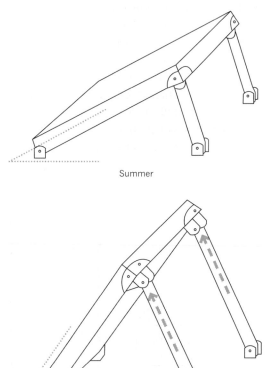

Summer

Winter

Figure A.2 Adjustable array tilts for summer and winter solar angles
Source: Polar Power

daily movement of the Sun. As a result, more stationary modules may be required. On the other hand, there are no moving parts to fail. Consequently, stationary arrays are often used for remote or dangerous locations.

Photovoltaic cell   Commonly known as solar cells, individual PV cells are electricity-producing devices made of semiconductor materials. PV cells come in many sizes and shapes, from smaller than a postage stamp to several inches across.

The size of an array depends on various factors, such as the amount of sunlight available in a particular location, and the needs of the consumer. The modules of the array make up the major part of a PV system, which can also include electrical connections, mounting hardware, power-conditioning equipment, and batteries that store solar energy for use when the Sun is not shining.

The basic PV or solar cell usually produces only a small amount of power. To produce more power, cells can be interconnected to form modules, which in turn can be connected in arrays to produce yet more power. Because

of this modularity, PV systems can be designed to meet any electrical requirement.

Solar cells are composed of various semiconducting materials, about 95% of which are made of silicon. One side of the semiconductor material has a positive charge and the other side is negatively charged. Sunlight hitting the positive side will activate the negative-side electrons and produce an electrical current.

A PV cell converts solar irradiance to electricity. It is the smallest semiconductor element within a PV module to perform the immediate conversion of light into electrical energy. A PV cell is a specialized form of semiconductor anode that converts visible light, infrared (IR) radiation, or ultraviolet (UV) radiation directly into electricity.

There are three types of PV cell: single-crystal or monocrystalline; multi- or polycrystalline; and amorphous.

- Monocrystalline rods are extracted from melted silicon and then sawn into thin plates. This produces a relatively high level of efficiency.

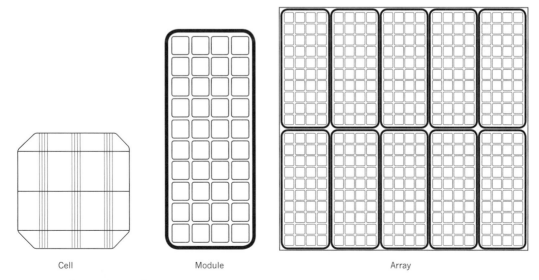

Cell   Module   Array

Figure A.3 Photovoltaic cells
Source: US Department of Energy, Energy Efficiency and Renewable Energy

- Polycrystalline cells are more cost-efficient to produce, but are less efficient than mono-crystalline cells.
- Amorphous or thin-layer cells are made up of a silicon film adhered to glass or other material. They are the least efficient and least expensive of the three types of cell. Because of this, they are primarily used in low-power equipment (watches, pocket calculators) or as façade elements. Their efficiency is half that of crystalline cells, and they degrade with use.

Photovoltaic device Solid state electrical device that converts light into direct current electricity. The voltage–current characteristics are a function of the light source, and of the materials and design of the device. Solar PV devices are made of various semiconductor materials including silicon, cadmium, sulfide, cadmium telluride, and gallium arsenide, and in single crystalline, multi-crystalline, or amorphous forms. The structure of a PV device depends on the materials used in the PV cells. There are four basic device designs: i) homojunction; ii) heterojunction; iii) p–i–n/n–i–p; and iv) multijunction.

Homojunction device Crystalline silicon is the primary example of this kind of cell. A single material—crystalline silicon—is altered so that one side is p-type, dominated by positive holes, and the other side is n-type, dominated by negative electrons. The p/n junction is located so that the maximum amount of light is absorbed near it. The free electrons and holes generated by light deep in the silicon diffuse to the p/n junction, then separate to produce a current if the silicon is of sufficiently high quality.

Some homojunction cells have been designed with the positive and negative electrical contacts on the back of the cell. This geometry

thickness of the solar cell: approx 0.3 mm
thickness of the n-semiconductor layer: approx 0.002 mm

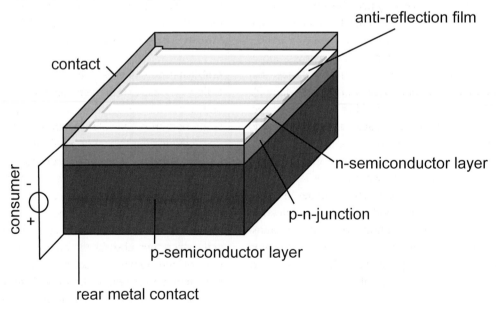

Figure A.4 Model of a crystalline solar cell
Source: Us Department of Energy

eliminates shadowing caused by the electrical grid on top of the cell. A disadvantage is that the charge carriers, which are mostly generated near the top surface of the cell, must travel further—all the way to the back of the cell—to reach an electrical contact. To be able to do this, the silicon must be of very high quality, without crystal defects that cause electrons and holes to recombine.

Heterojunction device   An example of this type is a CIS cell, where the junction is formed by contacting two different semiconductors—cadmium sulfide (CdS) and copper indium diselenide (CuInSe$_2$). This structure is often chosen for producing cells made of thin-film materials that absorb light much better than silicon. The top and bottom layers in a heterojunction device have different roles. The top layer, or window layer, is a material with a high bandgap selected for its transparency to light. The window allows almost all incident light to reach the bottom layer, which is a material with low bandgap that readily absorbs light. This light then generates electrons and holes very near the junction, which helps effectively to separate the electrons and holes before they can recombine. Heterojunction devices have an inherent advantage over homojunction devices, which require materials that can be doped both p-type and n-type. Many PV materials can be doped either p-type or n-type, but not both. Again, because heterojunctions do not have this constraint, different PV materials can be investigated to produce optimal cells. Also, a high-bandgap window layer reduces the cell's series resistance. The window material can be made highly conductive, and the thickness can be increased without reducing the transmittance of light. As a result, light-generated electrons can easily flow laterally in the window layer to reach an electrical contact.

p–i–n and n–i–p device   Usually, amorphous silicon thin-film cells use a p–i–n structure, whereas cadmium telluride (CdTe) cells use an n–i–p structure. The basic process is: a three-layer sandwich is created, with a middle intrinsic (i-type or undoped) layer between an n-type and a p-type layer. This geometry sets up an electric field between the p-type and n-type regions, which stretches across the middle intrinsic resistive region. Light generates free electrons and holes in the intrinsic region, which are then separated by the electric field. In the p–i–n amorphous silicon (a-Si) cell, the top layer is p-type a-Si, the middle layer is intrinsic silicon, and the bottom layer is n-type a-Si. Amorphous silicon has many atomic-level electrical defects when it is highly conductive. So very little current would flow if an a-Si cell had to depend on diffusion. However, in a p–i–n cell, current flows because the free electrons and holes are generated within the influence of an electric field, rather than having to move toward the field. In a cadmium telluride (CdTe) cell, the device structure is similar to the amorphous silicon (a-Si) cell, except that the order of layers is flipped upside down. Specifically, in a typical CdTe cell, the top layer is p-type cadmium sulfide (CdS), the middle layer is intrinsic CdTe, and the bottom layer is n-type zinc telluride (ZnTe).

Multijunction device   This structure, also called a cascade or tandem cell, can achieve a higher total conversion efficiency by capturing a larger portion of the solar spectrum. In the typical multijunction cell, individual cells with different bandgaps are stacked on top of one another. The individual cells are stacked in such a way that sunlight falls first on the material having the largest bandgap. Photons not absorbed in the first cell are transmitted to the second cell, which then absorbs the higher-energy portion of the remaining solar radiation while remaining transparent to the lower-energy photons. These selective absorption processes continue through to the final cell, which has the smallest bandgap. A multijunction device is a stack of individual single-junction cells in descending order of bandgap (e.g. see Figure A.6). The top cell captures the high-energy photons and passes the rest of the photons on, to be absorbed by lower-bandgap cells.

A multijunction cell can be made in two different ways. In the mechanical stack approach, two individual solar cells are made independently, one with a high bandgap and one with a lower bandgap. The two cells are then mechanically stacked, one on top of the other.

In the monolithic approach, one complete solar cell is made first, then the layers for the second cell are grown or deposited directly on the first. This multijunction device has a top cell of gallium indium phosphide, then a "tunnel junction" to allow the flow of electrons between the cells, and a bottom cell of gallium arsenide (GaAs).

Current research in multijunction cells focuses on GaAs as one (or all) of the component cells. These cells have efficiencies of more than 35% under concentrated sunlight, which is high for PV devices. Other materials studied for multijunction devices are amorphous silicon and copper indium diselenide.

Photovoltaic generator   All PV strings of a PV power supply system, which are electrically connected.

Photovoltaic module   The PV module is made up of single solar cells, which are interconnected

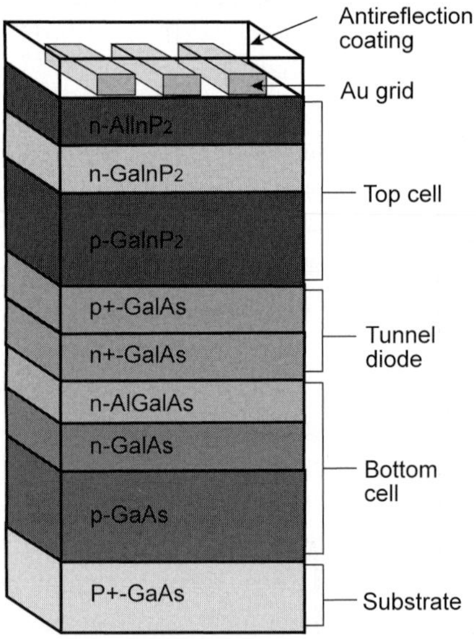

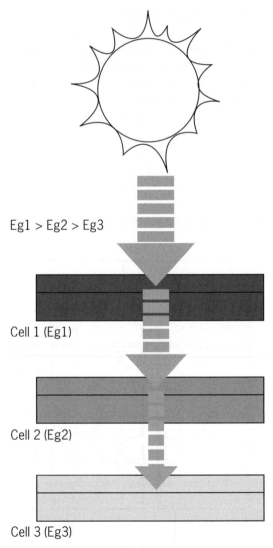

Figure A.5 A multijunction photovoltaic device–mechanical stack approach
Source: US Department of Energy

Figure A.6 A multijunction photovoltaic device–monolithic approach
Source: US Department of Energy

to form larger units to generate electricity or voltage for different uses. Cells connected in series have a higher voltage, while those connected in parallel produce more electric current. The interconnected solar cells are usually embedded in transparent ethyl vinyl acetate, fitted with an aluminum or stainless steel frame and covered with transparent glass on the front side. A junction box on the underside of the module is used to allow for connecting the module circuit conductors to external conductors.

A system of PV modules functions as an electricity-producing unit. The modules can be connected in series, in parallel, or both to increase output voltage or current. This also increases the output power. The electrical current increases when modules are connected in parallel. Figure A.7 shows three modules that produce 15 volts and 3 amps each, connected in parallel. They will produce 15 volts and 9 amps.

If the system includes a battery storage system, a reverse flow of current from the batteries through the PV array can occur at night.

This flow will drain power from the batteries. A diode is used to stop this reverse current flow. Diodes are electrical devices that allow current to flow only in one direction. Diodes create a voltage drop, so some systems use a controller that opens the circuit instead of using a blocking diode. If the same three modules are connected in series, the output voltage will be 45 volts, and the current will be 3 amps.

If one module in a series string fails, it provides so much resistance that other modules in the string may not be able to operate either. A bypass path around the disabled module will eliminate this problem. The bypass diode allows the current from the other modules to flow through in the "right" direction. Many modules are supplied with a bypass diode at their electrical terminals. Larger modules may have three groups of cells, each with its own bypass diode.

Isolation diodes are used to prevent the power from the rest of an array from flowing through a damaged series string of modules. They operate like a blocking diode. They are normally required

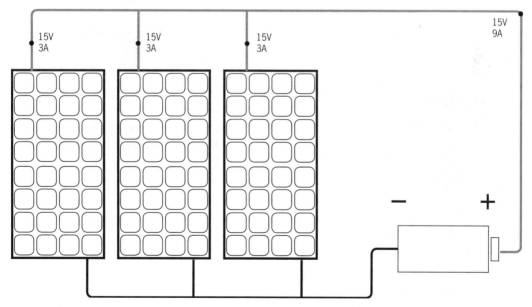

Figure A.7 Three modules connected in parallel
Source: US Department of Energy

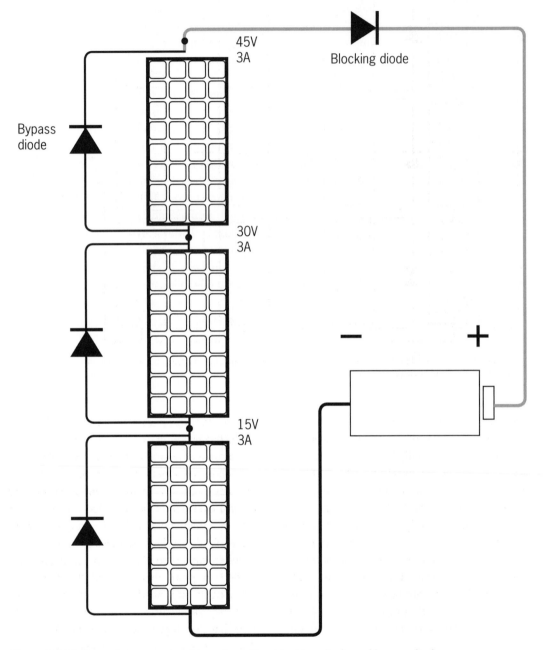

Figure A.8 Three modules connected in series with a blocking diode and bypass diodes
Source: US Department of Energy/Polar Power

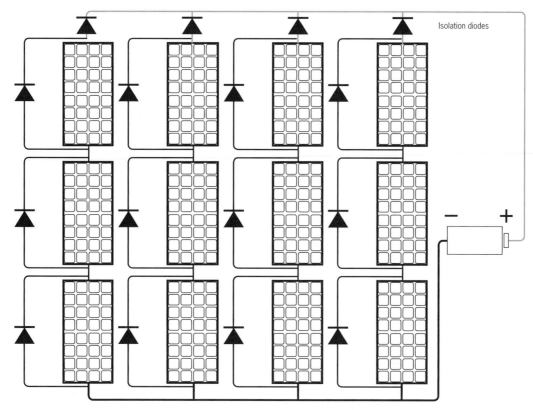

Figure A.9 Twelve modules in parallel-series array with bypass diodes and isolation diodes
Source: US Department of Energy/Polar Power

when the array produces 48 volts or more. If isolation diodes are used on every series string, a blocking diode normally is not required.

Modules should be installed within 200° of true south. In areas with morning fog, the array can be oriented up to 200° toward the west to compensate. Similarly, arrays in areas with frequent afternoon storms can be oriented toward the east. If the array is in the Southern Hemisphere, the array must face true south. Small portable arrays are usually pointed at the Sun, and moved hourly to track the Sun's path across the sky. *See also main entry:* **Photovoltaic module**

Photovoltaic system   A PV or solar cell is the basic building block of a PV (or solar electric)

system. An individual PV cell is usually quite small, producing about 1 or 2 watts of power. To boost the power output of PV cells, they are connected together to form larger units or modules. Modules, in turn, can be connected to form even larger units, called arrays, which can be interconnected to produce more power. By themselves, modules or arrays do not represent an entire PV system. Structures are needed to point them toward the Sun, and components are needed to convert the DC electricity produced by modules and "condition" that electricity to AC electricity. There may also be a need to store some electricity, usually in batteries, for later use. All these items are referred to as the "balance of system" (BOS) components.

Combining modules with the BOS components creates an entire PV system. This system is usually designed to meet a particular energy demand, such as powering a water pump, or the appliances and lights in a home, or, if the PV system is large enough, all the electrical requirements of a whole community.

A complete set of components for converting sunlight into electricity by the PV process, including the array and balance of system components, is composed of three subsystems.

- Power generation—includes a subsystem of PV devices (cells, modules, arrays) and converts sunlight to DC electricity.
- Power use—requires a subsystem consisting mainly of the load, which is the application of the PV electricity.
- Balance of system—between these two, a third subsystem that enables the PV-generated

electricity to be applied properly to the load.

See also main entry: **Photovoltaic system:** *Figure 57*

PV systems can be classified into two general categories: flat-plate systems or concentrator systems.

Flat-plate PV system The most common array design uses flat-plate PV modules or panels, which can be either fixed in place or allowed to track the movement of the Sun. They respond to sunlight that is either direct or diffuse. Even in clear skies, the diffuse component of sunlight accounts for between 10 and 20% of the total solar radiation on a horizontal surface. On partly sunny days, up to 50% of that radiation is diffuse; on cloudy days, 100% of the radiation is diffuse.

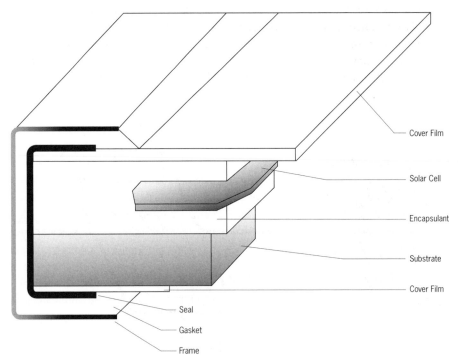

Figure A.10 Flat-plate PV system
Source: US Department of Energy

A typical flat-plate module design uses a substrate of metal, glass, or plastic to provide structural support in the back; an encapsulant material to protect the cells; and a transparent cover of plastic or glass. The simplest PV array consists of flat-plate PV panels in a fixed position. The advantages of fixed arrays are that they lack moving parts, there is virtually no need for extra equipment, and they are relatively lightweight. These features make them suitable for many locations, including most residential roofs. Because the panels are fixed in place, their orientation to the Sun is usually at an angle that is less than optimal. Therefore less energy per unit area of array is collected, compared with that from a tracking array. However, this drawback must be balanced against the higher cost of the tracking system.

Concentrator PV system This system uses optical concentrators to focus direct sunlight onto solar cells for conversion to electricity. It includes concentrator modules, support and tracking structures, a power-processing center, and land. The PV concentrator module components include solar cells, electrical isolating and thermally conducting housing for mounting and interconnecting the cells, and optical concentrators. The solar cells are predominantly silicon, but gallium arsenide (GaAs) solar cells are being developed for high conversion efficiencies. Current concentrator types include the Fresnel lens (both linear and point focus), the Graetzel cell, the reflecting parabolic trough, and other innovative optic devices.

Photovoltaic tracking array Array that tracks or follows the Sun across the sky. Tracking arrays perform best in areas with clear climates. The ability to follow the Sun produces significantly greater amounts of energy when the Sun's energy is predominantly direct. Direct radiation comes straight from the Sun, rather than the entire sky. Tracking arrays can follow the Sun in one axis or in two.

One-axis trackers normally follow the Sun from east to west throughout the day. The angle between the modules and the ground does not change. The modules face in the compass direction of the Sun, but may not point exactly up at the Sun at all times.

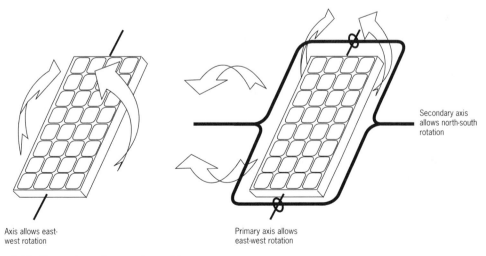

Axis allows east-west rotation

Primary axis allows east-west rotation

Secondary axis allows north-south rotation

Figure A.11 One-axis and two-axis tracking arrays
Source: US Department of Energy/Polar Power

Two-axis trackers change both their east–west direction and the angle from the ground during the day. The modules face straight at the Sun all through the day. Two-axis trackers are considerably more complicated than one-axis types.

Various tracking systems can be used. The first uses a simple motor, gear, and chain system to move the array. The system is

Figure A.12 Photovoltaic cell used as solar sensor
Source: US Department of Energy/Polar Power

designed to point the modules mechanically in the direction of the Sun. No sensors or devices actually confirm that the modules are facing the right way.

The second method uses PV cells as sensors to orient the larger modules in the array. This can be done by placing a cell on each side of a small divider, and mounting the package so it is facing the same way as the modules.

An electronic device constantly compares the small current flow from both cells. If one is shaded, the device triggers a motor to move the array until both cells are exposed to equal amounts of sunlight. At night, or during cloudy weather, the output of both sensor cells is equally low, so no adjustments are made. When the Sun comes back up in the morning, the array will move back to the east to follow the Sun again.

Although the methods of tracking with motors are quite accurate, there is a "parasitic" power consumption. The motors take up some of the energy the PV system produces. A method that has no parasitic consumption uses two small PV modules to power a reversible-gear motor directly. If both modules are in equal sunlight,

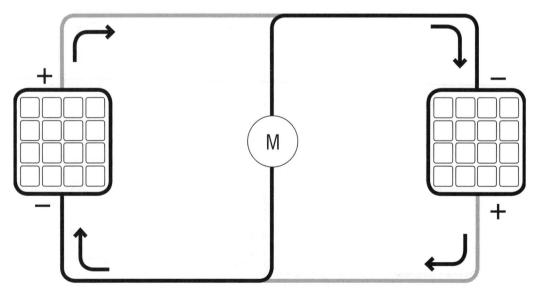

Figure A.13 Current flow with both modules in equal sunlight
Source: US Department of Energy/Polar Power

current flows through the modules and none flows through the motor.

If the right module is shaded, it acts as a resistor. Now the current will flow through the motor, turning it in one direction.

If the other module is shaded, the current from the right module flows in the opposite direction. The motor will turn in the opposite direction as well.

The motor must be able to turn in both directions.

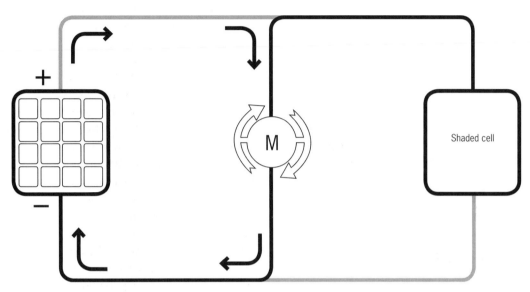

Figure A.14 Current flow in one module (shaded)
Source: US Department of Energy/Polar Power

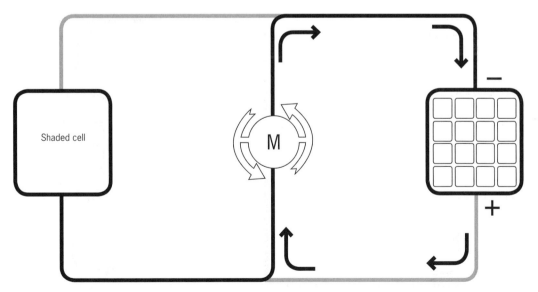

Figure A.15 Current flow with the other module shaded
Source: US Department of Energy/Polar Power

A third tracking method uses the expansion and contraction of fluids to move the array. Generally, a container is filled with a fluid that vaporizes and expands whenever it is in sunlight. It condenses and contracts similarly when in shade. These passive tracking methods have proven to be reliable and durable, even in high winds.

Photovoltaic productive mode system Use of PV cells to convert sunlight directly into electricity.

Appendix 5

Population by country

Table A5 2007 United Nations estimates and country data

Rank	Country/territory/entity	Population	Date	Percentage of world population	Source
–	World	6,671,226,000	Jul 1, 2007	100	UN estimate
1	People's Republic of China	1,321,674,000	Nov 2, 2007	19.81	Official Chinese population clock
2	India [3]	1,169,016,000		17.52	UN estimate
–	European Union	492,964,961	Jan 1, 2006	7.39	Eurostat
–	Arab League	339,510,535	2007	5.09	UN estimate
3	USA	303,273,466	Nov 2, 2007	4.55	Official US population clock
4	Indonesia	231,627,000		3.47	UN estimate
5	Brazil	187,434,000	Oct 29, 2007	2.81	Official Brazilian population clock
6	Pakistan	161,598,500	Oct 29, 2007	2.42	Official Pakistani population clock
7	Bangladesh	158,665,000		2.38	UN estimate
8	Nigeria	148,093,000		2.22	UN estimate
9	Russia	142,499,000		2.14	UN estimate
10	Japan	127,750,000	Jun 1, 2007	1.91	Official Japan Statistics Bureau estimate
11	Mexico	106,535,000		1.6	UN estimate
12	Philippines	88,706,300	Jul 1, 2007	1.33	Official Philippine National Statistics
13	Vietnam	87,375,000		1.31	UN estimate
14	Germany	82,314,900	Dec 31, 2006	1.23	Official Destatis estimate
15	Ethiopia	77,127,000	Jul 2007	1.16	Ethiopia Central Statistics Agency
16	Egypt	75,498,000		1.13	UN estimate
17	Turkey	74,877,000		1.12	UN estimate
18	Iran	71,208,000		1.07	UN estimate
19	France (including overseas France)	64,102,140	Jan 1, 2007	0.96	Official INSEE estimate
20	Thailand	62,828,706	Dec 31, 2006	0.94	Official Thai Statistics estimate
21	Democratic Republic of Congo	62,636,000		0.94	UN estimate
22	United Kingdom	60,587,300	Jul 1, 2006	0.91	Official ONS estimate
23	Italy	59,206,382	Feb 28, 2007	0.89	Official Istat estimate
24	Myanmar	48,798,000		0.73	UN estimate
25	South Africa	48,577,000		0.73	UN estimate

Table A5 (continued)

Rank	Country/territory/entity	Population	Date	Percentage of world population	Source
26	South Korea	48,512,000		0.73	Official Korean population clock
27	Ukraine	46,205,000		0.69	UN estimate
28	Spain	45,116,894	Jan 1, 2007	0.68	Official INE estimate
29	Colombia	44,049,000	Nov 2, 2007	0.66	Official Colombian population clock
30	Tanzania	40,454,000		0.61	UN estimate
31	Argentina	39,531,000		0.59	UN estimate
32	Sudan	38,560,000		0.58	UN estimate
33	Poland	38,125,479	Dec 31, 2006	0.57	Official GUS estimate
34	Kenya	37,538,000		0.56	UN estimate
35	Algeria	33,858,000		0.51	UN estimate
36	Canada	33,052,864	Oct 23, 2007	0.5	Official Canadian population clock
37	Morocco	31,224,000		0.47	UN estimate
38	Uganda	30,884,000		0.46	UN estimate
39	Iraq	28,993,000		0.43	UN estimate
40	Nepal	28,196,000		0.42	UN estimate
41	Peru	27,903,000		0.42	UN estimate
42	Venezuela	27,657,000		0.41	UN estimate
43	Uzbekistan	27,372,000		0.41	UN estimate
44	Malaysia	27,329,000	Oct 11, 2007	0.41	Official Malaysian population clock
45	Afghanistan	27,145,000		0.41	UN estimate
46	Saudi Arabia	24,735,000		0.37	UN estimate
47	North Korea	23,790,000		0.36	UN estimate
48	Ghana	23,478,000		0.35	UN estimate
49	Republic of China (Taiwan) [4]	22,925,000	Sep 2007	0.34	Official National Statistics Taiwan estimate
50	Yemen	22,389,000		0.34	UN estimate
51	Romania	21,438,000		0.32	UN estimate
52	Mozambique	21,397,000		0.32	UN estimate
53	Australia [5]	21,129,222	Nov 2, 2007	0.32	Official Australian population clock
54	Syria	19,929,000		0.3	UN estimate
55	Madagascar	19,683,000		0.3	UN estimate
56	Sri Lanka	19,299,000		0.29	UN estimate
57	Côte d'Ivoire	19,262,000		0.29	UN estimate
58	Cameroon	18,549,000		0.28	UN estimate
59	Angola	17,024,000		0.26	UN estimate
60	Chile	16,598,074	Jun 30, 2007	0.25	Official INE projection
61	Netherlands	16,387,773	Nov 2, 2007	0.25	Official Netherlands population clock
62	Kazakhstan	15,422,000		0.23	UN estimate
63	Burkina Faso	14,784,000		0.22	UN estimate
64	Cambodia	14,444,000		0.22	UN estimate
65	Niger	14,226,000		0.21	UN estimate
66	Malawi	13,925,000		0.21	UN estimate
67	Guatemala	13,354,000		0.2	UN estimate
68	Zimbabwe	13,349,000		0.2	UN estimate

Table A5 *(continued)*

Rank	Country/territory/entity	Population	Date	Percentage of world population	Source
69	Ecuador	13,341,000		0.2	UN estimate
70	Senegal	12,379,000		0.19	UN estimate
71	Mali	12,337,000		0.18	UN estimate
72	Zambia	11,922,000		0.18	UN estimate
73	Cuba	11,268,000		0.17	UN estimate
74	Greece	11,147,000		0.17	UN estimate
75	Chad	10,781,000		0.16	UN estimate
76	Portugal	10,623,000		0.16	UN estimate
77	Belgium	10,457,000		0.16	UN estimate
78	Tunisia	10,327,000		0.15	UN estimate
79	Czech Republic	10,325,900	Jun 30, 2007	0.15	Official ČSÚ estimate
80	Hungary	10,030,000		0.15	UN estimate
81	Serbia [6]	9,858,000		0.15	UN estimate
82	Dominican Republic	9,760,000		0.15	UN estimate
83	Rwanda	9,725,000		0.15	UN estimate
84	Belarus	9,714,000	end 2006	0.15	Official statistics of Belarus
85	Haiti	9,598,000		0.14	UN estimate
86	Bolivia	9,525,000		0.14	UN estimate
87	Guinea	9,370,000		0.14	UN estimate
88	Sweden	9,150,000	Jun 2007	0.14	Official Statistics Sweden estimate
89	Benin	9,033,000		0.13	UN estimate
90	Somalia	8,699,000		0.13	UN estimate
91	Burundi	8,508,000		0.13	UN estimate
92	Azerbaijan	8,467,000		0.13	UN estimate
93	Austria	8,316,487	3rd quarter 2007	0.12	Official Statistics Austria estimate
94	Bulgaria	7,639,000		0.11	UN estimate
95	Switzerland	7,508,700	Dec 31, 2006	0.11	Swiss Federal Statistical Office
–	Hong Kong	7,206,000		0.11	UN estimate
96	Israel	7,197,200	Aug 31, 2007	0.11	Israeli Central Bureau of Statistics
97	Honduras	7,106,000		0.11	UN estimate
98	El Salvador	6,857,000		0.1	UN estimate
99	Tajikistan	6,736,000		0.1	UN estimate
100	Togo	6,585,000		0.099	UN estimate
101	Papua New Guinea	6,331,000		0.095	UN estimate
102	Libya	6,160,000		0.092	UN estimate
103	Paraguay	6,127,000		0.092	UN estimate
104	Jordan	5,924,000		0.089	UN estimate
105	Sierra Leone	5,866,000		0.088	UN estimate
106	Laos	5,859,000		0.088	UN estimate
107	Nicaragua	5,603,000		0.084	UN estimate
108	Denmark	5,457,415	Jun 30, 2007	0.082	Official Statistics Denmark
109	Slovakia	5,390,000		0.081	UN estimate
110	Kyrgyzstan	5,317,000		0.08	UN estimate
111	Finland [8]	5,297,300	Oct 23, 2007	0.079	Official Finnish population clock

Table A5 (continued)

Rank	Country/territory/entity	Population	Date	Percentage of world population	Source
112	Turkmenistan	4,965,000		0.074	UN estimate
113	Eritrea	4,851,000		0.073	UN estimate
114	Norway [9]	4,722,676	Nov 3, 2007	0.071	Official Norwegian population clock
115	Croatia	4,555,000		0.068	UN estimate
116	Costa Rica	4,468,000		0.065	UN estimate
117	Singapore	4,436,000		0.066	UN estimate
118	Georgia [10]	4,395,000		0.066	UN estimate
119	United Arab Emirates	4,380,000		0.066	UN estimate
120	Central African Republic	4,343,000		0.065	UN estimate
121	Ireland	4,301,000		0.064	UN estimate
122	New Zealand	4,239,600	Oct 24, 2007	0.064	Official NZ population clock
123	Lebanon	4,099,000		0.061	UN estimate
124	Palestinian territories	4,017,000		0.06	UN estimate
125	Puerto Rico	3,991,000		0.06	UN estimate
126	Bosnia and Herzegovina	3,935,000		0.059	UN estimate
127	Moldova [11]	3,794,000		0.057	UN estimate
128	Republic of the Congo	3,768,000		0.056	UN estimate
129	Liberia	3,750,000		0.056	UN estimate
–	Somaliland	3,500,000		0.052	Somaliland government
130	Lithuania	3,372,400	Sep 1, 2007	0.051	Statistics Lithuania
131	Panama	3,343,000		0.05	UN estimate
132	Uruguay	3,340,000		0.05	UN estimate
133	Albania	3,190,000		0.048	UN estimate
134	Mauritania	3,124,000		0.047	UN estimate
135	Armenia	3,002,000		0.045	UN estimate
136	Kuwait	2,851,000		0.043	UN estimate
137	Jamaica	2,714,000		0.041	UN estimate
138	Mongolia	2,629,000		0.039	UN estimate
139	Oman	2,595,000		0.039	UN estimate
140	Latvia	2,277,000		0.034	UN estimate
141	Namibia	2,074,000		0.031	UN estimate
142	Republic of Macedonia	2,038,000		0.031	UN estimate
143	Slovenia	2,020,000	Oct 23, 2007	0.031	Official Slovenian population clock
144	Lesotho	2,008,000		0.03	UN estimate
145	Botswana	1,882,000		0.028	UN estimate
146	Gambia	1,709,000		0.026	UN estimate
147	Guinea-Bissau	1,695,000		0.025	UN estimate
148	Estonia	1,342,409	Jan 1, 2007	0.02	Statistics Estonia
149	Trinidad and Tobago	1,333,000		0.02	UN estimate
150	Gabon	1,331,000		0.02	UN estimate
151	Mauritius [12]	1,262,000		0.019	UN estimate
152	East Timor	1,155,000		0.017	UN estimate
153	Swaziland	1,141,000		0.017	UN estimate
154	Cyprus [13]	855,000		0.013	UN estimate
155	Qatar	841,000		0.013	UN estimate
156	Fiji	839,000		0.013	UN estimate
157	Djibouti	833,000		0.012	UN estimate

Table A5 (continued)

Rank	Country/territory/entity	Population	Date	Percentage of world population	Source
157	Réunion	784,000	Jan 1, 2006	0.012	Official INSEE estimate
158	Bahrain	753,000		0.011	UN estimate
159	Guyana	738,000		0.011	UN estimate
160	Comoros [15]	682,000	Jul 2007	0.01	World Gazetteer projection
161	Bhutan	658,000		0.01	UN estimate
162	Montenegro	598,000		0.009	UN estimate
–	Transnistria	555,347		0.008	Pridnestrivie government website
163	Cape Verde	530,000		0.008	UN estimate
164	Equatorial Guinea	507,000		0.008	UN estimate
165	Solomon Islands	496,000		0.007	UN estimate
–	Macau	481,000		0.007	UN estimate
166	Western Sahara	480,000		0.007	UN estimate
167	Luxembourg	467,000		0.007	UN estimate
168	Suriname	458,000		0.007	UN estimate
169	Malta	407,000		0.006	UN estimate
–	Guadeloupe [14]	405,000	Jan 1, 2006	0.006	INSEE est. subtracting St Martin and St Barth
–	Martinique [14]	399,000	Jan 1, 2006	0.006	Official INSEE estimate
170	Brunei	390,000		0.006	UN estimate
171	Bahamas	331,000		0.005	UN estimate
172	Iceland	312,851	Oct 1, 2007	0.005	Hagstofa Íslands
173	Maldives	306,000		0.005	UN estimate
174	Barbados	294,000		0.004	UN estimate
175	Belize	288,000		0.004	UN estimate
–	French Polynesia [14]	259,800	Jan 1, 2007	0.004	Official ISPF estimate
–	New Caledonia[14]	240,390	Jan 1, 2007	0.004	Official INSEE estimate
176	Vanuatu	226,000		0.003	UN estimate
–	French Guiana [14]	202,000	Jan 1, 2006	0.003	Official INSEE estimate
177	Netherlands Antilles	192,000		0.003	UN estimate
178	Samoa	187,000		0.003	UN estimate
–	Mayotte [14]	182,000	Jan 1, 2006	0.003	Estimate based on last INSEE census
179	Guam	173,000		0.003	UN estimate
180	Saint Lucia	165,000		0.002	UN estimate
181	São Tomé and Príncipe	158,000		0.002	UN estimate
182	Saint Vincent and the Grenadines	120,000		0.002	UN estimate
183	US Virgin Islands	111,000		0.002	UN estimate
184	Federated States of Micronesia	111,000		0.002	UN estimate
185	Grenada	106,000		0.002	UN estimate
186	Aruba	104,000		0.002	UN estimate
187	Tonga	100,000		0.001	UN estimate
188	Kiribati	95,000		0.001	UN estimate

Table A5 (continued)

Rank	Country/territory/entity	Population	Date	Percentage of world population	Source
189	Jersey	88,200		0.001	States of Jersey Statistics Unit
190	Seychelles	87,000		0.001	UN estimate
191	Antigua and Barbuda	85,000		0.001	UN estimate
192	Northern Mariana Islands	84,000		0.001	UN estimate
193	Andorra	81,200	Dec 31, 2006	0.001	Andorra Servei d'Estudis
194	Isle of Man	79,000		0.001	UN estimate
195	Dominica	67,000		0.001	UN estimate
196	American Samoa	67,000		0.001	UN estimate
197	Guernsey	65,573		0.001	World Fact Book, 2007
198	Bermuda	65,000		0.001	UN estimate
199	Marshall Islands	59,000		0.001	UN estimate
200	Greenland	58,000		0.001	UN estimate
201	Saint Kitts and Nevis	50,000		0.001	UN estimate
202	Faroe Islands	48,455	Jun 1, 2007	0.001	Official statistics of the Faroe Islands
203	Cayman Islands	47,000		0.001	UN estimate
204	Liechtenstein	35,000		0.0005	UN estimate
–	Saint-Martin [14]	33,102	Oct 2004	0.0005	October 2004 supplementary census
205	Monaco	33,000		0.0005	UN estimate
206	San Marino	31,000		0.0005	UN estimate
207	Gibraltar	29,000		0.0004	UN estimate
208	Turks and Caicos Islands	26,000		0.0004	UN estimate
209	British Virgin Islands	23,000		0.0003	UN estimate
210	Palau	20,000		0.0003	UN estimate
–	Wallis and Futuna [14]	15,000	Jul 2007	0.0002	UN estimate
211	Cook Islands	13,000		0.0002	UN estimate
212	Anguilla	13,000		0.0002	UN estimate
213	Tuvalu	11,000		0.0002	UN estimate
214	Nauru	10,000		0.0001	UN estimate
–	Saint-Barthélemy [14]	6852	Mar 1999	0.0001	March 1999 census
215	Saint Helena [16]	6600		0.0001	UN estimate
–	Saint-Pierre and Miquelon [14]	6125	Jan 2006	0.0001	January 2006 census
216	Montserrat	5900		0.0001	UN estimate
217	Falkland Islands	3000		0.00005	UN estimate
218	Niue	1600		0.00003	UN estimate
219	Tokelau	1400		0.00003	UN estimate
220	Vatican City	800		0.00002	UN estimate
221	Pitcairn Islands	50		0.000001	UN estimate